THE erotic

anime MOVIE GUIDE

HELEN McCARTHY & JONATHAN CLEMENTS

TITAN BOOKS

THE EROTIC ANIME MOVIE GUIDE

ISBN 1 85286 946 1

PUBLISHED BY

Titan Books
42-44 Dolben Street
London SE1 0UP

First edition September 1998
10 9 8 7 6 5 4 3 2 1

Several parts of this book have previously appeared, in a substantially different form, in *Anime UK*, *Anime FX*, *Manga Mania* and *JAMM* magazine.

British Library Cataloguing-in-Publication Data. A catalogue record for this book is available from the British Library.

Printed and bound in Great Britain by MPG Books Ltd, Victoria Square, Bodmin, Cornwall.

ILLUSTRATION CREDITS

All images used in this book are intended for the purposes of promotion and information only. No infringement of the rights of the copyright holders is intended. For British and American availability of the titles illustrated, please see individual entries in the title listing.

The authors and publishers would like to thank the following people and organisations whose kind assistance in lending pictorial material has made this book possible:

AD Vision Inc and AD Vision UK Ltd, with special thanks to Glenda Runnalls and Sharon Papa; Central Park Media, Inc, with special thanks to Jeff Zitomer; East2West, with special thanks to Chris Smith; Kiseki Films Limited, with special thanks to Simon Gale; Steve Kyte; Manga Entertainment Limited, with special thanks to Rod Shaile; Otaku Publishing Ltd, with special thanks to Alex McLaren; Pioneer LDCE Limited, with special thanks to Ben Jolliffe; Western Connection Limited, with special thanks to Sasha Cipkalo.

Front cover image:
The erotic interactive computer game *Ring Out* © CD Brothers Japan/Otaku Publishing Ltd.

Back cover images (top to bottom):
Sword for Truth © Jo Toriumi, Promise, Toei.
Junk Boy © Y. Kunimoto, Futabasha, Victor Entertainment.
The Sensualist © Groupier Productions.
Wicked City © Japan Home Video.

801 TTS Airbats © Toshimitsu Shimizu, Tokuma Shoten, JVC. *Adventure Duo* © Toshio Maeda, WestCapeCorp. *Armitage III* © Pioneer. *Bronze: Desperate Love Since 1989* © Minami Ozaki, Shueisha. *Countdown* © Hiroyuki Utatane, Fujimi Shuppan, Akane Shinsha, Pink Pineapple. *Cream Lemon* and *New Cream Lemon* titles © Fairy Dust, Soeishinsha. *Crying Freeman* © Toei Video. *Cutey Honey* © Go Nagai, Dynamic Planning Inc, Toei Video. *Devil Hunter Yoko* © NCS, Toho Video. *Devilman* © Go Nagai, Dynamic Planning Inc, Bandai. *Dragon Knight* © Polystar, elf RPG, All Products. *The Elven Bride* © Kazuma G-Version, Mediax, Pink Pineapple. *End of Summer* © elf/Pink Pineapple, Cinema Paradise, Hero. *F3: Frantic, Frustrated & Female* © Wan Yan A Gu Da, Pink Pineapple. *Ghost in the Shell* © Masamune Shirow, Kodansha, Bandai Visual, Manga Entertainment. *The Gigolo* © Tetsumi Doko, Seiyo, Jackpot. *Golden Boy* © KSS, TBS. *Hummingbirds* © Toho Video. *Kekko Kamen* © Go Nagai, Dynamic Planning Inc, Japan Columbia. *La Blue Girl* © Toshio Maeda, Daiei Co Ltd. *Little Witch Sally* © Toei Co. *Macross Plus* © Big West. *Megami Paradise* © Megami Takada Kensetsu Iinkai, Medai Works, King Records, MOVIC. *Miyuki-chan in Wonderland* © CLAMP, Sony Music Entertainment, Kadokawa, MOVIC. *New Angel 2* © Studio Angel, U-Jin, Pink Pineapple. *Pataliro!* © Mineo Maya, Toei Co. *Phantom Quest Corp* © Pioneer, AIC. *Plastic Little* © Kinji Yoshimoto, Satoshi Urushihara, MOVIC, Sony Music Entertainment. *The Professional: Golgo 13* © Saito Productions, Tokyo Movie Shinsha. *Rei Rei* © Toshimitsu Shimizu, Shonen Gahosha, Pink Pineapple. *RG Veda* © CLAMP, Shinshokan, Sony Music Entertainment. *Rose of Versailles* © Ryoko Ikeda, Tokyo Movie Shinsha. *The Sensualist* © Groupier Productions. *Sol Bianca* © NEC Avenue. *Space Adventure Cobra* © Buichi Terasawa, Tokyo Movie Shinsha. *Space Firebird* © Tezuka Productions. *Sword for Truth* © Jo Toriumi, Promise, Toei. *Timestripper* © CD Brothers Japan/Otaku Publishing Ltd. *Twin Dolls* © Daiei Co. *Urotsukidoji/Legend of the Overfiend* © Toshio Maeda, WestCape Corp, JAVN. *Wicked City* © Japan Home Video.

DEDICATION

To Fred Schodt, in affection and awe.

THANKS

The following people provided valuable expertise, support, criticism or comments on early drafts: Lee Brimmicombe-Wood, Jeremy Clarke, Youri Foster, Dave Hughes, Ru Igarashi, Ben Jolliffe, Simon Jowett, Mary Kennard, Steve Kyte, Yumeko Murasaki, Keiichi Onodera, Kate Pankhurst, Bill Paris, Rod Shaile, Jim Swallow, Motoko Tamamuro, Jason Taylor, Ellis Tinios, Simon Tomlin, Rumi Vyse, Steve Whitaker.

Special thanks to the people who've supported and encouraged us throughout this project: our editor Adam Newell, senior editor David Barraclough, designer Vanessa Coleman, production whiz Bob Kelly, and Steve and Kate.

TRANSLATION NOTE

For those who need to know, these are the translation policies we have followed in this book. Romanisation is Hepburn with the modifications listed below. Creators' preferred romanisation has been used, even where unorthodox, eg Masamune Shiro<u>w</u>. Chinese follows Pinyin romanisation except where an English precedent is well established, eg *Hong Kong* not *Xiang Gang*. Macrons have been omitted in the main text, but are signified with umlauts in the filmography translations. Katakana have been rendered directly into English where recognisable. Where a work has been professionally released in the English language, we use the English title, however far removed from the original. Where the English and American releases have differing titles, we have plumped for the one we like best (with the other to be found in the alternative title index). For untranslated titles, adherence to title precedents is not guaranteed, especially where the precedent has been set by doubtful sources. Japanese is often ambiguous about genitive cases and singular versus plural, thus 'House of Kittens' may in fact turn out to be 'Kitten's House'. Terms such as chapter/tales/stories have been rendered as best can be inferred. We have used our discretion with words like chapter and edition, mainly because nomenclature in Japanese is confused further by, for example, long 'books' like the original *Hakkenden*, published in dozens of 'chapters' each one a self-contained 'book' in its own right. Where an orthodox hierarchy exists for particular genres (eg myth=gods/legend=heroes/folktale=commoners), this has been followed. Unless present in Japlish, all deictic words are to be considered discretionary, eg *[The] Elven Bride*. Silent consonants have been dropped from the accusative modifier '[w]o', and the prepositional particle '[h]e'.

Crying Freeman

CONTENTS

INTRODUCTION

Why Write About Porn?

The subject of this book is a sound commercial choice. Whoever first said 'sex sells' was massively understating the case. I'm sure some readers of this introduction are here for other reasons than an intellectual interest in the subject. This includes all those who flicked through to check out the pictures first. But there's more to it than simply wanting to make money, although this is a reasonable objective which neither Jonathan nor I would be sorry to achieve. So what's our hidden agenda?

When I wrote *The Anime Movie Guide*, I deliberately left out most pornographic anime in an attempt to show the breadth and diversity of the medium. After all, the massed ranks of the Western press — quality as well as gutter — had already decided that Japanese animation was nothing but sex and violence; I didn't want to give them any further signposts down that road. Instead, I hoped that the book would help to broaden our thinking on the subject of anime in general. I should have borne in mind Dorothy Parker's justly famous epigram on horticulture. Asked to construct a sentence including that word, Miss Parker came straight back with, 'You can lead a whore to culture, but you cannot make her think.'

Despite an increasing awareness of anime's wider remit, both the press and the market have persisted in thinking almost exclusively along the same old lines. In the fine tradition of giving the customer what he wants (and the anime customer is still usually he), the number of pornographic anime now on Western release has climbed steeply, which looks set to continue. It seems that Western obsession with Japanese pornography will not go away, yet there is still little serious critical examination of the genre itself, or our own attitudes towards it. This book has given Jonathan and I a chance to explore some of the byways of erotic anime and our reactions to it, byways for the most part still untrodden by the Western media, for all their obsession with 'sick Japanese cartoons'.

SO WHAT EXACTLY HAVE WE DONE?

As you may have noticed if you walk in the mountains, straight paths can turn into adventure trails looping the loop over the same piece of difficult ground and sometimes seeming to go nowhere. In just the same way, the history and development of erotic anime is made up of many interwoven strands which double and twist on themselves. This is not a straightforward narrative. You will often find yourself referred back, or forward, as you read. I'm sorry if this is inconvenient, but uncluttered linear narratives only exist in writers' workshops. If you set out to explore unknown territory, you have to expect a few kinks in the route.

We start with a short history of erotic anime before the advent of video. Erotic expression in anime has developed slowly, contending with domestic restrictions and social attitudes just like that of other countries, ours included. Far from being isolated in a hermetically sealed world of oriental weirdness, Japanese writers and artists have had the same struggles and problems as writers and artists all over the world.

Separate chapters examine aspects of erotic anime which have come into their own since the arrival of video. Sex comedy, erotic horror and the female-oriented erotica, which grew from innocent entertainment for girls, have all developed in reaction to the legal, economic and social influences of the day. Computer games and mass-media formats are also covered, to demonstrate how the many devices and images of porn are used every day in the mass media. The most renowned Japanese anime porn to hit the Western market, *Legend of the Overfiend*, is considered in most detail because of the importance conferred on it by its foreign viewers and reviewers. Special consideration is given to censorship issues as they relate to anime.

There is also a title listing. This covers neither every erotic anime ever made, nor every title mentioned in the book. (To develop the historical background or make particular points we have sometimes referred to items which are not erotic in themselves, but since eroticism is only one of a wide range of human responses, it shouldn't be surprising to find it mixed in with everyday stories, or to catch occasional glimpses of the erotic in a wide range of non-genre titles.) The title list does, however, provide an overview both of the range of erotic anime and the growing quantity available in English. To the best of our knowledge, as with my last book, some of this material has not previously been documented in the West, but with the market for erotic anime expanding at the current rate, many at present 'unknown' titles may be available in the shops before this book hits the shelves. While making our final revisions we had to amend several listings to reflect forthcoming Western release plans.

Potential viewers should be aware that 'spoilers' pop up in many places in both the chapters and the listings. This will be your only warning. If you think that the one reason to watch a movie is to find out how it ends, this book could wreck your viewing pleasure!

For those who are using this book for research purposes, I would like to draw your attention both to the extensive footnotes and to the bibliography, which deliberately incorporates non-Japanese sources to demonstrate the universality of some of our subjects.

WHAT DO WE HOPE TO ACHIEVE?

A Nobel or Pulitzer nomination seems unlikely. Jonathan and I would settle for a little less hysteria and a little more research in the general treatment of anime in the Western media. Don't just take our word for anything, but don't believe what our domestic press tries to feed you either. Read, watch, evaluate and decide for yourself. If you come to the conclusion that anime *is* just sick oriental porn, as the average pundit says, at least you've given the matter some serious thought; which is more than he or she can claim. ●

La Blue Girl

HIDDEN ROOMS

○ Erotic Anime Before the OAV

From the earliest years of the cinema to the coming of made-for-video animation in 1983, erotic material had to thread a devious and often hidden path through the more conventional products of the Japanese mass media and the development of Japanese society throughout the twentieth century. The old artistic references to sexual matters were supplemented by new filmic metaphors like those being developed in the West. In this, as in so many other fields, the great Osamu Tezuka was a leading pioneer.

In America, the early days of the cinema were a rather low-rent affair. Eccentric men in darkened rooms messed about with foul-smelling chemicals and bulky boxes. All kinds of people paid pennies to get in and gawp at the spectacle, in civic halls, in barns, anywhere there was a suitable space. Cinema rapidly became the common man's preferred way of escape from mundane life. Anyone with parents or grandparents born before World War Two probably remembers hearing tales of collecting jam jars or empty bottles to swap for cinema admission. Relatives who didn't mind admitting to a disreputable past (and setting us a bad example) would confess to sneaking in while the manager's back was turned, or pooling coppers to admit a little brother or sister who would then open the emergency exit for the impecunious horde waiting in the alley.

In Japan, it seems, things were different. The cinema had more social cachet from the start. When an enterprising businessman called Shinji Takahashi waylaid Prince Komatsu in a Kobe hotel and showed him some Kinetoscope images in 1894, the Prince was much amused and declared himself impressed with this remarkable new invention from the West, bestowing a royal seal of approval. There was a slight hiccup when the great actor Danjuro XI objected to the use of the Kabuki-za, home of Japan's traditional 'comedy' theatre, for the first Vitascope screening in 1897, but a new venue was found. Danjuro XI eventually relented, and even appeared in the first ever

film of Japanese classical theatre, the drama *Maple Viewing*, shot in 1899 with an eye to promoting future sales by Tsunehiroki Shibata of the Mitsukoshi Department Store's new, high-tech photographic department. With princes of the blood and kings of commerce involved in the new art form from the beginning, it's no surprise that it was viewed as eminently suitable for artists, intellectuals and the well-to-do.

The earliest animations in Japan were made as collaborations between those interested in this new art of the cinema and artists wanting to expand the scope of their graphic work. The first of Japan's great animation directors, Seitaro Kitayama, gained experience for his early experiments in animating Indian ink drawings on paper by drawing title cards for silent movies. In 1917 he was producing and showing short films like *The Monkey and the Crab*, *Cat and Mice* and *The Naughty Mailbox*, and in 1918 his version of the Japanese legend of *Momotaro*, the magical little boy born from a peach stone, was touring not just in Japan but in France, attracting enthusiastic audiences. By 1921 he had founded his own studio, and an industry was born.

Others were working in the new art form too; Junichi Kouchi made two successful animated films, *The Lazy Sword* and *Hanahekonai's New Sword*, in 1917, when he was thirty-one, and by the twenties he was among those experimenting with the technique of animating wash drawings, adding a further dimension to the simple line animations previously developed.[1]

IMAGES IN HIDING

It was at this stage that erotic imagery in anime began its slow, hidden development. Anything too explicit was avoided, but directors and animators began to employ a visual lexicon to put an erotic charge into what might seem a perfectly innocent situation. Western directors were developing the same kind of tricks, and many — from broad hints such as lingering glimpses of stocking tops or panties, to imagery like surf rushing onto a beach or trains rushing into tunnels — have passed into the international language of film cliché. But in addition to this, each culture has its own erotic symbology. A girl nibbling the ends of her hair or scarf might seem quite innocent, but anyone versed in Japanese history, with its woodblock images of great courtesans doing the same thing, would know that she was ready, willing and available.

Until the coming of made-for-video animation, most of anime's erotic ideas had to be conveyed in this way, and trawling for them is a difficult process for a foreigner. To take a modern example (as the symbology is indeed still in use), the sequence in 1991's *Sword for Truth*, which introduces the character Orin, looks to Western eyes like a simple pickpocket scene. Some of the irony of hero Shuranosuke's actions in literally exposing Orin for what she is, by slicing her clothes off in the middle of a crowded street with one flick of his blade, is lost on those who don't realise the implications of her nibbling the ends of her scarf in her very first shot. Such viewers also miss the full significance of her later visit to his run-down lodgings, when she gives him a lavish free sample of her wares.

The first animated films credited with containing stories directly aimed at an adult audience, with hints at erotic elements in the relationships between the characters and in the iconography, come in the work of Noboru Ofuji, who was more celebrated for his technical innovations. He developed a new technique of working on semi-transparent paper, placing figures and backgrounds on different sheets which could be moved about in relation to each other for each shot. The greater fluidity and depth given by this advance was much admired, and won him a European distribution deal for his film *The Whale* in 1929. Galvanised by his success, Ofuji went on to even

greater technical heights. In 1930 he used sound in *The Control Room*, and by 1937 was working with colour on *Princess Katsura*.

The first Japanese animated talkie was *The World of Power and Women*, directed by Kenzo Masaoka in 1932. Reflecting the new world of commerce and modernity into which Japan was heading, it's an office romance, the tale of an impoverished young clerk engaged to a hugely fat and terrifyingly bossy woman, but in love with a beautiful and gentle typist. Old legends, history and folklore continued to provide subjects for animation, just as they did for live film, but Japanese directors and authors were already using the new arts to explore new ways of life.

Eroticism, though, was only part of the mix, and only hinted at. This trend was to continue as Japan's involvement in World War Two diverted animation, like all the other arts, to the war effort. Animators, like comic artists, film directors, writers and actors, in the West as well as Japan, were pressed into service by their country's propaganda machine. Relationships with Europe were interrupted, but after hostilities ceased Japanese artists resumed their contacts with their counterparts in the West. It was harder than before to communicate closely with the Yugoslav, Polish and Czech animators now corralled behind the Iron Curtain, but by way of compensation there was much to be gained from closer contact with the Americans. Many American servicemen and aides were now permanently stationed in Japan, as part of the peace settlement (indeed, a number of American bases remain in Japan today), and their attitudes, habits, entertainments and way of life had a huge impact on the average Japanese citizen's perception of the outside world.

A big difference was the attitude to nudity, sex and eroticism of the various Western advisers stationed in Japan to ensure that militarism didn't rise again. Of course, the Japanese had encountered Christian attitudes when the Spanish and Portuguese came to their shores in the sixteenth century, and ever since Commodore Perry's[2] ships sailed into port it had been obvious that there were many things which the Japanese accepted as part of life, but foreigners just didn't care for — like

---

[1] Kouchi lived until 1970, and saw his art become a true mass medium with the success of anime on television in Japan and America.
[2] Perry was the commander of the American expedition which re-opened Japan to the West in the nineteenth century.

mixed public bath-houses, homosexuality, cross-dressing actors and toilet jokes. Before the defeat of Japan, it was possible to just write off any differences as foreign weirdness; afterwards, Japan had to ask itself whether maybe the foreigners had a point. After all, they had won, and, in Japan as elsewhere throughout history, winning has given the winners authority to impose their way of thinking on the defeated.

In any post-war nation there is usually a good deal of deprivation. Japan was poor and starving. Huge areas of productive rice land had been fire-bombed. Industry was in tatters. Large numbers of young men had died in the forces. Even among the old, who had stayed at home, there had been heavy casualties. Changes in Japanese society and social attitudes were inevitable. With families so poor that even married women had to sell themselves to bring home some food money, Japanese girls facing much reduced marriage prospects and the whole country ravaged, freedom of erotic expression was not foremost on the agenda. It was to be some years before the situation began to change. The erotic aspects of anime, like those of manga, were to remain a subtext, embedded in iconography and only occasionally glimpsed, until Japan, like the rest of the world, went through even greater social change. If there were any Japanese 'underground' animated erotica, underground is where they have remained to date.

Erotic manga had also taken its first steps before the war, when artists like Saseo Ono depicted 'decadent' Tokyo society, with its slouching men

and mannish-clad, chain-smoking women, in pictures described as 'ero guro nansensu', Japlish shorthand for erotic grotesque nonsense. Yet, as Schodt points out, erotic comics per se, in the sense in which Westerners tend to use the term, are a relatively recent development.[3] The tradition of earthy expression in Japanese popular art was long established as part of adult entertainment, but not until after the war did it make its way into comic books, then still regarded as children's reading.

Sex and violence in comics worried those concerned for the new moral standards set by the occupying Americans very early on, and in the mid fifties the Campaign To Banish Bad Reading Matter censured even such luminaries as Osamu Tezuka, some of whose manga work was explicit in its imagery and scripting.[4] In the sixties, Fujio Akatsuka set the stage with tales of sex, violence and scatology in his numerous gag manga[5], and by 1968 Go Nagai was scandalising the Japanese PTA with *Shameless School*, a story of high school sex and slack classroom discipline which was publicly burned. The difficulties of Japanese censorship were skilfully circumvented in manga using techniques adopted later for animated porn (see chapter two) — genitals were not shown, or were blurred, or substitutes like eggplants, eels or snakes were used.[6]

THE TEZUKA EFFECT

One of the greatest of Japan's modern artists, Osamu Tezuka, a man known to millions as 'the manga god', grew up during the war and started his artistic career during the occupation. His influence on anime and manga was so immense that it is impossible to discuss either post-war industry in any depth without taking him into account. He was himself influenced by Western popular art and made no bones about his debt to animators like Walt Disney and the Fleischer brothers. An avid cartoon fan from the moment he saw his first Disney short as a schoolboy in 1938, all his spare time was devoted to films, writing and drawing his own comics, or studying insects.

The techniques he observed on film in *Silly Symphonies* and *Popeye* began to influence his own comic art, and by the time he was in his mid-teens he had already developed a highly individual style. About 3,000 pages of his juvenile works survived the war, evidence of a precocious talent. But no amount of evidence could have prepared anyone for what was to come. Tezuka was one of

---

[3] Schodt, *Manga! Manga!* p133

[4] See Groensteen's example from *Ayako*, p39

[5] Akatsuka is still active as one of the most popular manga artists in Japan, despite his current battle with cancer.

[6] It was not until 1993, as the vague regulations against depiction of pubic hair were increasingly ignored, that any form of realism could be allowed in drawing genitalia, but this has not prevented the continued use of the old, accepted iconography by many artists. There has, however, been a shift in the content and focus of erotic manga since the mid eighties. Prior to that point, adult comics were aimed at adult males and showed people they could identify with, interacting with grown-up women. With the rise of lolikon (see chapter five) the use of much younger sex objects with exaggeratedly cute, childlike characteristics grew more widespread. As erotic anime developed, and teenagers and young men began to form a larger part of the erotic comic market, this trend has continued.

those phenomenal beings who tear into their chosen field and, by sheer force of talent and strength of vision, shred its established conventions and change it forever.

All the more remarkable was that he accomplished this feat in two separate art forms (comics and animation) while also making time to study for and attain academic honours as a fully qualified medical practitioner. Tezuka wasn't just a great creative artist, he was the Japanese work ethic made flesh. Even at the end of his life, his work-rate left many younger men standing,[7] and in the first years of his career stories poured from his pen. But through his early years as a manga superstar and student doctor, he hung on to his dream of making animation. After early work with major studio Toei Doga, establishing a reputation abroad as well as in Japan, he founded his own studio, Mushi Productions.

At last, the young artist could make films his own way, and he plunged into animation with the same ferocious energy he had used in his manga. The renowned television series *Astro Boy* was followed by other work, including the seminal girls' series *Princess Knight* (discussed in more detail in chapter three) and *Vampire*, which mixed animation and live action. Meanwhile his manga production schedule carried on as frenetically as ever. Sadly, making films his own way was less successful commercially than artistically. Tezuka was so devoted to making animation to his own high standards that he employed large numbers of skilled craftsmen, and despite his best efforts to balance the books, the studio lost money. Tezuka tried everything he could think of to keep Mushi solvent, including a foray into adult film-making.

Mushi made their first film intended and marketed specifically for the adult audience, *The 1001 Nights*, in 1969. Eiichi Yamamoto directed a tale from the Arabian Nights for the studio, and the story of Aladdin, not quite as told by Scheherezade in the Sultan's harem, was a box office success.[8] Tezuka produced, and also co-wrote the script with Kazuo Fukuzawa. Hero Aldine, paying tribute to his creator's interest in Western film and possible Western audiences by looking like Jean-Paul Belmondo, loves and loses the beautiful slave girl Miriam in one hectic night of passion, changes his name to Sinbad in the course of his exotic escapades, many involving scantily clad houris, and finally meets the daughter he never knew he had. The film also employed the talents of Isao Tomita as composer

and Kazuko Nakaouma as chief animator to create a sophisticated package far outside the range of the standard kiddie fare which was most people's idea of animation.

In the following year, Tezuka's manga version of another exotic story was filmed for Mushi by Eiichi Yamamoto. *Cleopatra* added an unusual twist to the tale of the serpent of the Nile. The story opens in the future. Aliens are about to attack the Earth. The Time Patrol, looking desperately for a solution, travels back in time to Egypt in the last days of its Empire, and asks the obvious question: if Cleopatra managed to seduce Caesar and Mark Anthony to keep her land and people safe from the might of Rome, could she manage the same feat with an alien commander to save her planet and the human race? The film was released in America as *Cleopatra, Queen of Sex*. The addition of the subtitle did the box office no harm, but along with the scenes displaying Cleopatra's sizzling seductive talents it did earn the film its American X certificate, the only animation to be so distinguished until the appearance of Bakshi's *Fritz the Cat* a little while later.

Despite these successes, the studio was closed in 1970, later to reopen under new management. The failure of Mushi left Tezuka deeply disappointed — his childhood dream had come true, only to vanish again — but his energy and optimism led him to set up a new studio, Tezuka Productions, which plunged almost immediately into the same frenetic schedule of television and film productions inspired by its founder's manga works. It was not until 1980, however, that he was to make the film which most fully expressed his ideas about the role of erotic and romantic love, the magnificent *Space Firebird*, a segment of the ongoing *Phoenix* saga which he described as his 'life's work'. Under the direction of Taku Sugiyama, 700 animators spent a huge

---

[7] Schodt recounts a story of how Tezuka visited Walt Disney World with a Japanese television crew, and Schodt as his interpreter. After a full day's filming he took the artist back to his hotel and said goodnight. Early next morning, when they met to start filming again, Tezuka had a pile of comic pages, mostly completely inked, ready to hand over to the editor who accompanied him almost everywhere for shipping back to Japan. For most of his life he was said to complete about 300 pages of comic art every month. (*Dreamland Japan*, p241.)

[8] Bendazzi, generally scathing about commercial animation in Japan, remarks approvingly on its pioneering eroticism (p411).

sum (reportedly 800 million yen, then a record for a Japanese animated film)[9] on bringing Tezuka's epic tale to life.

FLIGHT OF THE PHOENIX

The story is set in a far distant future, when man has exploited Earth's resources almost to exhaustion and is able to live on satellites and settle other worlds far out in space. The social order is repressive and authoritarian. Only the elite know and live with their children; other babies, conceived in test tubes, are graded at birth according to the abilities revealed by their genetic code. They are then brought up by robots to fill the roles society assigns to them, as soldiers, workers or administrators. Administrators can rise to the ranks of the elite, but there are very few opportunities for others. Love and marriage are also privileges reserved for only a select few.

Hero Godo is first seen as a baby, and his nurse arrives in a neat red package with a handle, looking surprisingly like a modern ghetto-blaster sound system. Baby Godo soon finds that within that sleek red exterior is a whole world of marvellous things, if he can just work out how to handle the remote control that opens the package. Tezuka makes gentle fun of the infantile idea of a woman as a controllable plaything in a dazzling comic sequence; the red case transforms into a racing bike, a flying machine and all manner of strange and wonderful toys for boys before ending up as Orga.

Beautiful, blonde and curvaceous, Orga is dressed all in red strapping like an alien movie queen, a fetishist's dream come true, yet has the sweetest, gentlest and most giving nature imaginable. But she is not one of the changeable, disposable, emotionless doll-women which makers of animated porn would later create. Godo's baby consciousness views Orga as a toy, but as he matures through puppy love, experience of the world outside his safe and comfortable home and real suffering, he comes to see and value all the subtler, stronger qualities he had relied on and taken for granted all his life.

Orga cares for Godo as tenderly as any human mother. Her instructions to care for him are programmed into her circuitry, but they grow beyond mere programming into love. She feels for him in

Space Firebird

ways a robot cannot; she even weeps when he finds another love, although her robot body should not be able to produce tears. Finally she gives her life, the human consciousness she evolved through the power of love, for him. Inspired by her and not wishing to live without her, Godo in turn gives his own life to power a rebirth for his home planet.

Orga shares superficial characteristics with Maria from *Metropolis*, perhaps the first sexy robot in science fiction film. (Orga is certainly the first I've found in anime.) The tender 'maternal' qualities of generosity and gentleness embedded in her programming enable Orga to develop along very different lines from Maria, without sacrificing her beauty or attractiveness, but because Godo views the world in an immature fashion for much of the film, he doesn't see these qualities as anything but maternal. He views Orga purely as his carer, and a rich beauty from an elite family is his first love.

This brief romance is based purely on physical attraction and the thrill of crossing the tracks for both parties, and despite an attempted elopement it crumbles once faced with separation. The girl marries Godo's brother and, in a sequence which points up her essential shallowness, later tries to persuade Godo to save her from danger by hinting that they could pick up

---

[9] Groensteen, *L'Univers des Mangas*, p77.

their old relationship. But by now Godo has learned from experience that not everything in a pretty package is worth keeping.[10]

Although *Space Firebird* has some of the period's sexiest imagery, it contains no explicit sex scenes. Its erotic and romantic impact comes from the power of the writing, supported by superb art and design. The film powerfully states Tezuka's basic philosophy of love for life and all living things. The erotic and romantic sides of love, with their excitement and danger, are part and parcel of this larger way of love, essential components of human life, but not the most vital of human pursuits. Godo moves from the simple idealism and romanticism of youth, through danger and hardship, learning to value the good and faithful friends he has above the flashier attractions of power and wealth, until he finally realises that love and respect for life are essential to our survival.

Along the way, the artist has the opportunity to portray a couple of beautiful young women in skimpy futuristic outfits, and to play with our ideas of what an ideal woman should be and what her function in a relationship is, but that's just a bonus, a lure to glue the audience to their seats, like the spaceships, battle sequences and the stunning set pieces on the mining prison planet. Erotic and romantic imagery in Tezuka's works serve the overall scheme into which all his manga and animation slotted. The *Phoenix* cycle is life reborn through love.

THE HIDDEN AGENDA

Manifestations of eroticism in anime made for television were embedded in 'respectable' genres — a tender love story in the boxing series *Tomorrow's Joe*, some slapstick underwear shots or partial nudity in comedy shows. Though in general Japanese attitudes to nudity in the sixties and seventies were more relaxed than in the West, there were still definite limits on what could and could not be explicitly depicted on television.

One hugely popular expression of suppressed erotic longing was depicted in *Aim For the Ace!*, a television series about wannabe tennis star Hiromi, who loves Toda but sublimates her passions to her determination to be a tennis champion. Scenes of extreme physical effort were juxtaposed with the tensions between the characters, building an atmosphere of suppressed emotional energy channelled into the game itself. When the first *Lupin III* television series hit the screens in

1971, the eroticism of the relationship between Lupin and his leading lady Fujiko Mine, to say nothing of his constant attempts at seduction of every pretty woman who came within his reach, were toned down slightly from Monkey Punch's manga stories (in which genitals were depicted in a highly original fashion as three-dimensional versions of the scientific symbols for male and female, attached at the groin and often linked in ways not considered suitable for television audiences) but kept their saucy atmosphere.

Go Nagai began to produce anime for television in 1972, and, as discussed further in chapter six, made stories heavy with erotic overtones or completely daft with knockabout sex comedy. Also in 1972, the first series of *Science Ninja Team Gatchaman* (dubbed and edited for the American market as *Battle of the Planets*) sent a generation of boys crazy looking for glimpses of Jun's panties as she vaulted and twirled through her various athletic excesses, while their sisters sighed over brooding bad boy Joe, who was everything a Japanese father didn't want his daughter to bring into the family.

Gatchaman also featured Berg Katze, a villain who combined male and female elements — not surprising when you know that 'he' is a mutant created by an evil alien from a pair of twins, one male and one female. He can shapeshift between the two genders as well as change his age, appearance and voice. In *Battle of the Planets*, Katze became Zoltar, and his appearances without his mask were described as 'Mala, Zoltar's sister'. In Nagai's *Mazinger Z*, evil Baron Ashler was literally split down the middle — half-man, half-woman — enshrining gender confusion on prime time television.

Stories based on history might be thought more 'respectable', even educational, but film-makers seeking to fit erotic scenes into their movies found

10 A later version of the same basic story, Shinichi Masaki's 1986 OAV *The Humanoid*, took its inspiration from Hajime Sorayama's *Sexy Robot* illustrations. The imagery of Sorayama's work shares strong links with Tezuka's designs for Orga, using gleaming metal and the highest tech of his day to mix flesh with chrome for works of stunning visual titillation. Yet in animated form, the character fails to deliver any sexual charge whatsoever, and the story of a robot girl who is inspired by her human companions to emotion and self-sacrifice fails to convince. Its flabby writing is a feeble echo of Tezuka's film, confirming that sexy imagery alone isn't enough.

history a very good excuse. Western history, with stories like 1973's *Tragedy of Belladonna*, the last film directed by Tezuka for Mushi Productions, and based on Jules Michelet's story of medieval France, provided ample opportunity for bodice-ripping.

Later, as science fiction and action shows gained more popularity (and their audiences began to grow up), series like Buichi Terasawa's *Space Adventure Cobra* took the adventure and exoticism of foreign movies like the Bond saga, set them in space and threw in legions of scantily clad girls and the odd sexy robot. Lady, Cobra's constant companion, is a distant cousin of Tezuka's Orga, a faithful and devoted friend whose love can be utterly relied on and who looks sexy in metal. In the same year, 1982, the two-hour television special *Andromeda Stories* featured brief nudity and tenderly erotic moments in a science fiction romance based on the manga by Ryu Mitsuse and shojo artist Keiko Takemiya. To the Japanese audience there was nothing especially remarkable about featuring nudity in a prime time television animation. Even though attitudes in Japan had changed since the Second World War, there was still less fuss about flesh (especially painted flesh!) on show than would be the case with an American or British production, but the erotic aspects had to be kept low key. The explosion of anime erotica was still awaiting its trigger: the coming of mass market video.

Space Adventure Cobra

ALIENS AMONG US

Of course, sexual confusion and upsets in the social order can always be blamed on alien influences, as demonstrated by Rumiko Takahashi's hugely successful 1981 television series *Urusei Yatsura*. Creating a formula she was later to exploit with great success in *Ranma 1/2*, and with much more subtlety in the *Mermaid* series, Takahashi uses the alien outsider (in this case, Lum, princess of the planet Oni) as the ultimate fantasy babe, a calendar cutie habitually dressed in a skimpy tiger-skin bikini who constantly throws herself at her chosen human mate, Ataru Moroboshi.

Eventually, Ataru will do what any good Japanese boy should, and reject her for the girl next door, long-suffering Shinobu, who will make the perfect Japanese wife (as discussed further in chapter nine). Until then, he is the envy of all his classmates, with a glorious alien babe on a string, sleeping in his room and generally disrupting his life but never quite managing to stop him chasing after other girls. It's a teenage boy's wish-fulfilment formula which anime continues to exploit, right up to nineties hits *Oh My Goddess!* and *Tenchi Muyo!*. However, few have managed it with as much wit and grace as Takahashi and the Kitty Film studio in those early series.

Blaming the aliens worked in the cinema too, but selling to them was an even better excuse. One of the nastiest manifestations of sex in Japanese cinema occurred in 1983, when *The Professional: Golgo 13* was released (in Japan) to some success. The film had a strong directorial team in Osamu Dezaki and Akio Sugino, a solid, crowd-pulling comic tie-in to Takao Saito's long-running, best-selling manga and some state of the art computer graphics. These look absurd now, as they never blend well with the animation, and were obviously intended as a gimmick. The film was specifically constructed with an eye to possible sales in the West. The producers and writers studied the currently successful spy films and action thrillers coming out of America, and *Golgo 13* was their response. Seeing ourselves as others see us has rarely been more salutary.

Everyone in the film is either amoral or weak, a victim or an aggressor. Every woman in the film is a whore or a madonna, and entirely disposable. In a world where even strength only survives through low cunning, there is no room for concepts like equality. Professional assassin Duke goes to see an old friend when he's in trouble; he sleeps with her, casually availing himself

The Professional: Golgo 13

of sex as just another comfort of the house, and she dies. He meets, sleeps with and outwits a beautiful gangster queen, and she dies. He's on the run because he accepted a contract on the only son of a hugely influential businessman, and the bereaved father wants revenge. But in the ultimate ironic ending, it emerges that the person who took out the contract was the victim himself.

This proves to be an ultimate act of cowardice and selfishness, entirely in keeping with the mood of the film. For his father, faced with the horror of seeing his only child die before his eyes, what follows is a slow descent into madness by way of the implacable pursuit of revenge. For the son's wife and child left behind, the consequences are infinitely worse. The father is so determined to kill the man who killed his son that he uses his widowed daughter-in-law as payment to a deranged assassin. The character of the assassin is skilfully introduced with the full quota of horror; he's hideous, a long, seemingly boneless creature with deadly hands and a voice out of a nightmare, hardly seeming human.

The sequence in which the young widow is summoned down the long corridors of the stately mansion, admitted by the family butler to a darkened room, and abandoned to her fate despite her screams, is a masterfully paced stomach-turner. As for her little girl, now doubly bereaved of a dead father and a mother left catatonic by her ordeal, she and her cuddly toy are used as a bomb delivery service. There could hardly be a greater contrast with the sublime expression of love's unselfishness in *Space Firebird* than the exploitative and self-seeking use of love as weapon or commodity in *Golgo 13*.

In this, as in most other anime made for mass-market consumption, genitals are not depicted, or else are obscured, and the only things we see clearly are breasts and nipples. As the eighties became the nineties and the evolution of erotic anime pushed the boundaries of what could be shown on screen, in the realms of fine art there were other possibilities for suggestion and substitution. Despite the impact of the OAV on mass market erotica, some directors still choose to work on film, and to make films for an intellectually as well as physically adult market. The embedded iconography of the early years of erotic anime is still used, alongside more explicit imagery, to create a powerful erotic impact. *The Sensualist*, a ravishing film based on Saikaku Ihara's novel *The Life of an Amorous Man*, is a case in point.

A beautifully crafted evocation of life in the geisha quarter in the seventeenth century, its main story is that of a merchant who decides to help out a country yokel who's in trouble over some unwise sexual boasting, by using his long association with a great courtesan. Those scenes which actually show the courtesan coupling with her merchant patron are explicit without any display of genitals, but visual devices and metaphors are employed to powerful effect. Taking a cue from the highly mannered art style of that period in history, a slow-moving turtle's head progresses across the screen, its lines and movement suggesting the penis, changing just as we think we see a definite erotic outline; and an unfolding flower hints at the vagina.[11] We see a naked leg emerging from behind a lacquer screen, dazzlingly white-skinned and beautifully curved; the erotic charge is enormous. Because it's so obviously 'art', it can't possibly be offensive. How can a work in which leaves and fabrics were dipped into paint and pressed onto each cel to create texture and pattern possibly be classed alongside violent, shocking shelf-stuffers like *Legend of the Overfiend*? ●

---

[11] This technique from early art which had been extensively used in erotic manga is still popular with artists and animators; U-Jin has used it in his *Visionary* series in combination with the vogue for cute little animals.

VIEW FROM THE INSIDE

The Mechanics of Anime Pornography

A cartoon shows a young schoolgirl, watched secretly by an alien voyeur, surprised while undressing for bed, tied up, assaulted and groped by questing tentacles. The attacker then runs off with her underwear. Why do anime contain such imagery? Far from being a libertine orgy of sex and violence, Japan has its own censorship practises. Much of the strange activity in anime, assumed by Western critics to be some integral part of the Japanese psyche, actually developed from loopholes and evasions of Japanese obscenity law, or through mundane factors in production techniques.

We all live in a world steeped in visual media. We know that the newsreader is not really inside our television, and we know that the train rushing towards the camera will not crash through the screen and flatten us. We have all developed a visual grammar for reading film, and accept many conventions without a second thought. When two characters are on the phone with a split screen between them, we do not assume they are in the same room standing on either side of a black line. We do not think it is weird that Hollywood male leads seem to slip their boxer shorts on after sex just in case they are disturbed by an intruder in the next scene, that nobody in a film ever finishes a meal, or that starlets always seem to wake up with their make-up already applied.

Pornography has a visual grammar of its own, which has influenced the content and style of erotic film-making. A pornographic consumer will say that they want to see sex on screen, but this is a simple request that pornographers have learned to ignore. Do they really want to watch two people humping for a few minutes? Or is it the foreplay that interests them? Or even some innovative ideas for sexual technique? In fact, it is none of these things. The pornographic consumer does not want to *watch* sex at all. They want to *have* it, and the pornography itself is a poor substitute. It is in the interests of the film-makers to generate a *feeling* of sexual activity within the viewer, not merely its image.

In live-action porn, as the actors approach orgasm, the camera cuts from person to person at a faster and faster rate, in direct relation to the proximity of the orgasm. When performers kiss each other, they do so in a peculiar manner, mouths open but not touching, with visibly entwining tongues, because the image of touching tongues is more charged with sexuality than the more everyday image of kissing. The open kiss of pornography is an attempt to capture the feeling of a kiss 'from the inside', thereby making the image more immediate to the viewer.

Similarly, hardcore pornography invariably favours the 'come shot', in which the male ejaculates in full view of the camera. This hammers home the 'reality' of sex; as viewers we are assured that at least one of the participants has had a real orgasm, which helps convince us that the other has too. Participants rarely reach for a condom, need artificial lubrication or experience a loss of erection; of course they don't, because this is a fantasy, and a very specialised, almost interactive fantasy at that. For the masturbating viewer (and this is pornography's prime reason for existence) his aims (and this is the prime gender of the pornographic viewer) are the same as the characters on the screen — to achieve orgasm and think no more of it.

In areas where censorship is stricter, the visual grammar of pornography can adopt some peculiar traditions. Where an erect penis may not be shown, models adopt the positions of hardcore

Frantic, Frustrated & Female

pornographic tales. Text can address emotions and sensations that can only be implied by pictures, and this is why pornography still retains both components. Text can bridge the gap left by an inadequate image, and vice versa.

The introduction of a didactic element implies that a title has an educational value. Just as eighteenth-century pornographers could make their characters commit all manner of perversions, as long as they paid lip service to eventual salvation or retribution, modern pornographers can dress up a sex movie as a 'lesson' in marital relations. Similarly, the plot of a pornographic title may be used to circumvent cultural or legal taboos. Readers are assured that all models are over the age of consent, although the fantasies they provide may suggest otherwise. Perversions may be presented as dreams or nightmares, and thus another step removed from reality. In the subgenres of rape, sodomy and sado-masochism, it is often enough to claim that the victim is really consenting to the act, a device best achieved by having the victim themself 'tell' the story and assure us that it was all very enjoyable.

A similar device exists in the subgenre of homosexual porn in which one participant is above the age of consent and one is not. It less dangerous for the seductee to tell the story than the seductor, since we only have their word that it was not rape. This is also one of the many functions served by 'reader's letters', confessions and 'medical reports'. The fantasy of truth has as many uses as the truth of fantasy.

JAPANESE RESTRICTIONS

Although Article 21 of Japan's 1947 constitution proclaims: 'No censorship shall be maintained', Japanese erotic material is subject to both legal and practical tensions.[1] Japan's censorship system dates back to the period when the newly industrialised

pornography, but with the male member curiously flaccid. In countries where the penis cannot be shown at all, girls pose with suitably phallic substitutes. Bodily fluids are replaced with symbolic substitutes; there is a whole subgenre of sex among the soap suds, or in milk, or with body oil, in order to imply that which cannot be shown.

Some hardcore magazines are curiously cut; a woman may be shown drenched with sperm, but only if it is possible that it is actually something else. Thus it is that a photograph showing ejaculate leaving the penis may not be shown, but the aftermath may. Similarly, as we enter the softer hardcore world that may be sold outside specialist stores, genital contact is not permitted, but the implication of it is. Thus we can see a woman poised as if to fellate a man, with a line of saliva joining her mouth to his penis. Since they are not actually touching, this is permissible. A similar device may be utilised with respect to cunnilingus; the linguist (for want of a better term) may be shown about to commit the act, or pulling away from the act, but not actually in the process of committing the act itself.

These grammars also apply in the plotting of

---

[1] For example, before a film might be regarded by a legal authority, it must also pass muster with the self-regulatory body of the Film Ethics Sustaining Committee (the Eirin Iji Iinkai, or Eirin for short). The same film cannot be released on video without first receiving approval from the associated video body (known, in Japanese sources without the letter 'v', as Biderin). Television stations have their own, separate panels to review broadcast material, and the manga industry remains constantly wary of the Railroad Benefit Association (Tetsudo Kosaikai), whose disapproval can seriously damage a publication's sales. This last body is particularly powerful, since railway station kiosks are one of the major points of sale for manga magazines, and a successful complaint will not only remove the offending issue from sale, but also the next three issues after it.

country was trying to imitate the stuffy, prudish norms of its Western contemporaries. The two critical edicts on obscenity are Article 175 of the Criminal Code (1907) and Article 21 of the Customs Tariffs Law (1910), which attempted to codify the Japanese Government's desire to be taken seriously by the Western powers.

Regarded by the West as shameless and savage, the Japanese people were discouraged from public bathing or nursing, to regard flatulence, nose-picking and eating with one's mouth open as unforgivably gauche activities, and to be, frankly, less open and uninhibited about sex. One of the most influential phrases in Japanese obscenity law appeared in 1918, with the principle that '... pubic area need not be hidden, but there should be no anatomical details to draw the reader's attention.'[2] It is clearly an attempt to discourage gratuitous nudity, while allowing it where artistically necessary, but the 1918 edict has backfired in a spectacular manner. In a remarkable feat of sophistry, it was not regarded as a suggestion, but as a rule: there should be 'no anatomical details', whatever the context of the nudity.[3]

BENDING THE RULES

As in any other culture, the Japanese porn industry found many ways to circumvent this. There was, for example, a vogue in the sixties for 'pink cassettes', actors and actresses grunting and groaning in an erotic tape recording, which fast became popular listening material on the in-car player for the commuting salaryman. Sold from garages and roadside shops, these items flourished for over a year and presented considerable difficulty to the police, since the obscenity law had never been applied to a product devoid of visual image.[4]

Visual media were not permitted to show private parts, and instead viewers' attention was drawn

---

[2] Rubin, *Injurious to Public Morals*, p44.

[3] One of Bornoff's interviewees suggests that bitter, disenchanted officers, passed over for promotion, are the most likely policemen to be assigned the censorship job. He claims that this is an important influence on their over-literal interpretation of the Japanese law, since they genuinely have nothing better to do with their time. *Pink Samurai*, p405.

[4] See Constantine, *Japan's Sex Trade*, pp179-180.

[5] Chizuko Ueno, in her book *The Theatre Beneath the Skirt*, has suggested that another reason for Japanese erotica's obsession with female underwear is that underwear itself is an exotic, relatively recent foreign import. See also Constantine, pp191-196.

Ami — From Then On

to the space left by their absence. Just as the British *Carry On* films fetishised the cleavage rather than the breasts themselves, Japanese erotica avoided 'obscenity' by concentrating on bodily parts that were not deemed obscene, or acts that did not require the sight of genitals. White panties became an erotic commodity in their own right,[5] blank cotton spaces in the place of the body parts they concealed. Sexuality which could be realistically shown without the need for genitalia became an important part of erotica; voyeurism, especially up a skirt at the underwear within, became a standard device of visual titillation.

There is even the mysterious 'show-through' school of erotic photography, which depicts girls in sheer underwear that simultaneously reveals and obscures, or the 'pull-between' variant, where girls are shown in underwear wedged so tightly up into their crotch that it leaves nothing to the imagination. Because both methods show women who are technically clothed, they pass muster with the scrutineer, even though they can often be more explicit in what they reveal than straightforward pornography.

In Japan as with any other society, the limits defined by the obscenity law have had their own influence on the artistic representation of sex, even to the point of perverting it. It was no longer permissible, as it had been in the nineteenth century, to show a man and a woman having regular, explicit intercourse. Thanks to the wording of the law, it was now preferable to show images of men groping breasts (a 'safe' body part), or subjecting women to acts of sadomasochism (which do not require penetration and hence would not require the depiction of genitals).

There was another critical loophole in the 1918 ban, concerning the depiction of children's genitals. They were not included in the edict, since children were not assumed to be sexual creatures, an omission which has played a large part in the birth of the 'Lolita-complex' (or lolikon) subgenre of manga and anime. A image of a man having sex with a woman would be difficult to get past the censor, but two children 'playing doctor' would not be deemed a sexual act, since they are, by definition, 'innocent'. Such reasoning has encouraged many Japanese pornographers to fetishise the child or the schoolgirl, instead of the woman she replaces.

However, several cases started to test the mettle of Japanese obscenity law, resulting in a significant increase in the number of fully explicit images in all media. After a censorious peak in 1991, when an erotic fanzine was confiscated by police, the manga business has enjoyed a new lease of life. Retailers took adult manga off the shelves in reaction to a media frenzy, and then sneaked them back again when they realised how much money they were losing. The vocal minority was swiftly drowned out by the discreet majority that continued to buy such products.

BACK TO UNREALITY

The anime business has also capitalised on the recent period of publishing freedom. Until the mid nineties, sexual organs were depicted in anime as they so often were in manga, as areas in shadow or outlines devoid of detail. Characters would either be drawn with no genitals at all, or with a symbol in place of the offending object. Anime made after the mid nineties are likely to be more graphic in their depiction of the sexual act, sometimes to the extent of fully detailed genitalia, and unambiguous images of bodily fluids and unusual sexual acts.

Sometimes, however, a sense of complete freedom can be detrimental. Some pornographic anime adopt a self-censorship policy, not to prevent the unwelcome attentions of the police, but to push the right buttons with the viewer. If something is 'forbidden', it immediately becomes more titillating. Even if there is nothing untoward on screen, the presence of a censorship dot or blur can convince the viewer they are watching something so dangerous that it has to be cut.

In anime made before the mid nineties, there are several recurring ways in which the obscenity law is bent. The vagina is rarely depicted realistically, although there is some exploitation of the 'show-through' tradition. This rarely involves see-through underwear, however, since this is harder to animate. Instead, the viewer sees the shape or outline of the genitals beneath opaque underwear. Much can be done with animating highlights and shadows. In medium shots we will see the female's pelvic region, normally devoid of pubic hair, and possibly with the faintest hint of the outline of the labia majora. Close-ups are often depicted in false colour; *Frantic, Frustrated & Female* shows a detailed view of manual vaginal stimulation, in a deep blue hue entirely at odds with the fleshy pinks of other shots. This is clearly not a vagina, because it is blue. Therefore, the image can be shown of something not a finger massaging something that cannot be a clitoris.

There is an extra level of close-up unseen in live-action pornography for obvious reasons, which is the interior view. Uncommon in Japanese erotic art before the twentieth century, it was nonetheless present, and provided a 'camera angle' unavailable in real life. In the days of heavier anime censorship, the interior view performed a dual function. It both offered something unusual and circumvented restrictions by capitalising on the darkness and shadow within the human body. An interior view of fellatio, for example, can suggest the highlights of a tongue on a penis, without fully depicting either. More recently, interior views have been better 'lit', although there is still an apparent reluctance to show the penis in realistic detail. Thus in *The Elven Bride* we see a penis entering a vagina from both inside and outside, although it has been suitably doctored so that it looks like no penis known to man; the male is not in fact human, and hence has a prehensile penis with questing cilia around the tip.

Overfiend II:1

This device is often repeated, since the Japanese obscenity law is vague enough to permit film-makers to show perfectly realistic, detailed dildos committing the sex act, but not realistic penises. Several incidences of sex in the *Overfiend* series echo this, most notably in two scenes that were greatly trimmed in the British version, the Nazi Rape Machine from chapter II.1 and Caesar's metallic penis from chapter III.2. A dildo, vibrator or similar object is not a penis, and therefore not subject to the same restrictions. Similarly, women do not possess penises, and so the magical growth of one on a woman is permitted, since it cannot possibly be real. This device appears in the erotic PC game *Timestripper*, and also in *Frantic, Frustrated & Female*, where in both cases it is used as an excuse to pursue scenes of woman-on-woman sexual assault. Sometimes the surrogate penis may be replaced with something altogether more distressing to the censor, such as the gun-muzzles excised from the British releases of *Overfiend* III.3 and *Guy*, or one of anime's most infamous inventions, the wandering tentacle.

SUBLIMINALS AND SUBLIMATION

Animators have been known to embed jokes in the image itself, often by adding a subliminal image for a single frame (ie 1/24th of a second) that can only be seen if paused on a laserdisc player. The humour often borders on the erotic, and some fans will admit to pausing action shots to get a good look at the female characters' panties. One anime, *Junk Boy*, even features a protagonist for whom an obsession with freeze-frame pantie-shots is a claim to fame. His obsession lands him a top job 'road-testing' porn.

Some claim to have seen more explicit subliminals in supposedly 'clean' anime, including famous characters without underwear, but the habit is dying out. The prevalence of DTP software has made it so easy to alter images that some websites are stuffed full of unlicensed depictions of cartoon characters, ranging from the mildly naughty to the hardcore. When more explicit material can be found elsewhere, the subliminal variety is redundant, although some pornographers take the opposite route and insert tiny jokes to lighten up the erotic. In *Lady Blue*, for example, there is an explicit scene of a finger teasing a vagina, but deep inside a tiny, smiling cartoon character can be seen.

The erotic elements buried in mainstream anime are brought to the foreground in pornography, which has literally nothing to hide. It is unlikely that a frame-by-frame trawl through an erotic anime will turn up any subliminals, since there's no need to give fans a surreptitious peek at a girl's underwear if it will be ripped off any minute.

Finally, many erotica provide something that fans cannot usually see in their mainstream equivalents: the sight of popular characters, or at least their spitting images, in compromising positions. There has always been an interest, especially in the fanzine field, in pornographic versions of popular titles, in which characters are portrayed in a radically different light. In the realm of anime itself, where pornalike homages have to be paid for by producers and protected by lawyers, we can occasionally find thinly disguised erotic variants on popular shows and characters, such as *The Elven Bride*, a perfect masturbatory opportunity for all those fans of *Lodoss War* who ever wondered what the elf-princess Deedlit would look like with her clothes off.

PICTURE THIS

Imagine: a bored Californian housewife seduces a workman in her home, but the two are surprised by her office-worker husband returning home early. The two men both have sex with the woman, finishing by standing over her and ejaculating in her face as she reaches her climax.

This non-existent yet rather typical set-up from an American porn movie has been built from technical limits, not imagination. It suggests a small crew, a tight schedule and a non-existent set (in fact someone's home). The sex is presented for the benefit of a male audience, to the extent of including actors from two class backgrounds and a finalé that implies the sexual fulfilment of the male will automatically equate with that of the female. It can tell us a lot about the American porn industry, but what it tells us about America is vague and indirect.

Imagine: a cartoon image of a young schoolgirl, watched secretly by an alien voyeur, surprised while undressing for bed, tied up, assaulted and groped by questing tentacles. The attacker then runs off with her underwear.

Equally, the scene described above is not from a real anime, but has been constructed from a number of mechanical considerations. As a cartoon image, it is one step removed from reality, and does not require the consent of live actors. As science fiction, it is a further step away from normality. The schoolgirl is not a woman, and hence, by the rationale of the censorship law, not a sexual being. The striptease scene extends and prolongs the suspense, while titillating the male viewer as he identifies with the male

voyeur, permitted secret access to the inner sanctum of the girl's bedroom. He can then assault her (violence not involving genitalia), attack her with penis-substitute tentacles and then escape with her panties, a symbolic representation of that which the underwear covers. Is it really any stranger than the images presented by its American counterpart?

These are just some of the artistic and legal restrictions that have moulded anime pornography. All these elements combine to form its distinctive tone and style, and the erotic anime we see today are the product of several decades of development within Japan's domestic film business. It all makes perfect sense, insofar as pornography ever makes sense. The problem comes when such images are exported to a country which does not share the same mechanical restrictions.

Compared to live-action porn, anime often takes place in more exotic settings. Science fiction, fantasy or horror hybrids are common, whereas the live porn market is often restricted by practical considerations to hotel rooms and private houses. Japan is an exotic setting in itself to the Western viewer, and this often adds a certain appeal. As a foreign country, of course, we are able to map our own perversions and hang-ups onto the distant aliens of the Far East.

We are not sick-minded individuals if we watch *Overfiend*, but the Japanese (yes, all of them) *are* because they made it. The average Western viewer has never been to Japan, but has grown up reading stories and articles about the incredible culture and lifestyle of these inscrutable aliens. Japan does not exist in the real world, Japan does not shave its legs or steal your seat on the train. Japanese girls, if you ever met one, would become your willing sex slaves at a moment's notice. Japan is *Shogun*, or *Black Rain*, or *Empire of the Senses*, or *Akira*. There's honour and ninja and all sorts of weird stuff. It is the most foreign of foreign places, and its entertainment is equally alien. Isn't it?

The Japanese, we immediately assume, must be very strange if they prefer animated porn to the 'real' thing, if they find underage girls sexually attractive or if they continually 'demand' more scenes of abuse and perversion. In actuality, it is the non-Japanese consumers who are the weird ones, because they are the ones who have volunteered to impose these traditions on themselves. ●

MAGICAL GIRLS GROW UP

The Development of Shojo Anime

Much of the anime available in the West is made for the adolescent or young adult male market, but in Japan there is also a healthy and diverse sector aimed squarely at girls and young women. With its powerful manga tradition and merchandising machine, shojo material can be used, like its Western entertainment counterparts, for marketing gain and social engineering. To its young consumers, it's all about fun. Later, powerful emotional drives kick in, and these too find expression in the shojo universe. The role models and ideas presented have interesting ramifications.

In early 1998, the *New York Times* ran an article by Peter M. Nichols, prompted by the forthcoming Disney releases of Hayao Miyazaki movies. The image chosen to accompany the article was the Cyguard monsterborg from *Cybernetics Guardian*. Given the usual press stance on anime, that's no surprise, but the content showed evidence of some change in editorial attitudes:

'There's an air of anticipation in the land of anime, the risqué and warlike corner of Japanese animation that has become hugely popular on video in the United States. Amid characters like the genetically enhanced MD (Most Dangerous) Geist, liberator of the devastated planet of Jerra, and Doreimon, a scantily clad android from the twenty-second century, a youngster named Kiki is about to arrive — representing, of all things, the forces of civic-minded youth... Kiki, the young star of *Kiki's Delivery Service*, isn't from Jerra but from a magic kingdom many galaxies removed called the Walt Disney Company. The film, which will be released straight to video later this year, represents Disney's cautious entry into Jap-

anese animation. But don't call the film anime.'[1]

The article went on to claim that in America 'these days' anime refers strictly to adult Japanese animation, which the writer also labelled 'pornimation'; yet this wasn't just another attempt to demonise anime. The article's main point was that the Disney deal would widen the market for Japanese animation and legitimise all kinds of material not currently sold widely in the States: 'By importing samples from the vast selections of child-oriented animation from Japan, Disney may well clear shelf space for all kinds of work from Japan... Disney's link to a family film may open the way for Japanese animation that's not all sex and violence.'

John O'Donnell of American anime distributor Central Park Media, quoted in the same article, observed: 'In America, cartoons are for kids; in Japan they slice up the market into both sexes and every age group... We say anime is all violence and sex, and so far that's right, because the other ninety-five per cent hasn't been released here yet.'

Of that ninety-five per cent, a large proportion is aimed partly or wholly at the female market. In the West, where female comic and animation fans are in a minority, this may come as a surprise; in Japan, women and girls who enjoy comics and animation are catered for in just the

---

1 Nichols, 'At Mickey's House...' The deal between Disney and Miyazaki's backers Tokuma gives the Disney organisation distribution rights worldwide outside Japan on screens, and in Japan on retail video, for a number of titles by Miyazaki and his Studio Ghibli colleagues, as well as several other Tokuma properties.

Little Witch Sally

same market-oriented manner as those who watch wrestling or buy cosmetics. For a television series to succeed on television and in merchandising terms in the increasingly cash-strapped and competitive anime market, it helps to portray women who get a fair share of the action as well as having unfeasibly large bosoms, but good-looking male characters and strong relationships are an important factor as well.

As the historical outline in chapter one shows, the erotic elements of anime developed slowly and furtively, almost in hiding. Before the coming of videotape, it was difficult to watch porn without attracting attention. As Japan's affluence increased, and teenagers increasingly had their own televisions and VCRs in their bedrooms, or access to the family set-up while their parents were busy working, it became easier for young males to watch in privacy.

For females, however, the situation was different. Much as in the West, girls in Japan still share a greater proportion of household tasks than boys. All over the developed world, parents still tend to supervise girls more closely than boys, although this attitude is breaking down as more parents work long hours outside the home. It was generally more difficult for girls and women to find time alone with a video and no chance of interruption. Their choice of television programming, and to some extent of video programming, tended to be restricted to material which would not seem out of the ordinary to a casual viewer.

This attitude to female entertainment, as well as a complete misunderstanding of the style and purpose of shojo anime, leads many English-speaking fans, especially male ones seeking to assure females of their politically correct nice-guy credentials, to assume that such popular

romantic comedies as *Ranma 1/2, Oh My Goddess!* and *Tenchi Muyo!* are 'shojo', whereas they are all more correctly described as teenage male wish-fulfilment. Their style sometimes employs shojo elements, usually to make a point English-speaking audiences don't have the background to appreciate, but their main focus, in all three cases, is a boy pursued by a string of beautiful, gifted girls.

Tenchi, Ranma et al are different only in approach, not in kind, from the breast-fetishism of *Plastic Little*. They present all teenage girls as stereotypes, potentially available (even to a complete no-hoper) if you get the magic right, wholly fixated on getting a boyfriend and scoring over other girls. While girls the world over watch and enjoy shows aimed primarily at their brothers, and there are many female fans of such romantic comedies, these females are not the primary intended audience. The real development of anime for girls, shojo anime, meandered through a number of semi-concealed byways as it split into several major story types.

THE MAGIC BEGINS

The groundwork was laid in manga, which continues (for the reasons outlined above) to be the major arena for women's erotic and romantic entertainment in Japan.[2] The first televised stirrings of this new growth floated innocently onto the airwaves in 1966, when *Little Witch Sally* was screened on Japanese television. This delightful children's series was based on Mitsuteru Yokoyama's manga, but owed a good deal of its inspiration to the American television comedy *Bewitched*. In the American series, the cute witch who came to live in the human world to study these strange creatures was a fully-fledged babe, and her eventual decision to stay and marry the hero was a male wish-fulfilment fantasy made curvy flesh, with a cute crinkly nose thrown in. In the Japanese version, which was on the air for two years, the cute witch who came to live in the human world was a little blonde girl, whose pointed hat topped off an ensemble that included knee-high white socks and sensible shoes.

---

2 For a detailed history of the development of the women's and girls' comic market, see the works of Schodt listed in the bibliography. Since comics are outside the scope of this book, I refer to them only briefly, but it is impossible to develop a full and detailed understanding of Japanese women's erotic entertainment without studying them, and Schodt is by far the best English language source.

The 'magical girl' genre, which was to have such a huge influence on anime for years to come, was born.

Little girls just loved Sally. Her mama and papa were magical beings, she had magical friends (the magic familiar, whether humanoid, avian or animal, was to be an important factor in future magical girl series), yet she also knew ordinary human kids like them, and had the same kind of problems they did with school and everyday life. They entered completely into Sally's world. The voice actress Megumi Hayashibara, veteran of roles ranging from the female Ranma in *Ranma 1/2* to the consumptive Rei in *Evangelion*, credits the series with inspiring her own attitude to her work:

'When I was a little girl watching TV, I used to love a character called Sally-chan — not the voice actress who played her, but Sally herself. Now, when I work, I want people to think of the character I'm playing, not me personally.'[3]

Sally's adventures were so popular that when she retired, another little girl was needed to take her place. Step forward Akko-chan, of *Akko-chan's Secret*. The mysterious gift of a magic compact mirror endows the human Akko-chan with the power to transform herself into any person or animal she might choose. This introduced another vital element of the magical girl mix — the magical accessory or item which bestows power on an ordinary little girl, provided she fulfils certain requirements.[4] Another witch-girl followed in Sally's footsteps in the 1972 series *Little Witch Chappy*, wielding a pretty magic wand with a rose at each end, and there were more to come, cast from the same mould. These characters were all cheerful, self-reliant, obliging, perfect role models for well-mannered girls. If the little viewer identified with the heroine, she would see that the 'magic' worked more effectively because she did her best and wanted to help others. Her baby dreams were used to shape her future behaviour into socially acceptable desires and actions.

---

[3] Hayashibara, quoted in McCarthy, 'The Voice of Anime', p9.
[4] As time wore on the merchandising of these accessories was to assume major importance, culminating in the epic success of the series *Sailor Moon*, which contributed a large slice of Bandai's revenue from 1993-96. The Sailor Scouts save the world through the power of love and make-up; they certainly saved Bandai.

ALL CHANGE

The little girls who first followed the adventures of Sally got older. They needed new heroines whose dreams and ambitions grew with them, and their little sisters would also need older role models as they 'graduated' from repeats of Sally and her successors. Big sister of the three most noteworthy successors was the 1982 *Minky Momo*, who remains the only magical girl until *Sailor Moon* to have an English-language outing — one of her movies has been released on video in the West as *Gigi and the Fountain of Youth*.

Minky Momo is the quintessential magical girl. Her very existence depends on magic. She is the princess of the land of dreams, sent to Earth by her real parents because humans have forgotten how to dream, and as a result the magical land of her birth is crumbling away. By living with adoptive human parents and using her magic powers, she has to try and revive the ability of humankind to dream and hope. She will achieve this by helping to solve the problems and troubles which burden humans. Of course, there are limits to the problems a nine year-old girl can solve, so she magically transforms into various adult guises, and her transformation sequences, while never actually revealing anything remotely sexual, began a trend which became an increasingly important (and increasingly daring) element of the genre's appeal.

Transformation has a long history in fairy-tales and legends, but in Japan it is also important in the giant robot series and team shows, where fighting machines combine in different configurations during a sequence of stock footage which forms a vital part of the merchandising armoury. The magical girls' transformations followed the same rules; the sequence was always identical, usually between a minute and ninety seconds long, repeated at least once in every show. It involved elements of ritual and magic, such as special words or gestures, changing the nature of the participant in a delicious flurry of colour, light and glamour as she acquired her all-important accessories and her magical costume.

Creamy Mami, an early work from the pen of Kazunori Ito, whose later scriptwriting triumphs included *Patlabor* and *Ghost in the Shell*, followed *Minky Momo* onto television in 1983. An elementary schoolgirl, Yu can magically become a famous sixteen year-old idol singer with the help of an imp, a magic baton, and another of those transformation scenes. Little Yu has a restriction not common to all magical girls; she can become Creamy Mami for one year only, and if anyone finds out her secret she'll lose her magic powers. Her parents and friends are huge Creamy fans, and must be kept completely ignorant of Yu's dual identity, which causes all kinds of problems. When her friend Toshio accidentally sees her transformation sequence, she does indeed lose her powers, and the pair set off on a quest to recover them, which results in Toshio's loss of memory. He stays in this state until Creamy's final concert, when the restoration of his memories is accompanied by the final loss of Yu's power to transform. But now the time is right for this, and Yu is happy to return to being her normal, everyday self, while Toshio, having atoned for his unwitting act of impiety in spying on the magical secrets of his idol, values the real Yu above her transformed self.

By the time *Magical Emi,* in which an elementary schoolgirl becomes a famous and very cute teenage magician by magical means, hit television screens in 1985, the transformation sequence was as firmly established in anime folklore for magical girls as for giant robots. Vital elements of the change might be blurred or impossible to follow, but the end result was that the smaller and less powerful had transformed into the larger and more powerful. The robots, however, didn't lose any clothing during the process.

The similarities between magical girl shows like *Creamy Mami* and lolikon porn series (discussed in chapter five) are very marked. The ability to become an adult 'magically' by a secret transformation ritual, without needing to go through the painful process of puberty and experience, whilst retaining the ability to return to the innocence and beauty of childhood, is one of the foundations of both genres. In the best of the magical girl series, it's a positive thing; the young heroine can learn from her experiences, and 'try out' adult life without being scarred by her mistakes, while adults who witness her magical powers at work can recapture a little of the child in themselves. In reality, as any honest pornographer must admit, it's impossible. The magic which enables a child to take part in the adult world as an equal, and yet return to the unsullied innocence of childhood afterwards, is impure fantasy.

The magical girl genre remains marked by the encroachment of lolikon invaders on its flower-strewn turf. Shows as different as *Ranma 1/2, Megami Paradise* and *Oh My Goddess!* have borrowed some of its clothes and accessories for their own purposes, which have nothing to do with female

entertainment and wish-fulfilment, and none of its incarnations since *Cream Lemon* have been able to flash their underwear or run through a nude transformation sequence without attracting leering pre- and post-pubescent male attention.

Sailor Moon, the most recent of the great magical girl shows, has a following in English-speaking fandom which is very different from the massive audience of ten year-old Japanese girls who propelled it up the ratings at home. Many of these Western fans shave, mostly their voices have broken, and they're the last people you would expect to see buying Japanese dolls, though maybe you won't be surprised to see them freeze-frame through those transformation sequences. It's interesting to note that in *Sailor Moon*, as in all the classic magical girl shows, genitals are never revealed in the transformations. This didn't stop the American release company from using computer animation to cover the heroine's indistinctly depicted body in a leotard on every frame.

Nude transformation sequences have now become regular elements in many mainstream shows. Sometimes the sequences are used for comedic effect, as in the OAV series *Moldiver*, where both heroine Mirai and her brother Hiroshi are caught out by a design flaw in his Mol unit. When the power runs out and the superhero powersuit vanishes, the transformation sequence reverses and the wearer is left defenceless and stark naked, usually in a public place and in imminent danger of discovery. Sometimes they're presented for the amusement of the female viewer, as in *Voltage Fighter Gowcaizer* and *Teknoman*, where the young male leads are stripped to the (non-explicit) buff before magical armour forms round their muscular bodies (and all of them, including the elegantly slim ones, have muscular bodies for purposes of a transformation sequence). Even in a genre so far removed from shojo as the game tie-in, the influence of the magical girl persists. Studios making television anime will use any device available to sell merchandise and add to the viewing figures, and the magical girl's devices have been proven to work.

POWER AND SUFFERING

The magical girl genre was only one strand in the development of shojo anime. There were other forms of female escapism. Just a year after Sally came along, another manga starring a young girl was animated with great success. Osamu Tezuka, creator of *Astro Boy*, put part of his own child-hood on the screen when he dug into his memories of afternoons spent with his mother at matinee performances of the Takarazuka theatre troupe. The resultant *Princess Knight* defined the adventure-romance element of shojo.

Takarazuka is a group of female performers whose elaborate stage shows are a cross between musical and melodrama, with an enthusiastic audience which is predominantly female. The lead male roles are taken by actors from the company who specialise in playing men. The lead character of *Princess Knight*, a royal child born female because of a mistake in Heaven, has been brought up from birth as a boy because she is her parents' sole offspring and only a boy can inherit their throne. Compelled to live out a masquerade where discovery would have dangerous consequences for the stability of her homeland, she must not only acquire so-called 'masculine' skills — horsemanship, swordsmanship, statesmanship and so on — but master them convincingly enough to lead men.

This introduced an element of action and danger to the show, which won it many male fans and gave its female viewers a more adventurous role model to aspire to. It also gave them a foretaste of the costs of stepping into a man's world — when the princess falls in love, the possible consequences are unthinkable, and she is faced with the stark choice between abandoning her people and her destiny, or giving up the chance of marriage and a family of her own.[5] For the Takarazuka players, who sign a contract specifying no marriage until they retire, and for many other women in Japan and elsewhere, this is a familiar

---

[5] As Friedan points out in *The Second Sex*, much social upheaval and confusion in the immediate post-war years was deliberately suppressed under feelings of relief and gratitude; but the fact remained that women who had been running every aspect of domestic life now had to go back into the home and become 'little women' again, so that their men could feel like heroes and face less competition in the jobs market. Women who were proud of their ability to run a heavy machine, keep a lorry on the road without spares or manage a minuscule budget and keep a family or a workforce operational, were expected not just to adopt dependency and triviality as desirable character traits, but to be grateful for the opportunity, because their partners, sons or brothers were home safely. Similarly, the impact on Japanese women of the many stresses of war and defeat contributed to changing views of Japanese society. *Princess Knight*, first published in 1953, echoes the confusion of those post-war years, from which women have yet to fully emerge.

dilemma. Breaking the glass ceiling is possible, with luck, talent, hard work and the right help; but break the rules once you're on the other side, and you crash down again, possibly taking others with you.

In the manga version of *Princess Knight*, Tezuka deployed many of the visual tricks and metaphors which were to become part of shojo manga's everyday vocabulary: the use of hearts and flowers as fillers in or frames for the picture, the starry eyes indicating characters' true feelings whatever the script might require them to do, the feathery lines, the sweeping drapery used to substitute for detailed background or to focus in on a particular element of a large scene, the elaboration of details of costume, jewellery or hair adornment, all enriched by colour and movement. He also exploited the romantic aspects of the neo-European, pseudo-historical setting. These two useful distancing devices were quickly adopted for other shojo manga and other television shows, such as *Haikara Passing By*, set in Japan at the turn of the century, and the sublime *Rose of Versailles*, which takes place in the years leading up to the French Revolution.

Based on the manga by Riyoko Ikeda, *Rose of Versailles* owes a great debt to *Princess Knight* in terms of theme and style. It too has a heroine named and reared as a boy for inheritance reasons, though her real gender is not entirely secret. This heroine also finds her way of life a terrible barrier to the achievement of true happiness, though in her case the barrier is not assumed gender, but class. She comes to realise that she loves her childhood companion Andre, born a servant of her family, but in pre-Revolutionary France such a love is as unthinkable as if they were both men.

Stylistically, the similarities to *Princess Knight* are obvious. The heroine, Oscar François de Jarjayes, greatest swordsman in the realm and head of the Queen's Guard, plays out her tragedy of love and power in an elaborate frame of roses, drapery and glittering costumes. Her impossible love for Andre is paralleled by the impossible love of the young Marie Antoinette, whom she serves and admires, for Count Axel Von Fersen — a doomed romance, played out in full Court garb in the mirrored salons and ornate gardens of Versailles. Romance may be gritty and action-packed, it may be emotionally wrenching and sincerely felt, but if it's going to work for its intended audience, it must always be suitably dressed.

Rose of Versailles

rather than dropping out for marriage at the earliest legal age, the idea that there might be not just a choice, but a struggle between home and career or ambition emerged more strongly as a theme in anime, just as it had in manga.

Aim for the Ace! and its successor *New Aim for the Ace!* took a perennially popular wish-fulfilment theme, the girl with no obvious outstanding abilities but with great determination, as the starting point for the story of a tennis player's struggle to the pinnacle of her sport, and the problems of combining a gruelling professional schedule with a happy private life. Sumika Yamamoto's manga original was animated for television in 1973 and was still popular enough to sustain the release of new made-for-video stories in 1990; its popularity continued both in repeat screenings in Japan and in translated screenings overseas. Mitsuru Adachi's sports manga were also very successful in this area, with *Touch* a significant title in the thematic development of the female's struggle to reconcile her own dreams and ambitions with her need for love.

This prevalent notion of the price to be paid for happiness is reflected in another strand of shojo anime, the hardship genre. A number of titles fall into this category, but the defining one is Toei's weepie marathon *Candy Candy*, first televised in 1976. Set in that pretty yet undefined Middle-European place and time beloved of so many anime television directors (including those working on series of a very different style, like *Lupin III*), the series follows the life of orphan girl Candy, whose many travails start when her best friend is adopted, inspiring her wish to leave the orphanage and find a family of her own. Unfortunately she becomes a paid companion to the spoiled, malicious children of a wealthy couple, dreadful brats who make her life a misery. A chance meeting leads to love and escape, but the prospect of happiness is snatched away again when her beloved is killed during a hunt. Sent to study in England by the stern head of her late love's family, she meets with old friends, as well as old enemies who try to destroy her chance at a new love.

In 1979, after 115 episodes of hankie-soaking suffering and pain, Candy finds her happiness at last. None of the huge audience who followed her trail of misadventure every week could doubt that she earned it. What they may not have

Beware, though, of making the assumption that because this ravishing confection has been wrapped in spun sugar roses and glitter dreams, it has no more substance than a syrupy Mills & Boon romance novel. Schodt considers that although Ikeda's work was presented in comic-book form, it could be more aptly characterised as literature.[6] The skilful use of emotional tension and the twists and turns of plot and character are as carefully crafted and deployed as they would be in a conventional Western novel. Appropriately, the Takarazuka troupe, one of the original inspirations for *Princess Knight*, paid their own homage to its lineal descendant by turning *Rose of Versailles* into a highly acclaimed stage production.

This active, action-embracing vision of the capable yet truly romantic heroine catered for the viewer who had outgrown the original magical princess fantasies, opening the door for love stories in which girls did more than sit around and dream. The heroes and heroines were in the right age bracket for junior high school girls to aspire to and for their older sisters to identify with. As Japan's prosperity grew and more girls moved through the complete state education system,

[6] Schodt, in 'Berusaiyu No Bara', p15.

realised was that after so much trauma it was unlikely she'd be anything but thoroughly grateful to be safe, cared for and loved. Not for Candy the struggle to maintain a career and family life; she'd had enough struggle. Now her destiny was to be a happy and fulfilled wife, and eventually, no doubt, a happy and fulfilled mother.

WHAT'S LOVE GOT TO DO WITH IT?

Love is important to every aspect of shojo anime. In the magical girl genre it is focused as love of family, friends and cute fluffy animals; in the historical and sporting romances it is the obstacle to achievement or the impossible dream; in the hardship stories it is the reward for our heroine after her sufferings: a pink, flower-encircled 'happy ever after' in which she will be safe and secure from the cruel outside world. But romantic love is the foundation of a hierarchical relationship in which the heroine must, of necessity, sacrifice her own autonomy to care for a home and raise a family. One of the roles of the shojo formula is to convey the subliminal conviction that the sacrifice is worth it.

Very few anime, for whatever audience, look in detail at what exactly constitutes 'happy ever after', because the reality is hardly wish-fulfilment. *Slow Step* gives an indication, all the more revealing because the Japanese writer and director use it as a signpost, as well as comic relief. Heroine Minatsu gets a visit from her teacher Mr Yamazakura, whom she will eventually marry. He turns up unannounced and, because she's home alone, decides to wait and see her parents. Minatsu (who is already established in the series as a feisty girl and nobody's doormat) drops everything and spends the entire time running around after her uninvited guest, providing drinks and emptying the constantly filling ashtray. He doesn't utter a word of thanks, and neither of them regards this as anything out of the ordinary. He's just a man who needs a good wife to look after him, and she's a well brought up girl with nice manners who will make someone a good wife.

Domestic bliss is constantly serving others and, if you're lucky, sometimes being told how important and loved this makes you. Take off the glass slipper, Cinderella, and come and be measured for your glittery designer apron. Luckily you're a nice, well brought up young woman with the right education and the right attitude, so you'll like it, or at worst be reasonable about it.

The hierarchical aspects of the love relationship not only require that the female partner should be able to carry out the domestic and social roles required of her, but also that both she and the male should be 'suited'. In social terms this usually means that they are of roughly equivalent standing, interests and ambitions; romantically it's considered desirable for the couple to be broadly similar in age and physical type, and to complement each other's personalities. Practical, cheerful Minatsu will be a perfect partner for her kind-hearted but domestically muddled teacher. Martial artist Ranma Saotome will suit the martial artist daughter of dojo-owning Mr Tendo down to the ground. Cross-racial marriages, wide age gaps or 'Beauty and the Beast' stories are expected to end in tears, and surprise is mixed with the conventional expressions of delight when they don't.

One of the most interesting and erotically focused videos of 1985 was *Leda: Fantastic Adventures of Yoko*. Made ostensibly as a science fiction adventure for teenagers, it was aimed at girls even more than boys, with its powerful romantic storyline and elements of shojo style and story structure, though plenty of action and a couple of bikini'd battle babes made it perfectly acceptable to most young men. Yoko is a teenage girl with a talent for music. She's in love with a boy at her high school, but is too shy to let him know it. Yoko pours all her feelings into composing a beautiful romantic melody for the piano, and plans to give him the tape and hope it will convey her feelings where she can't find the right words. But on another world, one in a parallel dimension to ours, a treacherous ex-priest of the Goddess Leda is planning to bridge the gap between dimensions and invade Earth.

Yoko's melody is the only thing that can power up the mystical engine he needs to make the link, and so Yoko is snatched into the world of Leda. Here she unknowingly triggers her own transformation sequence and, much to her surprise, learns that she is Leda's Warrior, the only one who can power up the Wings of Leda (an armoured flying machine) and fight the evil which is devastating this strange world and threatening her own. But her adversary, the ex-priest and would-be conqueror of Earth, is a very attractive, intelligent being, a sophisticated and sexually aware older man who is confident that he can secure Yoko's cooperation by locking her into a 'sweet dream of love'. He thinks he knows just what she wants, but does he?

The difference between their ideas of love surfaces in an erotically charged dream sequence in which normal teenage romantic fantasies are stalked by serpentine winged terrors, and the face of the loved one — in which we might read his identity and his true motivation — is always hidden. In the end, these sensual and self-absorbed dreams can't provide the honesty and innocence Yoko really wants from love, and she breaks the seducer's domination of her mind through her unwavering quest for a genuinely loving first romance.

It might be argued that this is reading too much into a teenage adventure fantasy, but for the power of that dream sequence and the fact that Yoko's two main allies, Lingam the talking dog and Yoni the girl warrior, are named after the ancient Hindi terms for male and female genitals. There are no exposed tits and the tentacles don't penetrate, but, with its imagery of serpents and swords, its character names drawn from erotic literature and the safety of two worlds depending on a powerful man's seduction of a young girl, *Leda* is a video with profound erotic impact. Its ties to the shojo tradition are also unmistakable. Yoko becomes both a magical girl, complete with cute animal companion and accessories, and an action-adventure heroine with a mission, as she tries to overcome her shyness, save her world, and make the right choice for her own life and love.

CONTROLLING THE FUTURE

A vitally important consideration in any view of a woman's right to choose her life is its impact on future generations. The little girls watching magical princesses transform into teen idols are not even vaguely aware of this, but as they grow up that awareness grows with them. Shojo anime usually stops short at this point, when reality strips away the possibility of further romance, but the mainstream has something to say on the subject.

Yoshikazu Yasuhiko's 1986 movie *Arion* uses strong erotic elements in a story designed for the mass cinema audience, but is as conventional as *Leda* in its view of what constitutes a 'proper' sexual choice for young women, and more so in its view of who should make that choice. The main erotic focus is on two characters, the god-siblings Apollo and Athena, and the object of their very different but equally selfish desires and ambitions, the innocent young slave Lesfeena. She's a classic example of the heroine as object —

a young girl with immense potential to help settle the social order, a potential of which she is unaware and which she is completely unable to use for herself. Only in the right relationship with the right man can that potential be properly exploited. Of course, this will lead to her own happiness, but the social dimension is the more important one.

Lesfeena is fated to marry Arion, the young hero. This will link her divine blood and his Titan heritage to the human race and will enable the son of Prometheus to lead Greece out of its superstitious chaos into a new age of reason. It will also be an entirely suitable relationship, in traditional terms, linking two young people of similar ages and backgrounds to the benefit of both parties and society as a whole. At one point in the film it seems that this 'ideal' relationship is in fact a forbidden one, since Arion thinks Lesfeena is his sister. The relationship of brother and sister Apollo and Athena, which already hints at past incest and its terrible present results, is more than enough to convince him that taboos are there for a reason.

Once the tangle of lies and relationships that is the film's view of Greek mythology is resolved, it becomes evident that Arion wasn't following forbidden desires, but doing the right thing all along. The dramatic tension of this possible impropriety heightens the classic happy ending. There's also a subplot involving an urchin who befriends Arion and later reveals that 'he' is really a girl in disguise and has fallen in love with our young hero. But a love relationship between them is impossible; Arion thinks of her as a boy and a friend, and she's much too young for him. If they had met a few years later, things might have worked out, but he has a destiny and needs a suitable partner now, while she has to wait through the pain of feelings awakened too young and hope a suitable partner can properly direct those feelings in the future.

Apollo, whose relationship with his sister is best not closely examined, wants Lesfeena to bring her genes to the Olympian line and enable their rule to extend into the coming modern age with himself as its enlightened head, succeeding his father Zeus, who in his time similarly supplanted his own father. As in *Leda*, the union of an innocent young girl with a much older, much more sophisticated lover who possesses a suspected perverse past and a political agenda, is less socially and morally desirable than a marriage of innocent equals. Athena, meanwhile, is a raging torrent of repressed and perverted sexual energy whose frustrations emerge as spite, torture and instability on an epic scale, a warning to those who love their brothers in unorthodox ways and a contrast to the tender feelings growing between Arion and Lesfeena.

The climax of the film takes place literally inside the cavernous red womb of the ancient Mother Goddess Gaea, who is held largely responsible for the whole sorry mess of human history — though the father god Zeus (her grandson), takes his share of the guilt as a weak and self-deluding male whose prime imperatives are self-justification and self-preservation. The message is that forbidden fruit can never be truly sweet; only a properly ordered relationship can lead to a happy ending.

THE GENETIC IMPERATIVE

The breeding potential of women is usually only hinted at in anime — it's another part of the 'happy ever after' on which reality impinges too closely for fantasy's comfort. A few writers and directors, however, have made powerful capital out of allowing it to be the focus of the story. Yoshiaki Kawajiri's 1987 film *Wicked City*, though made primarily for a male audience, tackles this theme with considerable force and sexual energy, and the opportunities it provides for Freudian analysis are endless.

Women are shown as strong, sexual beings — in the opening sequence the leading man, Taki, goes home with a girl he's been trying to pick up for months, only to find, at the end of an energetic sex session back at her place, that she's really a spider-woman who, having drained his manhood in several more conventional ways, attempts to remove it completely with a few swift chomps of her transformed vagina dentata. The predatory and emasculating woman is thus firmly established as alien and therefore evil, but Kawajiri and scriptwriter Kisei Cho aren't interested in simply presenting stereotypes — they turn them in many directions to play with our preconceptions throughout the film.

Our preconceptions include the idea that this demonic-war adventure won't hold anything of relevance or interest for women, usually cannon-fodder in such battles. The development of the story proves differently. Taki, ostensibly just another salaryman, is a member of an elite force, the Black Guard, defending and policing a centuries-old treaty between the human world

Wicked City

and the Dark Realm. The denizens of this other world can look like us, but that loaded opening sequence establishes them as emphatically *not* like us. They can transform into all kinds of shapes, take over the bodies of humans dead or alive, and perform acts of magic such as transferring their life energy to another of their kind and fighting with bolts of power in lurid colours. Some of them are renegades, and don't want peace.

To protect the VIP whose presence is instrumental to the treaty, Taki is to be assigned a partner. Makie is a member of the Black Guard, a citizen of the Dark Realm, and a beautiful woman to boot. And although we have already been told that alien women are sexual predators and not to be trusted, her arrival throws a new element into the mix. She's working for peace between the two worlds. She's dressed in male clothing — professional and almost untouchable. And she saves Taki's skin in a tense fight with two of her own kind on the tarmac at Narita Airport. Like Oscar in *Rose of Versailles*, she doesn't need any help to function on equal terms in a male-dominated world.

As the film unfolds, we realise that the treaty is not the main focus of events, and the VIP isn't the tiny, wrinkled and very lecherous Dr Guiseppe Maiyart, but a child as yet unborn. Makie and Taki grow from their initial antipathy and wariness to respect and eventually to a mature, equal relationship. Maiyart's lechery subplot lets Taki compare Makie with other Dark Realm women, predatory and ruthless to the core, and to evaluate the maturity of her response to Maiyart's own crude approaches. We've already seen that Taki is a normal, sexually active man, and we learn that Makie is no shy virgin — she's had relationships with at least two of her own people, both of which she ended. (Paradoxically, this makes the two demon-rape sequences even more painful, precisely because she is a woman who can make her own sexual choices.) She doesn't hesitate to kill one former suitor when he threatens her mission, and uses her sexuality to lull him into a sense of false security before attacking, though Taki shares the kill.

Taki and Makie are suitable partners in every way; and by a strange genetic anomaly, they are among the very few members of both races who can interbreed. Their children (and presumably others like them) will eventually be the seal of peace between the two worlds. Maiyart, the Black Guard chief and the Dark Realm politicians and renegades are all working either to bring them together or keep them apart. Taki and Makie are the only characters who are completely unaware of their destiny and who are not consulted as to their wishes. For both of them, biology is destiny.

This shameless manipulation also has benefits for both. Taki can find fulfilment in caring for his woman and their child. From being a rootless adventurer, he now has a stake in the future. He has, in fact, become exactly the solid salaryman he seemed to be, even though he'll continue to earn his crust killing renegades rather than selling electrical goods. For Makie, however, the benefits are immeasurably greater. She discovers new emotional capacities (symbolised by a new-found ability to weep, unique among her kind), but that's not all — the moment she becomes pregnant, her magical and psychic powers increase immeasurably. It is she, not Taki or Maiyart, who finishes off the leader of the Dark Realm renegades. Appropriately he is one of her former lovers; no past ties of love or loyalty are going to threaten the child she carries. Taki may have found his focus in caring for her, but she has awakened to the power and responsibility of motherhood, and no force on Earth or beyond it can stand in her way now. In the closing moments of the film, after she has finished off the power of evil, a rain of light falls gently from Heaven, signalling the benign nature of her power despite its destructive potential.

Before we see motherhood confer this huge power, we've witnessed its perversion. In a crude yet compelling sequence in the lair of the Dark Realm renegades, Taki is sucked back to the womb by a woman whose whole belly opens in a grotesque parody of a vagina ready for penetration, and draws him inside, eyes

closed like a sleeping foetus. She's analysing his genetic structure to try to confirm the possibility of his breeding with Makie. He escapes only by blasting his way out of her devouring womb with his gun. For the intended (male) audience, the messages about good and bad women making good and bad mothers are loud and clear. For any female viewers, the subtext is that promiscuity and aggression get you blown apart; to gain real power, women have only to do the right thing, with the right man, at the right time. This prime example of boy's adventure fodder sends out the same message as any magical girl series.

INTO THE UNKNOWN

From 1993, the *Margaret* video series fulfilled the need for more adult, real-world stories for grown-up shojo fans by depicting popular romances, mostly conventional, sometimes with a twist, occasionally with a difference. The most successful manga in *Margaret* magazine are turned into one-shot videos. Titles such as *A-Girl* and *Singles* depict relationships in today's world to which readers can relate their own experience, while historical adventures like *Sleepless Oedo* take them back to more romantic times, yet with characters close enough to their own modern dreams and hopes, in the manner of *Rose of Versailles*. The contemporary female market is increasingly well served in the cinema too, with films like Isao Takahata's *Only Yesterday* (part of the Disney/Tokuma deal referred to earlier). It is the story of a woman in her twenties, at a crossroads in her life, who takes a sabbatical in the country to try and decide whether she wants to marry or go on with her career, and finds that her childhood memories can guide her.

Yet we're still dealing, for the most part, with women's relationships as defined by convention and society. Not even the most romantic dreams of shojo anime can escape the real world altogether; authors and readers alike are inevitably influenced to some extent by their society's view of what is possible. To break free of these all-pervasive subliminal constraints, a further step was necessary. In an attempt to remove the element of social custom from romance altogether, some authors dispensed with female protagonists. Women would become observers, voyeurs at the love trysts of proud, independent beings with free choice. Those trysts are depicted in the sub-genre usually known as shonen ai, or boys' love: a subject for a chapter in itself. ●

PRETTY BOYS IN PAIN

Shonen Ai Anime

A large and commercially viable market exists for stories about beautiful young men locked together in passionate, and usually doomed, romances or caught up in melodramatic situations. The audience is neither gay nor male; it consists of girls and young women, from high school age to maturity. It developed from shojo anime and manga, but is now an established genre in its own right. With strong roots in fanzine culture and with its own marketing mechanisms, it is almost entirely independent of the fads and fancies of mainstream anime viewers, but its influence can be seen even on television.

The scene: late at night in one of the smaller screening rooms at a British anime convention early in 1997. On the screen, a tear-jerking tale of impossible love is reaching its conclusion. Both protagonists are male. Packed into the chairs and spilling onto the floor are about thirty fans, male and female. The majority of them are known to me personally and they are all heterosexual. Several are in tears. For most, it's their first taste of shonen ai.

There is no published research in English on exactly why Japanese women began writing 'slash fiction' — stories with mostly male (and not necessarily, in fact preferably not, homosexual) characters in romantic and erotic situations, often involving elements of danger or tension so extreme they slip into melodrama. There is some valuable work on English-speaking fans who produce slash, pioneered by Henry Jenkins, but I am reluctant to use it to draw analogies, let alone conclusions. I have received generous help from Japanese and Japanese-speaking women in considering this phenomenon, but for the most part it remains uncharted territory. Everything that follows should be read with the caveat that so far our knowledge is very limited. These are my opinions only.

There are two reasons why so little material on shonen ai anime is available in the West, and so little known outside Japan about the genre's existence. One is very practical. The videos are most-ly based on manga and novels already published in women's and girls' magazines, and produced by the magazines' own video labels. The mainstream anime and video publications don't feature them unless they are very popular, and the producers don't bother much with advertising — they already have their own magazines to advertise in, which sell directly to the target market. However, magazines such as *Margaret, June* and the like do not filter through to English readership to the same extent as *Newtype* and *Anime V*. Western fans can easily see high-profile articles on *Tenchi Muyo!* and *Ghost in the Shell*, but are less likely to pick up on *Bride of Deimos* or *My Sexual Harassment*.

The other reason is the knee-jerk reaction of our society against anything perceived as 'gay porn'. Most people who buy anime and manga in America and Britain are male. They don't have a problem with the slew of lesbian anime that is available on American labels, but they react very badly to any suggestion that women might enjoy gay anime. They are the brothers, boyfriends, husbands and in some cases fathers of the target audience for that anime. Social pressure is a powerful weapon, especially when wielded at home. Of several hundred anime titles to be translated and released in English, just one, *Kizuna*, falls into the shonen ai genre. Additionally, the prevalent idea that nice girls don't have any use for sexual material outside their one-to-one heterosexual relationship restricts many women's ability to even consider pornography as something for their own enjoyment.

In Japan there is still a certain amount of social pressure along the same lines, which has kept the number of pure shonen ai anime relatively low. Magazines produce story tapes and CDs as well as videos. These can be listened to on a personal stereo with headphones; nobody knows you're not listening to the latest chart sounds. The listener probably already has the manga or the novel — and many of these novels are illustrated — as well as her own fantasies of what the characters look like. She doesn't need to worry about being 'caught' watching a video of which her parent or partner might not approve. An article in *Anime V*, talking of the relative lack of shonen ai anime compared to manga, seems to confirm this:

'You might think they too would be adapted for video, but the female audience is significantly different from the male one. Readers are office ladies and housewives, who are not the kind of people you can expect to spend 5,000 yen on a video. And you'd have trouble explaining it to your mother if she caught you watching one.'[1]

MEDIA MIXING

This diversity of media is another factor which I cannot accurately quantify, but its impact must be acknowledged. It's most easily observed with mainstream shows like *Tenchi Muyo!* or *El Hazard*, because their various forms are most widely publicised. A title can start off in a single medium — this could be manga, a novel, an OAV or a game, even a radio drama. It goes on, perhaps, to a CD drama release and then a limited OAV series, testing whether the already-established audience will transfer. If its track record holds up, it will cross into all the other media before making the leap to the pinnacle of major prime time television release and a massive merchandising campaign.

In *Tenchi's* case, two video series, radio dramas and CDs established the characters before movies, manga, merchandise and television followed. *801 TTS Airbats* had a successful radio drama spinoff which filled in more background and detail on the characters. Obviously, all of these provide far more detail and expand the story in directions anime alone can't take. The impact has already been felt in Western fandom. Many fans have written to me in my role as a magazine editor asking when to expect the concluding video of *RG Veda*, which doesn't exist. It doesn't matter to CLAMP's Japanese fans, who have the manga, but

this is unlikely to be translated into English. Similarly, the massive *Five Star Stories* manga provides all the detail fans of Mamoru Nagano's world missed in the hour long OAV, but its English publication in full is still awaited. This applies even more to the titles in a minority genre like shonen ai. Not only are they advertised in a closed circle of consumption, but the stories spread across a range of media which may never be accessible to the non-Japanese fan.

My own feeling is that girls and women may be drawn to the shonen ai genre because it depicts men, powerful beings for whom love and marriage are not the only option, under the pressure of emotions and situations more often connected with women. The darker areas of the genre have yet to be explored; but since, for many women, sexual relationships are a form of bondage, perhaps we shouldn't be so surprised to see the motifs of enslavement and possession employed so frequently. There's also the possibility that women like gay porn for the same reason men like lesbian porn: if you like to watch attractive members of the opposite sex in sexual situations, then gay porn gives you twice as many men for your money as straight material.[2]

It should be noted that very few shonen ai anime and manga actually show genitals; they were constrained by the same laws which hampered such depictions in 'straight' porn, and are now still working in the same traditions. While depictions of sex can be quite unmistakable, organs are rarely if ever shown effecting penetration or in a state of erection. Many dojinshi are much more explicit, but even in the specialised fan market caution is still observed. After all, if your mother thought it was shocking that you were watching a video with two men kissing, how much more shocked would she be by a close-up of their sex organs in use in a fanzine?

---

[1] Heart Hakase, in 'Lectures on Heart Mark Video Anime', pp40-41.
[2] It should be stressed that to the best of my knowledge, here in the West and in Japan there is no gay male audience for shonen ai anime or manga. As far as I am aware no research has been done on this topic and therefore no reliable data is available, but in a conversation in the summer of 1996, Gary Peet of Kiseki Films, one of Britain's anime labels, told me that shonen ai would not sell in the British gay market. Kiseki's parent company, the Revelation Film Group, has another label serving that market and has done extensive research into what suits its needs. Gay men, according to him, are very like straight men in their tastes when it comes to porn. They want to see genitals and sex. The majority want to see real genitals, not drawings.

THE SECRET HISTORY

Pataliro!

In 1982, the year that Minky Momo made her début, a television series called *Pataliro!* also premiered. It ran for a total of fifty-two episodes, into 1983, and was followed by a theatrical film. Inspired by Mineo Maya's manga, it tells the story of ten year-old despot genius Prince Pataliro of Marinella, whose tiny island country has two principal exports — orchids and diamonds. A criminal syndicate is constantly trying to get their hands on the second export crop, and the Prince uses all the considerable powers at his command, not all of them natural, to frustrate these aims.

Aiding and abetting him is his bodyguard and adviser Jack Barbarossa Bankolan, whose fatal weakness is his passion for pretty boys and young men. He ends up compromised with almost every gorgeous young assassin or malefactor sent against the Prince, despite his British secret service background and supposed stiff upper lip. During the series he develops an ongoing relationship with one of the would-be assassins, a ravishing fourteen year-old German redhead called Mariahi. This was the first time homosexuality had been a major theme in television anime, and the first appearance of the shonen ai genre on television. The world didn't end. The male audience didn't reach, appalled, for the off switch. The female audience loved it.

Backtracking, we can trace the development of shonen ai to women's manga and magazines. Schodt discusses the development of the leading magazines in the field in some detail. But even prior to this, the notion of the beautiful male character, whose ambiguous and disturbing sexuality drew both men and women, had been embedded in Japanese fiction for generations. The idea of samurai on long campaigns or monks in remote monasteries fulfilling their sexual and emotional needs with beautiful boy pages or novices is long established.

The first Japanese 'novel', an eleventh-century literary partwork called *The Tale of Genji*, whose ongoing adventures far outdo any modern television soap for passion and drama, provides a per-

fect model of the beautiful hero in its Shining Prince, a scholar, poet, dancer, archer, courtier and lover of such renown that his lovers regularly died for him. When Gisaburo Sugii filmed the novel in 1987 to mark the anniversary celebrations of a media conglomerate, he chose to focus on the love story elements of the ancient text as a way of making it comprehensible to the modern reader. His Shining Prince is very definitely straight throughout the movie, but his appeal to women is on the same lines as that of the tortured heroes of shonen ai. He's beautiful, powerful, able to have anyone he wants. To choose a dangerous love, a love that could destroy him, is heroic and tragic at once.

Although, after *Pataliro!*, homosexual activity as a central theme was left to the video rather than the television market, elements of shonen ai began to sneak into the mainstream. It started with fanzines based on those time-honoured bastions of boy's adventures, the sports dramas and team shows.[3] Football series *Captain Tsubasa* kicked off in 1983 and inspired fan Minami Ozaki to begin a shonen ai football fanzine featuring the show's characters, which would be the basis for *Zetsuai*, her football-rock fusion manga in *Margaret* magazine. This in turn spun off two OAVs, *Desperate Love 1989* and *Bronze: Desperate Love Since 1989*.

Also in 1983, the mainstream science fiction series *Genesis Climber Mospeada* featured Yellow Belmont, cross-dressing biker and night-club singer, a kabuki theatre dream made flesh, as gorgeous and sexually capable a man as ever fought evil in lipstick. *Saint Seiya*, a television series in which heroic teenage orphans fight to defend a beautiful princess from evil (and mostly older) men and women, often involving very disturbing torture scenes, began to generate large quantities of slash fiction fanzines. This was mostly drawn by high

---

[3] One fan source claims that, although stories of the shonen ai *type* existed before, the explosion of shonen ai as a *genre* followed directly from the release in Japan of *Another Country*, a 1984 British film which centres on gay love outside social boundaries, distanced by location and history.

school girls, and some of it was very explicit indeed, appearing very soon after the television series began in 1986. The 1988 series *Ronin Warriors*, structured along the same lines as *Saint Seiya*, appealed even more strongly to the slash fanzine groups, but not even Akira Toriyama's slapstick martial arts show *Dragonball* escaped their attentions.

The fanzine market produced a number of professional artists. Moving into the professional field meant giving up certain freedoms, in particular the freedom to show explicit sex scenes in graphic form, but as fanzine artists took their differently developed skills and sensibilities into the mainstream, they pushed the line of what was permissible further. Apart from Ozaki, the biggest success to cross the line have been CLAMP, the female collective whose work is moving shojo and shonen ai elements into the mainstream with titles such as *Tokyo Babylon* and *X,* as well as playing with lesbian chic in *Miyuki-chan in Wonderland*.

Mainstream OAVs like *Tokyo Revelation*, in other respects a standard demonic attack story in which the take-over of Earth by the powers of darkness can't go ahead without tentacles and schoolgirls, involve shonen ai elements as part of their thematic structure. Made in 1996, the story highlights the passionate fixation of would-be demon-lord Akira, a self-deluding but very pretty teenager, on his only childhood friend. Ever since a chance conversation in elementary school revealed that said friend was interested in arcane lore and calling up devils, Akira has worked on his summoning skills until he can call up a whole demonic army, in the hope that one day he'll be able to impress the pants off the object of his desire. When the two meet again, he shows his feelings in a stolen kiss.

Television is using the same elements in new series; one of the class of 1998, *Virus*, still running as I write this chapter, is developing some interesting aspects. Despite the presence of pneumatic female 'leads', many of the male character relationships are ambiguous and hint at shared secrets. There's a scene in which the central character, Serge, kneels before the enigmatic leader Raven and accepts a collar from him, in one of the most powerful homoerotic moments yet screened on prime time television.

Science fiction, fantasy or pseudo-history are favoured settings for many shonen ai stories, since they offer a useful distancing device, but there are also OAVs set in the modern world, one of the most prominent of which is the ongoing series *My Sexual Harassment*. Spun off Be-Boy magazine's manga of office life, which began publication in 1993, it's the story of a rising young corporate star whose travels on behalf of his company get him into sexual situations with businessmen all over the place. With workplace harassment an increasingly open topic in Japan, the series stands the usual perception on its head for the amusement of the shonen ai audience.

The influence has moved full circle, back to its roots. Mainstream anime and manga titles inspire the fanzine market to take their stories and characters in directions their original writers probably never envisaged, and fan creators turned professional start a fashion for shonen ai elements in mainstream titles, giving them the chance to attract the female shonen ai audience as well as their usual constituency of young men. Authors better known for their mainstream work use these shonen ai elements to powerful effect. For example, Hideyuki Kikuchi, whose novels have inspired many anime aimed at the male market, has contributed to the female fan's enjoyment too. The 1985 film version of his *Vampire Hunter D* has been a favourite with American female fans since its inception, and the Vampire With No Name has become a hugely popular fantasy figure.

Perhaps even more interesting is the 1994 film *Darkside Blues*. It has only one explicit shonen ai reference — when the psychotic, but desperately attractive Enji Hozuki tells androgynous hero Darkside, 'I've fallen for you pretty badly', seconds before Darkside kills him. Yet its atmosphere is undiluted shonen ai, despite the subplots about more conventional, but equally doomed, loves. The fey child Katori is mirrored by the youngest child of the evil Hozuki family, another fey character who can't be pinned in one place or time. Her elder sister is pure evil, delighting in torture and determined to stamp her family's mark on everyone and everything in the world, dead or alive. The oldest of the Hozuki daughters has sought refuge in religion but, unable to shed her responsibility for her heritage, runs a resistance safe house from her convent. The eldest brother, the embodiment of the cold, passionless corporate suit, is deeply and shamefully in love with the head of the resistance. And to cap it all, Darkside is given a ravishing vocal performance by one of Takarazuka's star 'male' players, Natsuki Akira, in her anime début.

Often the men and boys involved in shonen ai relationships don't consider themselves homosexual. The person they fall in love with simply happens to be male. Darkside and Enji are never actualy labelled 'gay'. Darkside is definitely not of this world, and all the iconography around him echoes the powerful yet aloof persona of the vampire, one of the most potent of sexual fantasies. Enji is portrayed as a ladies' man, straight in his sexual tastes (he chats up one of the heroines after rescuing her from a bunch of street toughs just before his first meeting with Darkside) and wholly psychotic in every other respect. Time and again stress is laid on the idea that love of an individual transcends desire for a particular type, whether physical, social or intellectual. Just as Oscar de Jarjayes in *Rose of Versailles* faces the social and emotional problems of love between herself and Andre, the childhood friend who was born a servant of her aristocratic family, so a man who falls in love with another man must face the social and emotional problems involved in this relationship if it's to survive.

In the *Desperate Love* OAVs, Koji faces scorn and ostracism from his elder brother, who uses Koji's love for young footballer Izumo to coerce him into giving up control of the family business. Contemptuous of his younger sibling, whom he sees as an irresponsible dilettante, big brother threatens them both with exposure as homosexuals, which would end Izumo's promising international career as well as compromising Koji's rock-star status. By choosing a socially unacceptable relationship the pair have made the rest of their lives difficult and even dangerous; no one would choose such a love, so it must be irresistible, a matter of destiny. Even young, beautiful, rich, talented males can't escape the bondage of love if that is their destiny.

LOVE AND DEATH

One of the most powerful of shonen ai anime (and a personal favourite) is the remarkable *Love's Wedge*. This is an accurate but somewhat inelegant translation of the Japanese title, which is meant, according to one of the characters, to imply something that joins two people together whether they want it or not, rather than something that forces them apart and splinters their lives. The kanji also allow the translation *Ties of Love* or *Love's Bondage*, with an ambiguity of meaning akin to the English 'cleave to' and 'cleave *in* two'.

---

[4] A similar concept can be found in the film *Soylent Green*. There, though, the 'furniture' is always female.

The first of two parts was released in 1992 on June Video. An erotic science fiction story set in a distant future, it takes place in the huge city of Tanagra. Tanagra is governed by the Parthia syndicate, the elite of the elite, composed of elegant, well-bred men (almost in the upper-class English style) known as Blondys; but it is powered by a computer-like entity called Jupiter, which imposes order and inflicts unspecified but dreaded penalties on any of the elite who waver in their duty, or allow this order to be disrupted. There are women in this society, but in the story they are only bit-part players, with all the influential emotional roles, as well as the social ones, played by men. (It is perhaps an ironic reflection of the modern world that the one truly powerful 'woman' in the lives of the men who run Tanagra is Jupiter, a computer.)

In Tanagra, wealth and power mean you can have anything you want. Teenage sex slaves, or pets, both male and female, are freely traded at auction. Other teenagers are known as 'furniture' — they come with the apartment and you can change them for a different style if you want.[4] Some of the lower classes, scathingly referred to as mongrels, seek this life as a way out of the poverty and degradation of the slum area of Ceres, becoming rent-boys on a semi-permanent one-to-one basis. Others look for employment on the black market, or in the 'night city', the district known as Midas, where all kinds of entertainment can be found and crime ranges from petty to seriously political.

Disaffected elements are plotting to destabilise Tanagra by killing the most important member of the Parthia syndicate, Jason Mink, but he has other things on his mind. Jason is deeply — and embarrassingly — in love with one of his pets, a bit of rough called Riki whom he picked up on the streets of Midas three years ago, when the boy was just seventeen. Known as 'Riki the Dark', he had made a small name for himself as a black marketeer and aroused all kinds of petty enmities. Straying into the streets of Midas in daylight, he got himself into trouble with a gang of middle-class would-be toughs trying to keep scum like him off their turf, and was saved from a bad beating only by the arrival of Jason in a car the size of his shabby apartment.

Taking the older man back to said apartment, because he was proud enough to want to repay the debt and had nothing to repay it with but his body, Riki somehow ended up in Tanagra as Jason's new pet. But Riki is a true free spirit, and although Jason says later that it took three years to

Bronze: Desperate Love Since 1989

emerges as we see more of Riki and Jason's shared memories. The master/pet relationship involves the pet's unconditional availability for the master's use — as Jason puts it, a pet has no pride and no shame. There's a flashback to the three-year period of Riki's 'taming'; the boy is shown naked except for a collar, chains and leather straps, masturbating under a spotlight for the entertainment of his master in the darkness beyond. The images we see are the chain on his wrist moving up and down against the floor as he obeys the master's commands, and his feet arching off the floor as he comes, followed by Jason taking him, still chained, from behind. In another flashback, he and Jason are coupling in a huge bed; in yet another, Riki is showing off in a crop top and thong amid a crowd of other pets under the eyes of a group of masters, demonstrating when another boy tries to establish himself as top dog that nobody bests Riki the Dark.

The relationship, in the end, has become one of love. Oddly enough, it isn't Riki, the free spirit powered by his emotions, who uses that word, but Jason, whose face and manner never betray anything but cool good breeding. To Riki he says only 'you are mine and I will have you', but to his friend Raoul, another member of the elite, he obliquely admits his feelings. Raoul is horrified, seeing his friend's ruin in this emotional excess. There is no precedent for love between a master and a pet in their society. By the time a pet is twenty, it has usually been discarded, sold on to a whorehouse or, if very lucky like Jason's former furniture Katze, established as a minor functionary or a black market operator, doing the elite's dirty work. For a pet and a master to build an ongoing relationship is impossible, even if both are able to admit the extent of any feelings which have grown out of their association.

Guy, who also loves Riki, has finally worked out that his friend probably returned to Tanagra to save the gang from the tender mercies of the authorities. He decides that the only thing to do is to kidnap Riki and set him free, to attempt to bring back the old Riki, the free spirit. What he hasn't counted on is that Riki can never be free in that sense again, either figuratively or literally. Wherever he goes, his experiences go with him. Throughout the two episodes there have been occasional references to the 'pet ring', which serves as both a marker and a tracking device, enabling the master to keep a constant eye on his property's movements. When Riki hears the whole of Guy's scheme, he shows Guy his pet ring. The device is round his penis and only his

tame him, he isn't really reconciled to his new status. So Jason gives him a year's sabbatical to go back to the slums and find his old friends again — and almost immediately regrets it.

The first episode is concerned with Riki's realisation that you can never really go back. He picks up the threads of his old life with the biker gang he used to lead, and starts to rebuild some kind of relationship with Guy, who was once his lover; but things have changed. A new kid on the block, Killie, is jealous and wants Riki out. Riki himself has changed, though he fights the notion. Twenty isn't seventeen, and having been part of an intense and wholly committed relationship, it's not possible to go and run with the gang like a carefree kid again.

Guy and the others are delighted to have him back, and he tries to pick up the threads of his old life, but when Jason jerks the leash, he has to return to Tanagra — not only for his own sake, but to protect Guy and the gang from the revenge of a disgruntled pet owner who wants his property back. When he is finally forced to admit his relationship with Jason to Guy, his old friend rejects him violently, unable to reconcile the memory of the proud free spirit he loved with the idea of Riki as a rich man's willing toy. The episode ends with Riki walking back to Tanagra, tossing his past behind him like a discarded cigarette end.

The second episode shows things are never that easy. The past can't be recaptured, but it can't be escaped either, and the dark side of the system master can take it off without taking off the organ with it. Guy, however, doesn't let that stop him, and in a homicidal rage he sets out to lure Jason to his death as revenge.

Finally, in a violent confrontation, he succeeds in trapping himself and Jason in a deserted underground bunker, planning to kill them both. But Riki intervenes, with the help of Katze. As Riki pleads for Guy's life, Jason asks if he really cares for Guy so much, and Riki is finally forced to admit his true feelings. He tells Jason that their relationship as pet and master and the love between them drove Guy, his former partner, to desperation; it's not Jason's problem, but if Riki leaves his old friend to die after causing such pain in the first place, he'll be unable to live with his guilt. In the end, the two lovers die together, heroically and romantically. Guy and their other friends are left to mourn them.

The story's main impact comes with the gradual stripping away of the defensive mechanisms we use to shield ourselves from the truth of emotions. Images of bondage and sado-masochism are often used as metaphors for the compulsion of powerful feelings, our slavery to our desires. In *Love's Wedge*, Jason learns that owning Riki's body matters less to him than taking possession of Riki's heart and soul. While he fully intends to enjoy his feelings for Riki as a forbidden pleasure (just about the only forbidden pleasure in Tanagra) with the added *frisson* of Jupiter's wrath if he ever slips, he comes, reluctantly, to realise that the only thing which is really important to him is Riki's happiness. Riki, meanwhile, understands that not only can he never return to the freedom of his youth, but that even if he could, he would no longer be able to enjoy it in quite the same way.

Like the spoiled little girls of the lolikon videos, Riki has crossed the line into the adult world, but on this occasion there's no way to recapture the confidence and carelessness of innocence once it's gone. Guy learns that you can't fix your loved ones and happiness in time like flies in amber, unchanging and unchangeable, unless you kill them first. He survives, perhaps because in the end he loved the real Riki less than the idealised Riki he wanted to believe in. Jason and Riki die because, having finally come through pain, conflict and misunderstanding to an honest and sincere love, there is nothing they can do to make their world accept it. Like the *Overfiend* series, *Love's Wedge* tells us that, in the end, death is love's only safe haven and its only possible triumph.

SIX TYPES OF AMBIGUITY

When women and girls watch anime, whether shojo or mainstream, they can identify a range of male character types, conforming, as one would expect, to the kinds of men most girl viewers will meet in their everyday life: family members, teachers, friends and potential partners. These characters carry on the process of conditioning the little girl to be a useful and cooperative person by helping to demonstrate firstly, that all kinds of people can have good and bad qualities and secondly, that while many people have good qualities it's better to stay close to the ones who are most suitable for you. They are the ones who will fit into your life and your social setting, the ones who won't cause trouble and disruption. Every girl's romantic dream should, in fact, be the average Boy Next Door.

This fits nicely with the male viewer's hope that every girl he meets will see him as desirable. However, male and female perceptions of these character stereotypes are different, and their functions can change depending on the kind of story they are used in. These types may seem to fit with the stereotypes of female anime characters discussed in chapter nine, but I would hesitate to claim that they are useful in analysis of anime from the viewpoint of any audience but the female one. As their reception in a completely alien culture demonstrates, shojo and shonen ai anime obviously have some 'crossover' appeal outside their target market, but I am reluctant to read in any universal significance. My examples are drawn from mainstream anime because these are the titles most likely to be familiar to English-speaking audiences; it should be noted that their intended male audience will not necessarily perceive these characters in the way their archetypes are described here.

TYPE	FEATURES
Big Brother	*Protective, responsible, noble 'sempai'*
Boy Next Door	*Average, shy, bland*
Local Hero	*Tough, valiant, flashy*
The Older Man	*Mature, sophisticated, intelligent*
Kid Brother	*Immature, unsophisticated, idiot savant*
The Stranger	*Forbidding, dangerous, enticing*

There are, naturally, many characters who contain elements of more than one type, or who seem to change type as the story reveals more detail and our perception of them changes. A good director and writer will make use of this to add interest to the formula, both for shojo and mainstream stories. For example, Maiyart in *Wicked City* is a responsible Older Man masquerading as a naughty Kid Brother to create the sympathy and solidarity that will enable a relationship to grow between Taki and Makie. Duke in *Golgo 13* is both a threatening Older Man and a deadly Stranger. But identifying the basic character type is usually possible, and a very important clue to that character's function in the story, his impact on the heroine, and his eventual fate.

BIG BROTHER

Boys like him, find him a good sort, and usually don't feel threatened by him. The Big Brother (like the Kid Brother) doesn't necessarily have to be an actual brother. He might be your brother's best mate. Maybe he's the slightly older boy next door. He's well meaning, sometimes bossy or even downright domineering, but he can be relied on to look out for you and do everything in his power to make sure you're alright. Often good-looking, he can be a bit of a poser, and in his evil incarnation he can hide real trouble under that parent-friendly exterior. Nevertheless, he's the one most parents want their little girl to go out with, and he's the one she probably had her first crush on. There are some shows in which he'll get the girl, but he usually loses out to the next candidate.

Yasha in *RG Veda* is a typical Big Brother, and so is Daryoon in *Heroic Legend of Arislan*; both are constantly looking after and helping out, often at considerable personal cost. Bean Bandit in *Riding Bean* is a perfect example of the type; old enough and independent enough to know his own mind and go his own way, he's still soft-hearted enough to feel for bewildered, despoiled little Carrie after she's abandoned by the vicious Semmerling. Seishiro in *Tokyo Babylon* and *X* is a more sinister incarnation of the type; although in the *Tokyo Babylon* videos he is an entirely typical and reliable nice guy, by the time of the *X* movie he has become the lover of the innocent mystic Subaru and is about to kill him. (See what clues you can miss if you don't read the manga?) Big Brothers don't have to be capable, though; poor Hiroshi Ozora in *Moldiver* is constantly doing his best to look out for his young brother and sister, while they both constantly ignore

him, pinch his best inventions and modify them for their own use, and generally run rings round the poor, good-natured sap.

BOY NEXT DOOR

This is the character most boys subconsciously identify with, and the one they want girls to want. He's also the one all girl viewers know they'll probably end up with, because the other types are too dangerous, too unreliable or too rare. He's really good-hearted but he hasn't got much else going for him. In his worst incarnation he's the sad geek Ujita in *Visionary*; he'll never get a girl without supernatural intervention, and even when he does, he won't know what to do with her. In less obviously inadequate modes he's Tenchi Masaki in *Tenchi Muyo!*, Keiichi Morisato in *Oh My Goddess!* or Takuya Isurugi in *801 TTS Airbats*: a nice enough guy, but you wouldn't look twice at

RG Veda

him unless, by magic, you became aware of his true inner qualities. Given the wish-fulfilment element of anime, you probably will.

LOCAL HERO

He's the one boys really want to be. They look up to him and usually envy him. What a guy! He's got it all — looks, charm, courage, wit, even super-powers sometimes. More importantly, he's got the ability to be one of a kind but still one of the boys, a bit of a lad but still a ladykiller to the core. Female viewers smile indulgently and think how nice this *Boys' Own* fantasy will be if he ever grows up. He's Akira Fudo in *Devilman*, teasing his pretty cousin about her panties before heading off to save mankind from the demons, and getting shredded in the process. He's Goku in *Goku: Midnight Eye*, loving and leaving every pretty girl he meets, usually to die, but making sure they're thoroughly avenged. He's Keiji in *The Elven Bride*, setting off on a big adventure for the sake of his loved one and leaving her to cope alone with ostracism and ignorance, while he attends to the really important business of finding a magic gizmo so they can consummate their marriage in the shortest possible time. Well, it beats waiting until they're both ready. Meanwhile, he's availing himself of the facilities offered by foreign travel. Some women can't help but love this type, but only a child or a fool would marry him.

THE OLDER MAN

He's the kind of man boys hope they'll be when they grow up. He's mature, intelligent, knows his way around and could get appropriate attention in any establishment. People don't mess with him, at least not without regretting it. He has enough money to buy anything he wants and enough *savoir-faire* to know where to get it, and he takes responsibility. In his best incarnations he's the perfect father, the utterly reliable teacher and the uncle in whom you can confide anything; at his worst he's every pervert who ever betrayed a child. In the right circumstances, most girl viewers could fancy him; they know they couldn't settle down with him because he's too worldly, but it would be one hell of a fling.

Yonosuke the merchant in *The Sensualist* is this kind of man. So is Mikhail in *Plastic Little*, constantly looking out for his feisty little Captain. So, in more sinister mode, is Raven in *Virus*, and the eponymous *Black Jack*. Of course, the level of his sophistication is also relative to his setting; Sleepy Estes in *Mad Bull 34* is an Older Man too. Even in

the most innocent of stories, this type is usually marked off-limits for young female characters and viewers. If you're going to get mixed up in the grown-up world, you'd better be sure you can cope with the consequences.

KID BROTHER

Boys like to think they've left this stage behind a long time ago, and now look back on it fondly. Girls reserve judgement, but usually treat the little brat with maternal or sisterly indulgence. He's the opposite of the Older Man, full of innocence and energy, often quite bright yet completely defenceless. But he's useful in story terms to ask the leading expository questions that save so much time, to provide the pivotal hazard or the joke that ends the episode on a suitably corny note, like Keyop in *Battle of the Planets*. Children can also provide wisdom and guidance, coming in useful to point up the criminal irresponsibility of adults; Mamoru in *Phantom Quest Corp*, who keeps heroine Ayaka's rackety, drunken life in some semblance of order, is a case in point.

Kids aren't responsible for their actions; they can be scolded and punished but there is always a tacit acknowledgement that they aren't really to blame. Bud, the raven-haired wunderkind who ends up piloting the glamorous and deadly Griffon labor in some of the most gripping episodes of *Patlabor*, is still too young to understand the impact of what he's doing. To him, the huge machine which can crush buildings and kill people is just a really cool toy, and the games his adult minders let him play out on the streets are pure adrenaline, just for fun. His natural speed, flexibility and fearlessness are being exploited by unscrupulous adults, but as far as he's concerned, it's all a game. The eponymous prince in *Pataliro!* is a brat of the first order, but because he's just a kid, he'd get away with all but the most spectacular bad behaviour even if he weren't royal. Kid Brothers live in a world where all is forgiven. No wonder growing up can be so painful — but there's a reward at the end for men who manage to survive. When you enter 'second childhood', it's permissible to retrieve some of the giddy habits of your first, and the elderly are permitted, and even encouraged, to indulge in childlike behaviour.

THE STRANGER

He's fascinating. He can be dangerous. He's Not

From Round Here. Whether he's good or evil, human or alien, there's something odd about him, and tangling with him is only going to lead to trouble. Anyone who behaves differently from the norm is a Stranger, even if he was born locally. One of Minatsu's beaux in *Slow Step* turns out to be a Stranger when he decides to go to America to study, instead of staying at home in Japan. Yellow Belmont in *Mospeada* is a Stranger. Even if he's an elegant and heroic type and not a figure of fun like the Gay Blade in *Samurai Gold*, anyone who puts on women's clothing and hangs around in bars is a Stranger. Baron Ashler in *Mazinger Z*, who's split in two down the middle, half male and half female, is very definitely a Stranger. Joe in *Battle of the Planets*, with a chip on his shoulder the size of Tokyo Tower and a bad attitude problem, is a Stranger. Vampire Hunter D is a Stranger, and so is the fey, androgynous dream analyst Darkside in *Darkside Blues*.

Women find the Stranger absolutely fascinating and wildly desirable, but they all know there's no long-term future with him. Look at the choices: stay at home and have a partner who's always an alien, or go back with him to wherever he came from, away from all your family and friends, and be always an alien yourself. And if you are tempted to take a chance on a relationship with him, what will be left if and when he blows out of town again, as Strangers usually do? You'll be tainted by association. Strangers are gorgeous fantasies, but better the devil you know, however handsome and attractive the devil you don't.

MAD ABOUT THE BOY

Of course, all central characters in shonen ai are by definition Strangers, since they choose to live outside the established social norms. By extension, all characters who cooperate with them or sympathise with them must also be touched by Strangeness, whatever their other attributes.

In considering the male character types presented in shojo, and then looking at shonen ai anime, it seems to me there is a major anomaly. Shojo male stereotypes may be nice or nasty, their influence on our heroine may be positive or negative, but they all fit into a recognisable place in her world and there is only one of them (the Boy Next Door) who is really suitable for her. However many frogs she kisses, only one will turn into her particular handsome prince. However, in shonen ai, the prince isn't interested in the girl viewer but in one of his own male courtiers. Far from the viewer resenting this, it's one of the major attractions of the genre for her.

In male porn anime, the viewer is involved not merely as voyeur but as potential leading man. Even if he is absent from the action, watching a lesbian scene like the biker orgy in *Frantic, Frustrated & Female*, there is always the underlying but clearly understood subtext that were he to step into the action the women involved would eventually be won over to the implicitly superior pleasures of sex with a man. If they don't fall panting at his feet immediately, they will either succumb in the end or be made aware of the error of their ways. For the female watching shonen ai there is no such subtext. Converting the characters to the supposedly superior pleasures of heterosexuality does not figure in this fantasy universe, since many of them are heterosexual anyway. The whole point of stories like *Love's Wedge* or *Kizuna* is to demonstrate that once affection is fixed on a single object, mere gratification of desire with any available partner is not enough.

The shonen ai fan chooses to be a detached observer at the spectacle of passion and pain. She neither has nor needs any point of identification with the players, any wish-fulfilment icon on which to hang her own identity. The viewer's identification is with the emotional destiny of the characters rather than a mere fantasy of personal sexual desirability. She feels, not that she could step in and seduce Jason or Koji if she so chose, but that they are destined for a love which is deeper, more demanding and more dangerous than simple sexual pleasure, a love which values the other for more than the sum of their physical and social assets. It is the kind of love, perhaps, that she would like for herself, but it's not a simple fantasy of stepping into the shoes of the onscreen protagonist. It is the fact that the characters would *not* fall panting at her feet which makes their story one she can lose herself in.

While her male counterparts wish they could be players in the erotic fantasies of U-Jin or *Cream Lemon*, the shonen ai viewer doesn't seek to enter the erotic world onscreen. With her real-life desires and dreams of personal sexual fulfilment untouched and uninvolved, she gets off on watching others get off — physically, mentally, emotionally, through torture, pain and humiliation, or through romance and the joy of secret love. More than any other form of pornography, shonen ai is simple voyeurism. As such, it is more complex, and possibly more exploitative, than anything anime has yet produced to excite men. ●

A TWIST OF CREAM LEMON

Forbidden Fruit for the Mass Market

In 1984 the new medium of the Original Animation Video went explicit, and the erotic anime market of today was born. Through the development of both comic and gothic-horror themes, such early OAVs as the Cream Lemon series influenced the development of titles like Legend of the Overfiend. But this was not some fiendish oriental masterplan for world corruption; right at the outset, Cream Lemon's very title intimated that sex was not something to be taken lightly, though it could be played for laughs.

1984 was a landmark year for erotic anime. The Original Animation Video (OAV), born in the last days of the old year with the release of *Dallos* on 21 December, was about to make its first faltering steps into the dangerous world of sex. In the cinemas things looked normal enough. Lurve, rather than sex, ruled the big screen with the huge success of *Macross: Do You Remember Love?*, the tale of one boy, two girls and a universe saved by the power of the pop ballad. Television anime had its eyes fixed on the stars, with sci-fi series like *Southern Cross, Giant Gorg, L-Gaim* and *Dunbine*, while playing for laughs from old and young viewers alike. The erotic element was represented in the witty, wiseacre crackle of the third *Lupin III* series and the criminal capers of the spandex-wrapped lovelies of *Cats Eye*, but it was kept carefully under wraps, sublimated into social acceptability. As in the following year's movie *Lupin III: The Gold of Babylon*, there was plenty of flirtation and sexy banter in Lupin's life but everything was suggested rather than shown on screen.

The 1984 anime television series *Touch*, based on Mitsuru Adachi's hit manga, shows a love triangle involving twin brothers, and the effect on the relationship of the death of the elder twin, with more emotion and passion than any scene in *EastEnders* or *Beverly Hills 90210*. In 1985 the first television series of the *Dirty Pair* filled the dreams of pubescent boys with images of scantily clad futuristic goddesses of destruction. Heroines Kei

and Yuri are both representatives of an agency devoted to sorting out problems and patron saints of the cock-up, in more ways than one. The characters of both these series were not involved in any erotically explicit activity, yet they carried a powerful and unmistakable sexual charge for their audiences.

In *Touch*, the realism of the setting (a high school baseball team) and restraint of the depiction made this acceptable. For *Dirty Pair*, the combination of sci-fi and comedy distanced the erotic element enough for parents and television stations to overlook it. The erotic OAV opened up the possibility of showing erotica without such artifices; the intended audience would know exactly what they were getting. On video, with no possibility of accidentally offending the uninterested, erotica could thrive, and in this new market audiences got their first taste of *Cream Lemon* from Fairy Dust.

The importance of this series' impact on the development of the erotic OAV is enormous. Its overall content combined humour and wish-fulfilment, with none of the outright bloodletting which emerged in the late eighties as a major new trend; yet its use of horror and Gothic elements gave another spin to the erotic animation concept, which may have contributed something to the market for later shockers such as *Legend of the Overfiend*. The nineties' erotic OAVs with comic elements also hark back to this

EROTIC ANIME

seminal series. The other great influence on the development of this new, mass-market medium for erotica was the success of erotic manga. One manga creator in particular, Go Nagai, was to have a major influence on the development of the erotic OAV, and his first erotic OAV title, also produced by Fairy Dust, appeared in the same year that *Cream Lemon* made its début (Nagai's contribution is discussed further in chapter six).

SUGAR BABY LOVE

The first erotic OAV, the two-story tape *Reddening Snow/Girls Tortured with Roses* emerged early in 1984 from Wonder Kids. But the fun really started in August, with the first releases in the *Cream Lemon* series, which were part one of a two-parter entitled *Be My Baby*, and *Escalation*, which would become a trilogy. *Be My Baby* was to develop beyond its originally projected two parts into one of the most popular *Cream Lemon* segments. The animation and art of these first two episodes were fairly primitive — the OAV was still in its infancy and seen as the cheap end of the anime market. The linking factor between these first episodes wasn't one of character, though the characters in a few *Cream Lemon* episodes are almost interchangeable, but of theme. Both tackled popular sex fantasies from the lolikon (Lolita complex) style guide.

Writer Steven Smet attributes the emergence of lolikon as a force in Japanese pop culture to a social reaction to feminism, making Japanese men turn to images of young, unchallenging girls (and boys) in sexual situations. But Smet goes on: '... don't get on your high horses over supposed kiddie-porn yet. Lolikon is a socially acceptable exorcism of fantasies, which should never be taken for real life. The [sex] crime rate in Japan is one of the lowest in the entire world. As one reporter once said: "It's the girls in the manga who keep the girls on the streets safe".'[1]

The Japanese term 'Lolita complex' is derived from a Western novel, Nabokov's *Lolita*, so Smet's warning about high horses is one we should take to heart, even if one regards his view of the benign aspect of lolikon manga as naïve. Early in 1998 a coterie of Western film luminaries spent considerable time and energy on a media apologia for their new film version of *Lolita*. Their interviews and the articles which followed make disturbing reading, reflecting as they do a terrifying willingness in apparently intelligent and thoughtful men and women to make the child not merely complicit in but

responsible for sexual acts with adults.

The innocent face of lolikon, and its earliest anime roots, can be seen in the magical girls genre, discussed in further detail in chapter three. For the heroines of these stories, the ability to become an instant adult by magic, without the painful process of growth and experience, is a positive thing. The young heroine can learn from her experiences, having a go at adult life without being scarred by her mistakes, while the adults she helps with her magical powers can recapture a little of the child in themselves. In lolikon, however, it can be a way of mentally legitimising much darker urges and desires — the 'little girl' isn't really a little girl, since she can change into a desirable nymphet, but with her magical abilities she will never grow old, never become critical or demanding, remaining forever a child. And since this older, more knowing sexual being is always waiting to emerge from within, any sexual act involving the little girl is both 'asked for' by, and done *with*, the hidden adult and not intended for, or done *to*, the apparent child.

Cream Lemon, by its very title, acknowledges the impossibility of this particular wish-fulfilment scenario. Only in fantasy can a child remain undamaged by contact with the darker side of adult desires, and many of the stories, even those intended as comedies, acknowledge this. The phrase *Cream Lemon* is a powerful combination of images with an impact that ties in to many levels of contemporary Japlish. In both Japan and America, the lemon is a symbol of first sexual experience — it's a fruit, pretty and sweet-smelling, and it looks attractive, but if you bite into it the sharper, sour side becomes dominant. And cream, a well known American sexual euphemism for female arousal, is a favourite dessert topping in both culinary and sexual contexts, its foreign-ness (the Japanese don't use dairy products in their traditional diet) giving it an exotic, racy aspect.

A note of caution should be sounded here, and kept firmly in mind. Simply because erotic anime were now available for home consumption, and were to become more and more popular as time went on, this is no indication that they 'took over the market' in any sense. The number of explicitly erotic anime made in any given year is

[1] S. Smet, 'Cream Lemon; An Almost Complete Overview', p39.

rarely more than seven to ten per cent of the industry's total output, and these titles are targeted very specifically at the adult market. Of course, young people, in particular young boys, get hold of them whenever possible, but in this they are no more perverse or perverted than their Western counterparts. Neither the erotic anime industry nor Japanese society encourages or supports access to pornography for children, any more than the Western erotic film industry or Western society.

FIRST TASTE OF SWEET AND SOUR

Cream Lemon started on a serious note. *Be My Baby* is the story of a brother and sister caught up in an incestuous relationship. Ami lives with her stepmother and older brother Hiroshi. When their stepmother has to go away on business, Ami and Hiroshi begin to experiment with their feelings and realise that they are sexually attracted to each other. The build-up to the erotic scenes is gradual, and there is some care taken to establish background and character before the young lovers get their clothes off.

Ami was to become one of the most popular stars in the *Cream Lemon* firmament, with several further instalments of her adventures, her own four-part miniseries and a claim to links with the later, hugely popular *Project A-Ko* film and OAV series. (*A-Ko* itself parodies both the magical girls genre and the lesbian elements of lolikon. Kei, the biker himbo of *A-Ko* 3 and 4, names *Ami's Journey* as his favourite movie. In Ami's third adventure, the 1986 *Now I Embrace You Ami*, Ami and Hiroshi return the compliment when they meet in a pub called "A-Ko".)

Escalation, the second in the series, is set in that breeding ground for wish-fulfilment, a strict Catholic girls' school, and focuses on a lesbian schoolgirl triangle. Rie is entangled in an affair her parents don't approve of, and is sent to the school to get her away from those 'bad influences'. Readers of erotic fiction may well wonder how any parents could be so naïve, though most Catholic girls' schools really don't deserve the erotic power accorded them in fantasy. However, in Japan, where Catholicism is well established but still a 'foreign' religion, and all state schooling is mixed-sex, it's just another exotic element, a signal that this isn't real life. An older girl she admires, Naomi, asks Rie to be her room-mate, but one of Rie's less likeable classmates, the withdrawn and sullen Midori, is included in the invi-

Cream Lemon Climax

tation. The story that follows is predictable lesbian-bondage stuff, making it one of the better known episodes among Western fans.

A totally different tack emerged with the third in the series, *Superdimensional SF Legend Rall*; the elements of parody obvious in the title, and the tale of a galaxy-conquering hero who is fated to be stopped by a female warrior armed with a magical sword, made for lighter viewing that proved popular with the growing audience. The female warrior is utterly flaky, and has a cute flying creature as a sidekick, echoing many of the magical girl shows which had influenced the development of lolikon anime. The script parodies some of the many, many clichés of fantasy, as well as three of the popular television mecha shows of the time, all of which had the word 'superdimensional' in their titles — *Super-dimensional Fortress Macross, Superdimensional Century Orguss* and *Superdimensional Cavalry Southern Cross*. Standards of animation had also risen as the success of the first two episodes paid off. A number of other erotic titles appeared in the run-up to Christmas but *Cream Lemon 3* was the biggest hit.

A SECOND BITE OF THE LEMON

The series' second year proved even more revealing than the first. The first title of 1985, the fourth in the series, appeared in March and quickly established itself with fans as one of the most enjoyable. *Pop Chaser* tells the story of Rio, a biker chick with attitude if ever there was one, who saves a small town in the middle of nowhere from the attentions of the local heavy Zack and his gang. In gratitude, she gets a romp with lolikon goddess Mai, but next morning Zack's mob rolls back into town and carries off most of the women, Mai included. When Rio goes in to save her with all guns blazing, she faces Zack's mighty mecha. It doesn't look hopeful for our heroine until we realise that Mai is so firmly clamped on Zack's genitals that the poor sap can't even reach the controls properly, let alone join battle. And how can Rio possibly take revenge for her oversexed little friend's abduction when Mai pops out of her captor's mecha to announce their engagement and ask her not to hurt him?

Told with tongue firmly in cheek, this is a tale of everyone's gullibility where sex is concerned. It should also be noted that although Mai is presented as a classic lolikon dream girl, she is firmly marked out at the end as old enough to contract a binding engagement to marry.

The director and designer was credited as Yuji Motoyama, a pseudonym for *Project A-Ko* creator Yuji Moriyama. It's still quite usual for anyone in the industry working on erotic video to use a pseudonym, either to hide his or her identity or simply to distinguish the work from their more 'mainstream' material. Some commentators[2] cite

similarities of character and motivation between the characters of A-Ko and C-Ko and Rio and Mai, and point to a similar atmosphere of wacky, no-holds-barred mass mayhem in both titles. If you look closely, you'll find the barman from *Pop Chaser* among the many cameo appearances in *Project A-Ko*, the 1986 movie which opens the series.

The fifth instalment of *Cream Lemon, Ami Again*, goes back to our incestuous high school heroine and the problems she's having making relationships with guys her own age work after that episode of passion with her older brother. Mother has sent Hiroshi off to London to put a stop to the affair, and Ami's friends try to cheer her up by taking her for a night out. They go to a disco where she meets a young man called Kondo and, in that mood of maudlin camaraderie familiar to most of us after a few drinks too many, tells him more about herself than might be considered wise on a first date. She winds up in bed with him, drunk enough to dream that he's her brother, but not enough to forget what they've been doing the next morning.

Part six is another continuation, taking us back to *Escalation* at graduation time and the parting of the ways for our trio of schoolgirl chums. *Escalation 2: Forbidden Sonata* is set a year after part one. Naomi has already graduated, and Rie is spending more time with her old classmate Mari. An invitation to Naomi's mansion for her former room-mates (and lesbian bondage crew) Rie and Midori brings a strange discovery — Mari is there too, tied up. From here on the action differs little from the original, though the art is generally considered better.

Part seven, *Don't Do It, Mako! Mako Sexy Symphony Part One*, revolves around Mako, who's so shy she's almost psychotic, to the point of rejecting a boy who really loves her and understands her problem. Then she meets a strange and fascinating girl, and a supernatural relationship develops. The involvement of Toshihiro Hirano as designer and director ensures art of the highest quality in the series, and something of the emotionally charged atmosphere of his 1985 OAV *Iczer-1* (in which an ordinary schoolgirl also gets involved with a gorgeous supernatural alien female) is in evidence, combined with a refreshing dose of wry humour. Looking at this episode in combination with Moriyama's later contribu-

---

[2] Eg Smet, op cit p39.

tions, it's easy to see the attraction of working on *Cream Lemon* — all the sex scenes that could never be part of a director's mass-market television or video work could be included here.

The supernatural theme continues in *Cream Lemon's* take on *Romeo and Juliet*. Part eight, *Super Virgin*, is the story of psychic schoolgirl Mako (no connection to the heroine of part seven) and a group of normal (ie lecherous) teenage guys. Mako is one of a gang of psychic girls who keep these apprentice perverts in check, but then she falls in love with one of them. The ninth video, *Happening Summer,* is another standard wish-fulfilment tale, in which little sister Yuki gets her sister Keiko's nasty boyfriend into bed. It all ends happily when she finds love with a boy her own age, the clumsy but sincere Koji, who has loved her from afar for some time. Designer/director Ayako Mibashi went on to make more *Cream Lemon* episodes, bringing her sensitive portrayal of character and a nutty sense of humour into play. Look out for a cameo photoshot of Naomi, the schoolgirl bondage queen from *Escalation*, as a model in the nasty boyfriend's sex magazine.

For their last outing of 1985, the team returned to parody with *Star Trap*, a science fiction send-up in which lesbian lovers Lan and Kanaka share command of a renovated starship looking suspiciously like the *Enterprise* (but cautiously renamed the USS *Mischief*). Their mission is to investigate the continuing disappearance of ships around a strange planet, and they take swipes not only at *Star Trek* but also at other science fiction sources, from the venerable *War of the Worlds* to the more recent local heroines *Dirty Pair* and the big grey guy himself, *Godzilla*. It's tempting to wonder if the production team had access to some of the erotic *Star Trek* 'slash' fan-fiction which was circulating so widely in the West at the time, but this is a romp in its own right, and a wonderful companion piece to the third episode with its fantasy parodies.

PILING ON MORE CREAM

1986 saw the end of the original *Cream Lemon* series. The first of the six stories released that year, *Black Cat Manor*, steps back in time to 1941, when student Masaki heads out of war-torn Tokyo seeking safety in the country. He finds lodgings in an old manor house in the mountains, whose only occupants are Saiko, a

widowed lady, her daughter Arisa, and their maid Aya. Once again there are elements of the supernatural, though there's plenty of sex with Saiko while Arisa looks on. This story was edited, along with two other episodes, *The Evil Doll* (from *New Cream Lemon*) and *The Dark* (a 1987 *Cream Lemon Special*), into an American-released tape called *Pandora: An Erotic Trilogy*, which contains some of the strangest dialogue any actress was ever asked to repeat and the only human-scale anime character with a forked penis. This resulted in the classic line: 'Oh no, please don't double-dong me!'

Don't Do It, Mako! Mako Sexy Symphony Part Two is a direct continuation of the first Mako episode. After her strange experiences Mako seems to have gained confidence, and even spends time with would-be boyfriend Yu. But she still hates him to touch her, which makes her wild masturbation sessions at night rather puzzling. Then her ethereal girlfriend intervenes, telling Yu that two entities are fighting for control of Mako's body and soul, one wanting to make her a completely sensual being, the other aiming to repress her carnal self, and he must help to ensure that she can set her true self free. It's a parable of the need for both the physical and the emotional side of love, for body and mind to work in harmony.

Less subtly, *Now I Embrace You, Ami* (usually referred to as *Ami 3*) has Hiroshi coming back from London and telling his sister that they can never resume their sexual relationship because the world won't allow it. In need of consolation, Ami calls Kondo, the guy she met in part two, and most of the second half of the twenty-five minute story is taken up with sex scenes.

After these two relationship-driven, angst-fuelled episodes, *Naris Scramble* is back on the familiar knockabout turf of impure parody. Supercute heroine Naris anticipates Go Nagai's 1991 OAV *Kekko Kamen* by setting herself up as defender of right in her school, opposed by three lesbian Nazis and their giant insectoid mecha. Dad is the school principal, but that actually makes the job harder since he's a pervert who would rather play with little dolls than real women. Still, at least Naris gets to wear more than Nagai's heroine, even if she does go into Super Deformed mode, paying homage to the babes'n'battlesuits genre *en route*. Ayako Mibashi is in charge again and lets rip with comic invention on the anime in-jokes. Look for more guest appearances of other *Cream Lemon* charas, too.

Superdimensional SF Legend Rall 2 disappoints through having become the stereotype fantasy its first episode parodied, but *Escalation 3* wraps up the series by improving on its two earlier stories, so that taken as a whole the *Escalation* trilogy is a primer of obsession and decadence being passed from one 'generation' to the next. Rie, who started out as an innocent pawn, is now the dominant partner in her own circle, and as she prepares to graduate, accepts another invitation to visit her old friend Naomi, this time taking along her own protégée, Arisa.

LEMON GOES MAINSTREAM

The *Lemon* brand had proved popular enough to spawn imitators; in 1984 Five Star produced the twenty-five minute *Cutie Lemon Virgin Road*, and in 1985 followed up with *Cutie Lemon II Graduation*. The word 'lemon' had become synonymous with a particular type of content — and it was even used where the level of 'lemon flavour' might be less than was implied, in titles like *Lemon Cocktail Love 30 S*, a police story which, though it contains some saucy scenes between musclebound Goro Tatsumi and his underage inamorata Maki, is nevertheless not up to *Cream Lemon* levels of naughtiness. Much of the action involves rescuing the girl rather than ravaging her.

But 1986 also saw further developments in the incursion of the erotic into the mainstream video market. Not surprisingly, the lolikon elements of *Cream Lemon*-type titles were abandoned, but there was also a much more conventional view of male-female relationships in the titles made for a more general audience. *The Scarred Man* was the first of what was to become a five-part video series based on the manga by Kazuo Koike and Ryoichi Ikegami, recounting the adventures of a picaresque gold prospector and his various conquests. Keisuke Ibaraki, known as the 'blond devil', races through a series of adventures in the modern world's more remote and dangerous areas, living life on the edge.

The erotic content of this adventure series was relatively high, but unlike the various *Cream Lemon* episodes, these stories mimicked Western live-action adventure films and had a similar aggressively anti-feminist agenda. Tele-

vision journalist Yuko, who falls in love with Ibaraki in the first episode, follows him into his world of danger and is killed in episode two, in the jungle where he picks up a new girl, Peggy. Peggy is taken hostage by porn merchants in episode three, and becomes the reluctant star of their latest production until rescued by our hero. Parts four and five involve him in more rescuing, this time of his friend Misty, who is kidnapped by the same nasty set of pornographers. These last two parts appeared in 1988, the year in which Koike and Ikegami's more famous *Crying Freeman* OAV series, which also has a considerable erotic content, was launched in Japan.

Two 1986 titles which added erotic spice to the ever-popular supernatural or horror story were *Darling Betty* and *Witch Girl Demosteady*. *Darling Betty* combined the tale of a demon-slaying, dragon-destroying witch and her sidekick with nudity and sexual situations, while *Witch Girl*

Darling Betty

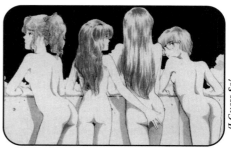

'I Guess So'

Demosteady is the story of a young man whose apartment is built in a dimensional warp, which first brings him his ideal partner, Mami, the 'witch girl' of the title, then tears them apart by dimensional shift. 1987's *I Give My All*, from Animate Film, and *Holey Pants: Desire on a Stroll*, from AIC, showed even top-ranked production houses getting in on the erotic act.

A new player came along in October 1987, and opened a new venue. Aichi's *Midnight Anime Lemon Angel* was a late-night television series which ran for forty-seven episodes and chronicled the adventures of Erika, Miki and Tomo, three well developed teenage girls whose erotic dreams were presented week by week for the delectation of their 'night-time friends'. The show was hosted by the voice actresses behind the three main characters, blurring the line between fantasy and real life, but the limited animation — in places resembling illustration more than moving pictures — was only compensated for by the superb Yuji Moriyama artwork. Although the arrival of the show indicated that erotic anime was already accepted by a wide range of different types of viewer, it nevertheless stuck firmly to 'traditional' erotica, the lolikon model, the underwear shots and the standard fantasy situations.

Over the first three years of the OAV's existence, erotic animation had become more widely available and more popular. Directors and writers had demonstrated that they could begin to move out of the lolikon straitjacket and combine with other popular male entertainment genres like the action-adventure, the horror story and the contemporary romance.

In 1987 the *New Cream Lemon* series had a major competitor when all these elements came together to create the title whose massive overseas success would eventually define the West's view, not merely of erotic anime, but of most Japanese animation. The first of the *Legend of the Overfiend* series was released on 21 January. *Overfiend*'s impact was considerably greater in Britain and America (where it was released in 1993) than it was in Japan, and the direction it took had already been mapped out by the work of Go Nagai among others, but it went further and faster than anything else on video. Violent erotic fantasies, taking their human protagonists either elsewhere in time or to other dimensions, became massively popular.

Meanwhile, recognising that lolikon was a fad-

ing force, and that not everyone would want *Overfiend*'s hardcore theatre of cruelty, *New Cream Lemon* had characters with a more mature look, and the growing interest in the supernatural evinced in other titles and other areas of anime continued to influence the stories.

ANOTHER DASH OF LEMON

The *New Cream Lemon* releases began with *Five Hour Venus*, the first of two *To Moriyama Special* episodes, based on the work of adult manga artist Naoki Yamamoto — Moriyama is a pseudonym. An active campaigner against adult censorship, Moriyama uses contemporary newspaper stories as a basis for some of his work, such as the 1989 OAV *Cream Lemon To Moriyama Best Hit 'I Guess So'*, but the characters in this episode, close high school friends Yachio and Shimeji, were created specially for *New Cream Lemon*. Some time ago, Shimeji needed to make money fast and starred in an X-rated video. A female art teacher finds out about this escapade, and uses it to 'persuade' Shimeji to pose nude for her art class. The action escalates from this point, but the predictable sexual content is sharpened by a strong satirical undercurrent, as both conventional male ideas of female sexuality and elements of lesbian/feminist dogma are shown with all their flaws and absurdities.

The second *To Moriyama Special*, *After School XXX*, came out a year later, but the story runs along the same lines, with the same satirical element and rather better animation. Shimeji and Yachio's classmate Asuka is being blackmailed with some compromising pictures. The girls manage to get the negatives back, but they have plans of their own for one of the pictures.

The second *New Cream Lemon* of 1987 was *White Shadow*, which came out four months after *Legend of the Overfiend* and could be considered to share some of the same story elements, since it centres around a trans-dimensional being of destructive power. The links to its lolikon origins are still visible, though — the love object, Mami, is a high school rhythmic gymnastics star. It also has some of the best art and animation in the series. Shota and Ichiro both fancy Mami, and in an effort to impress, Shota gives her an antique locket. Unfortunately, its cover is the door to another dimension and Mami is dragged in and imprisoned by a vampiric demon who takes her place. The unsuspecting Shota gets a thank you beyond his wildest dreams before she kills him and goes after Ichiro, while Mami struggles to escape.

The horror theme continues in episode three, *The Evil Doll*. This little classic was badly served by its inclusion in the appalling American edit *Pandora: An Erotic Trilogy*, but even there its quality shines through. It's the third contribution to *Cream Lemon* of the talented Ayako Mibashi, and its strange and powerful atmosphere lingers in the memory for longer than its erotic scenes. As Christmas approaches, Hiromu sees a strange girl in the snow, looking cold and lost. He gives her his scarf, but is taken aback when she seems to vanish. Next day, though, he sees her again, and she lures him to a strange place and promises to repay him for his kindness to her. This goes on for some time, with Hiromu's sister becoming increasingly concerned at his night-time disappearances. Then she realises that the girl he describes is very like an old classmate of hers, who vanished, never to return.

Mibashi creates a magical vampire tale whose tragic force springs from the implicit understanding that such stories can't possibly have a happy ending. This is possibly one of the best expositions of the *Cream Lemon* ethos — that however tempting forbidden fruit may seem, there's a price to be paid for it, and even the most light-hearted of sexual encounters can change things for everyone it touches.

This atmosphere of melancholy recurs in the sixth release, *Summer Wind,* in which a boy still mourning the death of his girlfriend meets a strange girl on the beach. They are both on holiday alone, and agree to move into a motel together. There's something odd about Mina (maybe sharing the name of one of the heroines of the Dracula myth isn't a coincidence) and by the end of the episode she and Yo have shared some beautifully depicted erotic encoun-

ters, but mystery and melancholy have left their mark on what should have been a beautiful summer.

Episodes four and five stick to more familiar, less disturbing territory. *Etude: Snow Heartbeat* is a tale of young love across the tracks, between rich classical pianist Yurika and biker jazz player Ryo, hindered by interference from Yurika's father. Their story continues in episode eight, *Etude 2: Early Spring Concerto*. She's still sad after her break-up with Ryo, and her mother tries to matchmake with an old school chum, while Ryo starts an affair with the singer from his band. Episode five, *Dream-Coloured Bunny*, is another wacky SD adventure, peppered with guest appearances — a girl from *White Shadow*, Wily E. Coyote and Roadrunner, even a Transformer. A lecherous lad hanging round the local pet shop is bullied

Ami – From Then On

in to buying a bunny to compensate the long-suffering shop owner for harassing his young female customers, and finds he has his very own bunny girl.

There's more cute animal parody in episode seven. The serious sounding title, *Two People's Life of Heartbreak*, and the opening frames of the 'MGM lion' lead us into a take on the hugely popular magical girl genre, for a story which could almost serve as its last hurrah. The similarities with *Creamy Mami* and the like are very marked. A little blue fox (one of Shinto's magical spirits) offers lovelorn Ruri a wish. She asks for the ability to change into someone else. She loves an older boy, but he's dreaming hopelessly of an idol singer nearer his own age. Now little Ruri can become the girl of his dreams, and she's acquired a cute animal sidekick of her own too! The final episode of *New Cream Lemon*, entitled *Part Zero* and released in June 1988, was simply the sex scenes from *Escalation* and *Be My Baby*, edited together and with some, though not all, of the censoring obscurities removed.

But there was still mileage in the *Cream Lemon* name, and in the character who had emerged as queen of the fans' hearts, Ami. An oddly assembled tape of sequences and images from earlier episodes, and new footage, showing how Ami got into the music business after leaving high school, appeared in 1986 as a *Cream Lemon Special* and did quite well. Its title, *Ami Image White Shadow*, runs the risk of confusion with the second *New Cream Lemon* episode, but it forms a prologue to *Ami — From Then On*. It also foreshadows the heroine's growing independence as she leaves Japan for London — where her brother Hiroshi is now based. *Ami's Journey*, a *Cream Lemon* movie also released in 1986, takes her off on her travels again to try and forget Hiroshi, this time to Hokkaido. Her friends take her on this trip as a birthday treat to try and cheer her up. But on her return, she finds that her stepmother, who insisted on her separation from Hiroshi, is now divorced from her father.

Then in 1988, Ami got her own four-part OAV mini series released under the *New Cream Lemon* banner, *Ami — From Then On*, tracking her life as a young woman trying to make it as a singer with a small independent record label. Her path crosses that of her high school boyfriend Kondo again when the large company he works for buys up Ami's label. Mean-

while Hiroshi has acquired an English fiancée in London. But the relationship between him and his sister, like hers with Kondo, still has many unresolved areas.

The most interesting thing about *Ami — From Then On*, apart from the generally high quality of the art and design (indicating the increase in budget since the first episode four years earlier), is the change in emphasis. All the characters are in their twenties now, and while there's still plenty of sex, Ami is much more in control of who does what with her — in fact, she always takes the initiative. Apart from an Ami compilation, with scenes from all her stories cut to music, and several edited fifteen minute episodes entitled *Cream Lemon Junior*, with the sex cut out of the more comic stories like *Pop Chaser* to render them suitable for a young teenage audience, *Ami — From Then On* was the swan-song of *Cream Lemon*.

SWEETENING THE LEMON

Fairy Dust had also produced erotica without the *Cream Lemon* brand name. The 1985 OAV *Magic Lipstick*, once again inspired by the magical girl genre, enabled a little girl heroine to transform herself into a grown-up sex siren with the use of a magical red lipstick. Like Ami, Yuma embarks on an erotic relationship with her brother, but unlike Ami, Yuma starts out very much in control of the situation. The material such shows parodied continued to be made for its original audience, little girls. Thus, a year after Yuma painted the town red, a magical girl with a very similar name, Yumi, provided cuter, softer colours and absolutely no explicit naughtiness in Studio Pierrot's television series *Magical Idol Pastel Yumi*.

Ami — From Then On had been the swan-song of the *Cream Lemon* series, but not quite its last gasp. In 1992, for the seventh anniversary of the line, a new *Cream Lemon* story was released. By now another new element had entered the media mix — laserdisc was all the rage and collected editions of earlier releases on LD were forming an increasingly important part of the market. *Cream Lemon Young Love: Angie & Rose* combined elements of its earlier fantasy precursors.

A young Japanese boy is far from home, spending the summer in the exotic wilds of Canada, where he encounters the beautiful Rose and her on, the audience had grown up, and in the increasingly complex marketing environment a new wave of pre-pubescent teenagers was looking for a different kind of package to satisfy those adolescent cravings.

Lolikon still has a foothold in contemporary anime. Sometimes its influence is recognised wryly, as in the sequence in the *Tenchi Muyo!* series where Ayeka and Ryoko realise that their pretty foreheads are both stamped with rapidly approaching sell-by dates. Meanwhile, Ayeka's little sister Sasami, still a child, will be a beautiful young woman able to claim hero Tenchi's heart when they are both past their prime. Sometimes jokes and slapstick are draped over lolikon in an attempt at disguise.

The 1997 OAV *Lunatic Night* is filled with corny references to venerated anime classics like *Space Battleship Yamato* and *Mobile Suit Gundam*. However, its heroines are three sex kittens with underage-looking faces and insatiable appetites who positively force the young hero into constant sexual exertion, while its elegant Atlantean queen (a *Sailor Moon* rip-off) masturbates under her flowing robes, and the villain's home-made sex toy transforms from vicious dominatrix to virginal-yet-obedient schoolgirl when her battery is repositioned.

Hardcore horror porn has a huge following but there is still a market which cherishes the impossible dream that inside every schoolgirl is not only a sex kitten waiting to get out, but also a cunning concealed mechanism by which she can pop back inside once playtime's over, no harm done and no one any the wiser. Whereas the magical girl series helped little girls grow up through fantasy into mature, sensible young women, lolikon anime catered to the perpetual infantilism of every underconfident, overoptimistic male.

Far from growing up and moving on to other roles in life, lolikon angels who outgrow the fantasies of their consumers are useless. *New Cream Lemon* allowed its heroines to grow up, whether or not its viewers were ready. From the beginning, *Cream Lemon* and the most honest of its cohorts stated that sexual experience was an irrevocable step past the boundaries of childhood, which once taken could never be retraced; but both on the fringes and in the mainstream, anime producers catering for the modern lolikon fan are still attempting to make those boundaries look negotiable. ●

Cream Lemon Young Love: Angie & Rose

rebellious teenage daughter Angie. Since he is abroad working for his emigrant uncle and Rose is his aunt, the story provides a lot of wish-fulfilment in one package; the thrills of foreign travel, foreign women, sex within the family, initiation by an experienced older temptress, 'normal' sex between two young people, and the possibility of an escape from all this adventure to the safe 'real world' of Japan at the end.

Although the art is beautiful, the running time — just thirty minutes — makes this more of a fond farewell present for the *Cream Lemon* aficionado of old than a serious attempt to recreate its former popularity. The world had moved

SLAP, TICKLE AND SCREAM

The Comic-erotic Horror of Go Nagai

Side by side with the development of lolikon anime, a new strand of erotic horror was emerging. To the modern tentacle-porn aficionado it may seem unlikely that this could also be combined with the broadest slapstick comedy, yet the two were not entirely ill-matched bed fellows. One man, the artist and writer Go Nagai, has had a profound influence on the development of the genre. While his work can be horrific in the extreme, it also contains humour, humanity and playfulness.

In 1984, the first year of the erotic OAV's existence, *Superpowered Girl Barabamba* was released by Fairy Dust. The thirty minute story was based on a manga by Go Nagai, *enfant terrible* of the anime world, a major influence on the progress of both erotic and horror anime. It involves a dimensional-travelling, non-human space pirate and her sidekick (who wind up transformed into a very human, very curvy cutie and a fluffy animal), a nasty alien called D'Rool, a nice young man and a trio of sympathetic lesbians with a fondness for romance. Like the contemporaneous Fairy Dust *Cream Lemon* series, Go Nagai's work combines comedy and horror with erotic elements, so it was perhaps appropriate that Fairy Dust should produce this OAV. Also like *Cream Lemon*, Nagai's work for video both points the way (in several directions) for the development of the erotic OAV and influences the work of others in the field.

Nagai entered the manga world in 1965 at the age of twenty, when he got a job as assistant to the great manga artist and writer Shotaro Ishinomori. Nagai worked hard — often not going home for days, grabbing a few hours' sleep between batches of completed pages, and even passing out at the drawing board. But after eighteen months of this grinding regime, his boss gave him a holiday. He spent it working on his own manga, a gag story which appeared in print in 1967. However, it was *Shameless School*, published a year later, which set the pattern for Nagai's future work in both manga and animation.

It was innovative, irreverent and caused a considerable scandal. Not only were characters featured nude and partly dressed, but — much more disturbing — it was set in a high school and depicted students as sex-mad, cheeky and lazy, and teachers as stupid, pompous, lecherous or otherwise absurd. Copies were publicly burned by the Japan Parent Teacher Association, who felt it brought the education system into disrepute. It's hard to imagine in the West of today, but in sixties Japan the state education system was so widely respected that the mere suggestion that teachers might not be entirely competent was shocking. Young people, however, lapped it up, and it inspired a live-action film and television series in 1970.

Nagai made a farsighted decision in 1969 when he set up a company to manage all production of his publications. Dynamic Production has been a family affair from the beginning — three of his brothers and various other family members work or have worked for the company — and this has given Nagai enormous creative freedom as well as management he can trust absolutely. He was astonishingly prolific from the early days of his solo career, with over thirty stories published in 1969 alone. Success followed success, with his many manga gaining in popularity and two themes emerging as his trademarks. One was large amounts of nudity and violence, often treated in a slapstick fashion, as in his yakuza family soap opera *Abashiri Family*. The other was a fascination with horror, in particular the traditional horror

Cutey Honey

ply a lump of metal, a vehicle to be driven, but somehow mystically alive and in rapport with its young pilot. Only one individual could develop the right symbiotic link with the robot to enable it to use its huge powers.

There's an echo here of the magical girl genre's powerful spirit sidekick and the special object which bestows the heroine's powers. For little girls the chosen manifestation was fluffy animal or fairylike being armed with a bracelet or baton; little boys preferred to play with something huge and metallic at the high end of technology. The uniqueness of the young pilot was an important factor in this and all the series which followed, both from Nagai himself and from his imitators. And although the audience for children's television demanded that he restrain his more outrageous impulses, he couldn't resist including an occasional element of naughtiness. In *Mazinger Z*, the young hero has a girlfriend with her own giant robot, Aphrodite-A, whose missile-loaded breasts are a very prominent feature. And the villain, Baron Ashler, is literally a split personality, half male, half female.

HONEY AND LEMON

Robots and eroticism were combined to even better effect in his 1973 television hit *Cutey Honey*, aimed at somewhat older viewers. Allowing his lead character to grow up ahead of his audience, leading them into a more adult world, Nagai moved on from a brightly coloured giant metal toy with breasts and braids to a beautiful android who wouldn't look out of place in a Wonderbra ad. But, like the girls his male viewers were noticing all around them as puberty hit, she was different, exotic, marvellous — not at all the same as themselves, but not just an object to be played with and put down, even though she was a robot.

Honey was created by a scientist whose own beloved daughter had met an untimely death. The Pinocchio theme has been popular in anime from the days of *Astro Boy* to the later stages of *Legend of the Overfiend*, but Honey is one of its more pneumatic exemplars. When her 'father' disappears, Honey learns of her origins, and of her unique talent. Contained in her not insubstantial chest is a wonderful gadget known as an airborne element solidifier. This enables her to change form, hairstyle and clothing at any time, to disguise herself in order to fight against evil

themes of Japanese folklore and history, demons, ghosts and ghouls.

In 1971, an animation studio asked him to make a television series of his latest manga hit, *Devil-King Dante*, a supernatural adventure tale. But Nagai thought the story wasn't suitable for animation. 'I went away and created a new hero, based on the American comic-book heroes of the time. That was *Devilman*.'[1] The manga appeared in the summer of 1972, with the anime series making its television début just a month later. Much less dark and erotic than the manga and later OAVs, the series was nevertheless pitched perfectly for the wider television audience and was an immediate hit. Nagai has continued to carefully coordinate his manga and anime works ever since, forming another family company, Dynamic Planning, in 1974 for the purpose of ensuring that anime based on his manga are made to his specifications.

By then, he had another hit on his hands. The giant robot epic *Mazinger Z* had appeared in manga and anime form in the winter of 1972. Robots were hugely popular with Japanese audiences. Building on the success of previous robotic creations in the works of Yokoyama and Tezuka, Nagai made an imaginative leap which changed and renewed the genre, by creating a giant robot which was not sim-

---

[1] Evans, 'An Interview with Go Nagai', p29.

wherever it finds her (and it does, of course, find her very frequently).

This more adult take on the magical girl genre is typical of Nagai's work. He often depicts extreme violence, against adults and children,[2] but in erotic situations he likes the parties involved to be over the age of consent. Whereas the magical girls' transformation scenes link into the darker side of the Lolita complex, Honey is depicted as a young woman well into her teens. In the *Cutey Honey* television series and later OAVs, Nagai runs through many of the standard lolikon situations depicted in *Cream Lemon* and other erotic fantasies — lesbian situations in and out of school, bondage scenes, chance encounters and so on — but as a girl above the age of consent, Honey can handle them.

Although her transformations involve her in a nude scene every time (like The Incredible Hulk, her clothes shred as she changes) she starts and ends as an attractive, competent, grown-up young female, not a child masquerading in an adult body. Honey went on to her own OAV series in 1994, and a new television series, *Cutey Honey Flash*, aired in 1997. Interestingly, when Nagai had the opportunity to create a 'real' magical girl series in 1978, *Magic Tickle* contained none of the comic-erotic elements one might have expected from the sultan of sauciness. In Nagai's world, sex is definitely not for small children.

Nagai's interest in the erotic was given room to expand when he was asked to write more and more for young adults. Violence and horror were the dominant notes in 1973's *Violence Jack*, a manga so profoundly steeped in both that it was not animated until 1990, and even then many of its most powerful and disturbing scenes never made it into the screen version. The erotic elements in this tale of an elemental being fighting for life in a Japan devastated by a terrifying earthquake are all dark, negative and bloody, even in the relatively muted anime version in which gang rape and the resulting bloody revenge are nevertheless brutally depicted. The casual murder of a group of innocent children, and the sequence in which a monstrous being, maddened by grief for its dead hermaphrodite lover, eats part of the body then runs amok, remain among the most horrific in anime. Despite the escalating amounts of violence in later productions, few have achieved the emotional impact of Nagai's work.

---

[2] Ibid, p29, his wife ascribed this to the influence of Sampei Shirato's ninja manga.

NAKED AVENGER

Returning to the theme of high school high-jinks which had scandalised parents in the sixties, Nagai created *Kekko Kamen* in 1974. This tale of life in a completely depraved high school run by perverts was an affectionate parody of one of his teacher Ishinomori's favourite genres, the masked hero story. In *Kekko Kamen*, the main character is masked, like the heroes of *Gekko Kamen*, or 'Moonlight Mask' (a popular live-action television series). The difference is that Nagai's heroine wears very little else. Casually twirling a pair of nunchaku, she hides her identity by ensuring that no one is likely to look at her face, and her long red gloves prevent the use of fingerprinting to reveal her secret. Like another giant of the anime and manga scene, Hayao Miyazaki, Nagai has never shrunk from using females as protagonists, and in *Kekko Kamen* he created a classic comedy heroine with a nicely ironic understanding of how her image works both for and against her, and a blithe refusal to be pigeonholed.

The first hour-long OAV appeared in 1991 and contains two adventures, each starting with the sweet but helpless Mayumi Takahashi, student at Sparta College, being picked on by her sadistic teachers under the supervision of Principal Satan Tochiz. Teachers at Sparta believe that any means are justified if the end of turning out pupils with good exam scores is achieved. Besides, they're all perverts who enjoy the various sadistic punishments inflicted on students whose grades fall below standard. However, when Mayumi is being tortured and humiliated, a naked figure appears — Kekko Kamen, the Warrior of Love and Justice!

With her magnificent physique and unparalleled command of such martial arts skills as the super muffocation grip, she defeats Nazi S&M queen Tapoko Gessha (in the Japanese name order, Gessha Tapoko, or Gestapo Girl) and treats her to a taste of her own medicine, much to her delight. One of the series' running gags is that, despite their determination to stop the masked intruder spoiling their fun, all the teachers from Principal Tochiz down are hugely grateful every time Kekko Kamen gets them in her grip. Since this is normally a thigh-grip round the head, the appreciative murmur 'Thank you, Kekko' is somewhat muffled.

But Kekko Kamen is not immune to the urges played out in such depraved fashion by the teachers at Sparta, as the second part of the first OAV shows. When hunky gym teacher Taro Schwarzenegger becomes the next Punishment Educator at

Kekko Kamen

should with her maths homework and faces the torturing tentacles of her new 'friend'. She's really an evil creation of Principal Tochiz and his staff, designed to give them another way of torturing the students and trying to get rid of Kekko Kamen. The queen of naked courage does come very close to losing her beautifully choreographed battle with the android on the rain-soaked rooftops of the school, but finally wins through by applying her intelligence and common sense, rather than her raw strength.

DEMONIC ACTIVITY

Though he continued to produce giant robot stories and gag manga, Nagai's interest in horror was still as strong as his penchant for the erotic. In 1976 he published *Shutendoji*, a manga which (like the earlier *Violence Jack*) was not animated until after the release of the first episodes of *Legend of the Overfiend*, appearing as a four-part OAV series in 1989. Based on Japanese folklore, the story of a young man born to the oni, the demons of Japanese legend, it is subtler than its violent battle scenes and flashes of nudity might suggest to the casual viewer. As Julia Sertori, writing about *Shutendoji* in the British magazine *Manga Mania*, remarked:

'Many of Nagai's stories present an uneasy view of the fantastic. The real, modern world of home and school is always his starting-off point, normally invaded by terrible creatures and events. While the invasion of the fantastic may provide Nagai's stories with their trademark sex and violence, these elements are also the very things that the characters fight against.'[3]

Jiro Shutendo wants to protect the human race from the terrible fate which awaits them, but mostly he wants to protect those he loves, his girlfriend and his adoptive parents. In a touching story twist, while her much-loved child is off saving the world, Jiro's adoptive mother is going mad with grief and fear at his loss. The half-world of insane terror into which she is being drawn is just as deadly as the horrors Jiro is fighting elsewhere, and only the affection of her family can save her. The horror of losing those we love, and the destruction of the everyday security of ordinary life, is bleaker and more terrifying than any demons the imagination can conjure up.

The first *Devilman* OAV made its appearance in

the college, his rippling muscles have just the same effect on Kekko as they have on the lesser females he teaches and tortures. She's so overcome by the vision of his manly beauty that she has to flee from the fight, and only the help and encouragement of senior student Chigusa shows her the way to win.

In the *Kekko Kamen* manga, it is revealed that Chigusa is Kekko's secret twin sister. Hence Kekko Kamen is able to appear at will to fight for justice, while her twin looks after the more mundane, day-to-day aspects of school life and helps and encourages her sibling when she runs into trouble. She suggests using the Ribbon of Love and Justice against Schwarzenegger — the only way Kekko Kamen can fight him is blindfold. And then our naked ninja finds he has a disadvantage — Schwarzenegger's overdeveloped physique creaks with every movement, letting her know exactly where he is, so she can hit him.

The second *Kekko Kamen* OAV, released in 1992, again contains two stories with parodies of anime, manga and film conventions aplenty. The British dub joyously picks up on these in both tapes, using a suspiciously Austrian accent for Taro Schwarzenegger and allowing the samurai snapper of the fourth episode to sound superbly Scottish in a hilarious take on Sean Connery's voice in *Rising Sun*. He's slicing the clothes off girls whose grades drop (it's never the boys) and snapping them in their semi-nude state, then pinning the pics on the school notice board in a novel show-and-shame system of grade improvement. The Polaroid pervert has been lured into this work by Principal Tochiz with the promise that he will be able to test his skills against our girl Kekko, but once again, despite initial setbacks, she wins the day.

Nagai's beloved robots recur in the first story of the second OAV, featuring an android schoolgirl so perfectly made she fools all the girls, and in particular the smitten Mayumi, into accepting her as the real thing — until Mayumi doesn't get on as well as she

---

[3] Sertori, 'The Devil Inside', p15.

1987. For his début in the less restrictive world outside the television series format, the character was redesigned, away from the spandex-clad American superhero look of the manga original and into something far more evocative, threatening and sensual. The contrast between young hero Akira Fudo, a quiet teenager into open-necked shirts and caring for small animals, and the post-transformation Devilman, a broad-shouldered, muscular half-beast exuding sex appeal while ripping the heads off demons, is stunning; Devilman is a teenage boy's fantasy of potency made flesh. He can even fly, unfurling huge, dark, leathery wings whenever he wants and simply having them vanish when he lands. In an interesting echo of magical girl series, this powerful adult being can return to his teenage human state. Akira agrees to be transformed into Devilman at the request of his friend Ryo, to try and protect the human race, including his own loved ones, from demonic attack.

These demons are not anti-Christian, but anti-human; relics from the far past, contained until now in another dimension, they are beginning to break through into our world once again, and we are their natural prey. No human is strong enough to defeat the demons, but a human-demon hybrid, with the strength of a demon but the gentle heart of a human, could be. To beat them, Akira has to join them. In between using his powers to battle evil in its most primal form, he returns to his every-day teenage self but, unlike the typical magical girl heroine, he is marked by his vicarious experiences in an adult body. A boy can't acquire such power without changing in some way, and Akira, while still possessing a kindly human soul, has lost some of his illusions and gained confidence and charisma, as well as the ability to run very fast and leap tall buildings (if not in a single bound, at least in just a couple of bounds).

The second *Devilman* OAV, released in 1990, was even more powerful, combining this ultimate male in flight and battle with an even more deadly female. Bird-demon Silene is as naked as Kekko Kamen, has great white feathered wings on her head, a cute feathered tail, and distinctly uncute claws on arms and legs — claws which, in a deadly echo of the giant robots of Nagai's early television series, can be fired off at an enemy. Like Devilman, she's an elemental force, but unlike him, she has no human side, no element of softness or gentleness about her. She is utterly devoted to the service of the great Demon King, and in that service she finally dies, after a bloody battle which leaves her

Devilman

opponent battered and bleeding in a ditch, hovering between life and death.

Silene is not just a bare-breasted bimbo thrown into the story for purposes of titillation; she is a deadly enemy, meeting Devilman on equal terms, and her defeat is not a foregone conclusion. The 'other woman' in the OAV, Akira's cute young cousin, a classic anime high school heroine, is absolutely no competition in terms of power or attraction. Just as *Cream Lemon* acknowledged the dangers and losses of sexual experience, so *Devilman* admits that females can be dangerous as well as dazzling. This bird comes from the very opposite of paradise, and knows how to sharpen her claws.

Akira pays a heavy price, both for defending his own people and for the head start in grown-up life which his experiences as Devilman have given him. He may have become stronger, faster and sexier than any other boy his age; he may have flown through the night sky with a gorgeous winged death-goddess; he may have lived more intensely than any teenager dreaming of 'life on the edge' could possibly imagine; but his innocence has gone and his life may be draining away with the last of his human blood.

In *Devilman* and *Shutendoji*, Nagai recognises the seductive power of violence, but he doesn't glamorise it. This is a difficult line to tread when both the heroes of these series are so attractive. With *Violence Jack* matters were simplified by Jack being a social outcast and seemingly not entirely human, but both Akira Fudo and Jiro Shutendo would fit in happily to most schools and clubs. Their transfer from manga form, where their motivations and feelings could be explored in much more detail, to animation, where shorter timespans compress character development, was masterfully handled.

Furthermore, the parallels with lolikon anime such as *Cream Lemon* are explicit but never laboured. Nagai recognises that for boys, just as much as for girls, there is no return to the innocence of childhood once the line into adult activity has been crossed.

PLAYING FOR LAUGHS

After such intensity, it comes as a relief to find that 1991's Nagai video output includes the crazy Super Deformed fantasy *Chibi Chara Go Nagai World*. This was made by a team of his protégés, but ties together many loose ends in the Nagai universe by putting the characters from *Devilman, Mazinger Z* and other Nagai manga into strange and comical situations in the bodies of children. Asked why this OAV was made, Nagai said, 'In *Devilman,* all the adults fight. The producer... thought it would be nice if they were young again and didn't have to fight.'[4] Yet it's not without moments of slapstick and erotic humour, like Akira Fudo's comic dismay when he realises that not only has he shrunk to child size, but so have all his organs.

The year also saw the release of Nagai's 'saucy seaside postcard' version of the great Hindu sex manual *Kama Sutra*, in which a young male virgin on an archaeological dig meets an ancient princess, gets his hands on the local version of the Holy Grail, and learns that for eternal life and eternal bliss he has to fill the cup with human sexual fluids. The British release was hampered by less than perfect subtitling, but *Kama Sutra* in any format was never likely to do as much for the profession of archaeology as the Indiana Jones movies. It's as cheap, cheerful and vulgar as a *Carry On* title, but with rather less wit in the *double entendres*.

In 1992 Japanese video fans could buy six new Nagai OAVs, three of which have made it to the West. Part two of *Kekko Kamen* has already been discussed. *The Abashiri Family* is a comic orgy of violence with nudity thrown in, based on his earlier manga of gangster family life but focusing on the adventures of the daughter of the family in a school which, like so many schools in Nagai's creations, turns out to be less respectable than parents might like to think. Nagai constantly urges his readers and viewers not to place blind faith in the symbols of authority, but instead to question and decide for themselves, even if the consequences are uncomfortable.

Hanappe Bazooka is a reprise of *Shutendoji* with a human hero and more gags. Interestingly, it's a collaboration with the great writer Kazuo Koike, of *Lone Wolf and Cub* and *Crying Freeman* fame. Hanappe is a hapless boy, a loser of the kind to be found in every classroom, but at heart he's a nice guy. He may have the usual run of teenage male fantasies, but all he really wants in life is for his family to get on with each other and not get at him too much, for the girl he fancies to fancy him back, and not to be beaten up by a gang of older bullies. When a pair of demons turn up and grant what he thinks is his greatest wish, he soon finds that not only does irresistible sex appeal have its downside, but that any kind of power brings with it all sorts of consequences, which are not necessarily what one had in mind. Seeing his mum having sex with the husky male demon, his sister engaged in lesbian bondage games with the cute female one, and his father living out his own fantasies, Hanappe finds himself longing for a bit of normal, conventional home life.

Meanwhile, his demonically bestowed powers of attraction only seem to get him chased by transvestites and man-hungry grannies, not the voluptuous young sex queens of his adolescent dreams. In the end, his sincerity and goodness of heart win over the demons to fight on his side in the battle to get himself and his world back to normal. Hanappe didn't need to get a life, in particular an exciting life full of sexual opportunity; he just needed to persuade himself and all those he loved to appreciate the one they already had.

The development of Nagai's OAV and television work has interesting parallels with the development of the erotic OAV in general. The escalating levels of violence (in particular sexual violence) permissible on video as the new medium of the OAV evolved enabled some of his most provocative manga work to be animated, though it must be said that without exception the anime versions are less horrific and less dense with plot and character than the manga. Yet throughout this development, Nagai's work and that of a few other creators in the genre retained those elements of humour and human sympathy which kept the sex comedy, in all its guises from broad to subtle, vital enough to survive the fashion for horror and re-emerge in the nineties, rude, crude and lewd, but still alive and kicking. Tentacles aren't the only things that can raise a reaction just by wiggling, and there are still audiences who prefer it if the reaction is a giggle rather than a scream. ●

[4] Evans, op cit p30.

'TITS AND TENTACLES'

Sex, Horror and the Overfiend

No other title apart from Akira has been so influential in the English-language anime market as **Legend of the Overfiend**. Creator Toshio Maeda has developed his central themes over several years, partly in response to commercial pressure and partly as a result of ideas that continue to obsess him. Looking over his animated works, we can see that **Overfiend** does not express a moral, but an underlying vision of the world which is bleaker and more terrifying than any of its onscreen excesses.

'Symbolic sites of power and control — the phallus, city architecture, a person's sanity — are possessed by energy. The latent becomes manifest as the dormant, hidden energy of *anything* is suddenly cast loose in an uncontrollable event of destruction. Typically puerile entertainment in most respects, the *Overfiend* series reveals a channelling of sexual energy and its coalition with social and cultural power.'[1]

The visual grammar permitted by the tentacle is extremely useful to the pornographer. With no restriction on length, it permits penetration without blocking the view. It can also be used as a form of restraint, permitting multiple penetration, sexualised bondage and ease of camera access. Best of all for the tentacle as a pornographic device, while it may often look suspiciously like a penis, to the extent of possessing a foreskin or glans, or even ejaculating upon climax, it is not a sexual organ by definition. The Japanese film-maker can thus show as many as he likes, doing whatever he wishes, without falling foul of the usual censorship restrictions. The only problem with the tentacle is that the film-maker must find an excuse for its appearance. This is best accomplished by making monsters a feature of the storyline, be

they demons, invading aliens or creatures from the id. And since such creations are evil by nature, it is a logical step in such porn to accentuate the incidences of rape and sexualised violence.

While there are many works in the 'tits and tentacles' genre, this chapter is chiefly devoted to the largest and most well known, Toshio Maeda's *Legend of the Overfiend* series (also known by its Japanese title, *Urotsukidoji*). A manga artist specialising in the erotic grotesque, Maeda's characteristic style was published in the right place (Japan) at the right time (when video distribution and censorship restrictions combined to create the ideal environment for its excesses). It was also released at the tail end of the eighties, when foreign distributors came looking for successors to the bestselling *Akira*.

In the West, the *Overfiend* series presents a problem for anime apologists. Its shock value is guaranteed to elicit a reaction from an audience, and it is a guaranteed bestseller with profits that can fund less popular releases, but it simultaneously generates adverse publicity for anime as a whole. With sales superseded only by *Akira*, *Overfiend* may be a money-spinner, but it is something that many find embarrassing, even in the industry itself. Only two Japanese actors were credited on the original production, and the English-language crews

---

[1] Anon, from *Kaboom!: Explosive Animation from America and Japan*, p142.

continued this custom by keeping most involvement suitably anonymous or pseudonymous.[2]

NOBODY LOVES ME

The story of the *Overfiend* is no more childish than any other fairy-tale, except Maeda's vision brings no hope of happy-ever-after. He has a psychologist's eye for the anguish of puberty, with a pornographer's talent for exploiting his audience's weaknesses. Maeda's world is an uncaring one in which youth and hope are continually sacrificed on the altar of adult complacency. For his characters, puberty is a satanic ritual that strips them of their innocence and turns them into evil adults. The action in *Overfiend* comes from youth's futile attempts to defy the system, accompanied by a deliberately infantile cycle of vengeance and vendetta.

Many of Maeda's characters brood over past betrayals, often waiting decades to exact their revenge. *Overfiend*'s cycle of rape and counter-rape is truly without end, the Chojin moves heaven and earth to keep the Kyo-O away, and yet their eventual, inexorable meeting is destined to become the very act of creation that starts the sequence once more. Munchausen and Yoen bide their time to exact their revenge on Amanojaku, and Kohoki broods in the fires of hell, waiting for a chance to get back at Megumi.

Maeda's world is fraught with pain and misunderstanding because it remains eternally frozen at the nadir of adolescent angst. There are so many characters because Maeda continually requires new blood to experience the pressure, pain and fear that comes with standing on the threshold of adulthood, staring out into the terrifying future. Time and again, his characters awaken to the knowledge that they are on their own in a heartless world, in which adults surround us with their strange perversions and hypocrisies. But entry

into the adult world brings powers, the literal magic of spell-casting and the figurative magic of power, responsibility and sex.

If you want to play the adults' game, you must become one of them. Sexual awakening can never be revoked; the energies it unleashes can be used for good or ill, but like magicians we must learn how to harness the power, and make it work for us, ever fearful that it can control us as easily as we can control it. Maeda's sorcerers need sex to cast their spells; they have a vampiric obsession with the power of orgasm. Ancient witches use it to stay young, warlocks draw potency from the pliant bodies of their sexual conquests and use it for war and destruction.

Initiation into the adult world also brings secret, hidden knowledge. The soul-destroying discovery in the *Overfiend* is that romance is a myth. The powerful, magical pangs of first love are destined never to be repeated, not the least because they too will fade and die. It is better, argues Maeda, to die happy in the arms of your beloved, than it is to grow weary of them, take them for granted or find yourself betrayed.

Maeda sees incredible tragedy in the rejection of love, all the more unbearable in his work because he sees the death of love as inevitable. Teenage affection is poisoned and corrupted as the lovers mature, children betray their parents, and human beings are incontrovertibly faithless. The survivors in *Overfiend* are not really survivors at all, they are merely those who retain some aspect, good or bad, of childhood. They stay children by remaining selfish, or by literally never growing up. Alecto is safe for as long as she remains Daddy's little girl.

When she rebels she is raped, first by her father and then by marauding demons as she searches for her lover amid the ruins of her childhood castle. The children of Eruth's kingdom will survive for as long as they reject the responsibilities and powers of adulthood; Yumi and Ken dare to fall in love, and they pay with their lives. Yufura's

[2] The only actors credited on the Japanese production are the voice-artist Tomohiro Nishimura (Amano) and the eccentric rock-singer Demon Kogure (Munchausen). In the American dub, some of the more colourful stage-names of the English-language cast include Rebel Joy, Pat McGroyn, Lucy Morales, Rose Palmer, Randy Woodcock and Jurgen Offen. None of Kiseki's cast in the *Overfiend III* dub were acknowledged, although the sleeve credited seven directors, but not the person who actually did it.

Overfiend I:1

WHO'S WHO IN THE OVERFIEND SERIES

AKEMI (I.1-III.1)
A college girl fated to give birth to the Overfiend. Assaulted by Miss Togami, desired by Nikki and impregnated by Nagumo.

ALECTO (III.1-III.4)
The daughter of Caesar, killed in an accident, then reborn as an android. She elopes with Buju, only to be slain (again) by her father's troops. Once 'repaired' she is raped by her father and then by marauding bandits.

AMANO (I.1-IV.3)
Full name Amanojaku, although many of the human characters address him as Amano because Hajime Amano is the false name he uses on Earth. Sent from the beast realm to find the Chojin, he is the brother of Megumi and the lover of Mimi (the daughter of the beast realm's ruler).

BUJU (III.1-IV.3)
A man-beast hybrid born in the aftermath of Nagumo's holocaust, Buju becomes the prime suspect in the hunt for the Kyo-O. Raised from the dead by the infant Kyo-O, he is convinced by Amano to rescue the baby from Caesar's clutches. After the fall of Caesar's Palace, Buju takes Himi to Osaka.

CAESAR (III.1-4)
An industrialist and religious leader, who becomes obsessed with the desire to control the Chojin's power. He captures Buju, thinking him to be the Kyo-O, inadvertently setting up a chain of events that will lead to the destruction of his empire.

CHOJIN (III.1-IV.1)
The fabled Overfiend, who is said to appear once every three thousand years and destroy the universe, only to make it anew. The series presents several candidates, but the True Chojin is the son of Nagumo and Akemi.

D-9 GENOCYDROID (III.4-IV.3)
An experimental cyborg soldier under development at Caesar's Palace. The incomplete D-9 fails in his attempt to rescue his ex-lover Pedro, and thereafter joins Kyo-O's followers.

ERUTH (IV.1-2)
The immortal child who rules the Secret Garden in the name of himself and his twin brother Paruth. Eruth believes that Himi's blood will restore his brother to life.

FAUST (III.1-4)
False name used by Munchausen while in Caesar's service.

HIMI (III.2-IV.3)
A small child found by Buju and Alecto in an ancient temple, Himi soon grows into a beautiful young girl with

magical powers, who demands to be taken to Osaka to meet the Chojin. See Kyo-O.

KEN and YUMI (IV.1-2)
Teenage lovers from the Secret Garden, threatened with certain death at the onset of puberty. They attempt to escape, but are caught by Yufura.

KOHOKI (II.1-2)
A creature from the demon realm, exiled as punishment for an affair with Megumi. He serves the young Munchausen in the hope to meet Megumi again.

KYO-O (II.1-IV.3)
A legendary creature said to be the Chojin's opposite, explained variously as Chaos to Law, Yin to Yang or even Good to Evil. See Himi.

MANTIS WOMAN (III.1-3)
Demonic lieutenant of Caesar, whose sexual favours are used to lure Buju into Caesar's clutches.

MA-O (I.2-3)
A giant demon beneath the sea, who caused the Great Kanto Earthquake in 1923. Summoned again by Suikakuju as a last ditch defence against Nagumo.

MEGUMI (I.1-IV.3)
Amano's sister and the former lover of Kohoki. Instrumental in thwarting the young Munchausen's schemes when he uses Takeaki against Nagumo.

MUNCHAUSEN SENIOR (II.1)
A Nazi diabolist and the inventor of the Rape Machine, which uses the combination of fear and desire to open gateways to other dimensions. Myunhihausen in some translations.

MUNCHAUSEN JUNIOR (II.1-IV.3)
He learns of the Kyo-O's existence in his father's diaries, and tries to 'bring forth' the Kyo-O in Takeaki. He reappears after the holocaust masquerading as the wizard Faust, and is presumed dead in a nuclear explosion near Osaka. He rejuvenates himself with the sexual energy of Yoen, and joins forces with her.

NAGUMO (I.1-III.2)
Suspected by Megumi of being the Chojin, Nagumo is regarded by everyone else as a geek. When he falls in love with Akemi, he develops magical powers, and many suspect that he is the Chojin. When he impregnates Akemi with the True Chojin, he transforms into a giant demon, to ravage the world in preparation for his son. He appears again to rout Caesar's army at the Gates of Hell.

NIKKI (II.1-2)
Another pawn in Suikakuju's attempts to destroy the

Chojin, Nikki sells his soul for the chance to have sex with Akemi.

OLD MASTER (I.2)
The high priest of the beast realm and Amano's one-time mentor.

OZAKI (I.1)
Class hunk at the college, suspected by Amano of being the Chojin. But Ozaki has merely developed facsimile powers through ingesting some of Nagumo's blood.

PARUTH (IV.1-2)
Brother of Eruth but never seen by the other denizens of the Secret Garden. It is revealed that Paruth has been long-dead, and his 'edicts' only exist in his brother's feverish mind.

PEDRO (III.2-4)
Caesar's female lieutenant, who leads a tactical retreat to Palace research centre, hoping to turn the tide of battle with the D-9 Genocydroid. D-9 incorporates parts of her former lover.

SUIKAKUJU (I.1-3, IV.3)
'Water-Horned-Beast', a demon lord and sworn enemy of Amano, who refuses to believe that the Chojin will bring peace. He is killed by Amano but raised from the dead by his concubines Fukakuki and Enkakuki (the Horned Devils of Wind and Fire respectively).

TAKEAKI (II.1-2)
Takeaki is given blood from his cousin Nagumo in a transfusion overseen by a disguised Munchausen, who hopes to turn him into the Kyo-O. The blood also bestows sub-Chojin powers on Takeaki. Eventually killed by Megumi, but several decades later, the True Kyo-O is born from his clotted blood.

TOGAMI (I.1)
A teacher at Akemi's school, who tries to introduce her pupil to lesbian sex, and when that fails, transforms into a rapacious demon.

YOEN [-KI] (IV.3)
Literally 'Devil of Charmed Fire', Suikakuju's younger sister joins forces with Munchausen to avenge her brother's death, although the 'flashback' scene of her brother's death in IV.3 bears no resemblance to earlier events in the series.

YUFURA (IV.1-2)
The chief torturer in the Secret Garden, Yufura holds back puberty with sorcery. When her magical energies are exhausted in a duel with Amano, she is forced to seek Buju's protection, and secures his aid, temporarily, with sexual favours.

spite is acceptable for as long as she is a 'good' child servant of Eruth; when she becomes a woman she is forced to prostitute herself for her own protection, and when that fails she is savagely murdered.

Sexual love is not the only doomed venture; the love of parents will also fail in *Overfiend*. Caesar's quest for power results in the death of his own daughter, Alecto. Wracked with guilt, he replaces her with an android, but rapes *her* when she prepares to leave him for Buju. Buju loses Alecto because she cannot leave her abusive father, but inherits Himi, an adoptive daughter. But Himi is fated to leave him for her symbolic marriage to the Chojin, the coming together of the worlds that will destroy Buju, yet also create him once more.

PORNS OF PROPHECY

Youth is determined to change the world, a revolutionary aim that the older, wiser adults feel obliged to oppose. Every generation repeats the mistakes of its predecessors, before eventually realising the folly of resistance and accepting the status quo. In *Overfiend*, only the young are stupid enough to imagine they can make a difference.

Love and romance are not the only myths. The story is riddled with portentous prophecies, all of which turn out to be incorrect. To viewers reared on Western fantasy, a prophecy is bound to come to fruition in the course of a movie, and can be used as a marker to demonstrate how far along the story we are. Not so in *Overfiend*, because everyone in the series operates under false pretences. Every time someone explains who is good and who is evil, which side we should be rooting for, or whose motives are honourable, the next episode reveals them to be wrong.

The Chojin, we are told, will unite the three worlds and bring peace and harmony. The Chojin will destroy the three worlds and bring chaos. Whoever defeats the Chojin shall inherit his powers. None can defeat the Chojin. The Chojin is Ozaki, no, the Chojin is Nagumo, no, the Chojin is Nagumo's unborn son. The Chojin can be defeated by the Kyo-O. The Kyo-O is Takeaki, no, the Kyo-O is Nikki, no, the Kyo-O is Buju, no, the Kyo-O is Himi. Actually, the Chojin and the Kyo-O will not fight at all.

In a bitterly human way, and a surprisingly

naturalistic one considering the fantastic nature of the series, Maeda forces us to watch, paralysed, as the juggernaut of destiny rolls ever onwards. Unlike many of his Western colleagues, he offers us no chance to feel comprehension or control, even for a moment. All victories are insignificant respites from doom. All defeats are crushing, and the uncaring Earth abides. Amano is the viewer's guide through the confusion, the titular 'wandering child' ('urotsuki doji'), but even he makes several errors of judgement, switches sides and mixes people up. He is an observer of the saga, but he is deliberately flawed.[3] He is granted a vision of the future, but not enough to change it. When, in the last episode, we see the nature of the new order, he is as surprised as we are. Maeda has no time for all-encompassing conspiracies, or omnipotent characters who know the secrets of the universe. The universe is just there, we are stuck in it and we will never, ever understand how it works.

LOST IN TRANSLATION

Thanks to the nature of its content and release schedules, *Overfiend* suffers more than any other anime in the transition to English. It is an adaptation of an adaptation of an adaptation, by several Japanese scenarists, then several different translators, few of whom had any knowledge of the original manga, or the direction in which the anime version was likely to go. The translators' scripts were rewritten, at least in part, by several others (ranging from qualified script doctors to interfering typists) with even less knowledge of the original, and altered still further in the dubbing studio for lip synchronisation and artistic licence. In Britain, the first five episodes were not sold as they originally appeared, but in the two Japanese feature-length movie edits. Effectively, it was cut twice, once by the Japanese to fit within the running time, and again by the BBFC, who snipped a substantial amount of footage.

It is a testament to both the original manga's density of plotting (or perhaps its lack of editorial coherence) that these aspects even appear to have confused the Japanese production staff. *Overfiend* was originally written in the way it was translated, piecemeal. Scenes and charac-

---

[3] An 'amanojaku' is a devil beneath the guardian deities of a temple. The term is sometimes used to describe someone who is deliberately contrary.

ters were cut, altered and conflated in order to make a suitable adaptation, but the confusing way in which the Japanese version was released implies that somebody, somewhere made a vital continuity error. The *Overfiend* synopsis in this chapter is set in chronological order with the benefit of 20/20 hindsight, but this was not within the power of the original production staff in either Japan or the West.

#	CHAPTER	EPISODE TITLE	ALSO KNOWN AS... (MOVIE EDITION)
1	I.1	Birth of the Overfiend	Urotsukidoji
2	I.2	Curse of the Overfiend	Legend of the Overfiend
3	I.3	Final Inferno	
4	II.1	Legend of the Demon Womb	Urotsukidoji
5	II.2	Battle at the Shinjuku Skyscrapers	Legend of the Demon Womb
6	III.1	The Birth of the True Chojin	
7	III.2	The Mystery of Caesar's Palace	Urotsukidoji
8	III.3	The Fall of Caesar's Palace	Return of the Overfiend
9	III.4	Passage into the Unknown	
10	IV.1	The Secret Garden	Urotsukidoji
11	IV.2	The Long Road to Divinity	Inferno Road
12	IV.3	Quest's End	

BIRTH OF THE OVERFIEND (I.1)

The year is 1993; the place, Japan. Beneath the surface of everyday life, strange forces are bubbling. There is not one but three universes: an ego, super-ego and id of opposing, but mutually dependent forces. These are the realms of the blissfully ignorant humans, the wise, changeling beasts and the rapacious, uncontrollable demons. Once every 3,000 years, the three realms will be destroyed and remade by a unifying force, the fabled Chojin (Overfiend).

Amano (Amanojaku) of the beast realm has been wandering the Earth for centuries, convinced that he can locate the Chojin while the power to destroy the universe is still in its infancy. Although he rarely discusses his motives, we can assume that Amano and the beasts wish to use the Chojin's powers for their own ends. But Amano is not the only supernatural creature searching for a new messiah among the unsuspecting human race. Over the centuries, he has fought many battles with the relentless Suikakuju, his *alter ego* from the demon realm.

Amano and his sister Megumi disagree over the Chojin's identity. They suspect he will be born in Japan, but have no idea who he could be. Amano is backing high school sports star Ozaki as a likely candidate, and refuses to believe that the nerdish Nagumo stands a chance. Nagumo is obsessed, as are the other local boys, with the It-Girl Akemi, although she is unlikely to ever glance in his direction. When we first see him, he is sneaking a peek into the girls' locker room and masturbating furiously, supposedly the act of a pervert, although later developments will suggest that it is merely a manifestation of the high sexual drive associated with godhood. The trials and tribulations of puberty are thus inverted, glorifying all that is suppressed in adolescent hormones. Like the ugly duckling of old, the onanistic, lonely, angst-ridden teenager should take heart, for who is to say he will not become lord emperor of the universe?

Viewers anticipating a swift resolution to the plot are in for a long wait, although it would appear that many of the translators who worked on the project were similarly expecting Maeda and his colleagues to follow a standard, unified narrative. Ozaki is not the Chojin, but nor is Nagumo. The true Chojin does not actually appear until much later in the series, after so many false alarms that some critics have understandably missed him altogether. Amano is confused by the behaviour of Ozaki, who ingests some of Nagumo's blood while teasing him in the gym, and consequently develops facsimiles of the Chojin's powers. It is Ozaki who taunts Nagumo in front of the entire school, prompting the cruel laughter of the young girls.

Meanwhile, Akemi is summoned to see Miss Togami, who might have the outward appearance of just another teacher, but is really a demon in disguise.[4] Togami reveals that her tongue is really a penile tentacle with an eye at the tip. She strips away Akemi's gym slip and molests her. Tentacles fly out from Togami's body, and surround the helpless victim, binding yet also revealing her naked breasts and body.

Owing to its chronological position as the first

demon-rape of the saga, and the presence of a still of Miss Togami's tongue-tentacle in the press pack, this scene is one of the most widely mentioned in mainstream criticism of anime. It is close enough to the start of the story to stand a good chance of being viewed, even by those commentators who were likely to turn off in disgust before witnessing the story's later excesses. And yet, it is surprising how tame the scene is, especially when considered in the light of what would follow.

The scene is engineered to set up the blossoming romance between Nagumo and Akemi, because his chance arrival saves the day.[5] Akemi is spattered with glowing pink seminal fluid, has a surrogate tentacle forced into her mouth and is (perhaps) sexually assaulted by Miss Togami, but remains a virgin. The sequence turns Nagumo into a kind of hero, but has at its core another form of adolescent sexual fantasy. Nagumo is an outcast in the world of his school (for half of the episode, he is only ever addressed in the English translation as 'Dickface') and would normally stand no chance whatsoever of appealing to the homecoming queen.[6] But, thinks the dark half of the human psyche, if only Akemi were threatened by some terrible fate, if only I could save her from a rapist, then she would look at me. Akemi the unattainable female can only be approached through the cycle of hurt/comfort, as a damsel in distress.

However, the male fantasist has no wish to place the object of his affections in real danger, nor does he want her 'endangerment' to lose what he regards as his sexual dues. Akemi must not be raped by a man, because Nagumo will lose his opportunity to claim her virginity for himself. Nagumo gains Akemi's attention by 'saving' her from a rapist, but Miss Togami, for all her

---

[4] In the original manga, Miss Togami was just one of several demonic teachers who preyed upon the sweet young things at the college. In panning shots across the school's frontage, we see it has the six-pointed star that is *Overfiend*'s symbol of magical power carved into it, a sure-fire sign of a rapacious adult institution.
[5] Actually, it is Amano who comes to the rescue, but Akemi never realises. The two boys watch the action through the keyhole until Amano comes to his senses. He heads off after defeating Togami, leaving Nagumo to comfort the dazed Akemi and take the credit.
[6] In terms of the anime archetypes discussed in chapter nine, Akemi is transformed into a Girl Next Door by talking to Nagumo. Until that point, she is an unattainable Maiden.

demonic horror, is actually a sanitised, rather childish threat. 'She' is female, because lesbian sex is less threatening to a man than the heterosexual alternative. And while surrogate penises may force their way into Akemi's mouth and spurt some kind of fluid over her body, we have already been told that these are not penises but tentacles. Miss Togami disappears once Akemi has been rescued, and no trace is left of the immense destruction wrought upon the staff room. The after-effects of her terrifying ordeal are no worse than waking from a nightmare, and Akemi remains eternally grateful to Nagumo because she believes he has saved her life.

Amano, however, still assumes that Ozaki is the Chojin, unaware that Ozaki's powers are merely the result of his drinking a drop of Nagumo's blood. The scene shifts to a party at Ozaki's place, and once again we are in the territory of teenage paranoia. Ozaki has his own apartment, coupled with prowess, popularity and a legion of adoring groupies. The teenage mind, insecure about its own looks, talent or potential, sees Ozakis everywhere. To the callow eyes of youth, everybody else has a girlfriend, everybody else is doing better at school, everybody else is going to be somebody. Ozaki is depicted as the luckiest man in the world, partying with three naked girls in a luxurious room. The camera dwells on one girl, bent face-down over a glass coffee table, her squashed breasts lovingly animated in a homage to the seventies European porn films

---

[7] These are the two errant episodes released out of order in the original series, an anomaly that has seriously damaged the potential for informed criticism. While it is possible that Noboru Aikawa's script for I.1-3 simply discounted the Munchausen/Kyo-O subplot as irrelevant, it is equally likely that the problem was noted but ignored. Since the Kyo-O story is only important in the later episodes, it may have been an editorial decision to leave it out, with the understanding that, should the series be successful, the gaps could be filled in at a later date. In his article on *Overfiend*, Steven Smet discusses other explanations, such as the possibility of II.1-2 taking place in a parallel universe, or even 3,000 years later in another cycle of apocalypse. My decision to shuffle the chronology is based on the evidence of the III.1 prologue, which similarly reorders events. However, this does not answer all of the questions, since I.1-3 seems to take place in Osaka and II.1-2 in Tokyo. Furthermore, the Japanese releases of II.1-2 were titled *Shin Chojin Densetsu*, or 'True Legend of the Overfiend', implying that they are somehow closer to the original story than the previous episodes.

that aspired to be 'art' through unexpected camera angles. But soon we are back in Maeda territory, as Ozaki's penis starts glowing with a ghostly light of its own. Ozaki's sexual organ has become imbued with the power of the Chojin, and conveniently, can now be shown on screen because an area of glowing, penis-shaped film is permitted, but not the penis itself. As in many other points in the saga, the manifestation of sexual power is a precursor to rapacious violence, and Ozaki's companions are soon dispatched.

Now convinced that Ozaki is the Chojin, Amano challenges him to single combat as the final proof. But Amano's powers make short work of Ozaki, and as he looks at the dying boy, Amano realises that it was Nagumo's blood that gave Ozaki the powers. Amano rushes to tell Megumi she was right all along, but he is too late. Nagumo has disobeyed a childhood law (looking both ways before crossing the road) and is hit by a car. The young may dare to flout adult rules, but only if they are strong enough to take the consequences. Nagumo dies in hospital on the operating table, only to be reborn as the Chojin-creature whose manifestation he has suppressed.

Experimenting with his sexual power, Nagumo forces a nurse to fellate him until he ejaculates in her mouth, and he then pins her to the wall and enters her. Once again, the camerawork is ambiguous, implying without revealing, since revelation would encourage censorship. Is the dripping liquid vaginal juices (suggesting she is enjoying it) or blood (suggesting a savage rape)? And here, in the third major sex scene, we have yet another 'magical' incident rooted in adolescent fantasy. The Chojin's orgasm, shown as streams of bright light emanating from the nurse's eyes, mouth and ears, destroys the body of his victim, while implying that it is her orgasm too. Like the pornography of many cultures, it implies that the satisfaction of the male is also the satisfaction of the female by default, regardless of her demeanour or degradation. The first flexing of Nagumo's sexual power transforms the hospital into a parody of a monster movie, as giant, wriggling tentacles, shaped unmistakably like writhing penises, break free and destroy all in their path.

LEGEND OF THE DEMON WOMB (II.1 & II.2)[7]

In one of the series' many flashbacks of the also-

Overfiend II

rans of demonology, we are shown the story of the Vrill Association in 1944 Berlin. In a great hall filled with valves and pistons of gothic biomachinery, amidst a hellish lightning storm that hides Allied bombers, Hitler is watching an experiment in progress. The mad scientist Munchausen Senior has invented a machine to bring powers from other dimensions, ideal for helping the Nazi war effort.

The Rape Machine is a vast wheel with female sex-slaves vaginally impaled on the spokes. Its activation causes pistons to chug into action, forcing metal dildos into the chained victims, setting up a resonant orgasm to break the boundaries between this world and the next. But something goes horribly wrong, and the demonic power destroys the machinery. The Führer is not amused, and orders the execution of Munchausen Senior. His son, however, survives, and watches in terror as the Allied bombs tear the city apart (the destruction animated in the same way, and using the same palette of colours, as the later demon-battles of series III). Munchausen Junior (Munchausen hereafter) gleans important information from his father's diary. He glosses over the story of the mythical Chojin (since the audience already knows it), but notes that the Chojin is not the only divine force in the cosmos. There is another creature, the Kyo-O,[8] the Chojin's dualistic opposite, and Munchausen believes that he who controls the Kyo-O will be able to defeat the Chojin and become the ruler of the universe.

The scene shifts to contemporary Tokyo, where Munchausen uses a virgin sacrifice to summon the demon Kohoki. He wants Kohoki to help him in his quest for power, but the demon is reluctant. Kohoki, one of the few sensible voices in the saga, warns Munchausen that he has misunderstood the prophecy, but Munchausen threatens to return him to Hell (an otherwise unexplained place somehow separate from the three worlds). Kohoki accedes to Munchausen's demands.

Meanwhile, Nagumo and his girlfriend Akemi are at the airport awaiting the arrival of Nagumo's cousin, Takeaki, who has been living in exotic, far-off London. No mention is made of the incident in the hospital, although we later discover that Nagumo has selective amnesia, and that the press have written off the incident as a gas explosion.

Unseen by the watchers on the ground, Kohoki attacks the plane and causes it to crash. Takeaki sees his parents dragged into a maelstrom of demonic energy, but is somehow protected while all the others on the plane die in the wreckage. At the crash site, a distraught Nagumo offers to give blood to save his cousin. He and his cousin are, he informs a disguised Munchausen, both O positive.[9] At this point in the series chronology, Nagumo has yet to be fully informed of the devastating effect his bodily fluids will have on mere mortals; the transfusion is fated to turn Takeaki into a monster, as Munchausen knows only too well.

Meanwhile (and there are a lot of 'meanwhiles' in these two episodes, since they are little more than a walk-through of scenes omitted from *Overfiend* I.1-3), Amano's sister Megumi has become very popular at the school martial arts club. In another of the teen wish-fulfilments at

---

[8] The 'Kyo-O', literally 'Mad Ruler', is described throughout II.1-2 as the 'Evil King' in the dubs using Michael Lawrence's script. In the English translations of subsequent episodes (Ryoichi Murata III.1-2, Jonathan Clements III.3-IV.3) and the satellite scripts prepared from them in other languages, the name is restored to Kyo-O, partly because the Kyo-O isn't evil, but mainly because the term 'king' is gender-specific. As events show, the Kyo-O is actually female.

[9] Nagumo even has a protagonist's heroic blood group. In the Japanese pseudoscience of blood typology, 'O' is individualist and enthusiastic. It is also commoner in the West than in Japan, where the largest blood group is 'A', regarded as conformist and gregarious.

which Maeda excels, her presence is masterful subversion of the adult order.

The sports club is one of the many establishment weapons in the fight against nascent sexuality. It separates the hormonally charged sexes and gives them something to sublimate their energies. How apt, then, that the beautiful Megumi should sign up with the martial artists. Instead of punching bags and each other, the boys now get to grapple with a tough tomboy, blessed with a rudimentary, penile sexuality like their own, an orally fixated interest in food and a slatternly dress code that has her permanently popping out of her clothes. The boys, however, don't stand a chance. Megumi has finally met her match in the form of Takeaki, newly recovered from the plane crash and enrolled at the same school. In one of the series' last occurrences of everyday drama, we see Takeaki and Megumi falling in love as they spar, with the rosy-cheeked embarrassment and stilted dialogue common to high school romance.

However, Takeaki has more to overcome than his shyness with women. Munchausen is awakening the Kyo-O within him by playing with his mind. In a Jekyll-and-Hyde realisation, Takeaki starts to suspect that his daytime self roams the streets at night as a killer. Like the characters of gothic horror before him, Takeaki metes out a jealous, spiteful justice upon a particular kind of victim: his prey are sexually active females and loving couples. He hunts them down under streetlamps and in lovers' lanes, committing a succession of sexual homicides tinged with anger and vengeance.

The spiteful envy of those with an active sex life is another device designed to appeal to the sexually immature viewer. It is the embodiment of adolescent jealousy, determined to make sure that if he's miserable, everyone else should be as well. When we see a bespectacled older man getting a blow-job from a young girl as he drives his sportscar, we are expected to act with rage. The man's terrible hubris (taking *our* woman, having a *fast* car, enjoying a *sexual* act) is punished when the demonic embodiment of jealousy overtakes his car, causes it to crash and drags away the woman for its own nefarious purposes. In a final, brutal touch, the unconscious girl still has her man's severed penis between her teeth.

But when Takeaki returns to his lonely apartment, the hallucinations of his happy parents are more real than the genuine memories of the murders he has committed. Munchausen raises the stakes by planting false data, instilling a paranoid delusion that Nagumo is plotting against him. The viewer has already seen an innocuous dinner discussion at which Nagumo and his family express their heartfelt concern for Takeaki's well-being. Now the same scene is replayed (a clever recycling of footage) but with new dialogue inserted in which Nagumo's family berate Takeaki for being a failure. They accuse him of being a burden and a loser, and lament that he did not die in the crash with his parents. As a typical teen, ever suspicious of adult hypocrisy, Takeaki is more than ready to believe, and so begins his slow fall into damnation. In his demonic Kyo-O form, he flies out into the night and rapes a girl atop a Ferris wheel; the fantasy this time of access, imprisonment and sex in public.

Unaware of Munchausen's brainwashing, Nagumo takes Takeaki to a strip-club, a pornographic initiation into the world of 'real men'. As the women dance and frolic (they are, of course, enjoying their job immensely), Nagumo masturbates in his private booth, but Takeaki remains nervous and embarrassed. He cries that he 'can't take it', and what appears to scare him is not the women's performance, but their direct gaze. While Takeaki is still agonising over ethics, and allowing the viewer to get a good look at the cavorting strippers, he is joined by Megumi. The two are pursued out of the club when their heavy petting destroys the booth, and Megumi helps Takeaki escape by carrying him off into the air. 'Guess you can tell I'm not human,' she comments, although she is referring to her power of flight rather than her masculine sexuality.

But the burgeoning love affair between Megumi and Takeaki is doomed, like any other in the *Overfiend* universe. This time, it is the demon Kohoki who interferes, as he reveals that his banishment to Hell was caused by his love for Megumi over a century earlier. He seizes her and ravages her high up on a bridge. Megumi accuses Kohoki of committing the murders (which we know to be the work of Takeaki), to which he replies echoing the thoughts of the masturbatory viewer: 'I don't know what you're talking about, I just want to fuck you.'

The sex that follows is one of the characteristic events that makes Maeda's work so popular and contentious. This is not the last time in the series that Megumi indulges in sex on the borderline between consensual bondage and actual rape. Megumi is that staple of pornography, the raped slut who secretly enjoys it, and the scene on the bridge is deliberately primal. Like a child accidentally walking in on a sexual act, the viewer is given an ambiguous set of signals that confuse pain and orgasm. Is Megumi consenting or not? The bodies meld in a sloppy mess of viscera, making the sexual act appear truly disgusting and sending an unconscious signal to the viewer: the next scene will be a flashback to someone's childhood days.

As if the muddle of scene-changes were not enough, we flash back to the young Munchausen. In a mirror of the hypnotic suggestion his adult self is forcing on Takeaki, the schoolboy Munchausen is disgusted with the hypocrisy of adults. When he is caught sacrificing pets at his Alpine boarding school, the authorities refuse to expel him because it might damage the school's reputation. Instead, Munchausen is soundly whipped by a blonde Aryan school mistress, from whom he extracts revenge in a bizarre ritual.

When she awakes from a drugged sleep, she finds herself in a magic circle, surrounded by burning candles and buckets of blood. As part of the ceremony she is then raped by an invisible demon, another circumvention of the censor, since the camera can show its shadow on the wall. The scene conflates power with orgasm, as the demon's muscular spasms literally tear her in two, a fittingly infantile denial of her humanity and punishment for her 'crime'.

Whereas the first series emphasised social fear and isolation, II.1-2 concerns itself with physical change. Takeaki is afraid of the strange things that are happening to his body, he does not trust his friends, and he suddenly finds girls much more interesting than he used to. He has fallen in love with someone who, despite all evidence to the contrary, he has placed on a pedestal and treats with kid gloves. But deprived of an outlet for his sexual fear, he roams the streets at night committing rape and murder.

In keeping with the anti-romantic attitude of the series, Maeda sets up and then subverts a classic rescue situation. Munchausen builds a replica of his father's Nazi Rape Machine, fits it with the requisite number of females and ties Megumi to the centre. His plan is to summon the Kyo-O by forcing Takeaki to have sex with Megumi on the central altar. Munchausen has already convinced Takeaki that friendship is worthless, but in order to succeed in the adult world, Takeaki must harden his heart and put aside the romantic feelings that are the last flowering of his childish soul. Munchausen tells him to, 'Kill her, eat her alive. Kill your lover, your woman, you must kill her first. After that, nothing can stop you. You'll never hesitate to kill again, not even your best friend.' Munchausen's ritual allows Takeaki to accomplish this doubly, both in the stated aim, which is to take a life, and in the tacit one, which is to lose his virginity.

Maeda is a master at stripping away the sublimations and rationalisations that hide man's dark nature. When Megumi is eventually rescued by Kohoki, who is mortally wounded in the process, he confesses that he only helped because he 'wanted to fuck you one more time.' To Maeda's cynical eye, even chivalry is motivated solely by lust.

In the final showdown, Takeaki is tormented by his deep-seated love for his friends, and the hatred which Munchausen has tried to instil. Like countless beastly symbols of sexuality before him, from werewolves to vampires, he begs the others to stay away from his affliction, but ends up impaled by Megumi (she punches his heart out, as all first loves eventually do). Takeaki tumbles off the roof, through a dimensional portal into the beast realm and into the temple of Gokumon, where he is slain by landing on a long spike.[10] But deep within, we can hear a heartbeat. The Kyo-O will eventually be reborn, and Munchausen goes into hiding to await the day.

NOT THE END OF THE WORLD (I.2 & I.3)

School life proceeds as per usual for Nagumo's girlfriend Akemi. But she has a new admirer, the class loser Nikki, who follows her around with a

---

[10] Later events (III.1 onwards) will show this to be the hilt of Buju's sword, which will protect the Kyo-O as she advances on Osaka. It is remotely possible that the character of Kyo-O/Himi may be a sly reference by Maeda to the 'Reply to Kyo-O', a work by the thirteenth century Buddhist leader Nichiren in which he exhorts a baby girl to overcome illness and fulfil her destiny. In a letter to the parents of Kyo-O, Nichiren says: 'Wherever your daughter may frolic or play, no harm will come to her; she will be free from fear like the lion king... A sword will be useless in the hands of a coward. The mighty sword of the Lotus Sutra must be wielded by one courageous in faith'. See Nichiren, pp119-121.

puppy-dog expression and even steals an ornament from her bag so he has something of hers
to cherish.[11]

We must follow another loser's obsession with
the most beautiful girl in the school, but surely
we have already been through this in the first
chapter? On the surface, these episodes begin
very like the first, with a hapless boy chasing
after the unattainable school beauty. What is
the real difference, if any, between Nikki and
Nagumo? To the cynical, Darwinian alpha-male
there is one crucial factor: Nagumo got there
first. He has now marked out Akemi as his
woman; it matters not how honourable Nikki's
intentions may be, Akemi is spoken for.

Nikki is slowly going insane with lust. Tormented by the other children at school, he
reaches rock-bottom when he is teased and
taunted by a gang of girls. The saucy bad-girl
makes him lick her foot, treating him like a
woman, in Maeda's terms, by forcing him to fellate a penis-substitute. This is more than Nikki
can bear, and he wishes an unpleasant death
upon all his tormentors. Before his very eyes, an
unpleasant death is exactly what they get.

Nikki is approached by two demons who offer
him the powers they have just demonstrated.
All he has to do is cut off his penis, replace it
with the artefact they give him, and drench his
new member with the blood of two humans.
The perfect candidates arise in the form of his
own parents, who regularly subject him to
drunken beatings. Here we have another aspect
of the teen's world taken to extremes. Teenagers are invariably at odds with their parents,
and commonly accuse them of being out of
touch or unfair. Nikki's parents are unfair in
the extreme, a pair of utter monsters who beat
their son to a pulp because there is nothing else
to do. Nikki murders them, cuts off his penis
and drenches it in their blood, thus conferring
upon him the magical power of the independent adult.

Meanwhile, Amano is showing Nagumo and
Akemi around the beast realm in an attempt to
explain to them (and the audience) what is
going on. Akemi is a parody of the ingenue,

Overfiend I

refusing to believe Amano's words even as she
stands in front of a hell-scene straight out of
Hieronymous Bosch. But the teen-angst pay-off
in this section is delivered by Amano's mentor,
the Old Master, who fearfully casts the trio out
of the beast realm. As far as the teenage mind
can see, old age is ever afraid of the power and
potency of youth, and it is this that the Old
Master cannot bear in Nagumo. As Amano
observes when the trio arrive back on Earth:
'That old fart's age must be getting to him.'

They return in time to see Nikki demonstrating
his new powers. He challenges the local bullies to
a fight, and beats them to a pulp. Flushed with
his success, he makes a move on Akemi, but is
repulsed by the Chojin's invisible scent-marking.
He settles instead for the pliable ex-girlfriends of
the boys he has just defeated, the shallow hussies
who are prepared to give their bodies to the
strongest fighter. He sulkily has sex with them,

---

[11] The lucky gonk reappears in the story over thirty
years later, in the post-holocaust Japan of episode IV.3,
when the makemono Idaten gives it to Himi as a gift
before her meeting with the Chojin.

accusing them all the while of being sluts. (What, we must ask, does that make him?)

When one of the girls complains he is hurting her (the uncut version shows his hands brutally mashing her breasts), he does not relent until he thinks he sees Akemi's face begging for mercy. The scene is presented as irony: Maeda's sex-magic requires female sacrifices, but their identity is not important. In the *Overfiend*'s mythology, Nikki's obsession with Akemi is a weakness. Love, or what he believes to be love, has distracted him from the pursuit of power. With his bestial outlook on life, Nikki assumes that Akemi will willingly submit to him if he can oust Nagumo, the current alpha-male.

Motive does not bother the Faustian demons. They do not care if Nikki has sex with Akemi or not, all they want is the demise of the Chojin. The demon lord Suikakuju is an arch-conservative and has no wish to see the Chojin's new order. Nikki is told that Nagumo's bodily fluids will make him even more powerful, and resolves that Nagumo must die.

Nagumo's parents have gone away to a funeral and, in a bizarrely everyday mixture of sex and death, their absence presents the opportunity to get Akemi alone again. Throughout the first few episodes, Nagumo and Akemi are shown edging ever closer to sexual congress, only to be thwarted at the crucial moment. On this occasion, they are interrupted by Nikki, who whisks Akemi away and demands that Nagumo fight for her return. More importantly, Nikki licks some of Nagumo's semen from Akemi's face, ingesting his enemy's powers along with his seed.

When Nagumo comes to reclaim his woman, Nikki tricks him into walking under a mass of falling girders. Believing Nagumo to be critically injured, Akemi begs for his life, which places her completely at Nikki's mercy. Such a device is common in pornography, since it rationalises a woman's unfaithfulness as the ultimate sacrifice for her man. It is also another of Maeda's brilliant uses of infantile logic: the Oedipal child's assumption that the mother only has sex with his father unwillingly, to protect her child. Akemi can consent to have sex with Nikki, but does so out of love for Nagumo, permitting the viewer the vision of her degradation without the loss of her virginal status.

However, Nikki gets no further than forcing Akemi to masturbate for him when he is attacked by Nagumo's blood, which metamorphoses into prehensile tentacles. Nikki is killed, and in a moment of Wildean pathos, it is noted that 'he really loved' Akemi.

Distraught at killing Nikki, Nagumo retreats to his house and shuts himself away from Akemi. But she tracks him down and offers herself to him, a Beauty submitting herself to the animalistic nature of the Beast. Nagumo and Akemi finally have sex, and the moment that his sperm reaches her womb, the world begins to end. In Maeda's anti-romantic terms, they have started to die because they have left their childhood behind. In the series' mythical terms, the moment sees the conception of the True Chojin, and as his life begins, so does the apocalypse. What we are not told is that the apocalypse will not be a swift disaster, but a slow, painful process stretching over decades.

Nagumo grows into a giant creature, and as he fights the demons' last line of defence (the Cthulhu-like sea-deity Ma-O), the beasts and demons break through into the human world and wreak havoc. Suikakuju begs his old enemy Amano to change sides and fight against the Chojin. Nagumo is not the True Chojin, but a figure who heralds his arrival. Nagumo must destroy the world, so his son can recreate it. Youth will always grow old and die, resisting in vain the new youth that will succeed it. Amano attempts to talk Nagumo out of destroying the world, but Nagumo is now a pawn of prophecy.

The annunciation of the True Chojin's birth is made to Amano. From Akemi's womb, the True Chojin tells him that his mother 'no longer has human emotions'. The Virgin-Mother of Maeda's universe, Akemi has crossed the threshold into adulthood, and is now little more than a broodmare for God's will. But, like the Christian Mother of God of whose myth she is a perversion, she intercedes to save Amano's life.

Akemi pleads with the monstrous Nagumo to kill her (in Maeda's world, this would be the ultimate victory since it preserves their love before it grows stale), but Nagumo is unable to do so. The Chojin promises to be born after a century in Akemi's womb, and Amano swears to wait and see the fabled new world order.

THE BIRTH OF THE TRUE CHOJIN (III.1)

The year is now 2013, and the three worlds

have crashed together. Japan has been ravaged by Nagumo and by American nuclear missiles in a holocaust that has literally split it in two (Caesar's map shows a new strait between Tokyo and Osaka).[12] The last American president turns out to have been a demon in disguise, who tried and failed to thwart Nagumo with atomic weapons.

The place that was once Japan is now a pornographic paradise of sex and strength: the planet of the rapes. Swashbuckling men and 'makemono' (a new human-beast hybrid) rape and pillage, and even though everybody seems too busy fighting and screwing to farm crops or rear animals, everyone is well-fed and healthy. People still wear clothes and spectacles, and use vehicles with internal combustion engines.

Within Osaka Castle, Akemi gives birth to the Chojin, who immediately drains the attending nuns of all their life energy. He has arrived early in order to fight his nemesis the Kyo-O, whom, it is alleged, has been reborn in Tokyo. Meanwhile in Tokyo, Caesar is also searching for the Kyo-O, hoping to use its power to defeat his enemies. Caesar is aided by an army of demons, as well as a disguised Munchausen.

As usual, everyone is barking up the wrong tree. The prime suspect is Buju, a vicious makemono rebel, but he is not the Kyo-O. When we first see Buju, he and his makemono accomplices are terrorising a family of humans. They are only interested in the sexually available women; all others are killed, including a mother and baby impaled on the same sword. Buju is pushing back the boundaries of bad taste, as are the animators, who allow Buju's penis to appear for a single frame before obscuring it once more with a censor-dot. In the midst of this, Buju has a revelation: he sees a red-haired princess (the adult Kyo-O). Buju is about to become a pawn of prophecy himself, for although he is not the Kyo-O, he is destined to be her guardian.

Mantis-woman, an agent working for Faust (a disguised Munchausen), lures Buju away for sex, transforming into a demon at the moment of orgasm and imprisoning him within her womb-

like thorax. Compared with other Maeda scenes, the sex is rather perfunctory, although it does show all the signs of having been made under lighter censorship restrictions. We have already seen Buju in a red-light district featuring real-life porn photographs as part of the animation; now we see graphic depictions of oral sex. But as usual, we are not looking at a penis, but a tentacle-like tail, thus circumventing whatever restrictions may remain.

When he discovers Buju is not the Kyo-O, Caesar throws him in the dungeons, where he is visited by an unlikely rescuer. Caesar's virginal daughter Alecto longs to leave the castle, but is kept locked away. Alecto is prepared to do anything to escape from the clutches of her overprotective parent, and offers Buju a deal. As the new Beauty salves the new Beast's wounds and soothes his troubled brow, she promises to let him out of the jail if he will liberate her from her father and show her the world outside her childhood fortress. Buju agrees, and flees with Alecto to the Gokumon Temple (in Japanese, literally 'Gates of Hell'), an ancient monument predating the time of the last Chojin. Although it is now in the human world, the Gokumon used to be in the beast realm, where its ancient inscriptions taught Amano's mentors about the legend of the Overfiend. It is also, you may remember, the last resting place of Takeaki, whose blood has congealed to create the True Kyo-O.

Alone in the temple with Buju, Alecto must now face the consequences of her teen rebellion. Buju makes her strip and display her body. Alecto tries to reason with him, demanding he show her more of the outside world, but Buju responds by throwing himself upon her, telling her what we have known all along, that there is little more to Maeda's big wide world than sex and sexualised violence.

Birth, sex and death eternally intermingle in the world of the *Overfiend*. As he lays in the afterglow, Buju is tormented by the cries of an infant somewhere in the temple. He is about to kill it, when his touch silences the child's cries. This is Himi, the infant Kyo-O. In not killing her, Buju accepts adulthood, and the Christ-figure of the *Overfiend* universe receives her adopted parents.

In thanks for rescuing her from her virginity, Alecto swears undying love for Buju, a claim that has proved to be the kiss of death for many a character in the series. Sure enough, Caesar has laid siege to the temple, and is determined to kill

---

[12] The *Overfiend* series playfully acknowledges the age-old rivalry between central Japan's eastern and western plains, pitching Tokyo against Osaka in the form of Kyo-O versus Chojin. Many of the inhabitants of the beast realm also have thick Osaka accents to distinguish them from the plummier, Tokyo-influenced demons.

Overfiend III

ten by Noboru Aikawa, but by several others, including the series director Hideki Takayama. This episode truly belongs to the character of Caesar, a selfish father-figure who harbours a desire for power and a barely concealed sexual attraction to his own daughter. But Caesar's Palace is not only the fortress built upon the ruins of Tokyo. The 'mystery' of Caesar's Palace ('enigma' is a better translation here of the Japanese 'nazo') is the contradiction of a father's love and a father's lust. Caesar builds the palace to protect his beloved daughter from the outside world, but it hides his own secret wish to keep her for himself. It is also a textual reference to Las Vegas, where the American dreams of power, sex and money are peddled to the faithful in small doses.

The young Caesar, we are shown, was not only a powerful businessman who dabbled in black magic during the eighties, but also a religious leader. In a scene largely cut from the British release, we see him presiding at an orgy of his followers, where three chosen believers are selected to service him sexually. As usual, Maeda turns sublimations from the real world on their head. Instead of the sanitised bread-and-circuses of 'civilised' titillation, Caesar gives his acolytes the sex and violence they secretly crave.

Unlike the glitter and sequins of a Vegas show, Caesar's performance to a packed house consists of graphic, sexualised bondage with three women. As he removes his clothes, we see that his lust for power has destroyed his humanity: part of his body is cybernetic, including a monstrous metal penis. The young sluts who flirt with their powerful high priest seem not to have thought through the consequences of dancing with the devil. The sex is initially unpleasant, but this is nothing unusual in the *Overfiend* series.

Buju and avenge the loss of his daughter's chastity. As we will eventually discover, it is not merely her betrayal that has brought his wrath, but the thwarting of his own incestuous desire.

When Alecto pleads with him for Buju's life, Caesar is fired with jealousy. Alecto is 'killed' trying to protect Buju, her wounds revealing that she is an android. Buju tells his dying lover that she is 'the best woman in the world' (because she isn't real, or because she volunteers for abuse and comes back for more?) and is also killed as he shields the infant Himi from Caesar's soldiers. Caesar orders his daughter to be 'repaired', demonstrating a possessive father's wish to restore his daughter's virginity, but the army is routed by the monstrous form of Nagumo.

The True Chojin is now an adult,[13] and announces to his mother Akemi that we are at the beginning of the end.

THE MYSTERY OF CAESAR'S PALACE (III.2)

From this point on, the script was no longer writ-

---

[13] Is this magically-accelerated growth or has a decade passed between the two scenes? Either is possible; since the main characters are all ageless or immortal, the matter of a few years might pass unnoticed. Few dates are given in the saga, but we can piece together a chronology. The Great Kanto Earthquake (caused in the series by the Demon Ma-O) is a real historical event, occurring in 1923. Amano tells Suikakuju it has been seventy years since that day, placing the events of the first two series in 1993. The prologue to III.1 claims another twenty years have passed, making the date 2013. But the opening to IV.1 gives the year as 202X. If born in 2013, both Himi and the Chojin would be 16 by 2029.

We see an internal view of one girl's mouth, where Caesar's giant organ is shown plugging her throat and causing her to gag. We also discover why the girls start whimpering in fear, as large spikes fly out of Caesar's penis at his moment of climax. This transformation kills the two women who are fellating him, the graphic shots of spurting blood and tearing flesh merely a precursor of the grand finale. Caesar's last chained conquest begs for mercy as he enters her vagina. This time we are not shown internal views of the consequences; the dreadful torture is left to the viewer to infer from the screams and cries of the dying victim.

Caesar claims that the future belongs to those who have the hard hearts of machines. His desire for power has almost turned him into a machine himself, and caused him to lose the power to love. Instead, he is only able to control and dominate, as we see when he berates the regenerated Alecto for her rebellion: 'Why did you sacrifice yourself for a beast? When I created you, the only feeling of love I programmed you with was love for me, your creator, your father.'

But Alecto is not the only character who has been raised from the dead. The power of Kyo-O has brought Buju back to life, and he is now infiltrating the palace. Buju has a double motive, avenging what he believes to be the death of his beloved, and also saving the life of Himi, the Kyo-O. Amano has confessed that he is under orders to neutralise the Kyo-O, but that he is now suspicious of the Chojin's aims. He suggests to Buju that Himi would be no threat if Caesar were dead.

Munchausen is tormenting the infant Himi in order to gain control of her powers. Himi uses her energy to teleport Buju inside the palace, where he rescues her. His mission to kill Caesar happens contemporaneously with a makemono coup, as Caesar's slaves decide to overthrow Caesar's yoke and resist their human masters.

But politics have no interest for Caesar any more, he just wants his daughter to make the impossible step backward into childhood. When Alecto hears that Buju is still alive, her elation is more than her father can bear. By refusing to love him and him alone, Alecto has forfeited the right to be regarded as his daughter. The tentacles of Caesar's rage fly out from his body and ravage her, and the incestuous

father swears to destroy both his daughter and her foolish love for another. He plans to use the rape of Alecto as bait to draw Buju, and to kill Buju before Alecto's eyes as the ultimate spite. He also forces Alecto to commit every act she committed with Buju, and ends by raping her anally, believing that Alecto's rectum is the last part of her to remain pure and untouched.

THE FALL OF CAESAR'S PALACE (III.3)

As Amano fights to hold off Caesar's attack on Osaka, his sister Megumi is inside Osaka Castle with the Chojin. She consents to help him cast a powerful spell, which, of course, demands sex-magic. As in her coupling with Kohoki on the bridge, Megumi's sexual activity borders on rape. Chojin infuses her with lust by his magical powers, and the feverish Megumi hungrily fellates him. By this point, either Megumi or the scriptwriter is hallucinating, because she begins addressing the Chojin as Nagumo. She begs him to have sex with her (her lust is part of the spell), and when he in his suave manliness deems her to be suitably prepared to receive his seed, he agrees.

But instead of having conventional sex, the Chojin creates a monstrous lover from the skulls and corpses that litter his lair. Megumi's lust is not enough to construct a powerful spell, so the Chojin also demands her submission and her terror. Each orgasm brings about a subtle change in Megumi. Her first merely prepares her to receive the Chojin's sexual attention; her second brings forth her bestial form, a visceral explosion of nails and claws and skin. Her third releases the magical energy bolt that repulses Caesar's attack.

Meanwhile, the makemono rebels overrun Caesar's Palace. Alecto, who has fled from her rapacious father, goes searching amid the ruins for Buju, but instead runs into a group of makemono. Hoping to draw her father out of hiding, they rape her in front of the entrance. This is another scene largely cut from the British release, since the makemono sexually assault her with the muzzle of a loaded machine gun. They threaten to shoot her in the breasts and in the vagina, and make her beg for her safety. Alecto promises to do anything they want, and is forced to submit to a gang rape. Unlike the other 'rapes' of the saga, many of which imply tacit consent on the part of the victim, the rape of Alecto features a sobbing, pleading victim, protesting all the while that her attackers are hurting her. While the camera still lingers on the multi-penetrative sex forced upon her, it also returns again and again to the tears streaming from her eyes.

Caesar is forced to sit and listen, and to face the bitter realisation that the makemono are copying his own actions, using Alecto's pain and degradation as a lure. Eventually, he can take no more and rushes out to save her. He cannot undo the damage he has done, but can sublimate his self-hatred by destroying Alecto's new attackers.

PASSAGE INTO THE UNKNOWN (III.4)

The *Overfiend* story takes a sudden turn at this point, partly because this episode alone features a script by a writer with a very different agenda. In the space of one episode, itself the ninth in a long serial, Gonzo Satsuka manages to alter the entire course of the events in the *Overfiend* storyline. Despite featuring the usual catalogue of sexualised violence, his episode still manages to inject a note of humanity into the proceedings that never quite fades.

Alecto is eventually 'rescued' by Caesar, wracked with guilt at his earlier behaviour. But there is no going back, for Caesar has betrayed his daughter for the last time. It is not enough for him to cause her death (twice) and deny her growth as a person. He has now raped her and left her for dead, and where the incestuous father has been, the rest of the world has now followed. The knowledge that he is directly responsible for his daughter's defilement pushes Caesar over the edge of sanity, and he wanders the ruins of his castle in a daze.

Caesar's female lieutenant, Pedro, is also subjected to a vicious gang rape, which, like the previous Alecto scene, is filmed without the usual implication of consent. The last hope for the palace is the experimental D-9 Genocydroid, a cyborg warrior in cryogenic storage. Pedro orders her soldiers to fall back to the research facility. Her motives are also personal, as the brain of D-9 is that of her dead lover, Yuji.

One of the few pornographic situations left unapproached by this point in the *Overfiend* saga is that of the frigid older woman. Pedro confesses to the sleeping D-9 that she has had no feelings since the day he became 'a creature of

metal'. D-9 tries to save Pedro from a group of makemono rebels, but falls to pieces and leaves her with nobody to protect her from the assailants.

However, as the palace falls, the combatants are enveloped in Kyo-O's 'Light of Judgement', a force which turns them upon their own allies. The Light originates in Himi's fear of the violence around her. Himi, who now has the form of an eight year old girl, stands and weeps once more. For as long as she cries, glittering rays envelop the surrounding area, causing all within their glow to lose control of the evil in their souls. The Light of Judgement works as a kind of anti-grail, visible only to sinners, sparing the pure of heart.

Thus Buju, Alecto and a few of the makemono warriors are unaffected. Buju, who had previously considered killing the infant Himi (in III.1), has changed to such an extent that he now soothes and comforts her. Unaware of the Light of Judgement, he simply wants to stop a child from crying, and demonstrates surprising tenderness.

The Light of Judgement also revives the D-9 Genocydroid, who attempts to rescue his beloved Pedro, but in a vicious twist to the plot, Pedro's own sins have found her out. The Light physically fuses her with one of her attackers, dooming her even as it saves D-9, her would-be knight in shining armour. D-9 dispatches the rapists, some of whom are heard to beg for mercy in an ironic replay of Pedro's own cries. But D-9 is too late. He kills the last of her attackers only to find that Pedro has been transformed into a hideous creature. In a heart-rending scene, she begs D-9 to kill her, telling him that it is now the only way he can show his love. The scene's violent resolution happens off-screen, a hallmark of Gonzo Satsuka's brief, thankless attempt to inject some sensitivity into the script.

It is a shock to see Pedro suffering worse at the hands of Kyo-O's justice than she did at the hands of her rapists. What is still more surprising is that while Pedro is made to suffer and die, her infinitely more culpable boss is offered redemption by the same force. Caesar remains unaffected by the Light of Judgement, as if he has already accepted his approaching death and is preparing himself for atonement. Just as in II.1-2, where Munchausen convinces the teen Takeaki that all kindness is rooted in hypocrisy and self-interest, Maeda now tries to convince us of the opposite.

In Maeda's brutal universe, which sees 'sex crime' as an oxymoron, Caesar's only offence is the desire to dominate and control Alecto, a perversion of a father's protective instincts towards a child. But Caesar's motives can be understood, if not condoned. He is wracked with guilt over the death of the original Alecto, for which he was partly responsible. His obsession with keeping her prisoner is merely an expression of this guilt; however corrupt his methods, Caesar is only trying to keep his daughter safe.

Caesar is fiercely protective of Alecto, but in a soliloquy delivered as the palace crumbles, he cries that 'even my power cannot protect you from the evils of this world.' Ever since his own attack on Alecto, Caesar realises that he himself is the most dangerous of these evils, and with his domain collapsing, he is now in search of a replacement guardian for her. He challenges Buju to a duel for Alecto, trading his daughter's favours as a prize in a contest, but also testing

THE FINAL CHAPTER
UROTSUKIDŌJI IV
INFERNAL ROAD

Episode One

ORIGINAL JAPANESE
LANGUAGE
ENGLISH SUBTITLES

18

Unreleased UK video cover

Buju's mettle. By the end of the episode, Caesar seems to be full of admiration for his one-time enemy, telling Alecto 'only Buju was strong enough to take you from me.'

While it can be argued that the Caesar/Buju duel with Alecto as the prize is the height of political incorrectness, this is not totally borne out by the outcome of the battle. Buju is victorious, but Alecto refuses to leave Caesar's side. Both father and daughter beg for each other's forgiveness; Alecto for running away, and Caesar for trying to make her stay. Instead of demanding that Caesar honour his promise, Buju admits defeat and walks away.

The aftermath of the Light of Judgement is portrayed in a similarly thoughtful manner. The camera dwells on a human child, bringing water to a dying makemono. The unnamed soldier weeps at all the bloodshed he has seen, both before and after he turned on his own kind, and says: 'why did we fight each other? Why did we fight at all?'

Similar feelings are expressed by the major characters. Two of Buju's companions discuss the sight of a human in love with a makemono, and decide: 'I guess it has to be better than killing each other.' The characters seem so ready to reject their violent past, and so eager to make a fresh start, it is as if they have become apologists for the past excesses of their creators.

Buju resolves to take Himi (the Kyo-O) to Osaka to confront the Chojin. His journey is the 'inferno road' of *Overfiend* IV, although why a series that can leap decades in a single bound needs to devote three episodes to a couple of hundred miles, only sales figures will tell.

THE SECRET GARDEN (IV.1 & IV.2)

It doesn't take a rocket scientist to see that the *Overfiend* series has become a very profitable franchise. Only IV.3 is really relevant to the main saga, and indeed, only the final episode duplicates the relatively mature, thoughtful storyline that characterised III.4. These two interstitial episodes have little function except to milk the story for a few more yen before it collapses under its own weight. This is particularly unfortunate for viewers in Britain, because it is the rapes, tortures and child abuses of IV.1 and IV.2 that led to the BBFC's refusal of a certificate for all three episodes. 'The Secret Garden' and 'The Long

Road to Divinity' are a vestigial meander in the overall plotline, two ox bow lakes of excess that have no bearing whatsoever on the overall saga.

As the travellers near Osaka, Chojin attempts to protect himself by shrouding the city in mist and leaping back in time to warp the minds of two Japanese schoolboys. One of the children, Paruth, will die, and the other, his brother Eruth, will be so traumatised that he will use his powers to construct a town of psionic children, who lord it over adults and refuse to grow up. This town is in the path of Buju and his followers, and Eruth gets the idea that if he drinks Himi's blood he will be able to bring his brother back from the dead.

The adults perform sexual acts in front of the children, who laugh and scoff at their degradation. Himi grows increasingly distressed at the sights before her, and is eventually whisked away by a kindly makemono chaperone. Buju happily joins in the orgy, not realising that he is partaking of a ritual to affirm Eruth's power. Eruth deems himself superior to adults because he is not ruled by sexual impulses. When two of the adult women attempt to arouse him, he is forced to kill them to prove to himself that he is disinterested. He does so by skinning them alive.

Ken and Yumi, two children from Eruth's town, reach puberty and fall in love, both capital crimes. They attempt to escape in a hang-glider, but are brought down when their nemeses buzz them with radio-controlled planes, yet another example, Eruth would argue, of the superiority of childhood. As the chief torturer Yufura leads them away to the great hall, she ridicules them for having 'the curse of adulthood' upon them. It is not enough for the two lovers to be imprisoned, they must be subjected to ritual sexual humiliation to destroy their faith in each other. Yumi is held down by a group of girls and raped by a demon, while Ken is forced to watch. The young Himi watches from the sidelines, paralysed with fear, clearly wondering why anyone would want to be an adult. In a rare moment of unambiguity, blood is shown running down Yumi's thighs. The lovers must then watch as each other's virginity is taken by strangers.

But the love of Ken and Yumi remains undaunted by their ceremonial dishonour, and Amano takes pity on them and helps them escape. One of the makemono delivers a stirring speech about love's power to conquer all, which brings a measure of unwarranted hope into the story.

Love might conquer most things, but Ken and Yumi already know that the moment they leave the mists around the town, they will be unable to survive. Nonetheless, they elect to die happily in each other's arms, leaving Amano to ponder Chojin's cruelty, while Buju's band get on with the messy job of rescuing Himi from Eruth's vampiric clutches.

Another sub-plot involves Yufura, who is one of the most vicious characters in the entire series. Yufura is an adult in a world of children, who artificially holds puberty at bay in order to stay alive. Despite living in constant fear of discovery, Yufura is the chief persecutor of those who reach adulthood; we discover her true nature when Amano strips her of her powers, and it's not unlike finding a Jew in the Gestapo. The hunter suddenly becomes the hunted, and the previously asexual Yufura is forced to seek a strong, adult male protector or suffer the fate that she so gleefully used to deal out to others.

Deprived of her former rank, the only power Yufura now wields is sexual, and so she offers herself to Buju in exchange for his protection. Yufura is cynically exchanging sexual service for power, but loses her guardian when Buju is temporarily removed from the scene by Eruth. He decrees that Yufura should be punished, and her final fate is implied to be too disgusting even for hardened viewers of the series. After a brief shot of the persecutors breaking splintered legs from a chair, Yufura is discreetly killed off-screen.

But it is Himi's growth from child into adolescent that forms the centrepiece of the series, to a degree that verges on the paedophilic. The children are particularly disturbing, with their literal decision that death is better than growing up, their utter hatred for adults, and the incredible cruelty which they inflict upon each other. IV.2 ends with a flashback showing how Chojin destroys the mind of the young Eruth, purely on the chance that he might be able to vent his insanity on Kyo-O thirty years later. With role models like these, Himi is understandably apprehensive about growing up herself, although we soon discover that the 'final encounter' of Chojin and Kyo-O will be directly related to her maturation.

QUEST'S END (IV.3)

Like Christianity itself, Maeda's theology recognises no genuine threat to the ultimate order. God's will *will* be done, and all humanity can do is look after its own kind or be trampled by the headlong rush of history. All the demons, devils and monsters that 'threaten' the Chojin are really his own creation (like the Christian Devil), and therefore pose no real danger to his plans. The first few episodes concern themselves with Amano winnowing out the false prophets, and in each case the final proof of their ineligibility for divinity is simply that they can be defeated. But there is space here for other religions too. Buddhism has its moment, when Amano explains how all things are inextricably linked; Maeda alludes to the Maya and the Norse myths with their cyclical approach to history, and even draws on Hindu lore for Nagumo's role as avatar.

Like the dualistic heresies of Christianity, Maeda sees salvation as the unity of opposites, as law and chaos, male and female unite to produce something altogether new, although as the credits roll on the final part of *Overfiend*, we are reminded once more that there is nothing new under the sun. Is this syncretism the result of ignorance on the author's part, or is Maeda deliberately making his point; that mere mortals can never comprehend the mind of God?

In the final episode, Munchausen rises from the dead and joins forces with Princess Yoen, whom a flashback reveals to be the vengeful sister of Amano's enemy Suikakuju. Buju's band of followers are then killed off one by one as they defend Himi. Finally, Kyo-O and Chojin meet. Himi reaches womanhood when she begins menstruating, Chojin drinks a single drop of her blood, and the world is destroyed (again). Amano wakes up and discovers to his terror the true meaning of Kyo-O's power. The Three Worlds have been restored, and he is back in nineties Osaka, ready to go through the whole terrifying saga again.

Like other parts of the saga, *Overfiend* IV contains moments of brilliance sandwiched between dead-ends, sub-plots and sex scenes. The film-makers seem torn between the contradictory impulses to drag their heels for the sake

---

14 Many manga have extremely detailed background depictions of buildings and machinery, but this can have less to do with an artist's interests than with the assistant's craft. A detailed background is the result of hours of painstaking work, but not necessarily the work of the creator whose name is on the cover. The page looks good and the creator looks good, and the draughtsman-like nature of the work leaves little opportunity for the assistant's distinctive style to show through.

of the money or wind everything up as quickly as possible. *Overfiend* IV does manage to convey a sense of the immense weight of all that has gone before, a suffocating desperation to end it all rather than live on in any more pain. The final episodes focus on Himi's existential crises about growing up, depicted as a choice between the cruelty of childhood (represented by Eruth and his psychotic henchwoman Yufura) and the blundering sensuality of adulthood (represented by Buju's continuing obsession with wine, women and song). The *Omen*-style conflict between Himi's historical role as the Kyo-O and her personal self (she's just a little girl, after all) is particularly well done, and the final scene is truly unexpected, although a careful study of the rest of the series reveals it to be inevitable.

MAEDA'S MINOR WORKS

Success brings financial security and more offers of work; the creator can afford to hire more assistants, but his or her role may diminish. An assistant in the manga business is not just someone who makes the coffee or answers the phone. They might draw detailed backgrounds, ink the art or do the majority of the pencilling.[14] Whatever the number and role of assistants, many successful manga artists follow a similar pattern. They will produce a significantly larger body of work, but be less involved at each stage of creation. Ideas and talent are spread thinner, and the material itself can suffer. They may even succumb to 'bottom drawer' syndrome, dusting off older, less successful material to plug the gaps.

In Maeda's case, the problem is not one of overwork, but weight of material. *Overfiend* got the publicity and the shock value, and the length of the series has ensured that few can compete purely in terms of shelf space and story ideas. *Overfiend* also had a budget far above that of its many imitators. A modern-day Maeda wannabe would have trouble securing funding from nervous backers, and would probably find their work turning into a one-shot OAV, rather than an ongoing epic.

The *Newtype Animesoft Compendium* rates each successive *Overfiend* sequel another notch down the critical scale, and the series does seem to run out of steam past the halfway mark. Maeda's success with the *Overfiend* saga has never been superseded, not even by anime adapted from his other works. There have been several other anime based on Maeda's manga, but without a similar budget or storyline to challenge his first success.

DEMON BEAST INVASION

Demon Beast Invasion replayed the theme of tentacled monsters attacking human girls, but added little to *Overfiend*'s accomplishment. True, the plot is slightly different. This time the Earth is threatened by monsters from outer space, planning their conquest of the planet by sending rapist-agents down to breed an invading army with young women.

Much of the shock element is supplied in the script rather than the visuals; the everyday event perverted into horror is pregnancy, childbirth and motherhood. The impregnated girls must give birth to horrific creatures. Futhermore, in an incestuous, Oedipal device, attacking demons mix sexualised violence with plaintive cries for maternal affection. There is also the ultimate tentacle as a cinematic device, taken to extremes when a girl has intercourse with a slug-like creature that is little more than a crescent with a penis/tentacle at each tip, thus permitting oral and vaginal penetration.

But the *Demon Beast* series demonstrates the fundamental problem with Maeda's post-*Overfiend* work. Audiences inured to *Overfiend* are unlikely to be shocked, and the low budget takes its toll. The quality of animation, and indeed other artistic aspects such as the music, are noticeably inferior to its predecessor, so much so that the producers stoop to cheap gimmicks. *Demon Beast Invasion* was the first of several Maeda-based anime to use Japanese porn stars as voice actresses; it is a bad sign indeed when the advertising blurb advises you to buy an animated video because the owner of one of the voices has a forty-three inch bust.

Furthermore, *Demon Beast Invasion* has inadvertently contributed to anime's foreign reputation as child pornography. Not surprisingly, the American release removed the various blurs, dots and mosaics of the censored Japanese version, not realising that the original animators had never intended the images to be seen uncensored. The genitals revealed are thus incompletely drawn, devoid of hair or distinguishing marks, and consequently give the wrong impression that all the sexually active characters are underage.[15]

ADVENTURE KID

Adventure Kid (aka *Adventure Duo* in Britain) similarly uses 'talent' from the live-action adult video field, but the stunt backfires. One thing that can normally be guaranteed with anime productions of any genre is that the voice-acting is of excellent quality, but this is not the case with *Adventure Kid*. The adult-video star Ai Iijima is noticeably substandard in the role of Midori, almost phoning in her lines while the other cast members enter into the spirit of the production with traditional anime exuberance. It only serves to demonstrate the importance of anime as a combination of image, script *and* sound.

The element of sexual fantasy in *Adventure Kid* is overwhelming, so much so that the story only makes sense when the trilogy is watched in one sitting. *Adventure Kid* may be pornography, but it is also raw fantasy, with all cultural inhibitions and limiters (including coherent plotting) stripped away. To an even greater extent than *Overfiend* itself, *Adventure Kid* is dominated by the erotic. And, like all dreams, sexual or otherwise, it tails away as it recognises its own incongruities, with a playful spoof on its previous excesses.

In 1945, Professor Masago devotes himself to his researches, losing all interest in sex with his wife Michiyo. When a group of marauding Japanese soldiers arrive, led by the dashing Captain Matsubara, she welcomes them into her home and her body. The professor is forced to watch as his wife is assaulted by the soldiers, a trying ordeal for him as he realises that she is actually enjoying it. He is then left to burn in the wreckage of his laboratory, and Japan falls to the foreign invaders. Fifty years later, the Professor's spirit is dug up along with his anachronistic computer, and he resolves to avenge himself upon the reincarnated soul of his faithless wife.

But Michiyo is no longer the person that she was. Her soul now resides in the body of a Japanese schoolgirl, Midori. Luckily for Midori,

15 Possibly, as the importance of the American market increases, the Japanese animators will start drawing fully rendered genitals to avoid this problem. In the manga business, some erotic artists have redrawn censored panels to make them more explicit for the American edition.

Adventure Kid

she is protected by a Japanese schoolboy, Norikazu, and the two of them are catapulted across space and time by the Professor's continuum-distorting device.

After winding up in a proto-mythical dreamtime, they jump back to their own world with the help of some of its magical denizens, and abandon the Professor's shade in the past, only to discover that the power of his rage has allowed him to survive. Love, it seems, is not the only emotion that can defy the space-time continuum. Eventually, the Professor colludes in his own destruction by being teleported into the middle of the Hiroshima bombing, and everybody lives happily ever after.

But beneath this superficial plot is a masterful tale of retribution and deliverance, in which a married couple take two lifetimes to realise how much they mean to each other. Norikazu, the

smart, computer-literate, loving boy is actually the reincarnation of Masago, making *Adventure Kid* a tale of redemption, as Masago/Norikazu learns to pay more attention to his eternal lover Michiyo/Midori. Masago's self-sacrifice is hence all the more touching, since he dies both to save his lover and kill his own beastly nature, so that another version of himself can live in happiness with an unsullied incarnation of his wife.

In the story's dreamtime 'Hell Zone', all males are key-masters, and all females are gate-keepers. Each needs the other sexually to cast the magic spell of growing up. Both Dakiniten, the queen of fairy-land, and her daughter, the sultry Eganko, can open portals to other worlds by opening their legs. In a triumph of innuendo, the demonic Kingan can literally turn into a key, but he can only be tamed by a woman who swallows his horn. When Midori does so, she gains control of the savage beast, but also cuts him down to size: the uncontrollable lusts of male desire tamed so that the now diminutive Kingan can be carried in Midori's underwear.

But before we can have our happy ending, the characters must replay one final part of the tragedy of Masago and Michiyo. Masago's lack of concern caused him to neglect his wife, but Michiyo was also a guilty party, destroying her marriage by welcoming the sexual advances of a stranger.

Fellow college student Yukimoto has secret designs on Midori, but passes the time blackmailing his music teacher into committing sexual acts in the classroom. Although he does not realise it, he is also the reincarnation of Captain Matsubara, the venal soldier who raped Michiyo/Midori in a previous life. Meanwhile, hellprincess Eganko refuses to leave Norikazu's bedroom. In a replay of the Ataru-Shinobu-Lum love triangle from *Urusei Yatsura*, the presence of this ever-ready sex goddess is playing havoc with the lead characters' romance.

On discovering that Yukimoto wants Midori for himself, Eganko offers him a deal. She will use a magic potion to drive Norikazu wild with desire for Saiki, his teacher, thus allowing Yukimoto to step in when Midori catches her boyfriend in the act. This is the ultimate test of Michiyo/ Midori's faith: now her eternal husband Masago/Norikazu has honoured her with his attention, can she honour him with her faith?

Beneath the normal gasps, grunts and groans is a script packed with quips and asides, many of which mercilessly lampoon the excesses, not only of *Adventure Kid*, but also the *Overfiend* series itself. There's even an obvious satire on the sorcerer Munchausen, in the form of Eganko's assistant Mephisto, who leaps into the human world only to discover that he's forgotten about the exchange rate. This final episode reprises the events of the rest of the story, but on the level of a teenage romance, with the fantastical love potions, the farcical mix-up over who gets which one, and Yukimoto's eventual downfall, when his dastardly plans mis-fire in public. All it lacks is a big chase scene for the audience to realise that playtime is over and they have to get back to the real world.

LA BLUE GIRL

A similar sense of playfulness dominates

Maeda's *La Blue Girl*. The whole thing is played for laughs, but features sex so explicit and kinky that its outright ban in Britain was a foregone conclusion. It cannot have helped the fortunes of the British version that the censor was shown the American release, which, like *Demon Beast Invasion*, restored explicit yet underdrawn genitalia previously hidden behind the mosaics of the Japanese censor.

La Blue Girl is another of Maeda's rites-of-passage tales, centring on a female protagonist, but presented for the sake of male gratification. It is a more blatantly pornographic retelling of *Devil Hunter Yoko* (see chapter nine), in which a similar high school heroine inherits a demonslaying mantle from her grandmother. It is also a homage to several popular motifs from Japanese legend, such as the power of the female genitals to subjugate beastly males.[16]

Maeda's version, however, is far more detailed, both in its open sensuality, and in the motivation of its characters. Many centuries ago, we are told, a clan of human ninja sealed a treaty with the Shikima dimension by marrying a human girl to a demon warrior. The unsuspecting Miko is the child of that union, a hapless student who discovers that her demonic heritage has literally given her blue blood.

As a princess-in-waiting, Miko is drawn into the power struggle between the human world, and the demon world, where her parents are still fighting the Japanese civil war of 400 years previously. Miko has much to bring to the conflict, because she is a 'kunoichi' (female ninja) of a clan that specialises in tantric sex-magic. She describes herself as a 'girl student who plays with herself to go where monsters live', because Miko's orgasms, like those of Dakiniten in *Adventure Kid*, will open interdimensional gateways.

The tentacle rapes of *La Blue Girl* are standard Maeda fare, but the combat between human beings is another of his absolute, uncompromising honesties in scripting. Instead of sublimating sexual tension into physical combat or snappy wordplay, Maeda shows the sex itself as a form of combat, in which whoever comes first, loses.

As in *Overfiend*, demons and sorcerers require

---

16 See Kawai, *The Japanese Psyche*, pp58-61.

the orgasmic submission of young women to achieve power, but *La Blue Girl* turns away from blatant horror. It is not that the women are not assaulted or degraded (they are), just that the straight-faced, serious plot and dialogue of *Overfiend* have been replaced by a horror/sex-comedy, in which all the characters admit how implausible the story is.

So it is that rapacious demons enter our world in search of nubile womenfolk to aid a pretender to the demon throne. In a typical Maeda touch, the portal from the demon world leads into the girls' locker room at Miko's school. There, the demons kidnap the volleyball team for a ritual to create an interdimensional gateway, itself a ludicrously gratuitous degradation of the female characters. They are ordered to 'turn their dripping holes towards the mirror of shame', and bend over a magic circle. The lower halves of their volley-ball clothes are stripped away, and lit candles are inserted base-first into their vaginas. The demon spawn then energetically masturbate the girls with the candles, to create a growing pool of vaginal juices.

Miko's mother, Maria, is dangled above the orgy by the chain that binds her wrists. She is then lowered and raised upon a giant phallus, with grooved sides that collect her bodily fluids for the pool below. When Miko's comedy side-kick rescues Maria, he cuts her manacles without thinking, and she is impaled vaginally on the phallus. As a cinematic device, the summoning ritual is as sickening as Munchausen's Nazi Rape Machine from *Overfiend*, but the attitude of the programme-makers seems to be that it is only a bit of harmless fun.

Similar 'harmless fun', liable to keep the British release of *La Blue Girl* ever unlikely, is the relationship of Miko's two rivals, Ranmaru and Bosatsu. An incestuous brother and sister, they seek to strip Miko of her magical powers through sexual assault. In the world of *La Blue Girl*, power and maturity are conferred in direct relation to one's ability to delay orgasm. Ranmaru drives his victim to a swift climax, only to discover that it is actually Miko's sister Miyu (a running joke throughout, possibly because Miko's character is arguably underage, requiring an older surrogate to vicariously satisfy her sexual yearnings).

A second 'combat' takes place between Miko and Ranmaru's bisexual sister Bosatsu. The hilt of a sword inserted in her own vagina, Bosatsu masturbates Miko with the tip of the blade,

La Blue Girl

before forcing Miko to lick her juices from the tip. Miko only defeats Bosatsu with one of the secret tricks of her clan (a recurring theme in mainstream martial-arts combat films), in this case her ability to inflate her clitoris into a phallic substitute. Miko eventually defeats her sex-ninja opponents when she discovers Ranmaru is a hermaphrodite, and is able to double his pleasure by entering him with her clitoris while manually stimulating his penis.

As befits a tale rooted in ancient dynastic marriages and threats to the security of the family, incest and incestuous subtexts permeate *La Blue Girl*. Ranmaru and Bosatsu practice sexual techniques on each other to perfect their magic, and Miko must enlist the sexual help of her sister Miyu in order to achieve the orgasm that transports her to the Shikima realm. The subtext reaches its climax when Miko's father admits that it is he who sent the Shikima hordes to assault her with sex-magic. In other words, the threat to Miko's own life is the sexual interest of her own father.

LADY BLUE

A similarly Freudian fairy-tale plot graces the sequel *Lady Blue*. This time the threat is past transgressions and old flames, threatening Miko's parents back in the Shikima realm. Something is preventing her parents from completing the sexual rituals that keep order in the universe, and Miko discovers, like Midori in *Adventure Kid*, that their troubles result from infidelity in the distant past. We know from *La Blue Girl* that Miko and her sister are the progeny of a dynastic marriage between a human female and a Shikima male. In *Lady Blue*, it is revealed that her parents' marriage was merely one of many such pacts made during a frantic power struggle that plunged both realms into a state of war.

Lady Blue follows Miko to college, where she is trying to hit the books and forget about her troublesome past as a sex-ninja. Her concerns are now that of her peers; in a flash of selective amnesia, she has forgotten her previous experiences with demonic rapists and now seeks true love. Miko puts her sorcerous background to good use, confessing with charming innocence that she wants 'to experience first love just once or twice', and using some of her hard-learned ninja techniques to predict her romantic future. She is thrilled to discover that she is destined to meet the man of her dreams, and rendered speechless and starry-eyed when the handsome college boy Hidemasa borrows her umbrella.

But, just like the many ineligible bachelors that beset *Devil Hunter Yoko*, Hidemasa is not all that he seems. He may be a nice boy, but he is also an unknowing descendant of Kyoshiro Karimara, a warlord betrayed by Miko's aunt four centuries previously. In his hobby as an appraiser of antiques, Hidemasa has stumbled across several artefacts left over from an attempted coup among the Shikima,[17] including the two flutes whose playing is causing all the marital strife back in the Shikima realm.

Aunt Shanahime intends to use the flutes and the powerful Spider Kettle to call forth Kyoshiro's shade from the underworld. He will inhabit the body of his descendant Hidemasa and live happily ever after with her, in the bliss that they were previously denied. But when Kyoshiro eventually returns, he spurns Shanahime, believing her responsible for his own death, and that of his mother.

The jeopardy in *Lady Blue*, like the wrath of Professor Masago in *Adventure Kid*, is based upon a misunderstanding. Kyoshiro is not evil, but has been turned into a vengeful spirit because he died believing himself betrayed. Kyoshiro is killed by his own father as part of a pact with demonic allies, but the act is another variation on *La Blue Girl*'s preoccupation with incest. The father perverts the institution of the family: threatened by youth and strength, he slays his son and vows to rape his would-be daughter-in-

law. Although not stated in *Lady Blue*, he behaves in accordance with the rules of Maeda's universe. Sex with Shanahime will confer her youth upon him, and he will remain eternally young.

The use of a historical background accentuates Maeda's interest in adolescent rites of passage, by drawing a parallel with adulthood. These strange things have happened to our parents, and their parents before them, and now they are happening to us. By involving ourselves in the preoccupations of our elders, we cross the threshold into adulthood and become one with them.

As the children must grow up, the adults must be prepared to make way, as evinced by the actions of Maria in *Lady Blue*. She orders Miko to defeat Shanahime by playing one of the magic flutes, even though she herself will suffer. Conversely, Shanahime is depicted as a Destroyer, a pale, misguided soul who seeks to steal Miko's would-be boyfriend just as his father sought to steal her. Like Matsubara/ Yukimoto in *Adventure Kid*, she has failed to learn from the past, and is destined to endure the cycle of suffering once more.

THE VALUE OF MAEDA

There are other creators in the tits and tentacles genre, but Maeda maintains his position as the original and the best. Constraints of budget and fluctuations in censorship restrictions have kept him ahead of the field, but I would argue that his work endures amidst that of the other creators because he brings something truly rare to his work: the combination of insight, exploitation and talent.

Shock value has gained him a lot of attention, as has the truly disgusting perversion, degradation and misanthropy of his works, but nothing can detract from his craft as a forthright pornographer. The result is a Freudian treasure trove of subtexts; there are psychosexual underpinnings in many films, but in Maeda's works they are so blatant that they can be spotted by anyone. His work is so honest in its perversity, and so conspicuous with its obscenity, that it highlights many of the undertones that lie buried in all those other shows that, at first, appear to be so innocent. ●

---

[17] It would seem that the attempt to seize control in the Shikima realm was contemporaneous with the end of Japan's long civil war in the early 1600s, a common device in fantasy that recognises that the mystic otherworld is no more or less than a mirror of our own.

'SNUFF OUT THESE SICK CARTOONS'

Anime Goes West

Erotic horror reached its apotheosis with the 'tits and tentacles' genre, and Legend of the Overfiend in particular. At around the same time, Akira broke video retail records and Western distributors began hyping anime as the Next Big Thing. Although mainstream and erotic anime have continued to grow and change, the Western reaction has remained stuck at this point in time, reeling from the excesses of the Overfiend, and disregarding all but the most controversial works in a varied medium.

'Outraged Members of Parliament are calling for a ban on horrific 'snuff cartoon' videos which show scenes of child-rape, mutilation and murder. These sick Japanese-made Manga films have reached cult status over the past two years among youngsters in Britain... A recurrent theme is sexual assault on young girls by supernatural beings.'[1]

The two titles that did the most to create the modern-day anime business in the West have also arguably damaged it, by encouraging false expectations from the foreign audience. 'Everyone' has seen *Akira*. 'Everyone' has heard of the *Overfiend*. Outside the dedicated area of anime fandom, these are the two anime most likely to be recognised by members of the public. But within the journalistic community, it is *Overfiend* that is most likely to get column-inches, and all anime, not just the erotic subgenres, are damned by association.

This adverse reaction has reached the point where the merest mention of the words 'anime' or, more often, albeit incorrectly, 'manga' are enough to set pulses racing. A full five years after the 'ban-this-filth' articles began appearing in the Western press, the announcement of the American release of Hayao Miyazaki's *Princess Mononoke* has to come accompanied by disclaimers to disassociate it from the negative connotations of the industry:

---

[1] Sengupta, 'Snuff Out These Sick Cartoons'.
[2] Mallory, 'Princess Goes West'.

'... audiences who are familiar only with American-made animated features, which continue to be targeted toward the kid trade, or even those who revel in the raucous, comic book-inspired, often graphically sexual and violent Japanese animation that travels the cult and art-house circuits, will find in *Princess Mononoke* something entirely new. "This is not 'anime'," says [Michael] Johnson [a senior executive at Buena Vista], "it's not effect-driven or violence-driven. This is true, full-cel, story-driven animation..."'[2]

In other words, if it isn't violent or pornographic, it can't be anime. The *Overfiend* series, regarded out of its historical and cultural context, has encouraged the foreign anime industry to release an unrepresentatively large number of erotic titles.

Whereas the extent, both in depth, breadth and variation in quality, of the Japanese anime business is known to Japanese consumers, the budget of *Akira* and the excesses of the *Overfiend* have encouraged many foreign anime buyers to make false assumptions about the rest of the medium. The term 'anime buyers', it should be stressed, does not merely apply to the consumer who purchases the tape in a store, but also the company representative sent to secure distribution contracts.

Anime have been available outside Japan for thirty years, starting with 'hidden imports' such as *Astro Boy*, *Marine Boy* and *Battle of the Planets*, whose Japanese origins were occluded by new music

Overfiend III:1

tracks and credit sequences. Many critics have reacted with horror at the erotic content of some anime, assuming them to be representative of the medium as a whole, though many might have tempered their response if they knew that the term 'anime' also described the cartoons they themselves watched as children. Writing off anime, as many critics have done, on the basis of the headline-grabbing minority of erotica, is as insane as decrying *all* cinema as a variation on *Debbie Does Dallas.*

STATEMENT OF BIAS

Although many of the examples in this chapter will ring true for any Western anime territory, they are primarily drawn from the United Kingdom. This measure has been adopted for a variety of reasons, chiefly that it is easier for me to discuss the place where I live. It is a small, concentrated market (worth £5 million against America's $75 million) with readily available data, and is a reasonable approximation of the non-Japanese anime market. Many of Britain's anime releases are bought in from American companies, but some are still translated, subtitled or dubbed in Britain, and exported to other countries. Britain does not possess Europe's broad base of other anime genres, and despite an attempt to redress the balance in the early nineties, the majority of its anime releases are American-made. It is thus as unlike Europe

as it is unlike America, yet familiar enough to all. I do not regard the United States as a single homogenous anime industry, but as four overlapping territories ruled by separate 'clusters' of distributors, each with their own geographical and ideological position. I am thus placing the United Kingdom between France-Germany-Italy-Spain on the one hand and California-Illinois-Texas-New York on the other.

Britain has a uniquely picky censorship system, marshalled by the British Board of Film and Video Classification (BBFC), which forces distributors (with very few exceptions) to submit all material for approval. The British censor has come up with some strange stipulations and opinions on anime releases, ridiculed by the British fan community (many of whom have not seen the uncut originals) yet often borne out by the experiences of freer markets elsewhere. The Motion Picture Association of America (MPAA) performs a similar role to the BBFC, but distributors are not obliged to seek a certificate from them. The absence of an MPAA rating may restrict the distributors' access to several domestic markets, but it also saves them several thousand dollars; a price that would otherwise make the release of more esoteric anime unviable. However, the lack of the MPAA rating also reduces the chances that someone will spot the erotic nature of a title in time to stop a child from watching it. One American company has found a novel answer to this dilemma. Central Park Media's erotic line is distributed under the title Anime 18, a name that implies adult certification without requiring it. Another method, particularly popular with the Texan anime distributor AD Vision, is to release pornographic anime in two versions, one with heavier cuts for distribution in less liberal states.

By studying the British censor's reaction to anime, we are thus able to examine not only the 'virtual' public reaction of the BBFC to the uncut anime, but also gain some idea of the rationale that governs what *has* to be cut in the United Kingdom, and what is cut by choice for distribution in some parts of the United States.

MANGLED BY MARKETING

There was no deliberate policy of misinformation about anime during the early nineties, but a succession of coincidences and errors caused anime to gain a significant bad press. Part of the problem lay in the need for media attention to stimulate buying behaviour.

In America, the term 'Japanimation' was popularised as a descriptive term that fully encapsulated anime's meaning. However, this term was not so widespread in Europe, where most journalists still cannot even distinguish between an anime (animation) and a manga (comic). To be fair, it is not wholly their fault. The largest anime distributor in Britain calls itself Manga Entertainment Limited (MEL), and their marketing machine has a vested interest in ensuring that the anime medium as a whole is associated with their company name.

Some commentators have attempted to read a conspiracy of ignorance into MEL's policy, but their motives are quite simple. Like any corporation, they have sought to create a brand identity that is easily recognisable and (unlike the confusingly vowelled 'anime') pronounceable to the man in the street. Their success has been incredible; MEL represent perhaps two-thirds to three-quarters of the British market share in anime. This can lead to great confusion, since beginning with incorrect terminology is liable to ruin any attempts at serious debate. I have been interviewed by many journalists about the British 'manga' business, although they had little interest in the sales of Japanese comics. Anime was their main concern, especially the more controversial titles.

MASSAGING THE FIGURES

Anime porn is over-represented in the works that make their way to Western shores. In 1997, there were thirty-five porn anime titles released in Japan. The *total* sales of all porn anime amounted to approximately 450,000 copies. Far from being a Japanese obsession, pornographic anime are a minority area, crowded out four-to-one that year by other video genres, and still further by nearly fifty television anime series and thirty-four mainstream anime films, mainly for the children's market. Porn anime sell, on average, a mere 13,000 units per title in Japan, compared to 110,000 for *Neon Genesis Evangelion*, 73,000 for *Toy Story* and 66,000 for Disney's *Sleeping Beauty*.

Furthermore, sales figures for certain pornographic anime abroad are greatly in excess of their sales back in Japan. This might imply that occidentals are far more perverted than their oriental cousins, but is rarely mentioned by journalists, who are liable to focus on the lunatic fringe of anime fandom because it makes for a more interesting story.

The academic community, the only interest group that could easily debunk the myths about anime, tends not to do so, partly due to a snobbish interest in 'literate' Japanese culture and partly because the initial media hype has been so adverse that many scholars were scared away. Discussion of anime for the general reader is in the hands of jobbing journalists. Expected to become instant experts on every subject they tackle, they are supposed to internalise the entire history of anime in the space of one phone call, to comprehend Japanese culture in an afternoon, and to view the 1,500 translated anime now available, all for the sake of a small article. Unavoidably, their conclusions often fuel the fire of adverse anime criticism, but should be taken in context, as the best they could do with limited time and resources.

RENTAL VS RETAIL: THE UK MARKET

The Western interest in anime came during a minor shift in entertainment media sales practises outside Japan. The physical way in which video is sold to consumers became a strong influence on what was *worth* releasing abroad for foreign distributors. In a time when many genres were proving volatile, pornography maintained a strong market share.

Many journalists believe that anime sprung fully

formed into the British market thanks to MEL, unaware that several of MEL's early releases were off-the-peg American dubs. MEL was able to pick and choose from a range of titles, but chose the ones most likely to gain publicity, either through entertainment or shock value. Their choices of release, however, have little to do with a Machiavellian desire to subvert Japan's image abroad. As modern day ventures, they are led by marketing, and as sensible business people, the staff of MEL, and the other major anime distributors who followed them, selected a predominantly male, teenage audience as the most likely to be prepared to pay hard-earned cash for videos they had never seen.

The British anime business might have been significantly different if it had arrived a few years earlier, before the brief boom in rental video was supplanted by retail 'sell-through' sales. During the eighties, when videos were not sold to consumers but rather to rental shops, a tape would cost around £80. Private buyers were very rare. Instead, the tapes would be sold in small quantities to video libraries, a captive audience who would then rent them to the public for a couple of pounds a night. Several of the smaller anime distributors, whose companies had previous incarnations in the live-action video market, seem to have been caught unprepared by the sudden reduction of profit margins when the retail boom began.[3]

Back in the good old days of 1985, it was a simple operation to shift 5,000 tapes to 5,000 rental stores. Individual consumers only risked a couple of pounds to watch something that took their fancy, and companies could charge a mark-up of anything up to £50 for the tapes themselves (that's ten times current profit margins). If the anime business had started a mere five years earlier, it could have produced a turnover of £250,000 per title.

The eighties video market would have easily supported sales of soap operas, comedies, love stories and other small niches within the anime business, because sales to the serious anime fans (around 4,500 per title in 1996) would have easily been matched by sales to the rental stores. The consumers would have risked less money per viewing, whilst the distributors would have made more money, even on titles with limited appeal.

But the eighties rental business was badly affected by the arrival of the retail video boom. Suddenly rental was less appealing than just popping down to the shops and buying your favourite films out-

right, and this had a knock-on effect on the kind of material sold. A cinema release or television showing became vitally important, because rental had ceased to be the natural preview medium. Trashy, straight-to-video exploitation movies declined, as the rental market in which they thrived was significantly reduced. People were happy to spend £10 or so on a video, but only if it was a film they *knew* they would like, and that tended to mean a film that they had already seen.

The straight-to-video niche markets (one of which was the newborn anime industry) were the worst affected. Curious viewers are now expected to pay £10 or more for a tape they haven't seen, as opposed to a £2 rental fee in the eighties. Rental libraries still exist, but they are far less likely to buy tapes unlegitimised by a previous appearance in the cinema or on television.

Japanese animation is often sold to the public with no discussion of its original context. The catch-all 'anime' can include cinema titles (*My Neighbour Totoro*), educational resources (*Animated Classics of Japanese Literature*), television serials (*Urusei Yatsura*) and niche-market video porn (*Rei Rei*), although all the average consumer sees is a row of identical video labels. This situation has led to the works of great directors being released out of their original order, to older, inferior anime jostling for space with the (sometimes) superior new, and to populist trash competing with arthouse cinema prints.

The nineties consumers are far more likely to buy videos with which they are already familiar, either through a previous cinema viewing or a liking for a well known name in the cast or crew. This has

---

[3] The Japanese anime industry is a multi-tiered system, that retains the good points of the eighties rental shops, along with the opportunity for retail. Many anime (with or without a prior media blitz on television) are first made available on rental video, which ensures a high profit to the distributor supplying the rental stores and a low risk to the rental consumer. A few months after the release on rental video, they are then sold on laserdisc for the anime connoisseur and collector. Such a system is not yet possible in Britain, where laserdiscs are rarer and more expensive than video, although Pioneer's long-term involvement in the British market could be based on the assumption that this will not always be the case. A possibility remains that digital television and pay-per-view may bring a return to the days of rental (in style if not substance), since viewers will not have to pay as much to sample anime on digital television as they would for video rental. At time of writing, however, the new technology is still untried.

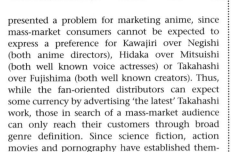

presented a problem for marketing anime, since mass-market consumers cannot be expected to express a preference for Kawajiri over Negishi (both anime directors), Hidaka over Mitsuishi (both well known voice actresses) or Takahashi over Fujishima (both well known creators). Thus, while the fan-oriented distributors can expect some currency by advertising 'the latest' Takahashi work, those in search of a mass-market audience can only reach their customers through broad genre definition. Since science fiction, action movies and pornography have established themselves over the years as the genres most likely to sell as impulse purchases, these have become the genres best represented outside Japan, with a consequent influence on the material available to journalists and commentators.

WHO BUYS THIS STUFF?

Although it is often assumed that the misrepresentation of anime can be rectified simply by releasing a wider bracket of material, this is not borne out by the experience of several video companies, whose ventures into neglected anime genres, unsupported by television or targeted marketing, ended in dismal failure. In one of the worst examples, the sales of the sporty soap opera *Slow Step*, released on British retail video in 1995 by Western Connection, did not even reach four figures. The problem here is that the fan community, while often vocal and opinionated, represents a tiny proportion of the overall market, both for video and for anime itself.

The average cinema-going unit is a boy/girl pair of twentysomethings with a disposable income. That mythical creation, the Average United Kingdom Anime Buyer, is *not* a commited anime fan. He, for it is a he, is fifteen years old and lives at home with his parents in an urban area. He likes computer games, but prefers consoles to PCs, and does not have a girlfriend or very many books. Such fans are on a two-year product cycle, remaining loyal customers for twenty-four months before finding something new to occupy their time, possibly the opposite sex, or more realistically, access to 18-rated films. Sadly, many companies tailor their releases to this bracket whether or not they were originally intended for it. The majority of the titles mentioned in this book, for example, are beyond the reach and ken of Mr Average United Kingdom Anime Buyer, as would be anything made for a female, a children's, an adult or a literate audience.

When science fiction staples like *Star Trek* can command convention attendances in their thousands,

and American anime conventions can also climb effortlessly into four figures, it is a very small sector of British anime buyers that even understands the misrepresentation of anime in the media.

UK SALES	GENRE/TITLE
>75,000	*Akira*
>60,000	*Overfiend* series, *Fist of the North Star*, *Streetfighter*
>40,000	*Ghost in the Shell*, *Ninja Scroll*, *Wicked City*
>25,000	Other erotic horror
>12,000	*Guy*, *Gigolo*, other erotic
>8,000	*Armitage III*, other SF
>4,000	Average dub (4,500)
>1,000	Average sub (2,500)
<1,000	Minority interest, imports (Average convention attendance: 500)

A mere 500 fans can be expected to attend British anime conventions. These are the people who write most of the letters, buy the fanzines and buttonhole disinterested telephonists about the fate of anime. Despite knowing most about the product, these consumers are essentially worthless to distributors because many have multi-format video recorders and can watch the tapes on Japanese or American import. Pleasing 500 people who may, or may not, respond with their wallets doesn't make good business sense.

A subtitled anime is selling well if bought by over 2,500 people. The average sales for a dubbed anime are about 4,500. At these levels, we can expect to find quite a large cross-section of titles. Soap operas, love comedies and historical dramas all jostle for space with science fiction, fantasy and horror on video shelves in better-appointed stores, but don't necessarily sell very well.

Above 4,500, we start to see a pattern developing. There are a few fantasy or horror titles, notably ones which have been out for some time and have built up considerable sales, but the majority in this bracket are science fiction or erotica. At any given time, the MEL fan club has about 8,500 members on its books; once we get above this number we are not only looking at sales to the fans, but also to 'floating voters', members of the public intrigued by advertising or media coverage.

The Gigolo

Sex comedies pan out at around 12,000, and from that point the only titles selling consistently are the very best science fiction (*Ghost in the Shell*, for example) and the more perverse erotica. Above 40,000 units the atmosphere is very rare indeed, and there is little here save the *Overfiend* saga, *Fist of the North Star* (which has had five years to build sales) and the game/movie-related *Streetfighter*. Above 60,000, there is a huge gap, after which a single title, *Akira*, plots a lone orbit at 75,000 copies.

THE GIGOLO MYSTERY

There are occasional anomalies caused by the way in which anime are marketed. *The Gigolo* is a dire anime fantasy about male prostitution, but one which seems to have impressed enough buyers to sell more than 20,000 copies. There are several reasons for this, not the least of which is that *The Gigolo* has been on sale for several years. Furthermore, it is an 18-rated title and has an obviously erotic content, as evinced by the cover art.

Anyone whose interest has been roused by a newspaper article on 'Japanese porn' is more likely to pick up *The Gigolo* than anything except perhaps *Overfiend*. Along with one other video (Anime Projects' *Kama Sutra*), it has a title that will stand

out from the *Devil-This*, *Demon-That* and *Unpronounceable-Thingy* confusion on the shelves.[4] This has worked wonders for *The Gigolo's* sales, probably to first-time anime buyers who were hooked by the accessible title on the spine, bought it as an impulse and never came back for a second try. Other erotica such as *Kekkou Kamen*, *Junk Boy* or *Hanappe Bazooka* might do similarly well, if it were not for their mystifying titles.

Non-erotic titles come and go, but have trouble competing with the erotica already on the shelves. To many store-owners, anime is equated with sex and violence, sex and violence sells, and more anime that fit the pattern will be welcome. Those that don't may be given a brief chance, but not much of one.

ENTER THE OVERFIEND

The Legend of the Overfiend cost over £100 ($160) per tape in Japan, where it was sold primarily for rental and to a very small niche market of fans. Although this price is far beyond the financial means of corruptible Japanese youths, the English-language version was a leading title for MEL in Britain (censored though it was). They released it on sell-through video, thus putting it within the grasp of anyone (over eighteen) who wandered into the right section of a video shop.

Accidental adjacence of important plot exposition to violent rape scenes ensured that much of *Overfiend's* story was removed along with the cuts made by the BBFC, making the final product a terrible melange of truncated soft porn and scenes of senseless destruction. Despite this, *Overfiend's* British sales are second only to *Akira*, and it remains one of the first ports of call for journalists

---

[4] This has less to do with idiotic Japanese titles than translators unaware of simple principles such as the equal frequency rule, deceptive cognates (aka false friends) or the contrast between communicative and referential language. More often, there is a simpler explanation, that a perfectly competent translator is hired too late and forced to repeat errors made by others. So it is that several anime have received an English-language release with a title that is badly translated (*Adventure Duo*), transliterated (*Ladius*) or transposed (*Demon Beast Invasion*). Interesting concepts such as *The Endragonning* are bastardised into the lame *Legend of the Four Kings*, and countless *Demon/Beast/Devil* titles only demonstrate the intellectual poverty of the English, not as some critics believe, that of the Japanese. To give one example, Miyazaki's film *Kiki's Delivery Service* (*Majo no Takkyubin*), would, if rendered by the industry's less sensible translators, come out as *Devil Girl Express*.

in search of an easy scapegoat. Far more interesting than *Overfiend*'s perverse content is its importance to the British anime industry. The success of *Overfiend*, with sales four times higher than the anime market average, made porn anime the glittering prizes of the business.

Pornographic anime are popular with distributors because they sell *outside* the dedicated anime market, and it is those consumers who make sales so profitable. As the figures demonstrate, anime fans actually buy *less* pornographic anime than members of the general public. Round up all the anime fans in Britain and you will seize no more than 5,000 copies of each title. Round up everybody else and you will find fourteen times as many of these supposedly corrupting videos. Far from trying to protect the man in the street from the anime-loving community, one could suggest that the gutter press start a campaign to protect serious anime fans from the man in the street.

However, the distributors must walk a dangerous line. Too soft and it has no value as pornography. Too hard and the censor will ruin it for you. The latter is one of the primary reasons why there are many more erotic anime on sale in the United States than in Britain, since dozens of the American releases would be refused a BBFC certificate if they were imported.

Distributors began by ignoring these two extremes and buying all they could find in the middle ground. Once the heart had been scooped out of the erotic animation industry in Japan, the distributors turned to the fringes and stumbled into several of the other genres covered in this book.

Much of the sex comedy and horror typified by Go Nagai had already been translated, but certain other subgenres, such as the 'Lolita-complex' (lolikon) serials, contain such explicit content that even a butchered British release would not be worth the tape it was recorded on. The homoerotic themes of shonen ai were deemed unsuitable for the 'beer-and-curry' target market of hormonally challenged males in their late teens. Faced with a dwindling supply, but unwilling (in fact, unable) to broaden their marketing focus to cover less controversial genres, some British companies sought controversy by turning to a practice already widespread in the American market: tailoring 'translations' to ensure that the language would be in

keeping with the expectations of the established customer base.

FIFTEENING

On occasion, the BBFC has even been steered towards upping the certificate, in a phenomenon known as 'fifteening', wherein the English distributors add gratuitous swearing at the dubbing stage to ensure that titles gain a suitably 'controversial' fifteen-and-over-only certificate. The fact that the swearing was not present in the original Japanese version is rarely reported, possibly because the public are reluctant to hear how much 'foreign rubbish' is really the product of local ingenuity, but mainly because only the translator and rewriter are likely to have any inkling as to how accurate a dubbing script is. Relatively innocuous titles such as *Appleseed* and *Patlabor* have appeared with artificially augmented dialogue. One BBFC examiner commented:

'... there's a lot of strong language in some anime, and sometimes it's counterproductive. An excellent film like *Patlabor 1* was [given a certification of] 15 solely on the basis of explicit language. I think that without the language it would have been passed as a PG.'[5]

In the fifteeners' defence, it is possible to argue that the effect of such dialogue on their foreign audience is impossible to replicate otherwise. Varying levels of politeness make it easy for Japanese scriptwriters to be viciously insulting through nothing but choice of verb conjugation. The differences in tone between translations can be incredible: depending on the English-language distributor, the same Japanese word, 'bakayaro', has been translated as 'idiot' in some anime, and 'motherfucker' in others. Similarly, whereas one company translates the words 'urusei yatsura' as 'obnoxious aliens', another has been known to translate the *same words* as 'fuck off, bitches'. With such varying degrees of potential obscenity, many anime distributors may be giving their clients what they want, but are simultaneously excluding many potential consumers, no longer permitted to see some films because the age-limit has been artificially, and often unnecessarily, raised.

Ultimately, fifteening is self-defeating, cramming square pegs into round holes and leaving no one satisfied. A similar policy was tried in the live-action film business, by the distributor of the 1993 comedy *Mrs Doubtfire*, who, according to the BBFC, '... conceded that [bad lan-

---

5 Imtiaz Karim, quoted in Ridout & Clements, 'Sense and Censorship'.

RELATIVE POWERS OF AMERICAN, BRITISH AND JAPANESE VIDEO CLASSIFICATIONS

AMERICA	BRITAIN	JAPAN
X	R18	ADULT
NC-17	18	
R		
	15	
PG-13		
	12	
PG	PG	GENERAL
G	U	

The X and R(estricted)18 have very limited distribution, film theatres are reluctant to take a film above N(o)C(hildren)17 in America and 18 in Britain. The American R(estricted) requires children to be accompanied by an adult. P(arental)G(uidance)13 is the same for children under thirteen. The British age minimums are far more restrictive; children under the required age are not permitted access, with or without parental permission or accompanying adult. Both systems are flexible: viewing requirements can be altered by the whims of powerful film companies. The British 12 certificate and the American PG-13 were introduced to allow blockbuster movies (eg *Indiana Jones and the Temple of Doom*, *Jurassic Park* and *Batman*) to reach their target audience without the necessity for cuts. Since their introduction, the higher age restrictions have supposedly become more explicit, since a film-maker can now argue that underage viewers are most definitely not admitted, whereas before there was always a chance they would sneak in.

These certifications are applied slightly differently to video; the BBFC works on the assumption that the potential for repeat viewings and the rewind function necessitate slightly stricter censorship on video releases than on the original film version. In the American market, the certifications are less relevant, because the cost of an MPAA certificate is too prohibitive for a small video publisher to bear. American anime censorship is voluntary, although some retailers are reluctant to stock anime because of the increased risk of selling a pornographic title to an underage consumer where both the retailer and consumer are unaware of the explicit nature of the title.

The Japanese system is far simpler, divided into those films that under-eighteens are permitted to see, and those that they aren't. The use of mosaics or black dots over offending genitalia can still be seen, but is becoming less and less of an issue. Some 'mosaics' scramble very little of the image, and some 'black dots' are translucent enough to leave nothing to the imagination. The only other difference in the Japanese system is that there are two separate censorship bodies, one for film and one for video. As in the United Kingdom, this is likely to result in slightly different versions receiving approval, depending on the medium of distribution.

guage] had been inserted solely... to achieve a more commercial rating.'[6] The language in *Mrs Doubtfire* was not quite as bad as that in the average anime, and so the film was awarded a 12 certificate. But this resulted in complaints from parents, demanding to know why they couldn't take their children to a family film. The film was eventually re-edited for a PG certificate, which it would have received originally if the swearing had been absent. The risk of such activities backfiring is multiplied ten-fold in anime, since distributors often have little idea of the tone of the original Japanese script.

SEXING SOL BIANCA

Sol Bianca, a science fiction tale featuring an all-female crew of space pirates, is distinguished in the field as being one of a handful of anime which, through reasons of international rights acquisition, exist in two separate English-language translations. It is thus possible to compare the approaches of completely different translators to the same text. In the British release, the script was a deliberately neutral, dispassionate reading, in reaction to the previousy released American version.

The language in the American script is most definitely 'R-rated', but the inclusion of so many four-letter words was clearly not absolutely imperative. If such language were truly integral to the script, it would have been repeated in the Graphic Visions comic adaptation of the series, which remains suspiciously curse-free. *Sol Bianca* is a real eighties science fiction extravaganza, with butch protagonists and racy plotting. If it had been made in Hollywood as a James Cameron live-action film, it would have had plenty of bad language, and this is presumably the main argument for putting such language into the translated product.

In the case of *Sol Bianca*, the characters are strong, confident, mature women. But because so many swear-words in English are physical or sexual in nature, their use in the American translation alters the original script by adding a sexist dimension that was not previously present. For example, in one scene, three characters are making their getaway on a stolen aircraft. The getaway driver Janny's feet won't reach the pedals, so First Officer April makes another girl, June, crouch down and operate them by hand.

---

[6] *BBFC Annual Report 1994-1995*, p6.

In the Japanese version, April reasons that June is the logical choice because she is so small, but in the American version it becomes a sniping reference to having to 'squeeze between [Janny's] fat thighs.' This immediately feminises Janny and April beyond the wishes of the original writer. It turns the attention, however briefly, from the desperation of the chase to whether or not Janny has a weight problem, and the viewer's thoughts to dieting, fashion and *double entendre*.

It may sound like a minor quibble, but such dialogue is repeated throughout, with simple phrases such as 'Hurry up' ('Hayaku nasai') transformed into 'Move your pink butt'. These lines eventually undermine the original characters, which is a shame because one of *Sol Bianca*'s most interesting features is the non-sexist characterisation. The end result may be watchable, but it is not necessarily the intent of the original creators. Ultimately, it also presents Western critics with more ammunition, since they are unlikely to have any idea how much has been altered in the transition.

VIDEO NASTIES

Whenever a journalist approaches an article on anime, the lack of source material brings with it a reliance on press releases and the work of other journalists, often with little opportunity to check the provenance of the material. Previous coverage of controversial anime leads to the inference that all anime are pornographic or sexual in nature. An unrepresentative sample in the English language can make it easy for journalists to assume that the Japanese (yes, all of them) spend all day watching demon-rape cartoons. And, thanks to fifteening, several quite innocuous titles are changed into embarrassing festivals of sexualised swearing, often turning mature, well written originals into B-movie juvenilia.

The controversial scenes and/or language in anime tend to provide journalists with their original rationale for covering the phenomenon, especially when it can be related to other events in the media. For example, in Britain, a rash of articles trumpeting the dangers of anime appeared around the time of the 1994 'video nasty' scare. This particular example of the periodic bouts of media outrage centred on the debate over a proposed cen-

Sol Bianca

sorship amendment to the Criminal Justice Bill, itself a reaction to the alleged 'copy-cat' elements in the James Bulger murder case.[7]

At the time, the Broadcasting Standards Council was quick to point out that the issue concerning anime had less to do with their alleged content, but more with the need for retailers and consumers to be aware of the difference between certain anime and 'normal' cartoons: 'The character of cartoons coming from newer sources of supply, including Japan, is tending to differ from traditions established with British audiences and an automatic assumption of their suitability for younger audiences may no longer be justified.'[8]

However, the Broadcasting Standards Council's sensible pronouncement was of little use to the newspapers, who preferred to continue reacting with rejuvenated shock in each 'exposé'. This quote in particular was to have an effect on the British industry, when the risk of being mistaken for a children's cartoon was cited as a very real danger for anime.

Cartoons have long been considered a juvenile medium, and some of the adverse reaction to anime in Britain can be traced to straightforward shock at the sight of sex and/or violence in what had previously been thought of as children's entertainment. This problem has been recognised, not only by the BBFC, but by the Government itself, who have essentially been forced, through their self-imposed operational policies, to reduce their own critical integrity to that of the lowest common denominator. In 1994, Earl Ferrers, the then Home Office Minister in the House of Lords, noted that:

---

[7] A case in which two boys kidnapped, tortured and eventually murdered a child, allegedly inspired by scenes in the video *Child's Play 3*, which has been banned in Britain since the incident.

[8] Broadcasting Standards Council, *A Code of Practice*.

'[The BBFC] must consider who is in fact likely to see a particular video, regardless of the classification, so that if it knows that a particular video is likely to appeal to children and is likely to be seen by them, despite its classification being for an older group, then the Board must consider those children as potential viewers. That does not mean that the Board must then ban the video altogether... but it must bear in mind the effect it might have on children who may be potential viewers.'[9]

In this case, the BBFC are imprisoned by a circular argument. Many people believe cartoons to be juvenile entertainment. Therefore, some viewers might be stupid enough to leave children unattended within reach of something like *Overfiend*. Since nobody in their right mind would wish children to watch something so horrific, the children of idiots must be protected from their parents' stupidity. This is not necessarily the BBFC's point of view, but it is one that the BBFC expects a significant portion of the less-informed populace to hold.

With this in mind, Toshio Maeda's *Adventure Kid* was heavily cut by the BBFC, who also insisted on a title change. The BBFC claimed that the presence of the word 'kid' might fool some buyers into making a purchase under the impression that the tape was for children's entertainment. Although the BBFC's pronouncement was met with hoots of derision from anime fandom, the American experience has nonetheless shown that some people are, genuinely, that stupid. The British fans argued that the 18-rated certificate and the cover art ought to have been enough of a hint. However, in the American market there have been several cases of retailers unknowingly selling erotic anime to children (or, on one occasion, their parents) assuming that as a cartoon, it must be suitable for children. The BBFC's fears are, it would seem, not unfounded.

THE JOURNALIST'S VIEW

When panic about video nasties, lack of understanding about Japan, misinformation about Japanese videos, fifteening, marketing practises and lack of resources are all combined together, what kind of reporting do you get? Something like this, by David Lister, writing in the *Independent*: 'Manga is known in the trade as Japanimation. The word Manga is Japanese for cartoons and the series is made in Japan... The Manga craze is prevalent among the 14-18 age group, almost exclusively with boys. The more adult videos have 18 certifi-

cates; but as one executive at Manga's marketing firm admitted, Manga fans of all ages will want to keep up with all the new releases, and 14-year-olds can purchase 18-certificate videos with ease...'[10]

If we assemble the actual 'facts' in the paragraph, it becomes abundantly clear that much of it is either incorrect or a simple restatement of the obvious, as if we should expect a Japanese media business not to behave like our own. The passage is hardly 'news' at all. For example, we could write a similar piece which argues, with equal validity:

Hollywood 'films' are called 'disneys'. The word means 'comics'.
14-18 year-old boys like watching 'films' made for 14-18 year-old boys.
Adult videos get 18 certificates.
'Film' fans like to see new releases, according to someone at a marketing firm.
There is only one marketing firm for 'films'.

Setting aside the word count expended on telling the readers what they already know, it is the potential for misinformation that is particularly interesting. Asking a busy marketing executive to explain the cultural background of Japanese animation is a little like asking a stranger in the pub to do your tax returns, but with no other sources of information, what other option did the early nineties journalists have?

An idle reader could easily infer that anime (which, like 'film' has many genres) is one long interconnected series, beginning innocently enough with PG-rated cartoons before plunging into a sordid abyss of sex and violence. The phrasing of the final sentence exists in a curious limbo, since it is actually reported speech from a nameless interviewee, not a statement of fact.

As the article continues, it lists a number of genuinely repulsive scenes from anime to illustrate the author's concern. However, these scenes are not from any or all anime, or even from a randomly selected sample.[11] The disgusting incidents Lister cites are all from the *Overfiend* series, inadvertently implying that they are typical. In fact, they are not,

---

[9] Ferrers, quoted in *BBFC Annual Report 1994-1995*.
[10] Lister, 'Cartoon Cult with an increasing appetite for sex and violence'.
[11] Actually, the chances of it being a random sample today are not inconsiderable. The available volumes of the *Overfiend* series, coupled with their high individual sales, could account for anything up to a quarter of all anime tapes sold in the UK.

even within the British industry. Although the unit sales are high for the *Overfiend*, the spread of 'adult', 18-rated material, even in the current teen-heavy customer base, is statistically in keeping with that in Hollywood films. Only twenty-five per cent of British anime titles are 18-rated,[12] and furthermore, at the time Lister was writing, the *Overfiend* series was a mere four per cent of available titles.

THE CENSOR'S VIEW

Overfiend's unrepresentative influence also caused waves with Britain's censorship body, further contributing to anime's bad press. The idea of animation as a solely juvenile entertainment has had less of an influence on the BBFC's censorship policy than the ongoing debate on media violence, and especially the depiction of sexual violence. The BBFC, often written off within fandom as a group of middle class reactionaries with no idea of the real world, have on the contrary given the issue of violence within anime careful thought, and their comments on the matter deserve to reach a wider audience of their critics. The text below is from the 1994-1995 report of the organisation:

'Rape is rarely treated as entertainment any longer in Western cinema, nor is it often nowadays a constituent of American or European pornography. Yet video tends to recycle some of the shoddiest products of our cinematic past whilst guiding us to the even more dubious products of cultures where the place of women is subservient and the right to sovereignty over their own bodies a vain hope...

'Worst of all, because most lovingly crafted, were the Japanese cartoons known as *anime*... [which] often feature scenes of women being gang-raped by lascivious, leering monsters, aliens with tentacles that entwine and bind the victim before multiply penetrating them through various orifices. Heavily cut by the Board was a scene in which a monster with a huge metal phallus rapes a victim orally, exploding in her mouth into spikes which penetrate the cheeks. Another woman was vagi-

---

[12] Ridout, 'Anime in the UK'. The media circus has ensured that the BBFC pays particularly close attention to the anime it receives for certification. In fact, the BBFC's attitude, 'informed' by the popular press, has often made its censorship of anime overly strict, and there are several cases where British anime distributors have pre-censored the tape they send to the BBFC in order to avoid a knee-jerk reaction cutting more footage than absolutely necessary.

[13] *BBFC Annual Report 1994-1995*, p20.

nally raped by a metal phallus which climaxed by blowing her to smithereens. [Both from *Overfiend* III.2.] In all, seven hour-length *manga* [sic] cartoons required cuts in sexual violence, in some cases quite substantial ones. Most appalling in human terms was a gang rape by aliens in which the muzzle of a rifle was used to masturbate a woman, first externally, then internally, with the victim forced to moan "I want it, I want it!" to stop them pulling the trigger [from *Overfiend* III.3]. In many of these cartoons, there seems to be an underlying hatred (or is it fear?) of women, which can only be slaked by the destruction of the female principle... It is frightening to view the exorcising of such violent fantasies in cartoons of such technical brilliance.'[13]

Many of anime's critics attempt to have their cake and eat it. English-language distributors generally send journalists uncensored preview tapes, rather than the cut version which the public will eventually see. In fact, as the BBFC's attitude towards anime began to eat into the value of the tapes, essentially removing much of the consumers' reasons for buying the videos, some distributors started playing up this angle, sending out press releases that described in detail the scenes which would be cut from the videos. The journalists were thus able to tell us all how disgusting it was, gaining column inches and free advertising for something which their readers would never be able to buy. The chance to tell the readers what was missing from the final release, of course, was also another excellent opportunity to imply in-depth knowledge without having to reach further than a press release.

The 'man on the street' can easily tell you how shocking anime are, even if he's never seen one, because his daily newspaper has told him all about them. He has been told to avert his eyes from a cataclysmic cavalcade of depravity, even though he will never see the most offensive material, because the BBFC will have removed it from the tapes he can buy in the shops. Witness the case of *Overfiend* IV, refused a British release by the BBFC on the grounds that it could conceivably be 'used by paedophiles to entice children'. British journalists are wasting their time calling for the 'filth' to be banned. It already has been. Everything available in shops in the United Kingdom has been *passed* by the British censor.

The viewing habits of consenting adults, at home, in private, are not subject to censure. In effect, you are perfectly entitled to watch an uncensored anime at home, you are just not permitted to buy it in Britain or show it to minors. Or in other words, if you are smart enough to know how to obtain uncensored anime, you are probably mature enough already (or irredeemably corrupt anyway) so that watching it is unlikely to turn you into a serial killer or flesh-eating cannibal. However, if you do not have the ability or inclination to find uncensored anime, you are probably the kind of person who could do without seeing it.

If you're prepared to look at the world in this way (and I certainly am), then the only losers are those consumers who buy a censored tape for its value as pornography, only to discover that it is not what they were expecting because its value *as porn* has been excised by the BBFC. This, however, is not uncommon in the world of pornography; surely the difference between good porn and bad porn is the difference between a satisfied customer and a conned customer.

THINGS TO COME

But what is it that sexually satisfies the anime viewer? It is one of the intriguing questions that arise out of the anime industry; how two-dimensional cels covered with acrylic paint can be regarded as erotic. It is possible that the draconian British censorship system, often regarded as anime's worst enemy, is actually its best friend. Thanks to the BBFC, anime porn is the most controversial material on the shelves in video stores, attracting a trendy audience of self-styled, defanged transgressors. Without the BBFC's actions, anime would be forced to compete with 'genuine' live-action pornography, and possibly suffer by comparison. Computer porn, the Internet and hardcore pornography from Europe are placing such strain on the British censorship system that it is heading for a radical reform. In 1997, the BBFC certificated two live-action hardcore films for the first time in a landmark decision that may be seen in retrospect to be a watershed in the history of British censorship.

Batbabe, an import from the libertarian California porn industry, was given an R18 (Restricted 18) certificate by the BBFC, which allowed the inclusion of thirty minutes of footage that would previously have been cut from a British release. Although the Home Secretary Jack Straw immediately clamped down and insisted on a review of the BBFC's policy, the fact remains that the BBFC had been prepared to countenance the release of an explicit porn film, on the understanding that its availability would be restricted to specialist venues. The BBFC, it turns out, has no objection to pornography, merely to unconsenting sex and sexualised violence.

The time is fast approaching when the strain placed upon the BBFC by the new ease of accessibility will force a change in censorship rules. Possibly, it will become easier for adults to obtain live-action pornography in Britain. If such a situation arises, what will it do to the British anime industry? In the short term there will be a brief boom in 'full length' director's cuts, as the original, uncensored versions are re-released to an eager market. Pornographic anime are currently dubbed in their entirety for the sake of the free market in America, so even British-made translations will be available in uncut versions.

But once the anime-buying public have access to 'real' porn, featuring 'real' people, will they have any reason to remain avid consumers? Few British sex shops make a good trade in anime, their oriental material is primarily live action, along with the other genres they stock. Even more so than the average member of the public, the buyer of hardcore pornography regards cartoons as a juvenile medium.

With a change in the censorship law, British consumers would finally have access to the uncut versions of many of the titles we discuss in this book, but would enough of them still be interested? If sales of anime porn subsided, it could cause trouble in the compact market of the British anime industry itself, since many of the less mainstream releases, outside the science fiction and fantasy genres for example, are supported by sales of pornographic anime. America's sheer size ensures that a niche market for uncut erotic anime can exist alongside the huge demand for live-action porn, with those sales similarly supporting a greater variety of anime releases. So it's fair to say that without the safe cash-cows of 'tits and tentacles' releases, many English-language distributors (both in Britain and the United States) might well turn their back on the industry altogether.

Meanwhile, back in Japan, the industry is still marching on. Before the Western market has fully comprehended the influences that caused 'tits and tentacles', already there are new developments in Japan, creating yet more 'strange' practices in porn anime, which continue to be sold to a foreign audience largely ignorant of the cultural background. ●

SEX WITH THE GIRL NEXT DOOR

The Roots of the Anime Erotic

Over-worked writers have always fleshed out their scripts with off-the-peg characters. Zany Best Friends and Mad Bosses are comedy show regulars. Good Cop, Tough-but-Loveable Cop and Lady Cop walk the mean streets of police dramas, following the orders of Minority Lieutenant. No soap would be complete without a Harried Housewife and a Nasty Neighbour. Modern-day anime has developed archetypes of its own, six kinds of wish-fulfilment woman used increasingly in both mainstream and erotic shows.

Because we regard the erotic as the extreme end of a continuum that begins in the mundane world, it is possible to see its roots in supposedly unerotic works. Media people all over the world have spent years searching for a guarantee of the greatest success with the largest audience. Nobody has managed to discover all the rules yet, but there are many derivative producers prepared to read some kind of winning formula into popular shows.

Many fantasy tales, and not just in Japan either, gravitate towards a cast roster that owes more to *Dungeons & Dragons* than the principles of good storytelling. There will be two warriors constantly duelling for control of the party, the thieving trickster (often also comic relief), the cleric and the magic-user. Or, to use different criteria, two heroes, a girl, a brain and a kid. Children's cartoons are especially likely to follow this cookie-cutter format, with (apologies to the *Teenage Mutant Ninja Turtles*) one who leads, one who 'does machines', one who is 'cool but rude', one who is 'a party dude', and of course a token female just in case any girls are watching. Such formulae are repeated across many media, (children can handle more, but a lot of marketing executives can't) and have found their most successful manifestation in the pop world, where prefabricated bands are designed to appeal to the widest possible bracket of consumers.

In the Japanese children's field, there has long been a vogue for teams of five, often colour-coded for ease of recognition. From the live-action superheroes that inspired the *Power Rangers* to their animated colleagues in *Battle of the Planets*, the team show encourages viewer identification with a particular favourite, but also promotes five times the usual amount of merchandising.

New developments in erotica have accompanied the arrival of staff who actually grew up watching anime. As the anime-viewing populace also ages, producers find new ways to take their money, and few have been more effective than the promotion of prefabricated gangs modelled like the moppets of short-term pop superstardom. There is little money to be made from promoting the cast and crew of children's cartoons, but the anime audience, because it covers a wider age range, encourages other forms of consumption more in keeping with traditional live-action film. Fans are not only invited to read the book and listen to the music, they can also follow the career of the voice actors across into different shows, with their own new merchandising opportunities.

To understand what the producers are hoping to achieve, we have only to look at the prefab anime group, the *Hummingbirds*. Five voice actresses who also sing (Kotono Mitsuishi, Yuri Amano, Fumie Kusachi, Sakiko Tamagawa and Hekiru Shiina) play five singing actresses, thus allowing for potentially infinite spinoffs. Beyond

Hummingbirds

the initial phenomenon of the *Hummingbirds* series itself, it acts as a jumping-off point for solo careers, novelty duets, nostalgic reunions and more publicity. As if anime synopses, stories, trivia, sketches and news were not enough for the magazines, they can now devote many column inches to the real faces behind the voices onscreen.

But when spin doctors and press officers are on hand to decide a definite formula for anime scripts to maximise returns, what kind of female characters do they come up with? And how does that effect the depiction of characters in erotic anime?

ANIME ARCHETYPES

Characterisation is rarely regarded as an important component in erotica. But insofar as the copulating creatures of pornography can be said to have characters, one can discern a few recurring types. When we are discussing pornography created for

TYPE	FEATURES
The Girl Next Door	*Bland, nice, clumsy*
The Tomboy	*Tough, boyish, feisty*
The Maiden	*Sweet, girlish, meek*
The Older Woman	*Mature, sophisticated, intelligent*
The Alien	*Sexual, disposable, idiot*
The Child	*Immature, unsophisticated, idiot savant*

men, the women we see are different combinations of very basic physical attributes. Women are seen as tall/short, fat/thin, blonde/brunette/redhead/mousey, large-breasted/flat-chested and so on. But a more careful examination of erotic novels or the 'girl-copy' that frames the pictures in many porn magazines will reveal that, even in a genre as supposedly characterless as porn, there are archetypes too. Think of any pornographic tale and you can summarise its participants, even if it's only with terms like 'virgin', 'bored housewife' 'lipstick lesbian', 'jailbait' or the 'girl next door'.

In anime, there are six basic types of female character. These formulae are by no means unique to Japan, but nevertheless turn up in anime with enough regularity to warrant a mention. Most importantly for some of anime's most fervent feminist apologists, it should be noted that all these archetypes are keyed towards *male* wish-fulfilment, which will be discussed below in both its mundane and erotic manifestations.

THE GIRL NEXT DOOR

This self-explanatory archetype is often the subject of first love, first kiss, and, in the case of some erotic anime, first sexual experience for male protagonists. She is also the same age as the targeted viewer, hence the presence of so many anime heroines who are high school students. An occasional damsel in distress, friend and mcguffin, the Girl Next Door represents all that is normal and everyday.

In all-female casts, such as *Hummingbirds* or *Sailor Moon*, the Girl Next Door will be the protagonist, because she best encapsulates the emotions of the average female viewer. Normally so bland as to almost be a blank slate, the only genuinely noticeable feature of the Girl Next Door is that she is a bit of a klutz. In those anime made specifically for a female audience, the Girl Next Door protagonist is often a fish out of water, a foreigner in the mysterious country of boys, fashion and make-up, a gawky teenager learning how to be an adult. But like all viewers of either sex, the Girl Next Door doesn't quite gel with the fantastic adventures and characters around her. She is the ugly duckling who doesn't yet realise her own potential.

In *Gunbuster*, the script informs us that piloting spacecraft is an extremely complex operation, best accomplished by the extremely intelligent Older Woman character of Kazumi 'Big Sister' Amano. But young Noriko is clumsy. Just like the viewer, she is useless at the controls of a fantasy spacecraft, but a vague 'natural' ability will prevail. Forget the Coach's continual insistence that only hard work will see her through, Noriko the Girl Next Door is at the front line of both wish-fulfilment and the suspension of disbelief, since no matter what the series chronology tells us about her hard work and extra lessons, the viewer watches her become an élite pilot in less than an hour. And in the ever-present sop to the male gaze, the Girl Next Door is still very pretty nonetheless.

Satsuki in *Hummingbirds* is another quintessential Girl Next Door. A singer who can't sing and a dancer who can't dance, she is also a military pilot who can't fly her plane, but she is the one with the 'natural talent' just waiting to bloom. It doesn't take much hard work on her part, or if it does, the camera will whisk us through the arduous training because that is not the thing we really want to see. We want to see her achieving

her goals, because that is also the fantasy of the couch-potato viewer.

Despite claiming to tell the tale of five sisters (one for each main archetype) and their two Alien competitors (dim, disposable, sexual, Other), *Hummingbirds* really focuses on the maturation of Satsuki. It is her crushes and her concerns that steer the plot; the other girls are merely supporting players.

Girls Next Door in romantic comedies tend to be long-suffering companions of the male lead, temporarily displaced by the arrival of a beautiful, but ultimately unsuitable rival. The best example is *Urusei Yatsura*'s Shinobu, Ataru's girlfriend, who is forced to move aside when her man marries an alien princess. But the Girl Next Door will always win in the end, because she is the safe, sensible marrying type.

With the exception of a tiny number of 'accurate' dramas such as *The Tale of Genji*, many anime characters have wildly unrealistic hair colour. This is a convention inherited from manga, where too much black hair means too much black ink, and not enough character differentiation. But amid all the rainbow hues of greens, blondes and blues, the Girl Next Door is more likely to have a 'normal' hair colour, and to display some kind of spiritual connection to traditional Japan. She is often old-fashioned, demure, adherent to old-time values and the kind of girl you could happily bring back home to meet your grandparents. She is also rather bland company, and likely to find herself kidnapped by the forces of evil. She is, after all, a symbol of the very normality from which the average anime viewer is seeking to escape, albeit temporarily. For while fantasyland is a nice place, the average viewer does not want to live there forever, and the storyteller must engineer some form of return to normality. Ultimately, when the hero rescues her, the Girl Next Door presents the potential for all to live happily ever after by marrying and settling down.

The eponymous *Devil Hunter Yoko* is a 'terminator of iniquity', seeking to right wrongs on the astral plane, but her secret concern is getting a man. Underlying much of the story's demonic action (itself openly or subliminally sexual in nature) are the simple concerns of an agrarian fertility cult; look after the land and make babies. Like the Japanese viewer, like us, and like our parents, Yoko is exhorted not to rock the boat, not to fight tradition or indulge in the wasteful

Devil Hunter Yoko

Frantic, Frustrated & Female

in the centre of the action. In more explicitly erotic anime, the Girl Next Door is more likely to be a character on the sidelines. In some stories, *Rei Rei* for example, she will be the humdrum harridan from whom the hero flees, thus beginning his many adventures with more willing sexual companions, possibly to return once he has learned how to treat her in bed. Perhaps, as in *Adventure Kid*, once the Hero has learned the arts of love from all these experienced Older Women, Aliens and Tomboys, she will be the faithful, marrying kind who will be eternally grateful for his education.

Frantic, Frustrated & Female features a textbook Girl Next Door, Hiroe, 'physically perfect' in every way save her inability to have an orgasm. Luckily, her 'big sister' Yayoi is on hand to help, with mysterious techniques including hypnotism, scientific experimentation and ancient Chinese sex manuals. The upshot of all this is multiple experiments in lesbian incest, the first episode culminating in three-way bondage sex between the girls and their mother.

The series concentrates on sex between women, including a competition between the alpha-lesbians to see who can make Hiroe reach her climax, after which the girls all sit around for a nice chat and a cup of tea. Supposedly, this is all for the benefit of Hiroe's boyfriend, who is unaware that his lover is faking it, but Yayoi's ceaseless mugging and winking to camera displays a self-referential awareness that the Boy Next Door is the viewer himself. Permitted fly-on-the-wall access to Hiroe's sexual awakening, the viewer is expected to enjoy watching 'his' woman become the perfect lover. Such a rationale is not uncommon in the pornography of many cultures, since it permits serial sex partners as an education for (of course) happy monogamy.

There is a militant heterosexual subtext; Hiroe the misguided Girl Next Door is always failing in her quest for fulfilment because she is looking in the wrong place. It is not an orgasm that she should be seeking, but the right man to give it to her; the moment he arrives she will settle down and be a faithful, sexually adept partner.

But eroticism is about transgression and fantasy, not a quiet night by the fire with your wife and a mug of cocoa. Even *Frantic, Frustrated & Female* recognises this, with its on-off pretence of incest (later episodes deny that the characters are related), as well as scenes of bondage, tentacles and sado-masochism. In the third episode, a haunted

activity of rebellion. And that means preserving her Girl Next Door status until she can find a suitable Boy Next Door. She has her devil-hunting, and that should suffice as a suitable career until she finds Mr Right. Since the loss of her virginity also means the loss of her powers, she is expected to retire upon marriage.

There are a lot of romantic dead ends in *Yoko*, but these are just as important as the devil-hunting, because Yoko's search for a man and her wars with demons are really the same thing. One of the theme songs sums it up by warning: 'devils are all men in disguise'. Yoko's mother, an ex-teen rebel herself, wants Yoko to lose her virginity as soon as possible, since this will save her from the mandate of devil-hunting; it also suggests that Yoko should turn aside from the magical powers she is offered, and accept her subservient role as a wife and mother. However, Yoko's grandmother wants her to wait and 'hunt devils', to sift through the available bachelors until she finds a more suitable mate. The demons that she destroys are also-rans, failing the test for being too forward, too foreign, too irresponsible and any number of other dreadfully sensible reasons. Naturally, most of the 'demons' attempt to defeat Yoko through sexual means; Yoko's mother lost her power the moment she lost her virginity, which was also the moment she fell pregnant with Yoko. Sex, in *Devil Hunter Yoko*, equals pregnancy, which in turn equals the end of carefree life and the acceptance of one's fate.

Devil Hunter Yoko is nominally a female rites-of-passage story, and so features a female character house drama, the girls believe that their sapphic household has been invaded by a man, but it turns out to be a demonic possession that allows them to grow penises. 'The truth is out! I'm a man!' cries Yayoi, admitting in the process that *Frantic, Frustrated & Female*, like most supposedly lesbian pornography, is really a male fantasy.

THE TOMBOY

If you went to bed as a teenage boy and changed sex overnight, a Tomboy is the kind of girl you would like to become. This is exactly what Rumiko Takahashi explores in her *Ranma 1/2*. The hero, Ranma, is a young martial artist, cursed to turn into a girl anytime he is splashed with cold water. And of course, the kind of girl that Ranma becomes is often tough, rude and Tomboyish. And while s/he can experiment with the notion of femininity and the farcical potential of living between two worlds, ultimately Ranma is 'really' a boy, just playing at being a girl.

The Tomboy is an athletic, often unfeminine individual, always fighting with the others, prepared to hold her own against men, and most likely featuring a short, boyish haircut and an interest in unfeminine activities like computers.[1] Tomboys are often, as some scriptwriters admit, unsettlingly radical, and sometimes writers provide rationalisations for their existence. *Streetfighter's* Chun Li is an accomplished female martial artist, but only because her father was one before her. She is thus inheriting a family tradition, not striking out on her own for independence.

Some even leave their existence unexplained, and take their characterisation out of the proto-real and into the *Twilight Zone*. 'Virgin Road', one of the short stories contained in the *Countdown* collection, features the Tomboy Jun, who manages to seduce both a bride and groom on their wedding day. But she is filmed in a strange manner, and often appears to have fully penetrative sex with her female conquests. The sex-crazy Tomboy might have been fun, but now it's time for Kunihiko (the groom) to settle down with a nice Girl Next Door, and he chooses

[1] Note that an interest in computers does not immediately make a character a Tomboy. Some scripts place so much value on the physicality of the Tomboy that the more sedentary, intellectual role of programmer/hacker goes to one of the archetypes that find themselves more redundant in action-adventures, such as the Child or the Maiden.

Akemi, who looks very like Jun, but is submissive and meek. We soon see his dilemma; when shopping for bedclothes he says to Akemi: 'Can't we get something more conservative?' Little could be less conservative than Jun, who not only is a dangerously decadent bisexual, but even kisses Kunihiko in full view of his mother.

The viewer's curiosity is further piqued when we see Akemi having oral sex with Jun, and the head movements imply fellatio instead of cunnilingus. It is only at the end when the Tomboy's true nature is revealed: she has both male and female organs, and the tale ends with the hermaphrodite watching with a smirk as the beautiful Akemi marches up the aisle to take her vows. It is their little secret that Akemi's panties are already soaked with Jun's semen, and dripping the stigmata of transgression onto the floor of the chapel, even as Akemi walks the 'virgin road'.

In erotic anime, the Tomboy's proto-masculinity is often treated as an unnatural trait, which the gods will punish. Pedro in *Overfiend* III is an efficient, military type; her aspiration to manhood is even signified by her possession of a male name. She is a competent officer at the expense of her womanhood, and, as the script eventually reveals, has become so in reaction to her long-term separation from her lover, Yuji. Yuji's mind has been incorporated into the armoured war machine known as the D-9 Genocydroid. Yuji/D-9 is emasculated by devotion to his work. Pedro's own frigidity has little to do with whether or not her lover is alive or dead. She loses interest in sex while he is in suspended animation, but cannot expect to be sexually fulfilled by his return.

Eventually, Pedro suffers the traditional consequence of trying to buck Toshio Maeda's misogynist system; she is gang-raped when her army loses the battle. Just as her emasculated lover turns her into a frigid creature by refusing her sex, he is also unable to save her from her new fate at the hands of her rapists. Despite bearing all the science fictional hallmarks of the ultimate warrior, all D-9 can offer his injured lover is the final release of death.

Another oft-depicted image of the Tomboy grows out of the sexist assumption that assertive, active behaviour from a woman represents a biologically impossible attempt to 'be' a man. The converse argument, that all homosexual men must be attempting to 'be' women, is also common in anime directed at a male audience, such as the

Ghost in the Shell

the inclusion of lesbian scenes. If the male viewer were female, he is reassured, he'd still prefer women to men. Thus, in Masamune Shirow's original comic, the only time we see Motoko Kusanagi as a sexual being is when she indulges in a three-way lesbian orgy (excised from many later editions). This is permissible to the readership because it avoids considering the alternative, that a 'real woman' might consider sex with men. If Motoko is the (male) reader's fantasy ideal, she must restrict her sexual behaviour to the sexual objects of the reader.

By using the katakana syllabary for the name Kusanagi,[2] the script even implies that it is an alias, and that 'Motoko' is a mask over a completely different character. She may appear to be a strong woman, but 'she' may not even be female. She has female attributes, but admits that her role and behaviour would be untenable without continual 'high-level maintenance'. Considering the number of right-wing, conservative ideas in the rest of *Ghost in the Shell*, it is even possible that Motoko is a deliberate contradiction. The super-competent woman, uninfluenced by troublesome hormones or maternal considerations, can be read as an extreme anti-feminist character. Her abilities, power and intelligence all rely on an advanced industrial civilisation created by men, and the patriarchal stewardship of the male government. Without them, she would be thrown onto the biological scrapheap along with some of Shirow's other victims: the old, the infirm and the unadaptable.

At the end of the *Ghost in the Shell* comic, Motoko's successful quest for potency is represented by her resurrection in a man's body. This is replaced in the film by that of a child; equally symbolic, but far more vulnerable. The child, it should be noted, is not so much Motoko, as the product of Motoko's union with the Puppet Master. In other words, she has married to secure her influence, a dynastic angle that was deliberately played up by Mamoru Oshii in his film version.

But the Tomboy's predilections are not restricted

camp, mincing character of The Gay Blade in *Samurai Gold*, or the fey, effeminate Tim in *Grey*. Toshio Maeda's *La Blue Girl* takes the idea to its logical extreme, by depicting two hermaphrodite characters. Miko is a female who can make her clitoris grow into a surrogate penis. Thus she is able to satisfy her nemesis, Ranmaru, who has both male and female sexual characteristics. She also becomes involved in perhaps the commonest Tomboy activity, lesbianism, when Bosatsu forces her to endure sexual assault with the hilt and blade of a sword as stimulation.

Many Tomboys are depicted as lesbians or potential lesbians, even in non-pornographic works such as *Ghost in the Shell*. The protagonist, Motoko Kusanagi, is a butch undercover operative blessed with female grace, pragmatism and spite. Never has there been a better example of the female of the species being more deadly than the male. But she is also typical of many women in military fiction; she is not a female so much as an adolescent's wet dream of how a female should be. She is, like Rei Ayanami of *Neon Genesis Evangelion*, 'a woman who does not bleed', a fictional creation that brings the viewer all the sexual accoutrements of womanhood, without the need to temper one's masculinity in response. She is, like the unthreatening, uncritical image of the pornographic centrefold, ready for anything the male viewer cares to imagine.

And yet, Motoko's competence and faux-masculinity contains the seeds of its own demise. She can only achieve her manliness by removing much of what makes her female. She may have a woman's curves, but they are made of metal. The male viewer identifies with Motoko as an action-*hero* role model, but also as a sex object. Is she a woman who acts like a man, or a man who looks like a woman?

Such a possibility presents a threat to the average male viewer, whose conscience is often salved by

---

2 In Japanese legend, Kusanagi ('Grass-Queller') is the magic sword that became one of the Emperor's Three Treasures. The wielder of Kusanagi was said to have the power to defeat an entire army, and it is currently at the bottom of the sea in the care of the Dragon King, awaiting the time when Japan requires its return. Thus, to the Japanese viewer, Motoko Kusanagi is loaded with symbolism, and suggests a *nom de guerre*. It sounds as 'normal' to Japanese ears as a heroine called Jane Excalibur.

to lesbianism; her masculinity often turns her into a sexual predator, the ever-present male fantasy of the selective nymphomaniac who wants just enough to keep both her and her man satisfied. Tony Takezaki's *AD Police*, by directly concerning itself with designing and creating the ideal woman, satirises the traditional ideals of male wish-fulfilment. Gena is a typical Tomboy, a truly masculinised creature who leads a detachment of élite police officers. Only slightly burdened with the cybernetics that are *AD Police*'s signifier of abused womanhood, Gena is a sexual predator, who makes a move on the virginal Leon before his previous lover is even cold. But she is also a critic of her society's treatment of women, confessing that she understands the dilemma of the robot-women she hunts down, *Blade Runner*-style.

In a gender-specific take on *2001*'s HAL, conflicting instructions in their programming have driven the robot-women mad. They are expected to be virgins and whores, wives and mothers, compliant women like the Maidenly Iris, or imitation men like the Tomboy Gena. These are the only choices they are given by the men who make the rules, and only desexualised females can expect to succeed in the male world. Thus in the second episode, the career-woman Caroline wins victories in the male business arena, but only after having her sexual organs removed. Her 'crime' against nature eventually catches up with her conscience, and Caroline becomes hysterical despite her hysterectomy. She becomes a serial killer on the train network, cutting out the wombs of her less motivated sisters, until she eventually achieves a truly perverse form of redemption when she is raped and murdered, dying, as one character sickeningly observes, like a woman at last.

The inherent contradiction in the Tomboy lies not in the depiction of strong female characters, but in many writers' and directors' equation of strength with masculinity. Many anime Tomboys are persecuted by the other characters for not being 'real women'. *Appleseed*'s Deunan Knute is an object of ridicule because, despite being competent in the male sphere, she is a bad cook. Yayoi in *Hummingbirds* has a flat chest and can't get a boyfriend. The android

---

[3] We did originally toy with the idea of calling this archetype the Virgin, as she invariably is in mainstream anime, but she rarely remains so for long in erotic ones.

stalker in *AD Police* can't decide whether to be a figurative, feminine, vampish *femme fatale* or a literal, masculine, psychotic one. Instead she alternates between the two roles before breaking down with the plaintive cry: 'It's all I know how to do! I can't take any more.'

THE MAIDEN

Just as the Tomboy is the active, masculine variant on the bland Girl Next Door, the Maiden is the feminine, frills-and-flounces flipside.[3] She is the type of girl that boys can most expect to encounter in the real world, less interested in traditional masculine pursuits and hobbies, and more likely to devote her time to home-making and needlework. The Maiden is the member of an all-female cast who cooks for everyone else or tidies up around the home. She will be the one who wears the least practical dresses, and who cares the most for pets and flowers. *Hummingbirds*' Uzuki is a typical example, but this is the least common anime archetype, because, like their real-life equivalents, they are better employed for decoration and maintenance than for advancing plots.

Maidens bandage wounds, like the sisterly Matsuri in *Legend of the Four Kings*, but they don't get too involved in the action. This very absence, however, is itself a form of fantasy. The humdrum Maiden is sidelined, because this is a fantasy world where only interesting girls get the camera's attention. The Maiden, voted in the real world Least Likely to Watch Anime and Most Likely to Tease Boys, is thus subverted by her exclusion.

Their rare appearances as important characters in mainstream anime continue this jealous subtext. *Sukeban Deka* has an ex-convict Tomboy for a protagonist, desperately trying to 'go straight' (or rather, become a Girl Next Door). Her opponents are a gaggle of prissy, snobbish Maidens who terrorise the entire school; their conversion into active villains makes it fictionally 'legal' for our *alter egos* to fight back at all who are prettier, richer or more successful than us, and lack the grace not to brag.

In erotic anime, Maidens are often victims of sexual assault, but normally so peripheral to the plot that, unlike the distressed Girl Next Door damsels, they are not deemed worth rescuing. Since one of the central *raisons d'être* of erotic anime is to portray as many sexual permutations as possible, there are likely to be many charac-

Phantom Quest Corp

ure, permanently asking the heavens what terrible fate has given her such a loser for a son. Like many adults in works aimed at children, Mrs Moroboshi represents a failed, misled opposite of the fun-loving kids. She stands for everything which keeps one young if avoided: responsibility, adulthood and marriage. Similarly, Ritsuko and Misato in *Evangelion* are burn-out cases; Ritsuko the chief scientist is a mother without a child, who throws herself into her computer programming as a substitute. Misato is psychologically damaged, shown to us in a flashback as a Child in jeopardy, whom nobody came to save. We then jump-cut back to the present day, where Misato is buttoning on her uniform, over the figurative and literal scars of her earlier experiences. In her scenes with the children in her care, Misato is depicted as a parody of an inept housewife. She can't cook anything except instant food, stays out late, oversleeps, drinks beer for breakfast, never cleans the house and never takes out the trash.

Another popular class of Older Woman is the old maid. In anime, these are the ones who have missed the sexual boat, or are perhaps marooned on the shore with one last chance for rescue. The best example in mainstream anime is Emu in *Crying Freeman,* whose adventures begin when the arrival of Freeman rejuvenates and transforms her into a fully fledged Girl Next Door, loaded with sexual potential.

Perhaps the most common form of anime Older Woman is the much-discussed older sister, either as a genuine sibling or a social 'senior', such as *Gunbuster*'s élite pilot Kazumi Amano, who even boasts the nickname 'Big Sister'. Senior to our Girl Next Door heroine Noriko in both years and experience, Kazumi is an excellent mentor figure, protector and, when the plot leaps an entire generation between two episodes, an eventual mother figure.

In mainstream anime, especially those which feature protagonists below the age of consent, Older Women have sexual experiences on behalf of the main characters. *Evangelion*'s Misato Katsuragi, billed as a 'Super-Big-Sister' in the pre-release hype, manages to combine many of the Older Woman's roles at once. She is not only a mother figure to the children in her care, there are also hints that she is a spinsterly burn-out case in the sexual stakes, preferring to drink herself into a stupor rather than deal with the people around her. But as the series progresses, it is Misato who dates the handsome Kaji, allowing

terless, humping Maidens in the background and superfluous scenes, like extras at an orgy. Just like their counterparts in non-erotic anime, they are primarily there for decoration. *Overfiend* IV.1 ends with the Maiden Yumi punished for attempting to flee the Secret Garden, and, naturally, the punishment takes the form of rape by a hideous, multi-tentacled monster. In any other episodic drama, such as a cop show or a superhero comic, this would be the point when the female foil is placed in ultimate jeopardy, only to be rescued in the nick of time by the arrival of the hero. But despite plenty of subplots and a large role in the episode, Yumi is a Maiden, and consequently not worth rescuing. The episode ends with Yumi soiled by the demon-rapist's triumphant orgasm; not with the last-minute rescue that a Girl Next Door might expect.

THE OLDER WOMAN

The Older Woman is one of the broadest categories of anime archetype, chiefly because adults in the real world will always outnumber the young population of viewer's peers that make up the other archetypes. Anime Older Women are often sophisticated, mature, intelligent creatures, mother-figures or even literal mothers. They are also embodiments of the teenage viewer's own fears, that crossing the threshold of adulthood is something to be avoided. For this reason, many Older Women are embittered creatures who hearken back to their glory days of youth.

Urusei Yatsura's Mrs Moroboshi is one such fail-the underage Asuka Langley to live out her crush on him vicariously.

Phantom Quest Corp's Ayaka is another textbook Older Woman. A confident career girl, she is nonetheless at odds with cultural tradition. At a time when the average woman should, conservatively, have tied the knot and taken up a new career as mother and home-maker, Ayaka is still hustling in the business world. She drinks away her troubles in karaoke bars, has a hangover every morning and can never hear her bedside alarm over the ominous ticking of her biological clock.

As they are almost always adults by definition, many Older Women fill the role of the villain. The adult nature of *Sailor Moon's* wicked-witch Queen Beryl is signified not only in her age, elegance and the perversion of youthful dreams, but in her very speech. Once again, this is not peculiar to Japanese fiction, but commonplace in many of our own stories, where the writers slip into the ease of archetypes, giving the evil characters a better command of the language, and a greater, more parental vocabulary and syntax than their childish adversaries.[4]

In erotic anime, we have all these devices and more, for the Older Woman's role as intellectual senior often manifests in the role of sexual initiatress. However, the idea of the embittered Older Woman who has somehow taken the wrong path is often eroticised as a symbol of

---

[4] See Westfahl, 'Wrangling Conversation...', p36, in which '... villains used longer sentences and longer words than did heroes. This difference reflects a widespread and age-old attitude of anti-intellectualism, a belief in admirable youth and evil elders, virtuous innocence and corrupt experience.'

[5] Lesbians are 'evil', of course, because they steal the women that are regarded as the rightful property of the male viewer. If they ask nicely they can borrow his woman, but only if he's allowed to watch.

[6] Kaguya is another legendary reference, to a beautiful foundling daughter bestowed on an old wood-cutter. She has many suitors, for whom she sets impossible tasks, but, contrary to the Western fairy tale tradition, none of them succeed. She eventually returns alone to her birthplace on the Moon. *Rei Rei* is thus an ironic epilogue to the legend, with the heroine as a frustrated spinster who missed the sexual boat, and a light-hearted sequel in which she returns to Earth to save humanity from making the same mistake. For the original story, see McAlpine, *Japanese Tales and Legends*, pp127-187.

corruption. Queen Beryl is matched in erotica by vast numbers of 'bad' Older Women, sirens and temptresses, lesbians[5] and sado-masochists, vamps and those who are literally possessed by the devil.

Nowhere is the Older Woman's complex role as sophisticate, mother figure, force of evil *and* experience better illustrated than in Toshimitsu Shimizu's erotic comedy *Rei Rei*. Its protagonist, the sexual trouble-shooter Kaguya,[6] lives near the Moon and watches over the hapless inhabitants of Earth. Her job is to save humanity from disaster by spreading the gospel of sexual freedom, assisted by her 'rude mechanical' sidekick, the goblin-come-butler Pipi.

Kaguya is a tart with a heart, a heavenly whore who's doing her bit for mankind by granting their wishes and fulfilling their fantasies, guaranteeing plenty of incidental action along the way. The first 'client' is Mamoru Tanaka, an all-purpose Japanese schoolboy, smitten with true love for the arrogant, dismissive Ikuko. Ikuko, of course, is merely a Girl Next Door who has lost her way, and Mamoru is not motivated by lust, but by honourable intentions to help her fulfil her archetypal role of becoming his girlfriend.

Ikuko has fallen under the spell of her former tutor, a bisexual Older Woman called Manami. But Manami now lusts after the hunky male doctor Okabe, and embarrassed by her youthful excesses, she is prepared to commit murder to forget them. Not only has Manami diverted Ikuko from the true path of sexual congress with the pure-hearted Mamoru, but she's also hatched a secret plan to kill Ikuko so that she can run off with Okabe, the new love of her life.

The homophobic identification of bisexuality and evil is a handy plot device to ensure that no one asks if Ikuko really *is* desperate for a 'real' man. Whereas some erotica (for example, the computer game *Ring Out*) recognise that homosexuality might be a genuine choice made by a consenting adult, *Rei Rei* demands that the viewer recognises it as a perversion. In time-old pornographic tradition, it has its cake and eats it too, titillating the male viewer with woman-on-woman action, before exorcising it with the timely arrival of a man to save the day.

If *Rei Rei* really were the meditation on life-choices that it pretends to be, Kaguya might instead offer Ikuko the chance to banish the annoying Mamoru from her life, but because this is fantasy for men, Mamoru's desire for Ikuko overrides any other concerns. He is, in mythic terms, pure of heart because he is most like the viewer. All Kaguya really cares about is Mamoru's unrequited lust, and Mitsuru Mochizuki's script ensures that there are plenty of reasons for the audience to sympathise with him.

After Ikuko is killed by Manami, Kaguya steps in to show the dead girl the error of her ways, in true *It's a Wonderful* [Sex] *Life* fashion, by taking the invisible girl to eavesdrop on conversations between Manami and Okabe. She also places her on the magical 'bridge of secret desires', and instructs her to make her fantasies real. The bridge represents sexual awakening (once across, you can never return), and Kaguya tells Ikuko to make up her mind. But there is a right and wrong answer to the supposedly open-ended question.

When Ikuko announces that she wants to remain forever in love with Manami, Kaguya laments: 'What a shame; wishing for a love that cannot be.' The script is unspecific as to whether Ikuko's love for Manami is bad because Manami does not reciprocate, or because Manami is malicious, or because Manami is a woman. Just in case the viewer still hasn't been brought round to Kaguya's way of thinking, Manami is depicted as an anti-mother, destroying young life instead of creating it, in a disturbing scene in which she is haunted by the ghost of Ikuko. The pale Ikuko begins by making sexual advances, but then perverts the process of childbirth by trying to crawl back into Manami's womb.

It is Kaguya's job to convince Ikuko of the error of her ways, and to ensure that she fully appreciates Mamoru's chivalrous behaviour. To his credit, Mamoru is certainly bending over backwards to get Ikuko back. He avenges the supposed death of his would-be girlfriend when Kaguya turns him into a nubile young girl, a disguise which allows him to seduce Okabe. When Manami comes home and catches them in bed together, Kaguya turns Mamoru back into a man. Thinking that she's lost everything, Manami storms out in tears, berating Okabe for being a pervert, an ironic statement considering that she herself has only recently been having sex with another woman.

Realising he's been had, Okabe is so stunned that he literally disappears from the story without a trace. Ikuko sees that Mamoru was the one for her all along and, after a timely rescue from her coffin just before she gets the oven treatment,

they all live happily ever after.[7]

Without a moment's pause, Kaguya is at it again, scanning Japan's cities for 'souls in pain' and setting her sights on Satoshi, a computer nerd with a heart of gold. Obsessed with astronomy, he only ever takes his girlfriend Mika to the planetarium and the gaming arcades, and she's getting angry because, like all Girls Next Door, whether they admit it or not, she's desperate to do the deed.

Kaguya discovers that Satoshi is afraid of contact with women, and reasons that the best possible cure for him is a bit of sexual healing. Thus fortified thanks to Kaguya's tender ministrations, Satoshi sets out to seduce Mika, but fails miserably. He immediately runs home to play with his computer, and ends up jiggling his joystick so hard that his spirit becomes possessed by his games console. Kaguya and Pipi rush in to save him, and in the process they discover Satoshi's real problem.

Satoshi was deserted by his mother at an early age, and was never properly weaned. His obsession with astronomy is rooted in a story told to him by his mother, about the Milky Way being the milk of the mother goddesses, flowing across heaven to make sure the godlets grow big and strong. Cue the amply-endowed Kaguya, who, as a fully qualified Older Woman, is able to take over the maternal role. Offering her breasts to Satoshi, she urges him to put aside the image of his mother, saying: 'You can't become a man until you've drunk your fill of me.'

His childhood now firmly behind him, Satoshi becomes a 'real man' at last, which, if this anime is anything to go by, means a brusque, arrogant toe-rag who veritably orders Mika to a seedy hotel as if he were doing her a favour. Once again, Kaguya and her assistant have pulled sexual triumph out of a hat, and the episode ends with Kaguya's teasing 'zaijian', the Chinese farewell that promises, or rather threatens, another visit in the immediate future.

---

[7] There was a final scene cut from the Japanese version during production, in which we see Manami and Okabe reunited over a dinner table. Where a Western script-writer might have finished with them both left alone, Mochizuki gives them what they really deserve: each other. But while Okabe has managed to talk Manami into coming back with him, she is a different person. She now has a pathological addiction to eating eggs (the food she used to poison Ikuko), and is an obese parody of her former self.

THE ALIEN

Foreign women stare out at hormonally challenged Japanese males at every turn. One only has to watch Hollywood films to see that all white girls are easy, and that anyone looking for a good time only has to wave a dollar bill at a passing American. No doubt a vast quantity of the 8,000 pornographic movies made in California each year is exported to Japan. Matters are helped by the pervasiveness of the Internet, which allows one culture access to the pornographic images of another. This is the downside of censorship practises in the modern age; they encourage the belief that sex doesn't happen in the homeland, that it must be a foreign import, like the videos smuggled back in your luggage, free of censorious cuts and unhelpful mosaics blotting out all the action.

Of course, the Japanese are by no means untypical. Just as every Englishman will tell you that all Swedish girls are boy-crazy wenches, and every Italian will tell you that British girls are desperate for sex, Japanese culture has mapped sexual permissiveness onto that which is Alien, that which is Other, that which is not in their own backyard. Erotica are often set in a time or place far removed from the viewer's own experience, since this accentuates the fantasy, and the reassurance that this world is far removed from our own hang-ups, guilt and fears of taboo.

Chapter eight has discussed how difficult it is to make generalisations about an entire culture

Armitage III

based on a limited sample of its media. But this problem is double-edged, because the Japanese have formed their own ideas about Western culture, and little of it is complimentary. A glance at *Mad Bull 34* is enough to convince the most liberal-minded of viewers that something has gone wrong. One too many cop show watched after one too many beers, and *Mad Bull 34* was born, in which a half-Japanese police officer is reassigned to the mean streets of New York, which is, of course, a land of happy whores, smiling strippers, drug addicts and gunslingers.

Foreign women are certainly very different. Different genes have given them a glittering cascade of different hair and eye colours. Foreign women are not only available in large sizes, they embody the many Western ideals of beauty foisted upon the Japanese by the invasive Western media. As Japanese girls seek to tone their muscles, pad out their breasts and bottoms, teeter on high heels or surgically alter their features to look more like their Western counterparts, the Japanese boys have got better things to do; watching foreign women in all their transgressional glory.

Just as this book argues for some sense of proportion when regarding *Overfiend*, it must be pointed out that such a sense is not always forthcoming from the Japanese. *Basic Instinct*, *Showgirls*, *Emmanuelle* and *The Lover* may be unrepresentative of the entire output of the Hollywood film business, but the average viewer abroad isn't necessarily going to know that. Just as foreign journalists assume that every home in Japan owns a copy of *Overfiend*, so the average Japanese kid extrapolates his media experience of the world without realising that he is confusing our fantasies with our mundane reality.

Another common form of Alien is the literal living doll, the robot or android. Taking a subliminally sexual cue from *Pinocchio*, the robot-girl is a figure of wish-fulfilment, a girl who needs the viewer's love to make her whole, like *Key the Metal Idol*, or a boy's toy with erotic potential in *My Marie*. The genetically enhanced Fatimas of *Five Star Stories* are beautiful women, and yet the final stage in their development must be artificially performed by their Masters. They may be dreams come true, but the fantasy is clearly marked by the author; the viewer cannot aspire to such perfection unless he too lives in the fantasy world of the story.

If there is no chance of escaping from robot-hood, then the robot girl must have built-in obsolescence. Thus Naomi Armitage in *Armitage III* is permitted to survive because she can become a nubile Girl Next Door and give birth, but the robot Antoinette in *The Humanoid* must sacrifice herself so that the hero can settle down with a 'real woman' without the guilty return of any old flames.

Because robots cannot normally be real humans, and because they are often depicted trying to understand the vagaries of human emotions, there is considerable scope within anime for them to be targets of abuse. Like the faceless Bond girls that charm 007 through the early reels until he meets the female lead, both *Armitage III* and *AD Police* feature robots designed for multi-purpose use, but with the 'female' type co-opted as cheap, disposable whores. They may enhance the bare flesh quota in any given show, but ultimately they must leave or transform themselves into something more acceptable. After all, what kind of hero would accept second-best? The male viewer wants his *alter ego* on the screen to get a real woman at the end, not a machine.

Real women are, by definition, neither robots nor Aliens, and so the throwaway, impermanent nature of Alien characters is often present, even where not expected in the non-erotic mainstream shows. There are many anime rooted in a comedy of manners, the farcical implications of having an unwelcome guest in your home, from the childhood fare of *Doraemon*, in which a young boy is forced to adopt the time-travelling pet robot sent to him as a gift by his distant descendants, to the adult porn of U-Jin's *Visionary*, which experiments with the erotic implications of inviting a sex-goddess to stay.[8]

The most famous Alien/foreigner is Lum, who features in the long-running comedy *Urusei Yatsura*. Our feckless hero Ataru Moroboshi is an average Japanese boy, who is forced to share his home with a beautiful devil-woman from space. Considering that Ataru is an incurable lech and that Lum is a loose-moralled foreign lass, one might expect the series to be over very fast. Takahashi maintains the dramatic tension by introducing some more bad luck into her hero's life. Lum's anger or lust will cause her to put out electricity like a small generator, frying all in the vicinity. Ataru is thus committed to a woman who continually offers him sex on a plate, but unable to accept her offer because they are ultimately incompatible. So he is now in a frantic double-bind, sworn to remain faithful to a woman he cannot have.[9]

However, in one of the earliest chapters of the original manga, the characters are taken out of the eternal circle of profitable farce and shown what fate awaits. Lum inadvertently sends Ataru a decade into the future, to the year 2001, where he gatecrashes his high school reunion and meets his as-yet unborn son. But more importantly, when all the chrononautical jokes have been laid aside, we see the woman with whom Ataru eventually settles down, and it's not Lum but Shinobu, the Girl Next Door.[10]

Alien girls, be they from another country or another planet, are good fun for a time, but there's no place like home, and our nice Japanese boy must eventually rid himself of these exotic odalisques and get himself a nice Japanese girl. The act of becoming a nice Japanese girl is far beyond poor Lum, even though she tries incredibly hard. She learns Earth ways, attends an Earth school, and tries to fit in.[11] One reason why we can never expect a truly satisfactory closure to the story of Lum and Ataru is that the only end that awaits is one where Lum is cast aside and Ataru settles down with Shinobu. The dramatic tension in many episodes of *Urusei Yatsura* springs from the dangerous moments when Shinobu's prissiness threatens to relegate her to the Maiden scrapheap, or Lum veers towards promotion to Girl Next Door.

---

[8] The beautiful Alien visitor in *Visionary* is even called Doreimon, in a punning reference to the children's series that inspired it.

[9] This is another common device. The protagonist has the wish-fulfilling easy option before his eyes, but has to defer gratification. Compare the eponymous *Kirara*, who similarly dwells in her man's bedroom, but is untouchable because she is a ghost. Such characters are mathematical problems in the erotic world; the hero must work out what makes her unavailable. They are too foreign, too sparky or too young; they can't cook or clean like good wives should; they are family members and hence subject to an incest taboo; they are fated to leave for other/better/worse things, etc.

[10] See Takahashi, *Urusei Yatsura*, pp33-52.

[11] In one scene she even has a throwaway line about collecting her Alien Registration Card, a play on the dual meaning of alien and foreigner, since all foreigners resident in Japan must do this in the real world, and many are indeed surprised to see themselves described with the same appellation applied to green-skinned invaders.

Fate has similar plans in store for Belldandy, the Alien figure in Kosuke Fujishima's *Oh My Goddess!* She is, as the title implies, a divine being, one of the three Norse fates who, in a mysterious conflation of Christianity and Paganism, grant wishes for God. But in a bureaucratic cock-up, the only way to get the Goddesses' help is to call them, and their phone number is ex-directory. Enter Keiichi Morisato, a lonely college student without a girlfriend to brighten those long evenings. He dials out for pizza, gets a wrong number and finds himself on the Goddess Helpline. When the beautiful goddess Belldandy promises to grant him a wish, Keiichi wishes for her to stay with him forever, and so she does. So now Keiichi the miserable loner has got a dream girlfriend, or possibly a doormat that wears perfume, depending on your point of view.

What kind of girlfriend is Belldandy? One who carries Keiichi's schoolbooks, hands him tools when he needs them and fusses broodily over the cooking and the cleaning. Keiichi, of course, loves her, and this is supposed to be reward enough, but the early episodes avoid reminding us that her presence is his wish, not hers. If this woman had freedom of choice, would she honestly choose to spend precisely nine months (yes) mothering him, until such time as God himself gets annoyed and demands that she return to heaven. This he does on Christmas Eve, which has of late become the conventional occasion for shy Japanese boys to pop the question. Her sisters Urd and Skuld[12] occasionally act like exuberant bridesmaids, and sometimes like reluctant in-laws. But this cannot go on, because this nice young Japanese boy seems to be on the verge of shacking up with an Alien female, and that cannot be allowed. Nice Japanese boys marry the Girl Next Door, that's the way these things are done.

Like Hans Andersen's little mermaid, Belldandy must leave her world behind if she is to stay. The sacrifice must be hers, because Keiichi's Japan, like the legendary Northern Europe from which Belldandy hails, requires a wife to leave her people and become at one with her husband's. She must renounce her status as Alien and settle down to be a Girl Next Door.

[12] The names are all Japanese attempts to pronounce the names of the mythical North European Norns: Fate, Necessity and Being.

But this is a difficult thing to accomplish, because Aliens are invariably disposable.

Fujishima employs an ingenious plot device to escape from this mess. The anime has written itself into a corner. Belldandy is an Alien, and by anime tradition, that means the time will eventually come when she has to make the bed, shut the door on her way out, and step aside for the faithful Girl Next Door, who has been patiently waiting for her man to finish sowing his wild oats. But *Oh My Goddess!* has no Girl Next Door to speak of. It begins in a strangely realistic way with Keiichi alone and forlorn, not the fantasy-within-a-fantasy of already beating away girls with a stick. Instead, Fujishima pulls off an incredible about-face. He throws in a flashback scene in which the tiny child-figures of Belldandy and Keiichi meet in the distant past, and swear eternal love for each other. This betrothal is then wiped from Keiichi's memory (for technical reasons, you understand) and we return to the present day, where we now realise that Belldandy's Alien status has been misappropriated. She is, and always has been, the Girl Next Door after all.

With a stroke, Fujishima solves the problem, but also destroys vast swathes of his story. Yes, Keiichi wished for a girlfriend, but the one he gets was actually preordained. Yes, she is putty in his hands and answers his every whim, but that is because of his chivalrous behaviour in an unspecified dreamtime, where they began as equals, but where she renounced her status to become his subservient wife-in-waiting. And yes, her sisters are interfering busybodies, but they now have no moral ground to stand on, because Belldandy is not a slave of circumstance, but an acquiescent partner who has sworn, by the very God they serve, to love, honour and obey.

A similar difficulty faces Milfa, the female star of the erotic OAV *The Elven Bride*. An elf married to Kenji, a human, Milfa must put up with familial interference, the responsibilities of marriage and, most crucially for the plot, the awful wedding-night realisation that her husband's penis is too big for her. *The Elven Bride* is a fantasy in which two childish characters play house when they marry against the wishes of their families. It's set in a deliberately unrealistic, cartoonish society. Milfa's mission, should she choose to accept it, is to transform herself from a blonde, Alien elf into a Girl Next Door, but the road is fraught with perils.

The Elven Bride

In mixing the magical with the mundane, *The Elven Bride* contains erotic reworkings of situation comedies like *The Flintstones* and *Bewitched*. Kenji has a day job as a soldier-cum-policeman in this medieval fantasy world. Milfa stays at home and pegs the washing out on the line, cooks dinner for her beloved, and tries to come to terms with the new adventures which married life brings.

Both her in-laws and her own family know that fate frowns upon racial miscegnation; the wedding is boycotted by both sides and the humans who live in Kenji's hometown are distrustful of foreigners. None of this bothers the couple so long as they have each other, but trouble ensues in the bedroom because Milfa's sexual organs are too under-developed for Kenji's virile human member.

Kenji resolves to go on a quest for Harpy Ooze, said to be the ultimate sexual lubricant. While Milfa sits at home waiting, Kenji travels far and wide, and eventually meets the beautiful, angelic Pyully. Pyully explains that she is a Harpian, a race that lives in secret within the great tree Yggdrasil. But Harpians cannot breed with each other; if they do they produce the ugly mules known as harpies. For a Harpian to produce Harpian offspring, she must mate with a human, and Kenji is the lucky candidate.

The story began with Kenji and Milfa's marriage, so viewers have not been given the vicarious thrill of watching Kenji sow his wild oats. His wife is still an Alien, but she will become a Girl Next Door soon, so why not indulge in a little extramarital activity with a new disposable Alien? While Pyully is arousing him, and he is half-heartedly fighting her off, he realises that she is using the mythical Harpy Ooze to ease his penis into her vagina. Seeing the end of his quest

in sight, he flips her over and milks her for a jarful of the precious fluid, impregnating her with Harpian triplets in the process.

Kenji returns home to drag his wife to the nuptial bed, but there are more problems. Milfa must face another sexy sitcom peril, the lecherous medic. She pops down to the clinic to see if the medieval gynaecologist has any suggestions, and finds herself amid an accepting gaggle of young wives and expectant mothers, many of whom are similarly involved in interracial marriages. One girl claims to be half-hobbit, and that she has double Milfa's trouble, since her boyfriend is a fully fledged beast, not a puny-penised human. What none of the women mention is that there is more to their attendance than meets the eye. The doctor is an ex-mercenary called Perio, who is using his powers of hypnosis to compel them all to have sex with him.

When Kenji finds out that Milfa has gone to see Perio, he rushes to the rescue, but not before Perio has almost brought Milfa completely under his spell. Whereas Kenji can have sex with Harpians to his heart's content, a sex scene between his wife and another man can only be the result of compulsion, and it is something from which her loving husband must save her.

Luckily, Kenji has the assistance of his grandmother, a suspiciously elfin succubus who, like many a Toshio Maeda witch, draws energy from human sperm to cast spells. Once Kenji has carried Milfa off just in time, it is granny who delivers the *coup de grâce* to the disgraced Perio. In a touch that truly makes the punishment fit the crime, she screws him to death.

The Elven Bride is intriguing for the way in which it deconstructs fairy tales and asks what happens in the 'after' of 'happily ever after'. The racial undertones are also strange, especially for an allegedly homogenous society like Japan. Milfa begins as a pariah in Kenji's home village, but soon discovers that many of the people around her are from foreign cultures too. Kenji and Milfa adore each other but are unsure of how they should deal with the perils of married life. But as Milfa shyly enters each new experience, she drifts further towards becoming the perfect bride, the perfect Girl Next Door, and further away from the doomed Alien figure that characters like her so often represent.

THE CHILD

Even more useless than the Maiden, but less rare thanks to the 'cute' lobby that calls for comic-relief mascots, is the self-explanatory Child. Asexual, selfish, but with an occasional accidental insight that changes the course of the plot, the Child is best used for asking dumb questions that allow the exasperated Tomboy, kindly Girl Next Door or maternal Older Woman to indulge in handy plot exposition.

Children are occasionally used as observers or comic relief, which in itself is enough to rouse the ire of many censors. In many anime, erotic or otherwise, the Child is not even human. *Tenchi Muyo!*, already overloaded with too many cast-members, has a real Child in the form of Sasami, and an animal one in the form of Ryo-Oh-Ki, the baby spaceship that looks like a rabbit. *Battle of the Planets* has a comic-relief Child in the form of Keyop, and *Ulysses 31* lost uncountable viewers with its incredibly annoying Child figure, Nono the robot. Such devices carry over, even into the supposedly po-faced melodrama of erotic horror. Witness the childlike kuroko[13] of the *Overfiend* series, tiny goblins who can often be seen running errands or staring from the sidelines of an orgy.

Beyond the symbolic Child of the kuroko, the

---

13 'Kuro' = black, 'ko' = child, although the word can also mean 'prompter' or 'stagehand'.
14 Like the Tomboy, the nymphet's demands '... are easily satisfied; she would rather have toys than boys and her sexuality is rudimentary enough to be inter-changeable with a boy's. The screen Lolitas are there to fulfil old men's fantasies as painlessly and covertly as possible. Where there is pain and recognition of suffering... the pain turns out to have been inflicted by a child whose innocence is only an illusion, a veil behind which a malevolent minx is waiting to lure a man to his ruin.' Haskell, *From Reverence to Rape*, p346.
15 The animation and art is conspicuously substandard, implying that the market and interest in such material is smaller than many tabloid writers would have us believe. Pornography is often an apprentice-ship for artists and creatives destined for better things, and some titles display considerable talent on the part of the animators. Several of U-Jin's *Pictures from High School* (see chapter eleven), for example, feature work from Satoshi Urushihara and Kinji Yoshimoto, who went on to put their experience animating female flesh to more mainstream use in the acclaimed *Plastic Little*. *Pictures from High School* includes some lovely backgrounds and parallax work that transcends the merely pornographic, but there is no such quality of workmanship in the Lolita Anime series.

real Child can also appear in a familiar con-vention to Western viewers, as the troublesome interloper that interferes with the adult charac-ters' flirtatious plans, by asking for a glass of water or refusing to go to bed when the two babysitters have secret plans for each other. She can also appear, like *Hummingbirds'* pre-teen Mina, as an *idiot-savant* on matters of the heart, uninterested herself, but able to comment on the older characters' attempts to woo members of the opposite sex.

It is undeniable that some children in anime are there to satisfy the lolikon obsession with young flesh on the part of some audience members. This undesirable element is, however, toned down in the mainstream.

In the original manga of *Gunsmith Cats*, the character of Minnie May is a diminutive blonde ex-whore, who becomes an assistant bounty hunter once she escapes from the brothel where she has been working since her childhood. Because this story takes place in Sonoda's fantasy Chicago, a place far removed from 'normal' Japan, these things can happen. May's saviour, Ken Taki, is a second-generation Japanese bomb expert, thus assuring the dom-estic market that not only could this not hap-pen in their own backyard, but that it is Japanese blood, and not the dangerously alien American kind, that can offer redemption. Ken is on the run from the mob, and so her beloved will recognise her when they meet again, May tries to keep herself as young-looking as poss-ible. That's the excuse, anyway. *Gunsmith Cats* presents a victim of abuse, desperately hanging onto her youth because that's all she thinks will hold a man's attention; an unpleasant subtext ignored by the majority of its readers,[14] and dropped completely in the anime version, which simply presents her as a Childish bomb expert.

Within the small dedicated niche market served by mail order video, there are more dis-turbing incarnations of the Child as sex object, such as the 'Lolita Anime' products from Wonderkids. The first ever erotic anime video, *Reddening Snow/Girls Tortured with Roses* was also the first Wonderkids release, beginning a series that ranged in the 1980s from risqué but unremarkable dramas of sexual awakening, to full-blown stories of paedophile rape.[15]

Variation features a schoolgirl of indeterminate age, who is taken in by an artist: a handy, com-mon device that puts male and naked female together in the same room (it turns up twice in the Wonderkids series). She stays for dinner, and the meal begins innocently enough, but slowly reveals its true colours as the camera pauses for long, lingering shots of the girl lifting food and drink to her mouth. It then pauses again on the decanter of sangria, which the paedophile intends to use to soften his victim's resolve. Protesting all the while, she is tied up, lifted off the ground and stripped. Paralysed with fear, she loses control of her bladder, and the man greedily drinks her urine as it falls down her legs. He then fondles her thighs and crotch until her distress becomes unbearable.

The scene changes to outdoors, where she is sobbing into his manly shoulder while he comforts her, bouncing her on his knee. But she is still naked, and bound with ropes hanging from a tree, as revealed when the man hoists her up, fingers her vagina and then begins to rape her from behind. The camera playfully juxtaposes the irony of a swing as a child's toy and sex toy, before the man ejaculates. And in the end, she, like all fantasy rape victims, seems to have enjoyed it after all.

There are several others along these lines, all featuring girls who may or may not be underage, it is often difficult to tell when the key animation is so ropey that their secondary sexual characteristics can grow and shrink at an alarming rate. In *House of Kittens*, two schoolgirls are inspired to experiment with sex by seeing their teacher at it, but the way in which paedophile links are drawn is insidious. Both the girls are arguably over the age of consent, but the protagonist, although a similar height to her friend, stands slightly further away from the camera to look smaller. She also goes in search of her junior at school to teach her what she has learned. If the girl we see having sex is not too young, there is always the chance that the next will be.

Several stories suggest that exposure to pornography or assault will make girls more easily persuaded to go further. *Dying for a Girl* features a schoolgirl who is sexually assaulted by a flasher in a playground. He pins her down, fondles her until she faints, goes down on her and then prepares to have full sex, when she is rescued in the nick of time by a fellow student, who takes her back to his place. There she has a nice relaxing bath, where she resolves to let her brave rescuer take her virginity instead of the would-be rapist. This includes a graphic depiction of his penis rupturing her hymen, as he proves himself to be the man that the old rapist never was. Beyond the apparent young age of the victim, the other shocking element is the way the script deals with her violation. It is depicted as a gift from heaven, softening her up for the hero's own enjoyment, and this attitude is far more distasteful than the actual visual content of the tape.

The Reddening Snow features a gang-rape, initiated by two thugs, but eventually concluded by a mild-mannered boy who harboured a secret love for the girl he assaults. He arrives with the heroic intention of rescuing her (or so he says, one suspects he could have tried running a bit faster), but eventually gives into peer pressure, mumbles that he hopes she'll forgive him, and then rapes her anyway. The incident takes place in a wintry forest, and the title refers to the pattern made on the snow as, left for dead, the girl bleeds from her injuries.

WHEN IS A CHILD NOT A CHILD?

Some female characters are often seen by foreign commentators as children, whereas that was not the original intent of the Japanese creators. *Overfiend* IV has three Child characters (Yumi, Yufura and Himi) who are untouchable until such time as their bodies reach adulthood. Adulthood and sexual maturity are crimes within the Secret Garden, and Yumi's attempt to flee is occasioned by her sexual awakening, and that of her lover Ken. Both in the case of Yumi and Ken, and in the later sex scene initiated by the vampish Yufura, the characters are no longer presented as children from the moment they become sexual beings. We may see scenes of first-time sex, but between sexually mature (albeit newly mature) adults. In the case of Yufura and Himi, this is particularly problematic, since in both cases their sexual development is magically accelerated.

In terms of *Overfiend*'s overall plot, we learn that the Secret Garden is organised along these lines because the fiendish Chojin can defeat Himi (destined to become his nemesis) if he catches her before the onset of her menstruation. Hence the creation of a realm of eternal children, in which adult sexuality is both a crime and a punishment.

A proportion of supposed child pornography in anime is nothing of the sort. Many female characters in anime (in fact, often all except the Older Women archetypes) are apt to behave in a manner that many Western viewers would describe as childish. They will often dress, talk and behave in a childish manner, a phenomenon that has led to some interesting miscasting in anime dubs. The best example of this in the English language is the character of Shoko in *Bounty Dog*. The mature, sensible voice actress who plays her in the English-language version sounds completely at odds with the manic, girlish figure who bounces all over the screen like a child at a birthday party. In the original Japanese version, she has a manic, girlish voice to match.

The oriental nude is naturally less hirsute than its occidental equivalent, a fact which has also helped spread misinformation about children in anime. Matters are not helped by the influence of Article 175 (see chapter two) and its supposed decree that pubic hair should not be shown, meaning that even supposedly adult girls are often shown without pubic hair. As a cinematic convention in any kind of porn, the removal of the pubic hair also allows the viewer to get a better look at the contact of genitals-on-genitals, all contributing to an apparent reduction in the age of the participants in anime.

The tradition of continuing to wear a school uniform at the junior college level is still enforced by some institutions, thus giving the impression to many foreign viewers that they are watching porn starring schoolgirls, whereas the protagonists are above the age of consent. The age of consent itself is problematic, and produces a significant 'grey area' that makes defining child pornography variant with the laws of the country in which it is seen. In America, for example, Central Park Media's Anime 18 label issues disclaimers with its pornography, stating that all involved in the production are at least nineteen years old. Such announcements would presumably not be necessary in some European countries, which have decriminalised sex in the early teens, especially between partners of the same age. A pornographic anime that contained, for example, scenes of a fifteen year-old boy having sex with a fifteen year-old girl, is technically child porn, but would present endless philosophical difficulties to certain censorship authorities in the West.

But these films are legal in Japan because they are not 'real'. The *thought* of paedophilia, and its representation in the media to consenting adults in private, is not illegal in itself, although the act is. Japan thus ascribes to the theory that pornography is cathartic, and makes imitation by the viewers of the acts depicted less, not more likely. It is therefore at odds with theories of media influence in many other countries, including America and Britain, which would argue that access to images of paedophilia would encourage paedophiles to commit the act itself and also aid child-rapists in encouraging children to acquiesce.

EXCEPTIONS TO THE RULES

Anyone watching a large number of anime is liable to discern the female character archetypes listed above, but also to ask themselves what possible point there is to the entire theory. After all, complete adherence to the rules makes for nothing more than predictable plotting, cardboard characters and hack-written scripts. In Japan just as much as in the West, many writers are working within creative restraints imposed by (to use a polite term) non-creative executives. There are also those who are forced to work within certain parameters in the initial stages of a show, in order to please networks or advertisers, who often require a guarantee that their 'original' show has enough in common with its predecessors that it will not rock the boat too much.

There is a further restriction on creativity, which is often imposed by executives, but is in fact rooted in audience expectations. There is nothing quite so soul-destroying to an artist as being told to give the audience what the audience *thinks* it wants. To adhere to such a principle is to be happy with pornography, in the literal sense. Pandering too much to audience demands is ultimately self-defeating, since the most vocal members are unlikely to be the most appreciative, or indeed the most loyal.

The reader is thus advised to take these archetypes as literally as a good writer would, with a pinch of salt. It is a triumph, not a disaster, every time an anime flouts the rules; the best anime break the mould with impunity, and the roster of writers responsible reads like a hit list of some of Japan's finest.

Chiaki Konaka's Naomi Armitage in *Armitage III* manages to work her way through every single archetype. An artificial woman who must break free of the constraints imposed by her male creator, she is a clinging Child, a super-

Sol Bianca

have an alien starship that can outrun any other craft in human space. The refugee, Rim Delapaz, convinces the pirates to help him rescue his mother, promising to lead them to a great treasure, worth more than they can possibly imagine. The pirates aren't sure, because like all stellar rogues they can imagine quite a bit, but they eventually agree to escort him to his destination. There they find themselves embroiled in a local revolution, led by Rim's father, and the story turns into a race against time to rescue Rim's mother, get the treasure and get out before all hell breaks loose.

The leader, Feb, is a classic Older Woman: calm, contemplative, and, in keeping with the sexist formulae of science fiction, not much good with firearms or technology. April and Janny are a pair of gung-ho Tomboys, active and competent military types. Janny 'Mann' even has a short crop and speaks in a male Japanese dialect. May is the ship's mechanic and robot specialist, which calls attention away from her Maiden frills. The ship's pilot, June, is literally an Alien; she is a highly strung, consumptive creature from another planet. There is no Girl Next Door, because the *Sol Bianca* crew have no place for a clumsy newcomer. They are a fully functional unit already, as our viewpoint character Rim Delapaz discovers. He is a Child whose role is to ask questions and get in the way.

This is what redeems *Sol Bianca* from the traditional trap of stereotype and formula. *Sol Bianca* is not a triumph of innovative storytelling, but it is undoubtedly enjoyable. Its real strength lies in the power of its characterisation, and the clever uses to which it puts such tired two-dimensional concepts as the anime archetypes.

There are other, more impressive stars of originality shining in the anime firmament, but it would be misleading to imply that anime has a greater proportion of masterpieces than any other art form in any other country. As per usual, ninety-five per cent of everything is trash, and it is rare indeed to find creators as talented as *Patlabor*'s Kazunori Ito, *Escaflowné*'s Shoji Kawamori or the transcendent Gainax collective who produced *Wings of Honneamise*, *Gunbuster* and *Evangelion*. The future does not look particularly bright, either, since more and more producers are ignoring writers' ideas in favour of concepts informed by that glorification of the lowest common denominator, market research. ●

violent, superefficient Tomboy, a cold-hearted, monstrous Alien, a party-going Maiden and a triumphant, home-making Girl Next Door, before driving off into the sunset as a mature, happily pregnant Older Woman. The cinema version of the story even continues after the film proper is over; finishing with a haunting music-box reprise of the main theme, to announce the happy arrival of a child. Naomi Armitage is a character fully aware that she begins life as a cipher. Like the robot women of *AD Police*, she berates her audience for its lack of imagination. 'If you hate me,' she yells in Alien/Tomboy mode, 'why did you make me?'

Sol Bianca makes a similar effort to exploit anime archetypes while still creating interesting characters. It is a 'female' film through its exclusion of men, in the same way that *Reservoir Dogs* is a 'male' film through its exclusion of women. In foregrounding female characters, *Sol Bianca* is able to make new demands of them.

The story calls for a stowaway to fall into the company of an all-female crew of pirates, who

CRUISE CONTROLS

Interactive Erotica and Digital Dating

Computer games are now as important a source of anime plots as manga, and are a major influence on the recent proliferation of one-shot exploitation videos that are high on hype and low on content. As a handy method of categorising the wishes and fantasies of the average player, the six female archetypes (discussed in the previous chapter) are deeply ingrained in the pornographic computer game market, reinforcing their use in anime. But few of the erotic games have been exported, making their powerful influence on modern anime hard for the outsider to spot.

Somewhere during the early nineties, there was an almost imperceptible shift in production statistics. Although there has always been a proportion of original ideas, or remakes of novels, the majority of anime used to be filmed adaptations of popular manga. But the current state of anime is heavily influenced by computer games, which, although not creating a new medium of distribution like the video cassette, have certainly altered the nature and content of many anime releases.

Movie producers are always keen to capitalise on trends, be it novels, comics or television shows, but the fad for game cash-ins has left a lot of burned fingers in the Japanese market, especially in the erotic field, where the value of game spin-offs is questionable. The original mathematics appear simple to company accountants: if a game sells a million copies, it is reasonable to expect enough of those consumers to pay for an animated tie-in. But what does their cash really buy them?

Novels appeal because of their complex detail, comics because they work as ready-made storyboards for the film version, but many producers fail to realise that the playability of a game is the one thing guaranteed not to transfer across other media. Consider the *Streetfighter* anime, obliged to make a coherent story out of a game whose prime subject matter is a dozen people hitting each other. In addition to the many problems of crafting a suitable story, which would beset a writer on any project, the game adapter is often forced to break many carefully learned rules of storytelling. Unnecessary subplots must be added to pacify fans of particular characters and, since many of the successful products are fighting games, combat becomes the central point of many anime with this pedigree.

In the erotic sector, the crossover brings a different sort of hazard. Many erotic games capitalise on providing the player with a semblance of control, naturally unavailable on the video version. With their multiple endings, they also reward repeat 'viewings', a benefit with which a video cannot compete. The erotic *Classmates* game sold over 100,000 copies in Japan, which left producers fighting for the video rights.[1] Software may be expensive, but lasts on average for fifty hours of game-time. The same kind of money will only buy around thirty minutes of animation. To get the same 'use' out of the *Classmates* video, the buyer would have to watch it twice a week, every week, for an entire year. Few of the 100,000 buyers of the *Classmates* game were likely to be as impressed with the anime version, and this factor has influenced long-term production planning. While mainstream television anime might be produced at anything up to twenty-six episodes

---

[1] The anime version was eventually made, and released in the West under the title *End of Summer*.

End of Summer

at a time, many game tie-ins (erotic or otherwise) are now one-shot wonders, so companies can take the money and run.

THE DEVELOPMENT OF EROTIC GAMES

Like the move from vaguely titillating, public film-viewing to the more-explicit, private accessibility of home video, computer erotica began in public gaming arcades before the advent of the personal computer made private, solo viewing the norm.

The earliest erotic games began with oriental variants on poker. The first arcade mah jong game, the imaginatively titled *Mah Jong Game*, appeared in 1978. Numerous imitators were soon on the market, and several held the attention of male players by providing a selection of female opponents. Some, like *Mah Jong Master*, employed photographs of real models, but were limited by memory considerations to fuzzy, low-resolution images. Others, like *Real Mah Jong Pai Pai*, opted to use anime-style images of girls, which saved valuable memory and added to the cartoony aspect of the games.[2] It wasn't until 1986 that such images were put to genuinely erotic use, with the strip mah jong variant *Second Love*.

The behaviouristic laws of pornography, where the titillating supply of virtually nothing creates a demand for just a little more, are perfectly suited to the coin-operated game genre. With a variety of

opponents and the requirement to hone one's skills at mah jong, the player is encouraged to return again and again.[3]

FIGHTING FIT

The mah jong games introduced the idea of reward and punishment to the erotica industry. The consumer was encouraged to keep on paying for replays, with the understanding that the better he became, the more likely he would be to see women with their clothes off. But mah jong games were merely the first incarnation; soon there were erotic variants on other types of popular mainstream game.

In *Bishojo Fighter*,[4] a *Streetfighter* clone, the actual combat is done by robots, but the erotic action is provided by the female 'puppeteers' who control them. After an animated 2D battle, the victor gets to see a still image of the defeated character removing their clothes. The more special moves the victor uses, the raunchier the images become.

There was only a single female, Chun Li, in the original *Streetfighter* game, although programmers learned that a female character, especially in the mainstream world, is a useful way of subliminally titillating the male viewer without resorting to overt pornography.

In *Bishojo Fighter*, all the characters are female, and designed to appeal to the widest possible

[2] Budgetary restrictions, both of filming and memory storage, have kept many of these games with an anime look to this day, although live-action CD-ROM erotica are on the increase. The anime look encourages the presence of an anime adaptation, and can also reach an audience through anime magazines, whose readers may be halfway through the text of an advertisement before they realise they are reading about a game. By that time, they may be interested enough to buy it anyway.

[3] Later refinements included animated stripteases, first seen in *Super Real Mah Jong III* (1988) and the advent of home versions that came accompanied by a video or laserdisc that stored live-action erotic footage. But *A[udio]V[isual] Mah Jong Video Fairies* and its fellow semi-interactive games, like their mainstream Western counterparts such as the video boardgame *Atmosfear*, were soon eclipsed by the more accessible combination of program and image on CD-ROM and other interactive media.

[4] I have used the title given by the British importers, although the game's actual Japanese title is *Ningyo Tsukai 2* (Puppet/Doll Masters 2). Similarly, *Heartbeat Memorial* is known as *Tokimeki Memorial* in Japan, and *Timestripper* has a longer title: *Timestripper Mako-chan*.

bracket of players. As if the sleeve notes' talk of her being 'well-brought-up and refined' were not enough of a hint, the Maiden character is called Sophia Rich. The disposable Alien is a Chun Li clone, the martial artist Li Xiaolou. Cris Canberra is a feisty Tomboy bedecked in leather and chains, while Miyuki Sonoda is an ice queen in her early twenties, a frigid Older Woman who has denied her own sexual fulfilment. The Child character Mika cannot be shown in an overtly sexual way, and so comes accompanied by her mother, another Older Woman to act as surrogate plaything for any Oedipally challenged gamers. And because the game has a two-player option, there are two Girls Next Door, flagged in the gaming manual as noble, honourable and, above all, nice.

THE CALL TO ADVENTURE

The adventure game genre was similarly exploited in the erotic market. Using an engine still popular today, the simplest versions combine scrolling text with occasional images onscreen. Following the popularity of the strip mah jong games, several companies began producing 'adventure' variants, copying the strip-games' policy of anime-style illustration and adding female voices to increase the realism. Many of the actresses employed were secretly (or occasionally openly) moonlighting performers from the anime business, strengthening the ties between games and anime still further.

These games also began to establish certain traditions in the field. Instead of a third-person perspective, in which the player watches the action as if a viewer with a camera, the majority of the pornographic adventure games preferred a first-person view. This prevented the male gamer from having to 'share' his conquests with a male character in the game. The female voices would address the male player directly, and images of the male character in the game would often avoid showing his face, or any other discerning features that could detract from the player's fantasy that it is he who is committing the acts shown.

In 1991, two popular games development companies, Just and Kirara, were warned by Japanese police that their games risked classification as obscene publications. Sales consequently rocketed, as did the number of high school boys caught shoplifting games which they were not old enough to purchase legally. The number of companies in the field swiftly multiplied, as did the number of games targeted at teenagers instead of the previously undefined 'adult' audience. In an attempt to

Timestripper

MOMM   :Your cock... it's so big...

convince their younger buyers that they were getting something truly naughty, the new games used censorship dots to give the illusion of titillation by 'obscuring' non-existent genitalia on the anime-style images.

Originally, all adventure games had a single acceptable ending. The hobbit would arrive home, the vampire would be killed or the world would be saved, although if players performed badly at certain points, their characters would be forced to retrace their steps to avoid a fatal error. In 1993 the games *Nova* and *Clan of the Kawarazaki* introduced the Japanese player to the idea of not one, but several endings of equal value, a development that would pay great dividends in the erotica business, where a player's personal preference for Older Women, Tomboys or any of the other archetypes, could result in a tailor-made story.

PRINCESS MAKING

There were other developments that did not quite run in tandem with Western gaming. Gainax, better known in anime circles for their high-quality, fan-friendly releases, have also had a part to play in the erotic market. Their accurate animation of bouncing breasts in *Gunbuster* (known as the 'jiggle effect') has been much imitated in the decade since they perfected it. A striptease game, *Battle Skin Panic*, caused controversy when it was revealed that this strip-poker variant could be purchased in Japan by minors. But it was another, apparently more innocuous Gainax computer game that has had the greatest effect on the Japanese world of erotic interactivity.

Princess Maker was a simulation game along similar lines to the American *Sim City*. But instead of designing and running a city, players were invited to rear a child. Fathers to a virtual daughter, their mission was to ensure that she grew into a well-mannered, well-educated, healthy young woman. In short, they had to create a 'princess' among her peers.

Princess Maker was to become the boy's toy of an entire generation, even though the whole idea was actually devised by a woman, Kyomi Akai. Each virtual girl has a list of scores that have to be improved or reduced, in order to create the perfect daughter and, by unstated association, the perfect girlfriend. The screen flashes up scores in areas as diverse as body strength, dexterity and general knowledge, and in such spiritual areas as stress, lust and moral fibre. Princess Maker's effects were far-ranging indeed; a direct line of descent can be traced from it to the ubiquitous tamagotchi virtual pets of the late nineties, and their distaff cousin, the virtual pop idol Kyoko Date. More importantly, Princess Maker created a vogue in the computer industry for simulation games that emphasised a sense, however illusory, of control.

Similar games have appeared which have taken the control element of Princess Maker a step further. Graduation places the player in the enviable position of a high school careers counsellor, whose job is to ensure that several female charges make it through school without flunking classes, playing truant or getting pregnant. One of its many spin-offs, Marriage, requires the player to set them up with the right husband.

HOW TO PICK UP GIRLS

Heartbeat Memorial puts the player directly into the action, so to speak. Instead of merely indulging in the vicarious pleasures of Graduation or Princess Maker, in which boyfriends are threats to one's established parental control, Heartbeat assigns the player to the role of the boyfriend himself.

The design of Heartbeat tells us a lot about its intended audience. The 'grand prize' is a girl called Shiori; a sixteen year-old high school student. She's not a knife-wielding psychopath or a large-breasted foreign female, instead she is the most average, bland person one could imagine. She is that ultimate in unattainable women, the Girl Next Door. As a player, you must try and steer yourself into Shiori's life and heart, make sure you're around at the right time, say the right things and suggest the right activities. With any luck, your witty repartee will get you her phone number. After that, you have to proceed to the next level, plucking up the courage and calculating the right moment to ask her out. The complex gameplay doesn't stop there; your next job is to keep control of her and get her to fall in love with you, with-

out causing any ructions among her friends.

This is not as easy as it sounds, since you are also forced to interact with them. Some of Shiori's friends will be interested in you for themselves. When her feisty associate Yumi tries to drag you out on a date, should you agree and risk getting found out by Shiori, or refuse and risk incurring Yumi's jealous wrath? The morose Miharu can be a valuable ally by putting in a good word for you, but devote too much time to her and she will get ideas above her station and assume that she can have you for herself. Can you keep Shiori's friends as your friends, and yet still get time with her alone? Only the skilful Heartbeat player can walk the tightrope and attain the ultimate prize: true love, be it with Shiori or one of her colour-coded friends.

No doubt there are those members of the moral majority who would regard Heartbeat as a far better thing to occupy young men's time than shooting demons in Doom. After all, there's no sex or violence, it's all good clean fun and it might even turn a few sad cases into more socially responsible individuals. It is not pornographic in the literal sense, or at least, it is only insofar as it regards women as objects and men as willing adherents to this principle. Like the worst manual on picking up girls, Heartbeat only tells its audience what to say. Listening to the girls' replies is not about getting to know another human being, it's about looking for behavioural clues for your next mission.

Despite the game's concentration on good manners and gentlemanly behaviour, it contains the underlying rationale that the women involved are objects. We know that they are not real people, and that their responses have been reduced to straightforward yes/no relays. With the women in Heartbeat, there is a right answer and a wrong answer, a way to charm and a way to scare them off. Ironically, the fact that their behaviour is part of a computer program turns them into objects, even though they themselves can argue against this. Shiori, for example, will cry foul if she suspects that she is being treated in a sexist manner, but the reduction of human interaction to such rules and cheats is itself an example of objectification.

TIMESTRIPPING

Many interactive erotic games combine elements of the Heartbeat engine with the more normal adventure game. This development has grown out of fundamental differences in buyer behaviour;

adventure gamers want plot and problem-solving, whereas porn consumers merely want porn. There is little point in making a pornographic adventure game too challenging; the real challenge is giving the consumer what they want. The combination of multiple endings and the yes/no relays of *Heartbeat* are the ideal solution.

Timestripper may appear on the surface like a modern 'erotic adventure' game, but it is very different. The basic technology, that of picture tableaux illustrating a text, has remained unchanged since the early days of the home computer, but *Timestripper* has a radically different reason for existence. As true pornography, it strips away all the 'unnecessary' elements of the other games to reveal the sublimated desires beneath. In fact, it is hardly a game at all, so much as a mildly interactive picture book, that only shows certain pictures if players follow the correct sequence of events.

The story of *Timestripper* unfolds in a linear fashion. There is no definite win/lose scenario, since whatever happens, the hero is destined to end up in bed with a beautiful woman. The difference lies in which woman it will be, decided by choices made during the game itself.

The gamer's 'choices' are actually hidden elements of a personality test. The events unfold in front of the player, with only a couple of minor subplots relying on the player's own decisions. Even these have no bearing on the ending. The chance decision to take a different route home might allow the player to see a sex scene he might otherwise have missed, but that's about it. Still more decisions are essentially red herrings. They may reorder certain blocks of text in the story, but make no other contribution to the game itself. But among these detours and branches are a few critical questions that will influence the outcome. Certain decisions made during the game provide the computer with yes/no answers to several questions about the player's own character and preferences, such as:

Would you cheat on your girlfriend?
Would you take pity on a frightened child?
Do you prefer one-night stands to long-term relationships?

Once the computer has the answer to questions like this, it sorts out the archetype that best matches the player, and tells the story variant with a fitting denouement. The story, and it is an ingeniously complex one, is an erotic variant on *Back to the Future*, in which two girls,

MAKO   : Ooh... aah.. do it more...

Timestripper

Nonn and Mako, are fighting over the same man in the year 2198.

The Alien blonde Nonn travels back to the present day, to wipe out Mako's ancestor, *Terminator*-style. Mako travels in time to stop her, and enlists the aid of the protagonist Shinji, who is also her boyfriend's ancestor. Nonn decides to seduce Shinji and stay with him, an alteration to history that will net her the man she wants. It also creates a paradox, because if Shinji doesn't marry his high school sweetheart Michiyo, his great-grandson will never invent the time machine and the girls will never be able to travel back to stop him.

But the history books don't mention that Shinji is/was an incorrigible womaniser and that he has just been dumped by the exasperated Michiyo. Mako knows that Shinji must propose to Michiyo at the graduation ball, or history will be irrevocably altered. But Nonn has realised this too, and attempts a double-pronged assault, seducing Shinji for herself, and simultaneously introducing Michiyo to the joys of bisexuality in order to ensure that she never wants her ex-boyfriend back.

All this is set against the superficially everyday machinations that surround the forthcoming dance. Shinji is on the organisation committee and is supposed to book a singer. If he wants to get anywhere, he'll have to consider seducing the singer's Older Woman manager, but even if he succeeds, the Childish singer will get stage fright and need some hands-on encouragement. Shinji also has to hold down a job at a local bar, where he is conducting a surreptitious affair with a Tomboy waitress, while quietly worrying that the camp barman has a crush on him. Meanwhile, the head of the dance committee is a spoilt rich Maiden who despises Shinji, and is just waiting for him to fail.

If you are kind, reasonable and sensitive, the story ends with normality restored, the time-travellers returning to the future and Shinji discovering that Michiyo's experience has turned her into a sex-crazed nymphet. Pragmatism, a realistic outlook and general honesty will net you a happy marriage to the poor little rich girl (gasping for a real man all along), getting a job managing her daddy's company while the time-travellers work in the family mansion as French maids. Indulgence of the idol singer's whims will win you her affection, although you'll have to repay her frustrated manager by having anal sex with her. In this scenario, the

time-travellers end up with their own television show.

The closest to a bad ending comes if you continuously plump for the arrogant, unfeeling decisions. You will be rewarded with the fickle Alien Nonn, while the heartbroken Mako plots her revenge as a woman scorned. But the star prize is Mako herself, with Nonn on the side when life gets boring. It's a happy ending that reveals what the canny reader may have suspected all along, that Michiyo was a false prophet and that the real Girl Next Door is Mako herself.

SELL-BY DATE: 2001?

The relationship of erotic games and erotic anime is likely to become less important as live-action pornography reduces the number of anime-style games. There are already CD-ROM games on the market that use the same adventure-game/personality-test engine, but replace the text and anime-style image with live-action footage. *Virgin Kyoko on the Trail of the Crescent Killer* pits a nubile female reporter against a serial murderer, with plenty of incidental, live-action porn footage. *Midnight Stranger* throws the first-person player into a dark, dingy bar with a beautiful foreign brunette. *Catch Sight of Figure* is a suspense thriller using live-action footage of detection and, of course, seduction. When the games are live action in their original incarnation, an anime adaptation would be a backward step, and is consequently less likely. Ultimately, however, anime-style games will remain for as long as there are anime.

In the immediate future, as the live-action games gain a greater market share, they will crowd out their anime-style predecessors. The first to disappear will be the modern-day stories that can be easily filmed with live models. As with the 'tits and tentacles' genre, the anime-style games will drift into increasingly esoteric perversions in order to justify their existence. The anime remakes that they generate will continue, although with less emphasis on contemporary tales like *Classmates*, and more on the fantastic elements typified by *Timestripper*. Eventually, faced with the bolder competition of 'real' sex, multi-ending interactive games and digital porn, erotic anime is likely to return, as it continually has done and will continue to do, to cartoon territory in short, staccato compilations of seaside-postcard naughtiness, pitched at an audience just a little too young or impoverished to afford the live-action, computerised variants. ●

PLAYBOY OF THE EASTERN WORLD

U-Jin's Pictures from High School

As a representative snapshot of where the erotic anime business is today, this final chapter is a look at a work by U-Jin, an artist specialising in compilations of short erotica, both in manga and on animated video. Examples are drawn from one of the few U-Jin productions not to have yet received a Western release, the anthology collection Pictures from High School, which not only exists in manga and anime form, but also as a computer game utilising the Timestripper engine.

The roots of erotica lie in humour (sublimating embarrassment), titillation (enticing desire) and transgression (fulfilling fantasy). This book has looked at many subgenres of erotica, but the chronological treatment of their origins offered in these pages is not to suggest that any of them have quite faded away. Today, they all exist alongside each other, and while fads and trends may come and go, there will always be a market for sex of some kind. There are still erotic horror anime and there are still shonen ai titles, but in the end sex is a very human concern, and today, by far the largest category in erotic anime remains erotic comedy.

U-Jin (the pseudonym is a pun on the characters for 'asobu' ['play'] and 'hito' ['person']) is one of the most successful of the many erotic manga artists in contemporary Japan. His works are so punchy and clear that very little needs to be altered for the screen adaptation. In some cases, the only additions are brief sketches in between the stories, in which U-Jin's cartoon *alter ego* appears as a kind of Master of Ceremonies. In the best music hall tradition, he tells dirty jokes, sings lewd songs and even tries to convince the audience to join in, drawing their attention to the sing-along subtitles handily provided onscreen. The emphasis is on fun above all else; U-Jin makes no apologies for sampling the beauties of the youthful female form, but nor does he shirk from presenting the male libido as a distasteful whirlwind of lust and self-interest. U-Jin's women are all gorgeous, but his men are without exception hapless

geeks and pathetic old perverts. In this manner, he ridicules the male audience even as he provides the pornography they crave.

U-Jin achieved considerable notoriety in Japan when his comic *Angel* became the subject of a censorship campaign. The Association to Protect Children from Comics, founded by a middle-aged housewife in 1990, sought to clean up what it perceived as the invasion of pornographic material into reading matter for children. Like *Angel*, *Pictures from High School* features a large number of brief scenes (five to ten minutes on video) in the U-Jin style, ranging from naughty comedy to hardcore sex. They are worthy of a detailed discussion, not only because they are well made, but also because they cover a wide range of erotic situations and give a good overview of the state of animated pornography in Japan today.

LOVE TRAIN

In 'Luck on the Long-Distance Commute', our protagonist is a salaryman running for his early morning train. A schoolgirl falls asleep in his lap and, shielded from fellow passengers by his open newspaper, he ejaculates in her mouth. On the train back that night, he is similarly blessed when, standing up in the crush in the aisle, he finds his crotch unwittingly pressed into the face of another dozing girl. The broken zip in his trousers does its plot-advancing job and his penis flops inexorably into her open mouth. The sensual rocking of the train does the rest of the work and he eventually disembarks after a hard day at the office, remarking on his incredible fortune.

'Luck on the Long-Distance Commute' is not so much hardcore pornography as erotic musings arising from a common public situation. It shares a common philosophy with a far subtler scene in episode four of *Evangelion*, where Hideaki Anno's camera takes an original angle in a train-travel scene. He focuses on his subject between two oblivious schoolgirls, whose blouses ride up when they grasp the overhead handrail. It is a beautifully observed moment, not the least because our angst-ridden hero ignores them completely.

People are often crushed together on the train, and U-Jin's work exploits much of the erotic potential. There is even a throwaway scene in 'Luck on the Long-Distance Commute' where a girl cannot get off at her stop, and has to be passed bodily down the carriage, permitting all the other dirty old men a good feel. It is also implied subliminally that the whole thing is a dream, since when the dozing lap-girl awakes, a few frames of the anime show that her head is actually in front of, rather than behind the salaryman's open newspaper, and that therefore she could not possibly have got near his penis. In fact, the only 'fantasy' daydream in 'Luck on the Long-Distance Commute' is when the salaryman muses on the consequences of being found sexually assaulting a schoolgirl in public, as his mind plays through the monstrous headlines, loss of job and prison sentence that would await if she awoke.

FEMININE WILES

There is a far more subversive message in 'The Little Match Girl', which works as a self-referential satire on pornography itself. It features another older man, this time from the country, who has come to Tokyo to work. Bonus in hand, he sets off to do his Christmas shopping, avoiding the temptations of the red-light district and resolving to buy some nice gifts for his loving family. We see him stride down a curiously Dickensian Japanese street where, with snow falling all around, he comes across a young girl selling matches. After some wrangling, she eventually makes him an offer he can't refuse. Her matches may be expensive, but they come with a special deal. He may look at her underwear for as long as each match burns. The old man has soon purchased all her matches, and rapidly burns his way though the supply for the chance to see her in various positions and states of undress.

Eventually, he has to burn all his clothes and possessions to keep the flame alive, until he finds himself naked and alone in the big city. Having relieved him of all his money, the little match girl politely bids him farewell, leaving him to wonder how he will explain his predicament to his family. But when the girl departs, she fades away, implying that the old man has become the victim of a seasonal spirit, the Ghost of Christmas Porn.

There is more gentle lampooning of the older man's obsession with young girls in another U-Jin short, 'Sailor-Suited Akko-chan vs the Giant Dirty Old Man'. In this spirited homage to Japan's long-running monster shows, we see a suited salaryman on his way to work, who happens to be watching when the wind lifts the skirts of two passing schoolgirls. The sight of their white panties transforms him into a 200-foot tall caricature of lust, and he stomps through the crowded city blowing great rushes of air at the ground to lift their skirts again. Akko, an everyday schoolgirl who moonlights as a monster-battling superheroine, gets a call from the control centre telling her to deal with it.

By this time the salaryman is masturbating furiously in the street, and giant gobbets of acidic semen are raining down on the town. He then starts enthusiastically humping a skyscraper, his giant penis battering through interior walls, desks and surprised-looking office ladies. Akko transforms herself into a giant schoolgirl and chases after him, as she herself is pursued by a crowd of vigorously masturbating perverts, who can now see up her dress to the giant underwear concealed within. Akko is spattered with some of the acid semen, but luckily the sperm only burns through her clothes, and she is otherwise unhurt. She then reveals her genitals and invites the salaryman to place his semen in her instead of threatening the safety of the city. With the full, legendary power of a woman whose dangerous desire cannot be sated once aroused, she sucks him dry and saves the world, warning her fellow girls to be wary of dirty old men.

FOREIGN BODIES

'High School Nurse' is a much simpler tableau. A girl working part-time in a hospital has to administer an injection to a troublesome patient, who turns out to be a gigantic Afro-American body builder. But no matter how many of his clothes they remove, they cannot find an area tender enough to admit a needle. Eventually, the schoolgirl starts to strip, and the foreign visitor gets increasingly aroused (the Japanese doctor is already gleefully masturbating as he watches through a peephole). The girl then jabs the needle through the foreigner's only soft spot (the base of his penis) and her job is done. 'High School Nurse' is particularly interesting for its depiction of the foreigner, who is an inarticulate, muscle-bound idiot. Partly playful urban myth (our hugely endowed male is not only a non-Japanese, but a *black* foreigner at that) and partly the height of political incorrectness, it is the Japanese doctor who gets his rocks off while watching the Japanese schoolgirl teasing the foreigner. The foreigner is not allowed to touch her — she belongs to Japan and the Japanese.

That local women must belong to local males is a common tradition in all cultures. Local boys are welcome to have sex with Alien women for fun, but the archetypal Girls Next Door (see chapter nine) are the prime crop of the sexual harvest. So while the black character in 'High School Nurse' is drawn in a racist caricature, he is nonetheless the inheritor of a long tradition in film, which is nowhere more prevalent than in Hollywood itself. Asian women in Hollywood films are often sexual objects for American men, but the pursuit of an American woman by an Asian man is often presented as an invasion to be thwarted. With such biased film writing as inspiration, it is no wonder that 'High School Nurse' turned out the way it did.

Caricatures of foreigners also feature in 'Qi Gong Girl', in which a nubile Chinese woman, Zhen-zhen, comes to Tokyo in search of fame and fortune on television. In being just far enough away to be unknown, China is often Japan's fictional otherworld of transgression, just as Europe is to the Americans, and America is for the Europeans. When a man at the airport tells Zhen-zhen that he is the contact from the television company, she leaves with him. However, we know differently, because the man has the rolled-r's and thuggish enunciation of a stereotypical gangster. He takes her to a whorehouse, the Health Iku-Iku, where she uses her mystical Taoist powers to bring men to orgasm without even touching them. There is some wordplay on the pronunciation of her name, 'Zhen-zhen' in Japanese becomes 'chin-chin', or 'penis', but then the television company track her down and she is swiftly bundled onto a plane before she causes an international incident. The bewildered Zhen-zhen heads back to China, remarking all the while that Japanese television was not quite what she expected.

JOKES AND SLAPSTICK

'Take Me Back to My Childhood' is intriguing because it features a rare case of a female paedophile, although that itself is the not the main point of the script. Our hero is a young man hard at work on a science project, who notices some very strange goings-on outside his window. Local children meet and play in the sandpit, where they are approached by a beautiful teenage girl. She appears every day, selects one of the boys and orders him to use a stick to stimulate her clitoris through her panties.

'Take Me Back to My Childhood' has a subtext that lies in men's subconscious jealousy of the affection and closeness with women that children (even their own children) are permitted to enjoy. Or in other words, men spend all their life looking for a mother, and when they eventually marry one she turns out to be somebody else's.

Our protagonist resolves to enjoy some of this attention, and designs an ingenious bunker in the sandpit that allows him to dig himself in and impersonate a small boy, with his legs hidden under the sand. When the girl arrives for the day's fun, he tells her that he's new in the neighbourhood, and then, somewhat forwardly, inquires if she would like him to poke her with a stick. After this comedy of manners, we return to the action in question, which consists of him caressing her vagina with one hand, while secretly masturbating underground. As the two of them achieve orgasm, the jealous local children throw rocks down the sandpit's slide, knocking the teenage boy unconscious in a slapstick ending.

Another strangely perverse work comes in 'The Scariest Story', which presents a common urban myth with little erotic content at all. Three girls sit round a campfire, slurp contentedly at their curried rice and spin vaguely naughty yarns and ghost stories. Each of these is animated briefly, but these are only red herrings for the titular punchline. Eventually, the others notice that the girl called Miyuki has hardly touched her food. When they ask her to explain, she tells them that when they were off drawing water for making dinner, she was squatting upstream, engaged in a particularly troublesome bowel movement.

What makes this an U-Jin production instead of a straightforward joke is the care with which the camera shows her squatting by the water's edge, straining to squeeze out a turd, and then watching as it floats downstream towards her unsuspecting pals. Unexpectedly, it is a scatological interest in the shit itself, rather than the girl who produces it, that is supposed to provide the erotic charge of the episode. Presumably, the majority of viewers without a sexual interest in human excrement are expected merely to enjoy the story for its comedic value, such as it is.

Most of U-Jin's tales are far more down-to-earth, many in fact seeming to stem from one-line ideas, or punchlines without jokes. Witness his 'Silver Lining', which is nothing more than an elaborate, cartoon-style set-up so that a pantie-less girl can land on the penis of a masturbating boy just as he reaches orgasm. This involves a carefully storyboarded approach to deliver her down two floors and remove her knickers *en route*, just so that her rich father can be shocked and appalled when he walks in and finds her having sex with the school idiot in broad daylight.

Similar high-concept japes await in 'How to Get a Free Pizza' in which three naked girls tease a pizza delivery boy to prevent him from handing them their order on time, and 'Back on Form', in which a baseball pitcher's inability to throw straight is cured when the catcher opens her legs to reveal she is not wearing underwear. From that moment on, he throws on target every single time.

Some even verge on the border of comedy without any sexual element at all. 'Aim for the A' implies a story with anal sex as its theme, but this gentle joke contains nothing of the sort. The story is an artful parody of the seventies television anime series *Aim for the Ace!*, in which a Japanese schoolgirl studies hard to become the greatest tennis player in the world. Despite a mere five-minute running time, 'Aim for the A' manages to sneak in many of the devices that fans of the original would appreciate. The obvious tips of the hat include long, nostalgic pans across the school grounds sparkling in the sunset, the distant chimes of the school bell, the team members' breathless cries when 'Coach' arrives and his gruff insistence on unnecessarily martial exercises.

It is one of these exercises that warrants U-Jin's attention. Every day after practice, one of the girls is selected by Coach for one-on-one tuition, an element of the student-teacher relationship fraught with innuendo world-wide. This involves standing blindfolded in one spot, attempting to hit balls fired from a machine while Coach shouts encouragement from the sidelines. But

unknown to his victims, Coach's voice is really on a tape, while he is lying on the ground and staring up at their pristine white underwear. He is observed one day by an ugly girl hiding in the bushes, who eagerly volunteers for one-on-one tuition the next day. While she waits expectantly with her blindfold on, the sun slowly sets. Everyone has gone home, including the lecherous Coach.

BACK TO THE BEGINNING

In 'Come for World Peace', U-Jin takes us full circle with a homage to the father of Japanese animation, Osamu Tezuka himself. In a knowing reference to *Astro Boy*, we see a brilliant scientist slaving away in his laboratory creating the ultimate superhero. For the sake of world peace, he has created a beautiful female crimefighter, but he hasn't quite got it right yet. As he beats his fists in exasperation against the side of the cryogenic tube, he notices how prettily his creation's breasts wobble. In a flash of lust, he forgets his work and has sex with the inanimate robot, before regaining control of himself and returning to his mission.

Soon, the robot is working almost perfectly, but when it takes its first tottering steps, it trips and lands face down with its pert bottom in the air. Once again, the scientist loses control of himself, throwing himself on top of her like a pig-witted Pygmalion. Whatever the scientist's noble ideals may have been, he is finally able to admit that world peace is not so much his concern as getting laid and, in another of the swipes at pornography itself that U-Jin tried before in 'The Little Match Girl', the camera zooms in on the robot's expressionless face.

It is these dead, staring eyes that live on in the mind after the story has finished. With them, U-Jin reminds us that pornography is, by definition, the creation of the human mind for the benefit of the human ego. The creatures that inhabit the pornographic world may be pretty, but their couplings are little more than the contact of similar superficialities. Nowhere is this more true than in animated pornography, where the characters are removed a step further from reality through inhabiting two-dimensional cels, drawn by hand. It is the rare moments of acute observation or genuine sensuality that make some of these tales worthy projects for study, since this is not only what makes them erotic, but also encourages us to consider their appeal to the Japanese, and indeed to ourselves. ●

A-Z OF TITLES

An Erotic Anime Filmography

Most of the titles mentioned in the chapters (whether or not they merit the label 'erotic') and a number more besides are included in the listing. The synopsis section of each entry aims to draw attention to the reason for the title's inclusion. All titles with coverage in the chapters are cross-referenced with the relevant page numbers. Names in the listing are given Western-style, family name last, although readers are warned that many creatives use pseudonyms for their pornographic work. Japanese and variant English titles are listed in the index at the back of the book.

CATEGORIES

P	Present day
H	Historical
D	Horror
SF	Future/science fiction
F	Fantasy
C	Comedy
T	Thriller/crime

RATINGS

N	Mild nudity
NN	Lots of nudity
X	Sexually explicit
XX	Very sexually explicit
V	Violent
VV	Ultraviolent
SM	Elements of bondage
G	Gay elements

We have also included these purely arbitrary classifications:

MAINSTREAM: A work in which sex and eroticism are not important factors, although they may still appear.

EROTIC: A work in which sex has a major influence on the story.

PORN: A work in which the story has a minor influence on the sex.

801 TTS AIRBATS
(Eng title for AOZORA SHŌJOTAI, lit Blue Sky Girl Squadron)

OAV series, 3 parts
JAPANESE CREDITS: 1994-96. Dir: Yuji Moriyama, Osamu Mikasa, Junichi Sakata & Tohru Yoshida. Screenplay: Yuji Kawahara (1), Ryoei Tsukimura (2), Ryoichi Yagi (3). Chara des: Yuji Moriyama. Music: Seigo Nagaoka. © T. Shimizu, Tokuma Shoten, JVC. Each 30 mins.
WESTERN CREDITS: US video release 1995 on AD Vision, sub; UK video release 1996 on AD Vision UK, sub, Eng rewrite by Matt Greenfield. ORIGINS: Manga by Toshimitsu Shimizu, pub Tokuma Shoten. POINTS OF INTEREST: Shimizu is also the author of the much raunchier Rei Rei. SPINOFFS: A radio drama using the same voice actors. CATEGORIES: P, C, F RATINGS: N, MAINSTREAM

A charming, lushly coloured and comic take on the future of Japan's defence forces, the strides made by women in modern society and the way human beings can screw up and still come through. Contains mild comic nudity but nothing to outrage the prudish. (See pp33, 39.)

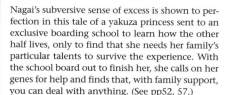

801 TTS Airbats

THE 1001 NIGHTS
(Eng trans for SENYA ICHIYA MONOGATARI)

MOVIE
JAPANESE CREDITS: 1969. Dir: Eiichi
Yamamoto. Screenplay: Kazuo Fukuzawa.
Anime dir: Sadao Miyamoto. Art dir:
Takashi Yanase. Prod: Osamu Tezuka.
Prod co: Mushi. © Mushi. 128 mins.
ORIGINS: The Arabian Nights and Osamu
Tezuka's manga based on this work.
CATEGORIES: F
RATINGS: N, EROTIC

The fantasies of the Arabian Nights are revamped for an adult audience, featuring a Sinbad who looks a bit like Jean-Paul Belmondo and plenty of exotic encounters with scantily clad houris. (See p11.)

THE ABASHIRI FAMILY
(Eng title/trans for ABASHIRI IKKA)

OAV
JAPANESE CREDITS: 1992. Dir: Takashi
Watanabe. Writer: Takashi Watanabe.
Chara des: Go Nagai. Music: Takeo
Miratsu. Prod co: Studio Pierrot.
© Dynamic Planning, Studio Pierrot,
Soeishinsha, NEXTART. 75 mins.
WESTERN CREDITS: US video release 1996
on AD Vision, sub.
ORIGINS: Manga by Go Nagai, pub Akita
Shoten.
POINTS OF INTEREST: Considered in the
UK as a release by East2West, but rejected
on account of the cheap animation and
the ethnocentric gags.
CATEGORIES: P, C, T
RATINGS: N, VV, MAINSTREAM

Lots of violence and nudity with lots of laughs.

Nagai's subversive sense of excess is shown to perfection in this tale of a yakuza princess sent to an exclusive boarding school to learn how the other half lives, only to find that she needs her family's particular talents to survive the experience. With the school board out to finish her, she calls on her genes for help and finds that, with family support, you can deal with anything. (See pp52, 57.)

AD POLICE

OAV series, 3 parts
JAPANESE CREDITS: 1990. Dir: Akihiko
Takahashi (1), Akira Nishimori (2 & 3).
Screenplay: Noboru Aikawa. Original story:
Toshimichi Suzuki & Tony Takezaki. Chara
des: Tony Takezaki, Fujio Oda & Toru
Nagasuki. Anime dir: Fujio Oda (1),
Hiroyuki Kitazume (2), Hiroyuki Kitazume
& Masami Obari (3). Planning: Toshimichi
Suzuki & Shin Unozawa. Prod co: Artmic,
AIC. © Artmic, Youmex. Each 40 mins.
WESTERN CREDITS: US video release 1993-
95 on AnimEigo, sub, dub, trans Shin
Kurokawa & Eriko Takai; UK video release
1995 on Manga Video, dub.
ORIGINS: Manga by Tony Takezaki, Eng
trans pub Viz (US), Titan Books (UK).
POINTS OF INTEREST: Set in the
Bubblegum Crisis universe.
CATEGORIES: SF, T
RATINGS: N, VV, SM, EROTIC

Three dark and ultimately misanthropic tales featuring violence, sexual perversity and exploitation wrapped up in a cyber-candy coat. Intended as an action-adventure, each story nevertheless has a strong sexual content. The first concerns the disposability of boys' toys. An android, who has been revamped for someone else's pleasure and profit, cannot rid herself of the image of the one human who made a powerful impact on her — by killing her. The second story talks sexual politics, as women have themselves adapted to fit in to the modern world. The third deals with the eroticism of control and the allure of high technology, as a police officer, all but killed in a fatal incident, is finally destroyed by becoming a cyborg. The scientist in charge of the project uses him to indulge her own warped cravings. (See pp100, 105, 111.)

ADVENTURE KID
(US title for YŌJŪ SENSEN ADVENTURE KID,
lit Demon Beast Battle Line; UK title
ADVENTURE DUO)

OAV series, 3 parts
JAPANESE CREDITS: 1992-93. Dir:
Yoshitaka Fujimoto. Screenplay: Atsushi
Yamatoya (1), Akio Satsugawa (2 & 3).
Chara des: Dan Kongoji (1), Ryunosuke
Otonashi (2), Yuji Takahashi (3).
Storyboards: Dan Kongoji & Hideki
Takayama. Music: Masamichi Amano.
Exec Prod: Hideki Takayama. Prod co: MW
Films. © T. Maeda, MW Films. Each
c40 mins.
WESTERN CREDITS: US video release 1994
on Anime 18, sub, trans Neil Nadelman;
UK video release 1994 on Kiseki Films,
same version (first 2 episodes are also
available as dubs).
ORIGINS: Manga by Toshio Maeda.
POINTS OF INTEREST: Scenarist Akio
Satsugawa went on to better things, script-
ing episodes of Neon Genesis Evangelion.
The BBFC insisted on the title change from
Adventure Kid to Adventure Duo, on the
grounds that consumers might buy the
tape thinking it was intended for children.
Adult-video actresses Ai Iijima (Midori),
Miki Mayazumi (Eganko) and Chiharu
Sato (Saiki) voice roles, but only Mayazumi
keeps up with the professional voice artists.
CATEGORIES: SF, D, C
RATINGS: XX, VV, PORN

A high school kid is hauled into a demonic adventure via his passion for computers. When an antique machine is unearthed, it triggers a nightmare scenario of rape and revenge from the days of World War Two. Our hero enters a world of raunchy demonettes and lust-crazed hellfiends with a panty fetish, who proceed to follow him back into his own reality for one of the strangest demon high school invasions of all. Listen out for Masamichi Amano's excellent music from *Overfiend* III, recycled here, as well as the *Tristan & Isolde* pastiche in part three. (See pp77-79, 81, 87, 91, 97.)

A-GIRL

OAV
JAPANESE CREDITS: 1993. Dir: Takuji
Endo. Script: Akinori Endo. Chara des:
Kazuhiro Soeda. Prod co: Madhouse.
© Nonko, Shueisha. c40 mins.
ORIGINS: Manga by Atsumi Nonko, pub
Shueisha in Margaret magazine. The
previous release in the 6-part Margaret
series was Kiss Me on the Apple of My Eye.

This is the final entry in the series.
CATEGORIES: P
RATINGS: N, MAINSTREAM

Sisters Mariko and May, and Mariko's bad-tempered boyfriend, become involved with Ichiro, a rather arrogant, womanising male model. A look at life and love in nineties Japan. (See p31.)

AIM FOR THE ACE!
(Eng trans for ACE O NERAE!)

TV series, 26 episodes
JAPANESE CREDITS: 1973. Dir: Osamu
Dezaki. Screenplay: Kazuaki Okamura et
al. Music: Akira Misawa. Prod co: Tokyo
Movie Shinsha. © Yamamoto, Takara.
Each c25 mins.
ORIGINS: Manga by Sumi Yamamoto.
POINTS OF INTEREST: Yoshiaki Kawajiri
was among the animators. The OAV series
Pictures from High School includes a brief
pornographic 'homage' to the series,
entitled 'Aim for the A'.
SPINOFFS: Another TV series, a movie and
a 6-part OAV series.
CATEGORIES: P
RATINGS: MAINSTREAM

Hiromi is determined to be a tennis champion, but while she pursues her goal, other areas of her life are neglected. Her triumphs and problems on and off court and her romantic mishaps have made this series popular in continental Europe as well as Japan. (See pp13, 27, 121.)

AKIRA

MOVIE
JAPANESE CREDITS: 1988. Dir: Katsuhiro
Otomo. Script: Katsuhiro Otomo. Chara
des: Katsuhiro Otomo. Music: Geinoh
Yamashiro Group. Prod co: Akira
Committee. © Akira Committee. 124 mins.
WESTERN CREDITS: US video release 1990
on Streamline Pictures, dub, Eng rewrite
Michael Haller; UK video release 1991 on
Island World Communications, now
Manga Video, dub, sub.
ORIGINS: Manga by Katsuhiro Otomo, pub
Kodansha in Young magazine; trans
graphic novels pub Epic (US), Mandarin (UK).
SPINOFFS: The Western anime industry?
CATEGORIES: SF
RATINGS: V, MAINSTREAM

Biker gangs fight it out in a Tokyo still devastated after World War Three, and become entangled with a project to enhance and control ESP in children. But the powers they are dealing with go far beyond any possibility of control. *Akira*'s female characters are amazons and sluts, not because of any overt misogyny on Otomo's part, but because he refuses to pander to the pretty-girl bimbo aspirations of his more commercial colleagues. Thus, for many fans, their first experience of anime sexuality was the brutal assault of Kaori by a biker gang, an implied rape with the rare, honest aftermath of a bruised, traumatised victim. (See pp58, 82, 86, 87.)

AKKO-CHAN'S SECRET
(Eng title for HIMITSU NO AKKO-CHAN, lit Secret Akko-Chan)

TV series, 94 episodes
JAPANESE CREDITS: 1969. Original story: Fujio Akatsuka. Prod co: Fujio Production. © Fujio Production, Toei Doga. Each c25 mins.
CATEGORIES: F, P
RATINGS: MAINSTREAM

Another stage in the growth of the magical girl genre. Akko is an ordinary little girl living in Tokyo. Then a spirit gives her a magic mirror, which can help the owner transform into any person or animal at will. With all this power at her disposal, Akko uses it to solve the everyday problems of her schoolfriends. Warm, gentle and sweet. (See p24.)

ANDROMEDA STORIES

TV MOVIE
JAPANESE CREDITS: 1982. Dir: Masamitsu Sasaki. Original story: Ryu Mitsuse & Keiko Takemiya. Music: Yuji Ono. Prod co: Toei. © Takemiya, Toei. 120 mins.
ORIGINS: Manga by Keiko Takemiya.
CATEGORIES: SF
RATINGS: N, MAINSTREAM

A living computer from outer space disrupts the lives of the inhabitants of planet Altair in its attempts to create a machine world. The young queen, Lilia, and her son flee with the help of a small band of survivors, including an android warrior from another world destroyed by the same entity. Their adventures will lead to the beginning of life on another planet — Earth. This contains some nudity, which would raise eyebrows on

Western prime time television. (See p14.)

ANGEL OF DARKNESS

OAV series, 3 parts
JAPANESE CREDITS: 1990-91. Dir: Kazuma Muraki (1), Suzunari Joban (2 & 3). Original Story: Ran Kotaro. Story: Yukihiro Kusaka. Supervision: Yukihiro Kusaka. Chara des: Kazunori Iwakura (1), Yuji Ikeda (2 & 3). Art dir: Kazunori Iwakura (1), Yuji Ikeda (2 & 3). Exec prod: Ran Kotaro. Prod: Jiro Soka. Prod co: Pink Pineapple. © Pink Pineapple. Each 50 mins. WESTERN CREDITS: US video release 1995-96 on SoftCel Pictures, sub trans Toru Iwakami & Doc Issaac.
POINTS OF INTEREST: 'Edited' versions of the US release have 5 mins cut.
CATEGORIES: P, F
RATINGS: NN, XX, VV, SM, G, PORN

Lesbian schoolgirls, cannibal trolls, small but perfectly formed elves and, of course, multi-tentacled demons in a 'story' which sometimes plays like a catalogue for designer bondage gear and sometimes like a St Trinians movie cross-dressing as *Little Shop of Horrors*. Part one has a pair of schoolgirl lovers fighting the forces of evil, which (like most forces of evil in erotic anime) feed on the 'emanations' of schoolgirls. A perverted professor and his S&M mistress are in cahoots with a demon-fiend, which is luring innocent girls with unusual wardrobes into its lair so it can feed. The elves, obviously, are outraged at this perversion of the forces of nature. Part two has the professor rearing demonic plants which need the 'bodily fluids' of schoolgirls to survive. In part three, a young woman who has escaped the horror decides to turn her experience to some use when she is abused by a girl gang, and lures them into the professor's murky hideout where, yes, you've guessed it, demons feed on whatever they're calling it these days.

A-PLUS FOR THE FASHION BOY
(Eng title for O-SHARAKU KOSO WA HANA MARU, lit Full Marks for Mr Fashion Victim)

OAV
JAPANESE CREDITS: 1993. Dir: Takuji Endo. Script: Akinori Endo. Chara des: Kazuhiro Soeda. Prod co: Madhouse. © Kuramochi, Shueisha. c40 mins.
ORIGINS: Manga by Fusako Kuramochi,

pub Shueisha in Margaret magazine.
First of a 6-part video series named for the
magazine in which the manga appeared.
SPINOFFS: Singles came next.
CATEGORIES: P
RATINGS: N, MAINSTREAM

Hodaka is a successful young businessman. He owns his own boutique and he's only twenty-three. Then his life is turned upside down when he falls in love. The problem is, she's still at school. In fact, she's only just fourteen.

APPLESEED

OAV
JAPANESE CREDITS: 1988. Dir: Kazuyoshi
Katayama. Screenplay: Kazuyoshi
Katayama. Chara des: Yumiko
Horasawa. Mecha des: Kiyomi Tanaka.
Anime dir: Yumiko Horasawa. Art dir:
Hiroaki Ogura. Music: Norimasa
Yamanaka. Prod co: Gainax. © Shirow,
Soeishinsha, AIC, Bandai. 70 mins.
WESTERN CREDITS: US & UK video
release 1994 on Manga Video, dub, Eng
rewrite John Wolskel; US video release
1994 on US Renditions, sub.
ORIGINS: Manga by Masamune Shirow.
CATEGORIES: SF
RATINGS: V, MAINSTREAM

Armitage III

The dark side of a Utopian future world is exposed in this story of a young cop's involvement with a terrorist group. Less complex and engaging than the manga on which it is based, the story plays down the love relationship between cyborg Briareos and female soldier Deunan, a complex pairing involving the shared history of a life as guerillas and both their memories of her father. The main love interest, the cop's relationship with his dead wife, provides the motive for the action through her suicide which happens before the story opens. As the young man tries to avenge himself on the uncaring, increasingly mechanised society which drove her to her death, we are asked to question our own increasing dependence on technology. (See pp88, 100.)

ARION

MOVIE
JAPANESE CREDITS: 1986. Dir: Yoshikazu
Yasuhiko. Writer: Yoshikazu Yasuhiko &
Akiko Tanaka. Chara des: Yoshikazu
Yasuhiko. Music: Jo Hisaishi. Prod co:
Tokyo Movie Shinsha. © Yasuhiko, TMS,
Nippon Sunrise. 120 mins.
ORIGINS: Greek myth; manga by
Yoshikazu Yasuhiko, pub Tokuma Shoten.
POINTS OF INTEREST: Note the
magnificent score by Hisaishi, better
known in the West as composer on the
films of Hayao Miyazaki.
CATEGORIES: F
RATINGS: XX, V, SM, EROTIC

I call a story whose climax takes place inside a womb erotic, whatever the author's original intention. This dazzling oriental twist on Greek myth is a film of great power and its simmering undercurrents of sex and violence have visceral impact, even though they break the surface only occasionally. (See pp29-30.)

ARMITAGE III

OAV series, 4 parts
JAPANESE CREDITS: 1994-95. Dir: Takuya
Sato. General dir: Hiroyuki Ochi.
Screenplay: Akinori Endo (1), Chiaki
Konaka (1-4). Chara des: Hiroyuki Ochi.
Opening animation dir: Hiroyuki
Kitazume. Anime dir: Kunihiro Abe (1, 3
& 4), Koichi Hashimoto (2), Shinya
Takahashi (3), Naoyuki Onda (3),

Hiroyuki Ochi (4). Art dir: Norihiro Hiraki (1 & 2), Tokuhiro Hiragi (3), Hiroshi Kato (4). Music: Hiroyuki Namba. Exec prod: Taro Maki. Prod co: AIC. © Pioneer, AIC. Part 1 50 mins, parts 2-4 each 30 mins.
WESTERN CREDITS: US video release 1995-96 on Pioneer LDCA, sub, dub, Eng rewrite Mary Mason & Quint Lancaster; UK video release 1996 on Pioneer Anime, dub only.
POINTS OF INTEREST: A movie version, combining edited episodes with approximately 5 mins of new footage (mainly the finalé), was released as Armitage III Polymatrix. Its voice cast included Elizabeth Berkley of Showgirls (Armitage) and Kiefer Sutherland (Ross). A new sound effects track was engineered in Hollywood for the movie version.
SPINOFFS: The manga seems based on an earlier version of the script, with baddy D'anclaude renamed Madonna, and a strange early scene in which Armitage is mounted by an amorous dog.
CATEGORIES: SF, T
RATINGS: N, X, VV, MAINSTREAM

Another dark future is the setting for this violent but thoughtful drama. The central theme — our attitude to our toys — is underlined with glimpses of sex-slave robots and a human/robot sexual relationship which finally takes the integration of man and his creations a stage further. The violence is considerable, but there's more erotic teasing than sexual action, except for one non-explicit scene where Armitage gets it together with her cop partner. (See pp86, 105, 110-111.)

BATTLE OF THE PLANETS
(Eng title for KAGAKU NINJATAI GATCHAMAN, lit Science Ninja Team Gatchaman)

TV series, 105 episodes
JAPANESE CREDITS: 1972-74. Dir: Nagayuki Toriumi & Hiroshi Sasagawa. Original story: Tatsuo Yoshida. Screenplay: Jinzo Toriumi, Akiyoshi Sakai, Satoshi Sueyama et al. Chara des: Tatsuo Yoshida. Music: Bob Sakuma. Prod: Ippei Kuri. Prod co: Tatsunoko. © Tatsunoko. Each c25 mins.
WESTERN CREDITS: US TV syndication 1978-79 dub, Eng rewrite Jameson Brewer

& Alan Dinehart III. Patchy UK video release on some defunct childrens' labels. The 1995 video series is also available in the US.
SPINOFFS: 2 further TV series, totalling a further 100 episodes, and a 4-part video series made in 1995.
CATEGORIES: SF
RATINGS: V, MAINSTREAM

A magnificent and often unintentionally comic take on the sentai (team) show concept, Battle of the Planets took five disparate youngsters and entrusted them with the awesome responsibility of defending the planet from alien invaders. Helped by high technology weapons and craft, and guided by a fatherly scientist mentor, they still had to face their own demons and sort out their own difficulties in order to defend the planet effectively. The villains managed to be both silly and threatening, and the leader of the attack forces wasn't gender-confused so much as gender-merged, an amalgam of male and female, welding together the characteristics of both — though in the Western translation they were presented as brother and sister to save frightening the kiddies. Bad boy Joe (aka Jason in the West) provided a brooding sexual charge for the female fans, while Jun (aka Princess) flashed her knickers with every breathtaking leap through the air, doing the same for little boys. There was also the constant puzzle as to whether Jun would end up with Mr Nice Guy Ken (aka Mark) or go off with dangerous-but-exciting Joe. The series was the first exposure to anime for many fans who didn't even know it was Japanese. (See pp13, 40, 41, 82, 94, 108.)

BODY JACK

OAV
JAPANESE CREDITS: 1987. Dir: 'Dojiro'. Screenplay: Takashi Tanigawa. Chara des: To Moriyama. Prod co: Bandai Visual. © Ross. 35 mins.
CATEGORIES: P, F
RATINGS: XX, NN, G, PORN

Weird science as Dr Toyama takes control of the body of beautiful high school girl Komaba with his strange invention. He lets the randy young Asagedani 'slip into' her body so he can see how it really feels to be inside a girl. Then Komaba's classmate, the equally beautiful Nakano, surprises him and mistakes his activities for a sexual advance from her friend. They proceed to

Countdown

demonstrate that three into two will go, whatever the laws of mathematics say.

BOUNTY DOG

OAV series, 2 parts
JAPANESE CREDITS: 1995. Dir: Hiroshi
Negishi. Original story: Takehiko Ito.
Script: Mayori Sekijima. Chara des:
Hirotoshi Sano. Anime dir: Hirotoshi
Sano. Art dir: Tadashi Kudo. Music dir:
Sho Goto. Prod co: Zero-G Room.
© Zero-G Room, Starchild, Toho.
Each 30 mins.
WESTERN CREDITS: US & UK video release
1996 on Manga Video, dub.
ORIGINS: 2 CD drama discs in 1994.
CATEGORIES: SF
RATINGS: MAINSTREAM

Three investigators check out a military project on the moon and learn that it's really an alien base full of beautiful cloned women. One of the women is already rather well known to one of the investigators, as they used to have a relationship, but Yoshiyuki is completely unaware of the horror awaiting him and his colleagues on the moon. Unfortunately, Yoshiyuki doesn't know that his ex-girlfriend is a clone, and that there's an entire army of them on the alien base who don't share their sister's warm feelings towards human males. Can the inves-

tigation team defeat an army of aliens bent on their destruction? (See p110.)

BRONZE: DESPERATE LOVE SINCE 1989
(Eng trans for BRONZE ZETSUAI SINCE 1989)

OAV
JAPANESE CREDITS: 1996. Dir: Kazuo
Yamazaki & Yoshiro Kawasaki. Prod co:
Shueisha. © Ozaki, Shueisha. 45 mins.
ORIGINS: Manga by Minami Ozaki, 1992
OAV Desperate Love 1989.
CATEGORIES: P
RATINGS: N, V, G, EROTIC

The love affair between Izumo and Koji seems doomed. Koji's father dies and his elder brother seems intent on breaking up the couple. Izumi has the chance to go to Italy and take his footballing career to a new level; the two of them would face terrible difficulties living as a gay couple. But they both learn that they can't give each other up so easily, whatever the consequences. (See pp34, 36.)

CANDY CANDY

TV series, 115 episodes
JAPANESE CREDITS: 1976-79. Dir: Hiroshi
Shidara. Prod co: Toei. © TV Asahi, Toei.
Each c25 mins.
ORIGINS: Manga by Kyoko Mizuki &
Yumiko Igarashi.
CATEGORIES: P
RATINGS: MAINSTREAM

This epic soap opera is one of the major influences on the development of shojo anime and contains many of its vital elements, including the cheerful and good-hearted orphan heroine encountering many hardships, the 'exotic' foreign backgrounds and the paramount importance of childhood friends. Set in a Japanese dream of Europe, it remains popular in France and Italy where the original manga still sells and the television series is occasionally rescreened. (See pp27-28.)

CLEOPATRA
(aka CLEOPATRA QUEEN OF SEX)

MOVIE
JAPANESE CREDITS: 1970. Dir: Eiichi
Yamamoto. Screenplay: Shigeru

Satoyoshi. Prod: Osamu Tezuka. Prod co: Mushi. © Tezuka Production. 113 mins. WESTERN CREDITS: US theatrical release 1971, dub, as Cleopatra Queen of Sex. ORIGINS: Manga by Osamu Tezuka. POINTS OF INTEREST: The US release was the first animated film ever to receive an X certificate. Future directors Gisaburo Sugii and Yoshiaki Kawajiri were among the animators.
CATEGORIES: H, SF
RATINGS: N, EROTIC

The renowned Queen of the Nile is visited by time travellers from a future Earth in danger of alien invasion. Can her fabled charms work their magic on an alien commander from the far future? The woman who seduced Caesar and Mark Anthony (but failed with Octavian, perhaps because she wasn't really trying) sets out to make a lasting impression on a man from another planet. Sex, nudity, drama and humour are all handled with intelligence and skill. (See p11.)

COUNTDOWN
(Eng title for YÛWAKU COUNTDOWN, lit Temptation Countdown)

OAV series, 4 parts
JAPANESE CREDITS: 1995-96. Dir: Shoichi Masuo & Naohito Takahashi. Chara des: Sanae Chikanaga. Prod co: Pink Pineapple. © H. Utatane, Fujimi Shuppan, Akane Shinsha, Pink Pineapple. Each 35 mins. WESTERN CREDITS: US video release 1995-96 on SoftCel Pictures, sub, trans Doc Issaac.
ORIGINS: Manga by Hiroyuki Utatane, pub US by Eros Comics.
POINTS OF INTEREST: Edited US versions of all 4 OAVs exist, each 5 mins shorter.
CATEGORIES: P, F
RATINGS: XX, NN, SM, G, PORN

Erotic short stories parodying various anime and manga staples. A modern day subway encounter leads to erotic confusion. A sword-swinging macho man meets his match in a girl who can tie anything down. A bride has a last-minute fling before taking that walk to the altar — in fact, right in the vestry, with her groom and her guests waiting in the pews! A policewoman has to deal with a giant statue controlled by a sex-mad megalomaniac, with only her own sex-maniac robot to help out. This latter story features one of the few scenes of gay male sex in non shonen ai anime. (See p98.)

CREAM LEMON 1 BE MY BABY
(Eng title for CREAM LEMON SERIES PART I BI MAI BABY, lit Flirting Younger Sister Baby. The English pun is quite deliberate.)

OAV
JAPANESE CREDITS: 1984. Prod co: Soeishinsha. © Soeishinsha, Fairy Dust. 25 mins.
POINTS OF INTEREST: The first in the long-running series and the first adventure of its most successful character, Ami.
SPINOFFS: Ami's story continued in Cream Lemon 5.
CATEGORIES: P
RATINGS: XX, NN, PORN

Ami and Hiroshi, brother and sister, have feelings for each other that no siblings should. When their stepmother goes away on business, they are left alone in the house and can explore those feelings. So they do. And Mum isn't happy when she finds out. (See pp43-44.)

CREAM LEMON 2 ESCALATION
(Eng title for ESCALATION KONYA WA HARD CORE, lit Escalation: Tonight It's Hard Core)

OAV
JAPANESE CREDITS: 1984. Prod co: Soeishinsha. © Soeishinsha, Fairy Dust. 25 mins.
SPINOFFS: 2 further episodes for this storyline, in Cream Lemon 6 & 16.
CATEGORIES: P
RATINGS: XX, NN, SM, G, PORN

Rie is in bed with her piano teacher when they are surprised by her mother. Exit Rie for a strict Catholic girls' school. Mari is her roommate, but as she settles in, Rie develops a crush on senior girl Naomi. When Naomi invites Rie to room with her, she's flattered, but then she finds that her gloomy, withdrawn classmate Midori is to join them. Naomi draws the two younger girls into an intense relationship based on bondage and domination. So much for Catholic schools. (See p44.)

CREAM LEMON 3 SUPERDIMENSIONAL SF LEGEND RALL
(Eng trans for CREAM LEMON: SF CHÔJIGEN DENSETSU RALL)

OAV

JAPANESE CREDITS: 1984. Prod co: Fairy Dust. © Soeishinsha. 25 mins.
POINTS OF INTEREST: Absolutely no censorship in this episode.
SPINOFFS: A second Rall adventure was released (Cream Lemon 15).
CATEGORIES: SF, F
RATINGS: NN, V, PORN

An evil overlord sets out to conquer the universe. The only thing in his way is a half-dressed warrior maid armed with a legendary sword. Parody of all the worst clichés in fantasy. (See pp44-45.)

CREAM LEMON 4 POP CHASER
(Eng title for CREAM LEMON: POP CHASER)

OAV
JAPANESE CREDITS: 1985. Dir: Yuji Motoyama. Chara des: Yuji Motoyama. Art dir: Yuji Motoyama. Prod co: Fairy Dust. © Soeishinsha. 25 mins.
POINTS OF INTEREST: The director/ designer is Yuji Moriyama of Project A-Ko fame, working under a pseudonym.
CATEGORIES: SF
RATINGS: NN, XX, V, G, PORN

Lesbian sex, group sex and sex in the pilot seat of a mobile suit all feature in this sci-fi spoof Western with more than a trace of *Battle Beyond the Stars* in both its story and its general air of cheerful cheesiness. The relationship of tough girl Rio and ditzy Mai is considered by many to mirror that of A-Ko and C-Ko in *Project A-Ko* (and it's true that we don't see A-Ko and C-Ko's first meeting in the original movie and OAVs…). Great fun. (See p45.)

CREAM LEMON 5 AMI AGAIN
(Eng title for CREAM LEMON: AMI AGAIN)

OAV
JAPANESE CREDITS: 1985. Prod co: Fairy Dust. © Soeishinsha. 25 mins.
ORIGINS: A sequel to the first Cream Lemon OAV.
SPINOFFS: Ami returned in Cream Lemon 13.
CATEGORIES: P
RATINGS: NN, XX, PORN

Ami is devastated when her stepmother sends her brother Hiroshi to London, ending their incestuous affair. Her friends try to cheer her up with a night out, but unfortunately she gets completely drunk and falls into bed dreaming that she's spending a wild night with Hiroshi once again. She wakes up next morning to find it was no dream, but her partner isn't Hiroshi… (See p45.)

CREAM LEMON 6 ESCALATION 2: FORBIDDEN SONATA
(Eng trans for CREAM LEMON: ESCALATION 2 KINDAN NO SONATA)

OAV
JAPANESE CREDITS: 1985. Prod co: Fairy Dust. © Soeishinsha. 25 mins.
ORIGINS: A sequel to the second Cream Lemon OAV.
SPINOFFS: The story continued in Cream Lemon 16.
CATEGORIES: P
RATINGS: NN, XX, SM, G, PORN

It's only when you leave school that you realise how much you miss your friends and the daft games you used to play together. Senior student and bondage queen Naomi has now graduated from her Catholic boarding school. She invites her old room-mates Rie and Midori, now seniors themselves, to her mansion for the weekend. They arrive to find that they are not the only guests, and that even though Naomi has joined the grown-up world, she doesn't intend to give up all her old hobbies. (See p45.)

CREAM LEMON 7 DON'T DO IT, MAKO! MAKO SEXY SYMPHONY PART ONE
(Eng trans for CREAM LEMON: IKENAI MAKOCHAN — MAKO SEXY SYMPHONY ZEMPEN)

OAV
JAPANESE CREDITS: 1985. Dir: Toshihiro Hirano. Chara des: Toshihiro Hirano. Art dir: Toshihiro Hirano. Prod co: Fairy Dust. © Soeishinsha. 25 mins.
POINTS OF INTEREST: Hirano is the director responsible for such atmospheric chillers as Iczer-1 and Vampire Princess Miyu.
SPINOFFS: Mako's story continued in Cream Lemon 12.
CATEGORIES: P, F
RATINGS: NN, XX, G, PORN

Sixteen year-old Mako can't bear the thought of sex or any form of physical contact. She won't even contemplate wearing a short skirt, and does all she can to get out of school swimming classes. Obviously this isn't helping Yu, a love-struck classmate who is trying to get to know her better. But then a beautiful, ethereal girl shows up. Is she some kind of demon or vampire, or is it just that Mako's own feelings, repressed since childhood, have taken on physical form in a desperate effort to break free? (See pp45-46.)

CREAM LEMON 8 SUPER VIRGIN
(Eng title for CREAM LEMON: SUPER VIRGIN)
OAV

JAPANESE CREDITS: 1985. Prod co: Fairy Dust. © Soeishinsha. 25 mins.
CATEGORIES: P
RATINGS: NN, XX, PORN

A different leading lady named Mako with a very different agenda this time, in a tale of high school lechery and girl power. The Super Virgin Group is a psychic girl gang whose aim is to keep the boys in line. When one of their number falls in love and starts to see that male lust has its positive side, the scene is set for gang war. (See p46.)

CREAM LEMON 9 HAPPENING SUMMER
(Eng title for CREAM LEMON: HAPPENING SUMMER)

OAV
JAPANESE CREDITS: 1985. Dir: Ayako Mibashi. Chara des: Ayako Mibashi. Prod co: Fairy Dust. © Soeishinsha. 25 mins.
CATEGORIES: P
RATINGS: NN, XX, PORN

At the start of the summer holidays, teenage girls plan their boy-hunting strategy. Yuki already has a guy who fancies her, Koji, but he is around her own age, clumsy, without much to recommend him — a real geek. She dreams of a much more sophisticated man, her older sister Keiko's boyfriend, Akira. Akira turns out to be not quite the dream lover she imagines, but of course she has to go a long way to find out. (See p46.)

CREAM LEMON 10 STAR TRAP
(Eng title for CREAM LEMON: STAR TRAP)

OAV

JAPANESE CREDITS: 1985. Prod co: Fairy Dust. © Soeishinsha. 25 mins.
ORIGINS: A parody of Star Trek and Japanese SF TV shows.
CATEGORIES: SF, C
RATINGS: NN, XX, G, PORN

Dyke defenders of the galaxy Kanaka and Lan are off to investigate the disappearance of several ships in a distant quadrant. Lan is superstrong, Kanaka is a shapeshifter, and both are completely nuts. All resemblances to the *Dirty Pair* are probably intentional, and look out also for the many other film and television references. (See p46.)

CREAM LEMON 11 BLACK CAT MANOR
(Eng trans for CREAM LEMON: KURONEKOKAN)

OAV
JAPANESE CREDITS: 1986. Prod co: Fairy Dust. © Soeishinsha. 25 mins.
WESTERN CREDITS: Edited for US release by Excalibur Films as part of Pandora: An Erotic Trilogy.
CATEGORIES: H
RATINGS: NN, XX, PORN

Student Masaki Murakami heads out of Tokyo seeking refuge from the bombings in the winter of 1941. In the mountains he finds a strange old house, empty but for the widowed mistress Saiko, her daughter Arisa and their maid Aya. The strange atmosphere of the old house makes Masaki feel uneasy, but that does not stop him embarking on an affair with Saiko. (See p46.)

CREAM LEMON 12 DON'T DO IT, MAKO! MAKO SEXY SYMPHONY PART TWO
(Eng trans for CREAM LEMON: IKENAI MAKOCHAN — MAKO SEXY SYMPHONY KŌHEN)

OAV
JAPANESE CREDITS: 1986. Dir: Toshihiro Hirano. Chara des: Toshihiro Hirano. Art dir: Toshihiro Hirano. Prod co: Fairy Dust. © Soeishinsha. 25 mins.
ORIGINS: A sequel to Cream Lemon 7.
CATEGORIES: P, F
RATINGS: NN, XX, G, PORN

Mako has changed. She has gained confidence and will spend time with her classmate Yu, but she still hates to be touched, which isn't helping him get the romance going. Then the strange girl who seemed to change Mako's attitude comes to see Yu and tells him that two entities are fighting for control of Mako's body and mind. Unless she can balance her sexual attitudes, one or other of them will possess her soul and all hope for a happy, normal relationship for Mako and Yu will be gone. Now it's up to him. (See p46.)

CREAM LEMON 13 AMI 3: NOW I EMBRACE YOU AMI
(Eng trans for CREAM LEMON: AMI III IMA YORETE AMI)

OAV
JAPANESE CREDITS: 1986. Prod co: Fairy Dust. © Soeishinsha. 25 mins.
ORIGINS: Follows on from Cream Lemon 5.
SPINOFFS: Ami's story continued in Cream Lemon: Ami's Journey.
CATEGORIES: P
RATINGS: NN, XX, PORN

Big brother Hiroshi comes back from London for a few days and arranges to meet Ami, but all he wants is to end the relationship, telling her that it will only damage both of them since the world can't accept an incestuous love. To try and forget her brother, Ami calls the guy she met in her drunken fling at the disco. (See pp44, 46.)

CREAM LEMON 14 NARIS SCRAMBLE
(Eng trans for CREAM LEMON: NARISU SCRAMBLE)

OAV
JAPANESE CREDITS: 1986. Dir: Ayako Mibashi. Chara des: Ayako Mibashi. Art dir: Ayako Mibashi. Prod co: Fairy Dust. © Soeishinsha. 25 mins.
CATEGORIES: F, C
RATINGS: NN, XX, V, PORN

A superdeformed heroine in battle armour and a giant mecha piloted by three wannabe Nazi lesbians slug it out for control of a local high school, parodying not only other anime but many of *Cream Lemon*'s own clichés along the way. (See p46.)

CREAM LEMON 15 SUPERDIMENSIONAL SF LEGEND RALL 2
(Eng title for CREAM LEMON: SF CHŌJIGEN DENSETSU RALL II — LAMO RU NO GYAKUSHŪ, lit Cream Lemon SF Superdimensional Legend Rall 2 — Lamo Ru's Counterattack)

OAV
JAPANESE CREDITS: 1986. Chara des: Nekoda Nyan. Prod co: Fairy Dust. © Soeishinsha. 25 mins.
ORIGINS: Sequel to Cream Lemon 3.
CATEGORIES: F
RATINGS: NN, XX, VV, PORN

The evil demon lord is still up to his old tricks, and it's not just the galaxy he wants to conquer — no female is safe from his wandering attentions. Carol takes up the magic blade of Rivers and gets on with the story, which has quickly moved from being a parody of the tired stereotypes of fantasy to being a tired stereotype of fantasy itself. (See p47.)

CREAM LEMON 16 ESCALATION 3: ANGELS' EPILOGUE
(Eng trans for CREAM LEMON: ESCALATION 3: TENSHITACHI NO EPILOGUE)

OAV
JAPANESE CREDITS: 1986. Prod co: Fairy Dust. © Soeishinsha. 25 mins.
ORIGINS: Sequel to Cream Lemon 6.
CATEGORIES: P
RATINGS: NN, XX, SM, G, PORN

Tying up the first series, the story resumes as Rie, Mari and Midori are about to graduate from their high school. The girls are invited once again to Naomi's mansion for a party, and they initiate Rie's young friend Arisa and other junior girls into the same lesbian bondage pleasures Naomi introduced them to two years earlier. (See p47.)

CREAM LEMON: AMI'S JOURNEY
(Eng title for CREAM LEMON: TABITACHI AMI SHŪSHŌ, lit Cream Lemon: Ami's Journey, Final Chapter)

MOVIE
JAPANESE CREDITS: 1986. Dir: Bikkuri Hako. Prod co: Fairy Dust. © Soeishinsha,

APPP. 90 mins.
ORIGINS: Follows on from Cream
Lemon 13.
SPINOFFS: Cream Lemon Special Ami
Image White Shadow followed.
CATEGORIES: P
RATINGS: NN, XX, PORN

Cut off from her beloved brother Hiroshi, Ami's friends try to take her mind off the separation by going on a birthday trip to Hokkaido. It cheers her up a little bit, but Ami is shocked to discover on her return home that her father and stepmother have divorced... (See pp44, 50.)

CREAM LEMON CLIMAX
(Eng title for CREAM LEMON CLIMAX ZENSHŪ, lit Cream Lemon Climax Compilation)

OAV series, 5 volumes
JAPANESE CREDITS: 1988. Prod co: Fairy
Dust. © Soeishinsha. Each 50 mins.
ORIGINS: Compiled from episodes of the
popular Cream Lemon OAV series.
CATEGORIES: P, SF, D, C
RATINGS: NN, XX, PORN

Compilation tapes of the series.

CREAM LEMON KEI AMAKI SPECIAL: CHERRY MELANCHOLY
(Eng trans for CREAM LEMON KEI AMAKI SPECIAL: CHERRY NO YŪTSU)

OAV
JAPANESE CREDITS: 1989. Prod co: Fairy
Dust. © Amaki, Fairy Dust, Pony Canon.
40 mins.
ORIGINS: Manga by Kei Amaki.
CATEGORIES: P
RATINGS: NN, X, PORN

Young girls desperate for a man bump into each other on the street and decide to improvise.

CREAM LEMON SPECIAL — AMI GRAFFITI
(Eng title for CREAM LEMON AMI SŌSHŪHEN: AMI SEISHUN GRAFFITI, lit Cream Lemon Ami Compilation: Ami Youth Graffiti)

OAV
JAPANESE CREDITS: 1986. Prod co: Fairy

Dust. © Soeishinsha. 80 mins.
ORIGINS: Compiled from the Ami
episodes of the popular Cream Lemon
OAV series.
CATEGORIES: P
RATINGS: NN, XX, PORN

If you couldn't afford all of Ami's adventures, this tape compiles the lot (up to 1986), including some of the naughty bits.

CREAM LEMON SPECIAL AMI IMAGE WHITE SHADOW
(Eng trans for CREAM LEMON AMI IMAGE SHIROI KAGE)

OAV
JAPANESE CREDITS: 1986. Dir: Bikkuri
Hako. Chara des: Yuko Kurata. Prod co:
Fairy Dust. © Soeishinsha. 30 mins.
ORIGINS: Follows on from Cream Lemon:
Ami's Journey.
SPINOFFS: The mini series New Cream
Lemon Ami — From Then On followed.
CATEGORIES: P
RATINGS: N, X, PORN

Left alone in a cruel world, Ami embarks on a career as an idol singer. Set before *Ami — From Then On*, this episode takes Ami on a trip to London for a secret meeting with Hiroshi. (See p50.)

CREAM LEMON SPECIAL — THE DARK
(Eng title for CREAM LEMON SPECIAL DARK)

OAV
JAPANESE CREDITS: 1987. Original story:
Nicholas Lloyd. Chara des: Mako Nitta.
Prod co: Fairy Dust. © Soeishinsha. 47 mins.
WESTERN CREDITS: Edited for US release
by Excalibur Films as part of Pandora: An
Erotic Trilogy.
CATEGORIES: D
RATINGS: NN, XX, VV, PORN

Two young men, one a priest, seek shelter in a castle in the middle of a dark, dense forest. The lady of the castle offers hospitality, but during the night she seduces and kills the priest. Using tricks from Western horror films and stories, this is a modern version of an old oriental horror story. Christian priests taste just as good as Buddhist ones, it seems. (See p46.)

CREAM LEMON TO MORIYAMA BEST HIT: 'I GUESS SO'
(Eng trans for CREAM LEMON TÖ MORIYAMA BEST HIT: 'SÖ KA MOSHINNAI')

OAV
JAPANESE CREDITS: 1989. Dir: To Moriyama. Chara des: To Moriyama. Prod co: Fairy Dust. © Soeishinsha. 35 mins.
CATEGORIES: P
RATINGS: NN, XX, PORN

A young boy finds a gun while out walking in a park one night, and uses it to coerce a girl on the train into giving him a blow job. This OAV also features public confessions, under-the-table masturbation scenes in a coffee house and some nasty uses for the casting couch at a television station. (See p48.)

CREAM LEMON YOUNG LOVE: ANGIE & ROSE
(Eng title for CREAM LEMON AOI SEI ANGIE & ROSE, complex pun on 'aoi': blue-pornographic, green-verdant, green-fresh/young, and 'sei/saga': sex/custom/nature.)

OAV

Crying Freeman

JAPANESE CREDITS: 1992. Chara des: Mon-Mon. Prod: Kazuya Miyazaki. Prod co: Studio Soft. © Fairy Dust, Studio Soft, Japan Home Video. 30 mins.
POINTS OF INTEREST: There is an astronomical number of possible translations for this title; we have plumped for the bland option above for alphabetical and chronological reasons. As part of the marketing for Angie & Rose, Fairy Dust offered 3 phonelines at 100 yen a minute: 'Dear Ami', 'Cream Lemon Theatre' and 'Lemon Confessions'.
CATEGORIES: P
RATING: N, PORN

When he accepts his uncle's offer of a summer job, a Japanese boy spends a hot summer in the sensual maelstrom that is Canada, witness to the adventures of his blonde aunt, the experienced Rose, and her eldest daughter, the sultry rebel Angie. Somehow out of place in the nineties, this spinoff seems created more as a bonus item for the laserdisc retrospective than as a genuine attempt to jump-start the series. (See pp50-51.)

CREAMY MAMI
(Eng title for MAHÖ NO TENSHI CREAMY MAMI, lit Magic Angel Creamy Mami)

TV series, 52 episodes
JAPANESE CREDITS: 1983-86. Dir: Osamu Kobayashi. Chara des: Akemi Takada. Prod co: Studio Pierrot. © Studio Pierrot, NTV. Each c25 mins.
ORIGINS: Manga by Yuko Kitagawa & Kazunori Ito.
POINTS OF INTERESTS: One of Japan's greatest screenwriters, Patlabor's Ito, is paired here with ex-wife-to-be Takada.
SPINOFFS: OAV and movie.
CATEGORIES: P, F
RATINGS: MAINSTREAM

Naughty imp Pino Pino gives Yu a magical baton with which she can, for one year only, transform herself into Creamy Mami, idol singer and magical being. Her parents and her oldest friend Toshio don't seem to notice this double identity, even though they are all huge fans of Mami. When Toshio actually sees her transform part-way through the story she loses her magic powers, and the friends go on a quest to recover them. They succeed, and Creamy comes back to her fans, but Toshio loses his memory. Not until the end of the series and Creamy's last big concert does he regain his memory and Yu finally lose Creamy's magical powers. (See pp24-25, 50.)

CRYING FREEMAN

OAV series, 5 parts
JAPANESE CREDITS: 1988-92. Dir:
Daisuke Nishio (1), Nobutaka Nishizawa
(2), Johei Matsuura (3), Shigeyasu
Yamauchi (4), Takaaki Yamashita (5).
Screenplay: Higashi Shimizu (1, 3 & 4),
Ryunosuke Ono (2 & 5). Anime dir: Koichi
Arai. Art dir: Masahiro Sato &
Mitsu Nakamura. Music: Hiroaki
Yoshino. Prod co: Toei. © Toei Video.
Each c50 mins.
WESTERN CREDITS: US video release
1993 on Streamline Pictures and 1994-95
on Streamline Pictures/Orion Home
Video, dub, Eng rewrite Gregory
Snegoff; UK video release 1994 on Manga
Video, dub.
ORIGINS: Manga by Kazuo Koike &
Ryoichi Ikegami, Eng trans pub
Viz Communications (US), Titan
Books (UK).
POINTS OF INTEREST: The anime chara
designs follow the manga almost line for
line.
SPINOFFS: A successful 1997 live-action
movie, directed by Christophe Gans. He
has announced that his next anime-
inspired production will be Patlabor 2.
CATEGORIES: P, T
RATINGS: NN, XX, VV, SM, EROTIC

A violent video with lots of sex scenes and some of the perviest bad guys (and gals) in anime. Crying Freeman is a Chinese assassin who rises to head the 108 Dragons clan with the aid of his wife, the only one of his intended victims ever to survive. The various trials and tribulations of criminal life involve a mad Barbie clone who wants to make him her personal sex toy and an African gang queen who believes in cutting right to the bone. The leading man gets his kit off — frequently — but otherwise most of the gratuitous nudity is female, and all of it is vague in the genital area. Not digitised, just not there. (See pp47, 57, 101.)

CUTEY HONEY
(Eng title for SHIN CUTEY HONEY YAMI NO GUNDAN HEN, lit New Cutey Honey Squad of Darkness)

OAV series, 8 parts
JAPANESE CREDITS: 1994-95. Dir:
Yasuchika Nagaoka. Writer: Isao Shiyuza.
Screenplay: Isao Shiyuza (1-4), Ko Uemura
(5 & 8), Higashi Shimizu (6 & 7). Chara
des: Go Nagai. Mecha des: Kunihiro Abe.
Anime dir: Osamu Horiuchi & Hitoshi
Horiwa. Art dir: Hiroshi Kato, Masaru
Futoda & Akira Kimura. Prod co: Toei
Video. © Go Nagai, Dynamic Planning, Toei
Video. Each c32 mins.
WESTERN CREDITS: US video release 1994-
96 on AD Vision, sub, trans Ichiro Arakaki.
ORIGINS: Manga by Go Nagai; 1973-74 TV
series.
POINTS OF INTEREST: Cutey Honey is very
popular with fans in France, where she is
known as Cherry Miel.
CATEGORIES: SF
RATINGS: X, N, V, G, MAINSTREAM

Honey is a glorious android girl, originally created to remind a now-deceased scientist of his dead daughter. She has a most unusual device implanted in her chest — an 'airborne element solidifier', which can create just about anything from thin air. This means that when Honey needs to change her appearance in her role as a fighter against injustice, she can create a new look from nothing; it also provides an excuse for at least one nude transformation sequence per story. (See pp53-54.)

DANCE TILL TOMORROW
(Eng title for ASATTE DANCE, lit Dance the Day After Tomorrow)

OAV series, 2 parts
JAPANESE CREDITS: 1990-91. Dir: Teruo
Kigure (1), Masamune Ochiai (2).
Screenplay: Sheila Nakajima (1), Tomohiro
Maruyama (2). Chara des: Jiro Sayama.
Music: Tetsuya Nakamura. Prod: Satoshi
Nishino. Prod co: Knack. © Yamamoto,
Tokuma Japan Communications.
Each 45 mins.
ORIGINS: Manga by Naoki Yamamoto,
serialised in Big Comic Spirits. Eng trans
pub Viz (US), serialised in Pulp magazine.
CATEGORIES: P, C
RATINGS: N, EROTIC

Women are only after one thing, unless that is, they stand to benefit from your inheritance. Another entry in the 'unwelcome guest' stakes, not because our hero can't have sex with his roommate (he can, and does), but because he has to

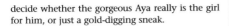

decide whether the gorgeous Aya really is the girl for him, or just a gold-digging sneak.

DARKSIDE BLUES

MOVIE
JAPANESE CREDITS: 1994. Dir: Yoshimichi Furukawa & Michitaka Kikuchi. Script: Mayori Sekijima. Chara des: Hiroshi Hamazaki. Key animation: Hiroshi Hamazaki. Prod co: Toho. © Ashibe, Kikuchi, Tokuma Shoten, Toho. 80 mins.
WESTERN CREDITS: US video release 1996 on US Manga Corps, sub, trans William Flanagan & Yuko Sato.
ORIGINS: Manga by Hideyuki Kikuchi & Yuho Ashibe.
POINTS OF INTEREST: Androgynous hero Darkside is voiced by Natsuki Akira, a male impersonator from the Takarazuka troupe.
CATEGORIES: F
RATINGS: V, MAINSTREAM

The future belongs to one company: Persona Corporation. Only a few places on Earth hold out against their dominion; one is in Kabuki Town, a ramshackle part of Shinjuku known as the Tokyo Darkside. To this place comes a strange, beautiful being who has the power to change worlds. Darkside describes himself as a 'dream therapist', but he's really a magnet for the dreams and desires of everyone who comes into contact with him. From the psychotic, sexy Enji Hozuki who tells him 'I've fallen for you pretty badly' (only minutes after making moves on a quiet, retiring young nurse), to the leader of the revolution, a young woman desperately in love with the eldest son of the oppressor, everyone seems to want a piece of his disturbingly beautiful person. There are some unsettling scenes of sexualised torture at the beginning, and the whole atmosphere drips with the suppressed eroticism of a vampire novel, but the overall impression is of a beautifully designed Gothic tale with a meandering plot, slow pace and non-existent ending, leaving you with the feeling that the real story is still to be told. (See pp35-36, 41.)

DEMON BEAST INVASION
(Eng title for YŌJŪ KYŌSHITSU, lit Demon Beast Classroom)

OAV series, 6 parts
JAPANESE CREDITS: 1990-94. Dir: Jun

Fukuda (1, 2, 5 & 6), Juki Yoma (3 & 4). *Screenplay: Joji Maki (1 & 2), Wataru Amano (3-6). Chara des: Mari Mizuta (1 & 2), Hisashi Ezura (3 & 4), Toshikazu Uzami (5 & 6). Monster des: Junichi Watanabe. Art dir: Naoto Yokose. Music dir: Teruo Takahama. Prod co: Daiei © T. Maeda, Daiei. Each c45 mins.*
WESTERN CREDITS: US video release 1995-96 on Anime 18, sub, trans Moe I. Yada.
ORIGINS: Manga by Toshio Maeda.
POINTS OF INTEREST: Features porn actresses in the main voice roles. Translator's pseudonym 'Mö iya da' means 'I can't take any more'.
CATEGORIES: P, H
RATINGS: XX, NN, VV, SM, PORN

Why do invasions of demons always start in Japanese high schools? In fairness, this time the demons aren't invading — they're coming home. An ecological disaster drove them from Earth aeons ago and now they want the old place back. And of course, they have to mate with human women (preferably high school girls or nurses, but they're not all that fussy) to create a new hybrid that can get the planet in good shape for Grandma and Grandpa's return. The Interplanetary Mutual Observation Agency is there to stop them, but not before lots of demonic tentacle rape scenes. (See p77.)

DESPERATE LOVE 1989
(Eng trans for ZETSUAI 1989)

OAV
JAPANESE CREDITS: 1992. Dir: Takuji Endo. Script: Tatsuhiko Urahata. Anime dir: Tetsuro Aoki. Art dir: Shinichi Uehara. Storyboards: Yoshiaki Kawajiri. Prod co: Madhouse. © Ozaki, Shueisha. 45 mins.
ORIGINS: Manga by Minami Ozaki, serialised in Margaret magazine.
SPINOFFS: Another OAV, Bronze: Desperate Love Since 1989, was produced in 1996.
CATEGORIES: P
RATINGS: N, XX, G, EROTIC

Izumo is a gifted young sportsman with a terrible secret in his past. Koji Nanjo is the son of a wealthy family who despise his career as a rock singer. When he and his friend Katsumi Shibuya enter Izumo's life, they change his entire future. Neither of the young men would describe himself as 'gay', yet they find themselves falling for each other. Their love is too strong to resist and they become emotionally and sexually involved in an affair which could end both their careers. Prime shonen ai material. (See pp34, 36.)

DEVIL HUNTER YOKO
(UK title/trans for MAMONO HUNTER YÖKO [pun on YÖ-bewitching, KO-child], US title DEVIL HUNTER YOHKO)

OAV series, 6 episodes
JAPANESE CREDITS: 1991-95. Dir: Katsuhisa Yamada. Script: Yoshihiro Tomita. Chara des: Takeshi Miyao. Anime dir: Tetsuro Aoki. Art dir: Takeshi Waki. Music: Hiroya Watanabe. Prod co: Madhouse. © NCS, Toho Video. Part 1 c45 mins, parts 2-6 each c30 mins.
WESTERN CREDITS: US video release 1993-96 on AD Vision, sub, trans Arakaki & Dwayne Jones; UK partial video release 1995 on Western Connection, sub, trans Jonathan Clements.
CATEGORIES: D
RATINGS: N, V, X, EROTIC

All men, the theme song tells us, are devils in disguise. Sixteen year-old Yoko is about to discover the truth for herself. Will she stay a virginal demon fighter in the tradition of the women of her line, or will she duck out of her responsibility and play around while she's still young and giddy? The demons who are invading the human world will do anything to diminish her powers, including enlisting the aid of a possessed classmate to try and 'persuade' her to abandon virginity by fair means or foul. With the help of good advice, good friends, a bit of luck and sheer determination, Yoko navigates the perilous world of love and magic and keeps her options open. (See pp81, 96-97.)

DEVILMAN
(Eng title for DEVILMAN TANJÖ HEN, lit Devilman: The Birth, aka DEVILMAN: GENESIS & Eng title for DEVILMAN YÖCHÖ SHIRENU HEN, lit Devilman Witch-Bird Shirenu Chapter, aka SIREN THE DEMON BIRD)

OAV, 2 parts
JAPANESE CREDITS: 1987 & 1990. Dir: Tsutomu Iida. Screenplay: Tsutomu Iida. Supervisor: Go Nagai. Chara des: Kazuo Komatsubara. Music: Kenji Kawai. Development Assistance: Kenji Terada.

Prod co: O Production for King Record. © Dynamic Planning, Kodansha, Bandai Visual. Part 1 51 mins, part 2 60 mins.
WESTERN CREDITS: UK video release 1994 on Manga Video, dub; US video release 1995 on US Renditions, sub, & Manga Video, dub, Eng rewrite John Wolskel.
ORIGINS: Manga by Go Nagai; 1972 TV series.
SPINOFFS: A third OAV was planned but is still awaited; distaff manga sequel Devilman Lady.
CATEGORIES: D
RATINGS: XX, VV, EROTIC

The change in the look of Nagai's characters from their manga and television series versions was considerable, and enhanced the overall air of sexual menace when the main character transforms from quiet high school kid to human/demon hybrid. The undercurrent of sexual attraction between Akira and his friend Ryo, so powerfully depicted in the manga, has been more or less abandoned, as has Ryo's origin story. (See pp40, 53, 55-56, 57.)

DIRTY PAIR

TV series, 24 episodes
JAPANESE CREDITS: 1985. Dir: Masaharu Okuwaki. Chara des: Tsukasa Dokite &

Devilman

Fujihiko Hosono. Prod co: Sunrise.
© Takachiho, Studio Nue, Sunrise, NTV.
Each 30 mins.
WESTERN CREDITS: The spinoff movie
Dirty Pair: Project Eden and the 2 OAVs,
Affair of Nolandia and Flight 005
Conspiracy, are all available on video in
the US from Streamline Pictures/Orion
House Video. Dirty Pair and Dirty Pair
Flash OAV episodes are due out on video in
the US from 1998 on AD Vision.
ORIGINS: Appearance in the 1983 Crusher
Joe movie and Haruka Takachiho's science
fiction novels.
SPINOFFS: OAVs, OAV series, movie and
a 'flashback' series, Dirty Pair Flash,
recounting the youthful adventures of our
heroines. There is also a US comic by Adam
Warren.
CATEGORIES: SF
RATINGS: N, V, MAINSTREAM

Kei and Yuri are the most feared pair of trou-
bleshooters for the 3WA. Codenamed Lovely
Angels to their faces, they are known behind
their backs as the Dirty Pair — because somehow,
even though it's never their fault, every job
they're assigned to ends in mass destruction,
sometimes on a planetary or even system-wide
scale. The girls are a study in contrasts, and often
fight like cat and dog, but cool, feminine Yuri
and hotheaded Kei are good friends and always
there for each other — except maybe just occasionally where men are concerned. Their sidekick
Mughi is a highly intelligent lifeform in the
shape of a huge pussycat, and their ship the
Lovely Angel is equipped with all the latest technology. Their uniforms set a new standard for
intergalactic cheesecake in the revered tradition
of *Barbarella*, and the girls are loved by fans

Dragon Knight

throughout the world thanks to video releases
and television showings all over Asia, in America
and Europe. (See pp42, 46.)

DOOMED MEGALOPOLIS
(Eng title for TEITO MONOGATARI,
lit [Imperial/Capital] City Story)

OAV series, 4 parts
JAPANESE CREDITS: 1991-92. Dir:
Kazuyoshi Katayama (1), Kazuyoshi
Katayama & Koichi Chigira (2-4),
Kazushige Kume (3 & 4). Supervising dir:
Taro Rin. Screenplay: Akinori Endo. Chara
des: Masayuki Goto. Anime dir: Koichi
Hashimoto. Art dir: Hideyoshi Kaneko.
Music: Kazz Toyama. Prod co: Madhouse.
© H. Aramata, Toei. Each c50 mins.
WESTERN CREDITS: US video release 1993-
94 on Streamline Pictures, dub, Eng
rewrite Ardwight Chamberlain; UK video
release 1994 on Manga Video.
ORIGINS: Novels by Hiroshi Aramata, pub
Kadokawa Shoten.
POINTS OF INTEREST: Ardwight
Chamberlain is the voice of Babylon 5's
Ambassador Kosh. The Kanto earthquake
also features in the Legend of the
Overfiend.
SPINOFFS: A live-action version is also
available in the UK from Manga Video.
CATEGORIES: P, D
RATINGS: XX, NN, VV, SM, EROTIC

Incest and its impact are creepily portrayed here,
and black magic is for once genuinely scary. It's
not the sort of story you expect to end with a rendition of 'All You Need is Love', which comes as
something of a surprise. Part one has a strong
turn-of-the-century opening with everything
from a resurrected sorcerer plotting to take control
of Tokyo's guardian spirit to the beginning of the
incest subplot which is finally resolved in part
four. Part two takes us up to the devastating Kanto
Earthquake of 1923, and sees evil sorcerer Kato
producing his own demonic offspring after the
rape of an innocent girl. Part three introduces two
new elements — the building of the Tokyo subway after the earthquake, disturbing ancient dragons, and the arrival of a Shinto priestess determined to save Kato's daughter from being sacrificed to further her father's lust for power. The
final part is heavy with Shinto symbolism, but the
demonic Kato is redeemed by the power of love,
and the dark secret within the family is brought
out into the open.

DORAEMON

TV series, 27 episodes
JAPANESE CREDITS: 1973. Dir: Yoshiro
Owada. Music: Shunsuke Kikuchi. Prod co:
Nihon TV Doga. © F. Fujio, NTV. Each c20
mins.
ORIGINS: Manga by Fujiko Fujio.
POINTS OF INTEREST: The OAV Visionary
takes Doraemon's basic premise and gives
it an erotic twist.
SPINOFFS: 1979 TV series, New Doraemon,
which is still running (c800 episodes to
date), movie series commencing in 1980
and still producing at least 1 movie per
year to date.
CATEGORIES: SF, C
RATINGS: MAINSTREAM

Doraemon is a robot cat sent back from the future by the hapless schoolboy Nobita's descendants to help him change his ways and ensure a comfortable inheritance for them. It doesn't work out according to plan, because Nobita left so little behind that they can only afford a cheap and cheerful robot — he doesn't even have ears the way a proper robot cat should! The comic capers of the pair have amused countless little ones in Japan and all over Asia and South America. (See p105.)

DRAGON HALF

OAV series, 2 parts
JAPANESE CREDITS: 1993. Dir: Shinya
Sadamitsu. Screenplay: Shinya Sadamitsu.
Chara des: Masahiro Koyama. Art dir:
Takahiro Kishida & Masahiro Koyama.
Prod co: Production IG. © Mita, Kadokawa,
Victor Entertainment. Each 30 mins.
WESTERN CREDITS: US video release 1995
on 1 tape on AD Vision, sub; UK video
release 1996 on AD Vision UK, same
version.
ORIGINS: Manga by Ryusuke Mita.
CATEGORIES: F
RATING: N, V, MAINSTREAM

The nudity is played for laughs and the violence is epically comic in this daft take-off of the fantasy genre by manga genius Mita. A huge fan favourite, it's the tale of half-human, half-dragon Mink and her teenage pursuit of her idol, singer and swordsman Dick Saucer, to whom she would happily Give Her All but for the slight technical hitch of Dick's alternative career as a dragon-slayer. There's a wacky subplot about a pervert King (who fancies Mink's dragon Mum) and his jealous half-human, half-slimeball daughter, plus lots of silly D&D-style fantasy stereotypes to add to the fun. One of the most bizarre versions of Beethoven ever orchestrated forms the theme song, which is all about cooking dinner for the object of your desire. Insane. *Dragon Half*'s many imitators have escalating levels of nudity but sadly none of the inspirational nuttiness of the original.

DRAGON KNIGHT

OAV series, 2 parts
JAPANESE CREDITS: 1991-94. Dir: Jun
Fukuda (1), Kaoru Toyo'oka (2).
Screenplay: Akira Hatta. Original story:
Masato Hiruda. Original idea: Dr Pochi.
Original concept: Yoshinori Nakamura.
Chara des: Ako Sahara & Akira Kano.
Anime dir: Yuma Nakamura. Prod co:
Polystar. © Polystar, elf RPG, All Products.
Part 1 40 mins, part 2 50 mins.
WESTERN CREDITS: US video release 1994-
95 on AD Vision, sub, trans Ichiro Arakaki
& Dwayne Jones.
ORIGINS: Adult computer game by elf
(Masato Hiruda).
CATEGORIES: F
RATINGS: X, N, V, SM, PORN

A disappointment to those who liked the monsters in the RPG, this has plenty of unclad girls to take the edge off their sense of loss. Armed with sword and Polaroid, Takeru is a knavish knight rescuing girls in distress only to cop a peek at their charms. True love and friendship redeem him in the end, but not soon enough.

DRAGON PINK

OAV series, 3 parts
JAPANESE CREDITS: 1994-95. Dir: Wataru
Fujii (1), Hitoshi Takai (2 & 3). Prod co:
AIC. © Iyotoko, Pink Pineapple. Each 35
mins.
WESTERN CREDITS: US video release 1994-
95 on SoftCel Pictures, sub, trans Doc
Issaac.
ORIGINS: Created by Iyotoko, best known
in Japan for computer RPGs and garage
kits, based on one of his games.
POINTS OF INTEREST: Edited US versions
of all 3 OAVs exist, each 5 mins shorter.
CATEGORIES: F, C

RATINGS: X, N, V, SM, PORN

It's getting to the stage where 'dragon' is a code-word for 'large breasts' in anime. Sex slave Pink and her sword-slinging master wander a D&D universe losing battles, treasure and clothing, helped by their friends Pierce the elf and Bobo the warrior. Very silly.

DYING FOR A GIRL/ALTAR OF SACRIFICE
(Eng trans for NANNICHI-KO NO SHINDE MO II/IKENIE NO SAIDAN)

OAV
JAPANESE CREDITS: 1984. Original Story:
Fumio Nakajima. Prod co: Wonder Kids.
© F. Nakajima, Wonder Kids. 25 mins.
ORIGINS: The first Wonder Kids Lolita
Anime release was Reddening Snow/Girls
Tortured With Roses.
SPINOFFS: The later Variation is a direct
sequel to Altar of Sacrifice. The next release
in the series was House of Kittens.
CATEGORIES: P
RATINGS: NN, X, PORN

The second Wonder Kids Lolita Anime release, and the last to include two short stories instead of one longer one. *Dying for a Girl* features a student who secretly admires the senior who is helping her with her tennis swing. Her desires find an opportunity when he rescues her from a would-be rapist in the park. *Altar of Sacrifice*, despite the *Overfiend*-soundalike title, is a tale of lesbian awakening, featuring two girls putting antique statues to novel uses. (See p109.)

EL HAZARD
(Eng title for SHINPI NO SEKAI EL HAZARD, lit El Hazard the Mysterious World)

OAV series, 6 parts
JAPANESE CREDITS: 1995. Dir: Hiroki
Hayashi. Script: Ryoei Tsukimura. Chara
des: Kazuto Nakazawa. Anime dir: Kazuto
Nakazawa. Art dir: Nobuhito Sue. Music:
Seiko Nagaoka. Exec prod: Taro Maki. Prod
co: AIC. © Pioneer LDC. Part 1 45 mins,
parts 2-6 each 30 mins.
WESTERN CREDITS: US video release 1995
on Pioneer LDCA, sub, dub; UK video
release 1998 on Pioneer LDCE, dub.
SPINOFFS: An ongoing TV series and more
OAVs followed.

CATEGORIES: P, F
RATINGS: MAINSTREAM

A glorious mishmash of the Arabian Nights and the Marx Brothers, *El Hazard* drops a bunch of ordinary kids and their teacher into a fantasy universe, then stands back to watch the resulting chaos. The school bully teaches the alien invaders the art of war, the hero has to spend most of his time pretending to be a girl, and between ditzy priestesses (the worst imaginable guardians for an Ultimate Weapon), lesbian seductresses and the bondage queen of the bug people, you can tell you're not in Tokyo any more. (See p33.)

THE ELVEN BRIDE
(Eng title for ELF NO WAKA OKUSAMA, lit A Young Elven Bride)

OAV series, 2 parts
JAPANESE CREDITS: 1995. Dir: Hiroshi
Yamakawa. Original story: Kazuma
G-Version. Prod co: AIC. © Kazuma
G-Version, Mediax, Pink Pineapple.
Each 30 mins.
WESTERN CREDITS: US video release 1996
on AD Vision, sub, trans Kuni Kimura,
Eng rewrite Matt Greenfield (1), Autumn
Rowe (2).
POINTS OF INTEREST: Milfa's uncanny
resemblance to Deedlit from Record of
Lodoss War.
CATEGORIES: F
RATINGS: X, N, PORN

Elves mature slower than humans, so when Milfa marries the human Kenji, there's a slight proportional difference in their anatomical development. After self-help in part one doesn't entirely solve the problem, Milfa goes to a doctor specialising in interspecies relationships — who is also an incubus and a grade-A lech. (See pp19, 21, 40, 106-107.)

END OF SUMMER
(Eng title for DŌKYŪSEI NATSU NO OWARI NI, lit Classmates: End of Summer)

OAV series, 4 parts
JAPANESE CREDITS: 1994. Dir: Kinji
Yoshimoto. Screenplay: Yuhiro Tomita.
Chara des: Ryunosuke Otonashi. Chara
concepts: Masaki Takei. Prod: KSS. Prod
co: Pink Pineapple. © elf, Pink Pineapple,
Cinema Paradise, Hero. Each 55 mins.

WESTERN CREDITS: US video release
1994-95 on AD Vision, sub, Eng trans
Ichiro Arakaki & Dwayne Jones (1 & 2),
Masako Arakawa & Chris Hutts (3 & 4).
ORIGINS: Based on the computer game
Classmates by elf (Masato Hiruda).
POINTS OF INTEREST: Note the presence
of Plastic Little's Kinji Yoshimoto.
SPINOFFS: The sequel, Kakyusei, was
released in the US as First Loves.
CATEGORIES: P
RATINGS: XX, N, PORN

Wataru really loves Mai, but with other girls
throwing themselves at him all summer long,
what's a boy to do? The typical teenage boy
dream; lots of gorgeous women just falling into
your lap, and a Girl Next Door who believes you
when you say you couldn't help yourself. The
artwork is really lovely. You can observe the
artists' skill with flesh tones in some detail. (See
p112.)

F³: FRANTIC, FRUSTRATED & FEMALE
(Eng title for NAGEKI NO KENKŌ YŪRYŌJI,
lit The Lament of an Otherwise Perfectly
Healthy Girl)

OAV series, 3 parts
JAPANESE CREDITS: 1994-95. Dir:
Masakazu Akan. Chara des: Kaji
Hamaguchi. Anime dir: Kaji Hamaguchi.
Planning: Kinya Watanabe. Prod co: Pink
Pineapple. © Wan Yan A Gu Da, Pink
Pineapple. Each 35 mins.
WESTERN CREDITS: US video release 1995
on SoftCel Pictures, sub, trans Ichiro
Arakaki, Eng rewrite Matt Greenfield.
ORIGINS: Manga by Wan Yan A Gu Da,
pub Fujimi.
POINTS OF INTEREST: The script back-
tracks on the incestuous characters of part
1, later claiming that they only look as if
they are related.
CATEGORIES: P
RATINGS: XX, NN, G, PORN

Hiroe seeks all kinds of aids for her feelings of
teenage frustration, from the appliance of science
to a lesbian biker bash with her mum and sister.
All this is supposedly to help her achieve orgasm,
without which she won't feel fulfilled by her
boyfriend. But all she's really looking for is the
'right' man to ring her bell (ie the viewer), turning
this sapphic satire into the logical extremes of the

Abba song 'The Day Before You Came', in which a
woman catalogues how dreary her life was before
the arrival of her perfect lover. Immortal dialogue
like 'I'll shoot you all with my cannon of love'
shows Matt Greenfield's editorial hand at work;
his apparent insistence on cheesy American ver-
nacular certainly pays dividends in the porn
genre. (See pp19, 20, 41, 97-98.)

FIRST LOVES
(Eng title for KAKYŪSEI, lit Underclassmates)

OAV series, 4 parts
JAPANESE CREDITS: 1995. Dir: Koichi
Yoshida & Kan Fukumoto. Screenplay: Yu
Yamamoto. Chara des: Yuji Takahashi.
Anime dir: Yuji Takahashi. Storyboards:
Kan Fukumoto & Hiroshi Yoshida. Prod co:
Pink Pineapple. © Pink Pineapple. Each c18
mins.
WESTERN CREDITS: US video release 1996
on AD Vision, sub.
ORIGINS: Based on Classmates, released in
the US as End of Summer.
SPINOFFS: There is now a special 'elf'
edition of the series, for those who like
their porn with pointy ears.
CATEGORIES: P
RATINGS: XX, N, PORN

The protagonists in this sequel to *End of Summer* are younger high school kids, though the American version points out that they're not legally minors. Kakeru follows Wataru's lead, trying to make it with his dream girl (his first) but getting distracted here and there, through no fault of his own, of course.

FIST OF THE NORTH STAR
(Eng title/trans for HOKUTŌ NO KEN)

MOVIE
JAPANESE CREDITS: 1986. Dir: Toyo'o Ashida. Screenplay: Susumu Takahisa. Chara des: Masami Suda. Prod co: Toei Doga. © Hara, Buronson, Toei. 110 mins.
WESTERN CREDITS: US video release 1992 on Streamline Pictures, dub, Eng rewrite Tom Wyner; UK video release 1992 on Manga Video, same version.
ORIGINS: Manga by Tetsuo Hara & Buronson; 1984 TV series.
POINTS OF INTEREST: This was the first release on the Manga Video label. Episodes of the TV series released in the US & UK by Manga Video in 1998.
CATEGORIES: SF
RATINGS: V, MAINSTREAM

Post-apocalyptic fantasy of death, extreme violence and martial arts. Loner Kenshiro wanders a devastated landscape looking for his brother, who has kidnapped his beloved. Although the tortured love story of Ken and Julia and the possessive jealousy which fires the conflict between the two brothers are the underpinning themes of the series, and although the mix of sadism and competition provides a homoerotic undercurrent, there is no explicit erotic content. (See p86.)

THE FIVE STAR STORIES
(Eng trans for FIVE STAR MONOGATARI)

MOVIE
JAPANESE CREDITS: 1989. Dir: Kazuo Yamazaki. Screenplay: Akinori Endo. Chara des: Mamoru Nagano & Nobuteru Yuki. Prod: Haruki Kadokawa. Prod co: Sunrise. © Nagano, Toys Press. c60 mins.
ORIGINS: Manga by Mamoru Nagano, still ongoing in Newtype magazine after 12 years.
CATEGORIES: SF
RATINGS: N, MAINSTREAM

A brief glimpse into Nagano's elegantly etiolated world in which fashion drawings play out huge passions and conflicts on a stage that spans a distant star system. The androgynous beauty Ladios Sopp isn't just a gifted girly-boy mecha designer but the Emperor of the whole system. The genetically engineered Lachesis is his betrothed, and also the control unit for a vital portion of the systems of a giant robot. When they eventually find each other they go straight on the run from a furious mob out to get them both. This is the point at which it can really save a lot of trouble to have a giant robot tucked away somewhere — if only our cute hero can remember where he hid it before they get zapped. (See pp33, 104.)

FOBIA

OAV series, 2 parts
JAPANESE CREDITS: 1995. Dir: Shigenori Awai. Screenplay: Naruhiko Tatsumiya. Chara des: U-Jin. Anime dir: Yoshinobu Yamakawa. Art dir: Junichiro Nishikawa. Sound: Noriyoshi Matsuura. Prod co: Gaga. © U-Jin, Leed, Tec, Gaga. Each c47 mins.
WESTERN CREDITS: US video release 1998 on Anime 18, dub, trans Kevin McKeown.
ORIGINS: Manga by U-Jin, pub Leed/Read Comic.
CATEGORIES: P, H
RATINGS: NN, XX, V, PORN

The drama group at Enoshima College is disrupted by the murder of a potential leading lady. Mutsumi suspects his fellow student Sato, but Sato has been possessed by repliniods from the future who feed on the blood of Japanese schoolgirls. Luckily Mutsumi's best mate turns out to be a time-travelling warrior princess who has come back from the year 2112 searching for a hero to wield a magic sword and fight the beasts. That hero is Mutsumi, a geek who gets an erection every time he's worried. He certainly wouldn't get one watching this slow, moronic, repetitive junk which takes recycling of footage and ideas to new depths.

GHOST IN THE SHELL
(Eng title/trans for KŌKAKU KIDŌTAI)

MOVIE
JAPANESE CREDITS: 1995. Dir: Mamoru Oshii. Screenplay: Kazunori Ito. Chara des: Hiroyuki Okiura. Mecha des: Shoji Kawamori & Atsushi Takeuchi. Music: Kenji Kawai. Prod co: Production IG.

© *Shirow, Kodansha, Bandai Visual, Manga Entertainment. c75 mins.*
WESTERN CREDITS: US & UK theatrical release 1995, video release 1996 on Manga Video, sub, dub, trans Taro Yoshida & Paul C. Halbert.
ORIGINS: Manga by Masamune Shirow serialised in Young Magazine.
SPINOFFS: A sequel to the manga is now appearing in Japan.
CATEGORIES: SF
RATINGS: N, V, MAINSTREAM

Oshii's film is richly sensual, with a visceral score and wonderful, almost subliminal detail. Ito wisely simplifies Shirow's right-wing manga down to the bare bones of a romantic metaphor, but the result is still powerful. Motoko Kusanagi and her colleagues in an elite government squad are on the track of a cybercriminal. As they learn more about him and his origins, Kusanagi questions the basis of her world and her own existence. She is largely a machine yet has a human consciousness; she wants to be free of the confines of the physical world, yet feels the need for ongoing relationships and contacts. The so-called cybercriminal holds the key to a new way of living, and Kusanagi wants to find out the truth about him. Interestingly, all the female shells in this story are just that, mere disposable dolls made to serve a function, with the exception of Kusanagi herself. The only character in the story who talks about a 'normal' relationship, with a wife and daughter, turns out to be a deluded low-life parroting the fictions fed to him by a superior intellect. The only relationship which challenges Kusanagi's loyalty to her team is the one which will enable her ultimately to shed her female shell and swim free in the currents of information which now circle the world as relentlessly as any ocean's. (See pp24, 32, 86, 99.)

THE GIGOLO
(Eng title for DOCHINPIRA: ONNA DAISUKI!, lit Vulgar Punk: I Love Women!)

OAV
JAPANESE CREDITS: 1993. Dir: Hiromitsu Ota. Screenplay: Amano. Art dir: Shigemune Kikoyama. Storyboards: Hironobu Saito. Prod co: Studio Kikan. © T. Doko, Seiyo, Jackpot. 45 mins.
WESTERN CREDITS: UK video release 1994 on Kiseki Films, dub, trans Ryoichi Murata.
ORIGINS: Story by Makio Hara & Tetsumi

Doko.
POINTS OF INTEREST: This title was among the UK top 20 selling anime videos for over 18 months after its release.
CATEGORIES: P
RATINGS: XX, NN, V, SM, PORN

It isn't often you get two for the price of one, but here you can have cheap and nasty in one video. Jin is a young man who drops out of college to make a living selling his body to bored rich women in Tokyo. A life of hanging round bars and shopping malls suits him to perfection despite the occasional rough client, but he gets involved with the wrong woman and finds himself up to his neck in gangland warfare. The plot, script, characterisation and pacing are all so banal and predictable that you could get more of an erotic charge out of watching paint dry. (See pp86, 87.)

THE GIRL FROM PHANTASIA
(Eng title for FANTASIA)

OAV
JAPANESE CREDITS: 1993. Dir: Jun Kamiya. Chara des: Kazuya Kise. Art dir: Kazuya Kise. Music: Toshiyuki Watanabe. Prod co: Starchild Records. © King Records, IG. 40 mins.
WESTERN CREDITS: US video release 1994 on AD Vision, sub, trans Ichiro Arakaki.
ORIGINS: Manga by Akane Nagano.
CATEGORIES: C, F
RATINGS: X, V, EROTIC

Everyone thinks magic makes life easier. But when Akihiro buys a new rug for his student digs, hoping it will help him seduce his girl by providing a comfier setting for his advances, he finds that's not always true. The gorgeous female sprite who pops out of the carpet might not be a problem in herself (though his girlfriend is unlikely to agree), but the rug is a gateway to another dimension and there are much less soft and cuddly things waiting to emerge. As evil spirits start to pour out of the rug and into our world, Akihiro has two big problems — get them back before they do any harm, and stop his girlfriend from finding out about the good-natured, generous, uninhibited and underdressed Malon (who is just one vowel away from being a pun on her own anatomy). All the jokes have been done before, so that's quite enough about shag piles at the back.

GOKU: MIDNIGHT EYE
(Eng title for GOKÜ: MIDNIGHT EYE, lit [Wu Kong/Awareness of Vacuity] Midnight Eye)

OAV series, 2 parts
JAPANESE CREDITS: 1989. Dir: Yoshiaki Kawajiri. Screenplay: Buichi Terasawa. Chara des: Hiroshi Hamazaki. Art dir: Mitsuo Kozeki. Music dir: Yukihide Takekawa & Kazz Toyama. Prod co: Toei, Madhouse. © Terasawa, Toei, Scholar. Each 45 mins.
WESTERN CREDITS: US & UK video release 1995-96 on Manga Video, dub, Eng adaptation John Woskel.
ORIGINS: Chinese legend of Sun Wu Kong; manga by Buichi Terasawa, pub Scholar.
CATEGORIES: T, F
RATINGS: N, V, MAINSTREAM

Updating his Cobra character with a twist of Philip Marlowe for a more cynical, cyber-crazed generation, Terasawa retells the Monkey King myth as a futuristic tale. Goku is given unusual powers to fight an evil villain who has the police baffled. The usual disposable Terasawa women meet the usual nasty ends, but some of them come in highly unusual forms. You've heard of *Girl on a Motorcycle*? Well, move over Marianne Faithfull, here's a girl who *is* a motorcycle. (And yes, she can really go…) There's also a young lady with a peacock's tail which has an unusually hypnotic effect (though since she never wears anything she could probably manage that pretty well without any special powers) and a catgirl with a serious attitude problem. The one non-augmented woman, a cop, makes the fatal mistake of sleeping with our hero, and of course gets killed. Despite its complete predictability, this one has its moments, especially on the visual side. (See p40.)

GOLDEN BOY

OAV series, 6 parts
JAPANESE CREDITS: 1995-96. Dir: Hiroyuki Kitakubo & Tatsuya Egawa. Chara des: Toshihiro Kawamoto. Anime dir: Toshihiro Kawamoto, Yasuhito Kikuchi, Masa Honda & Michiyo Suzuki. Art dir: Tatsuya Kushida & Yuji Ikehata. Prod des: Hiroyuki Kitakubo. Storyboards: Hiroyuki Kitakubo. Music: Joyo Katayanagi. Prod co: APPP. © T. Egawa, KSS, Shueisha. Each 30 mins.
WESTERN CREDITS: US video release 1996 on AD Vision, sub, Eng rewrite Matt Greenfield.
ORIGINS: Manga by Tatsuya Egawa, pub Shueisha.
POINTS OF INTEREST: Egawa is also author of the manga Magical Talruto-kun (also a TV series) and Be Free.
CATEGORIES: P, C
RATINGS: NN, X, EROTIC

The amorous adventures of a young man who sets out on his pushbike to seek the university of life, where all the professors seem to be female and gorgeous. Kintaro is a voyeur with a breast fetish almost as serious as his passion for computers, and he's given to practices Western males may find a little strange — sniffing toilet seats after ladies have used them, for instance — alongside the normal lechery and groping. Amazing art and some humour.

GREY DIGITAL TARGET

OAV
JAPANESE CREDITS: 1987. Dir: Tetsu Dezaki. Screenplay: Yasushi Hirano, Kazumi Koide & Tetsu Dezaki. Story dir: Toshiaki Imaizumi. Music: Goro Omi. Prod co: Ashi, Magic Bus. © Tagami, Tokuma Shoten, 80 mins.
WESTERN CREDITS: UK video release 1994 on Western Connection, sub, trans Jonathan Clements; US video release 1997

Golden Boy

on *Viz Comminications, sub.*
ORIGINS: *Manga by Yoshihisa Tagami, pub Tokuma Shoten, US pub Viz.*
CATEGORIES: *SF*
RATINGS: *N, V, MAINSTREAM*

This is a bleak, elegant and intelligent story, hampered only by a limited animation budget. In a future world devoted entirely to combat, the lower orders can only get out of the slums by fighting their way to full Citizenship. Underclass member Lips joins the army to escape further episodes of rape and abuse at the hands of soldiers. Her powerless lover Grey loses her twice, once to the army, and again when she is killed on her first mission. Consumed with self-loathing, Grey enlists and becomes a successful killing machine. This film can be read in two ways; as a romantic celebration of the resilience of human emotion, or as a tragic meditation on the futility of caring about anything. (See p99.)

GUNBUSTER
(Eng title for TOP O NERAE! GUNBUSTER, lit Aim for the Top! Gunbuster)

OAV series, 6 parts
JAPANESE CREDITS: *1988-89. Dir: Hideaki Anno. Original story: Toshio Okada. Chara des: Haruhiko Mikimoto. Mecha des: Koichi Ohata & Kazuki Miyatake. Anime dir: Yuji Moriyama, Yoshiyuki Sadamoto & Toshiyuki Kubo'oka. Art dir: Masumi Higuchi. Music: Kohei Tanaka. Prod co: Gainax. © Gainax, Bandai, Victor.*
Each 30 mins.
WESTERN CREDITS: *US video release 1990 on US Renditions, sub, trans Deborah Grant & Yuki Nakajima (1 & 2), Trish Ledoux & Toshifumi Yoshida (3-6), & Manga Video, dub; UK video release 1994 on Kiseki Films, sub.*
CATEGORIES: *SF*
RATINGS: *MAINSTREAM*

A beautifully made tale of space conflict, borrowing from Joe Haldeman's *Forever War* and Kihachi Okamoto's *Battle of Okinawa*. A loving homage to several classic serials, it shows schoolgirls in giant robots saving the world from aliens, but on a deeper level it dares to suggest that sometimes heroes can find themselves fighting on the wrong side in a war they are destined to lose. Notable for our purposes chiefly because of the 'jiggle effect', an animated rendering of female breasts much copied by

the porn sector during the nineties. (See pp96, 101, 111.)

GUNSMITH CATS

OAV series, 3 parts
JAPANESE CREDITS: *1995-96. Dir: Takeshi Mori. Screenplay: Atsuji Kaneko. Chara des: Kenichi Sonoda & Tokuhiro Matsubara. Anime dir: Toshimitsu Kobayashi & Tokuhiro Matsubara. Art dir: Kazuo Nagai. Storyboards: Takeshi Mori. Music: Peter Erskine. Prod co: OLM. © Sonoda, Kodansha, TBS, VAP.*
Each 30 mins.
WESTERN CREDITS: *US & UK video release 1996 on AD Vision, sub, dub, trans Masako Arakawa, Eng rewrite Matt Greenfield.*
ORIGINS: *Manga by Kenichi Sonoda, pub Kodansha in Comic Afternoon, Eng trans pub (US) Dark Horse Comics.*
CATEGORIES: *P, T*
RATINGS: *VV, N, MAINSTREAM*

A thriller which lacks the pace and immediacy of the manga original but has lovely art and the coolest opening credit sequence seen in anime for years. Rally Vincent and Minnie May Hopkins are both experts in their respective fields — firearms and explosives — and run a gun shop. Rally freelances as a bounty hunter and Minnie is an ex-child prostitute. The story is set in Sonoda's dream of Chicago as a white trash heartland of seedy thrills and broken innocence; but for all its atmosphere of realism, it's a kinder, more romantic view of the West than that of *The Professional: Golgo 13*. (See p108.)

GUY
(Eng title for GUY: YŌMA KAKUSEI, lit Guy: The Demon Awakes, & GUY SECOND TARGET ŌGON NO MEGAMI HEN, lit Guy Second Target Chapter of the Golden Goddess)

OAV series, 2 parts
JAPANESE CREDITS: *1988 & 1992. Dir: Yorihisa Uchida. Chara des: Yasuhiro Makino (1), Yorihisa Uchida (2). Mecha des: Yukio Tomimatsu (1), Eiichi Akiyama & Eiko Murata (2). Monster des: Masami Obari. Music: Nobuhiko Kashihara. Prod co: Friends. © Media Station.*
Each 40 mins.
WESTERN CREDITS: *US video release 1993 on AD Vision, sub, trans Ichiro Arakaki &*

Dwayne Jones; UK video release 1994 on Animania, dub.
POINTS OF INTEREST: The US version of part 1 retains the sequences edited from the UK release. However, there is also an edited version available in the US.
CATEGORIES: SF, H
RATINGS: XX, VV, SM, NN, EROTIC

Schlock horror porn for the wannabes of the MTV generation. It's trying very hard to be cool, but can't wipe off the drool. The infamous gun rape sequence of part one is the bit most likely to give offence to any thinking person (any thinking person who hasn't yet borrowed it for their own live action thriller, that is), but the whole premise is largely based on mindless titillation and spares no stereotype in pursuit of its goal. (See pp20, 86.)

HAIKARA PASSING BY
(Eng trans for HAIKARA-SAN GA TŌRU)

TV series, 44 episodes
JAPANESE CREDITS: 1978-79. Prod co: Nippon Animation. © W. Yamato, Nippon Animation, Pony Canyon. Each c25 mins.
ORIGINS: Manga by Waki Yamato, serialised in Shojo Friend.
CATEGORIES: H
RATINGS: MAINSTREAM

Set in turn-of-the-century Japan, this romantic tale of schoolday love affairs encompasses more of the exotica which made shojo romance so appealing — Western clothes, foreign travel in an expanding world, women's struggle to have careers and find freedom, and finally a happy, settled and suitable marriage. (See p26.)

HANAPPE BAZOOKA

OAV
JAPANESE CREDITS: 1992. Dir: Yoyu Ikegami. Chara des: Fujio Oda. Art dir: Fujio Oda. Prod co: Studio Signal. © Koike, Nagai, Dynamic Planning, Nippon Crown. 55 mins.
WESTERN CREDITS: US video release 1996 on AD Vision, sub, trans Ichiro Arakaki; UK video release 1997 on AD Vision UK, sub.
ORIGINS: Manga by Kazuo Koike & Go Nagai, pub Shueisha.
POINTS OF INTEREST: A more serious

study of the same themes can be found in Nagai's Shutendoji.
CATEGORIES: P, C, F
RATINGS: NN, XX, G, SM, EROTIC

Teenage loser Hanappe has a wildly disinterested (not to say dysfunctional) family and is constantly getting beaten up by a gang of bullies. Then his life changes for the worse. Two demons — one male, one female — arrive from the netherworld and give him the gift of irresistible sex appeal. Like all demonic gifts, though, the catch isn't clear until you read the small print. But Hanappe's sweet nature and kind heart win over the demons, and the girl of his dreams. All he really wanted was a happy family and a nice girl, and after lesbian bondage, demonic sex parties and hordes of rampant old ladies have disrupted the fabric of space-time, that's what he gets in the end. (See pp57, 87.)

HERE IS GREENWOOD
(Eng title/trans for KOKO WA GREENWOOD)

OAV series, 6 parts
JAPANESE CREDITS: 1991-93. Dir: Tomomichi Mochizuki. Screenplay: Tomomichi Mochizuki. Chara des: Masako Goto. Anime dir: Masako Goto. Music: Shigeru Nagata. Prod co: Pierrot Project. © Y. Nasu, Hakusensha, Victor Entertainment, Pierrot Project. Each 30 mins.
WESTERN CREDITS: US video release 1996-97 on Software Sculptors, sub, dub.
ORIGINS: Manga by Yukie Nasu, pub Hakusensha.
POINTS OF INTEREST: US edition has 2 episodes to a tape.
CATEGORIES: P, F
RATINGS: G, MAINSTREAM

One of the most gentle and affirmative OAV series of the nineties, Greenwood is the name of a dorm for misfits in an exclusive school. Kazuya comes here to get over his love for his elder brother's wife and come to terms with his suspicions about his brother's bisexuality. Since his brother is the school doctor, this may seem a foolish idea, but Greenwood and its inmates provide the supportive environment he needs. With boys dressing as girls, girls pretending to be boys, ghosts on the look out for love and all kinds of strange events, life is never dull. Despite the absence of so-called erotic elements, there's plenty about sex, love and other human urges.

HEROIC LEGEND OF ARISLAN
(Eng title for ARSLAN SENKI, lit Arslan Chronicle)

MOVIE
JAPANESE CREDITS: 1991. Dir: Mamoru Hamatsu. Script: Tomoya Miyashita & Kaori Takada. Chara des: Sachiko Kamimura. Anime dir: Kazuya Kise. Art dir: Yuji Ikeda. Music: Norihiro Tsuri. Prod co: Animate Film. © Tanaka, MOVIC, Kadokawa, Sony Music Entertainment. 60 mins
WESTERN CREDITS: US video release 1993 on US Manga Corps, sub, dub, trans Pamela Ferdie & William Flanagan, Eng rewrite Jay Park; UK video release 1993 on Manga Video, dub only.
ORIGINS: Novel by Yoshiki Tanaka.
SPINOFFS: Another movie and 4 OAVs continue the story.
CATEGORIES: H, F
RATINGS: N, MAINSTREAM

Elegant and beautifully directed historical fantasy which makes great virtue of limited animation and is stuffed with gorgeous young men doing heroic deeds against dastardly villains. The villains are not totally one-dimensional, however, despite their extreme cruelty. Young Prince Arslan goes into hiding from the invaders of his country and tries to raise an army to oppose them with the help of a loyal general. The style is pure shojo and the male-bonding theme running right through the story carries a strong undercurrent of homoeroticism — the only female character of any note, a warrior priestess, is a surrogate male, and the role of Arslan's mother, the captive Queen, is questionable in the extreme. (See p39.)

HOLEY PANTS: DESIRE ON A STROLL
(Eng trans for PANTS NO ANA: MANBO DE GANBO)

OAV
JAPANESE CREDITS: 1987. Dir: Nobuyuki Kitajima. Original story: Pants no Ana. © Gakushu Kenkyusha, Soeishinsha, Pony Canyon. 25 mins.
ORIGINS: Stories and letters in Bomb! magazine.
POINTS OF INTEREST: Supposedly written, directed, cast and scored with the aid of fan comments and questionnaires
returned to the production company.
CATEGORIES: P, C
RATINGS: N, EROTIC

The ad blurb claims that this is a sweet, humorous look at teen worries, born from the real-life concerns of correspondents with *Bomb!* magazine. An excellent excuse to blame the audience if a project is unsuccessful. Since there were no follow-ups, we can assume that the experiment was a failure. (See p48.)

HOMEROOM AFFAIRS
(Eng title for TANIN NO KANKEI, lit Human Relations)

OAV series, 2 parts
JAPANESE CREDITS: 1994. Dir: Osamu Sekita. Screenplay: Hiroyuki Kawasaki. Chara des: Minoru Yamazawa. Art dir: Akira Furuya. Music: Hiroyuki Takei. Prod co: JC Staff. © Arima, Hakusensha, Jam Creation, JC Staff. Each c45 mins.
WESTERN CREDITS: US video release 1994 on Star Anime Entertprises, sub, trans John T. Carr III.
ORIGINS: Manga by Ichiro Arima, pub Hakusensha.
CATEGORIES: P, C
RATINGS: X, N, V, EROTIC

This constantly promises more than it delivers in erotic terms. Just as the heroine can't decide whether she's really a bad girl or just a confused child in need of a strong man to look after her, so the script and direction can't decide if they're a soft porn flick or a tender romance with bits of sexual titillation. Through a series of wildly unlikely coincidences, a young man in his first teaching job finds himself living with one of his pupils. It's all innocent, despite her best efforts, but he'd get sacked if he was caught. Then her ex shows up, there's a bit of trouble, and Teacher gets beaten to a pulp saving her from a gang rape. In the end there's a proper engagement, with a wedding planned for when she graduates.

HOMOSEXUAL REPORT
(Eng trans for OKAMA HAKUSHO)

OAV series, 3 parts.
JAPANESE CREDITS: 1991-92. Dir: Teruo Kigurashi. Screenplay: Ippei Yamagami (1), Sheila Yamazaki (2 & 3). Chara des: Teruo Kigurashi. Music: Jiro Takemura. Prod co:

Knack. © *Knack. Each 45 mins.*
ORIGINS: Manga by Hideo Yamamoto,
serialised in Young Sunday.
CATEGORIES: P
RATINGS: N, G, EROTIC

A gay man troubled by his own uncertainties
decides to test out his feelings by approaching his
close friend's girlfriend in this contemporary tragi-
comedy.

HOUSE OF KITTENS
(Eng title for KONEKO-CHAN NO IRU MISE,
lit Where the Kittens Are)

OAV
JAPANESE CREDITS: 1984. Original Story:
Fumio Nakajima. Prod co: Wonder Kids. ©
F. Nakajima, Wonder Kids. 30 mins.
ORIGINS: The previous Wonder Kids Lolita
release was Dying For a Girl/Altar of
Sacrifice.
POINTS OF INTEREST: According to the
Newtype Animesoft Compendium, this was
the most popular of the Lolita Anime
series.
SPINOFFS: Variation was the next release
in the series.
CATEGORIES: P,
RATINGS: N, PORN

The third Wonder Kids Lolita Anime release, in
which two schoolgirls catch their teacher in the
act and decide to experiment with each other.
Another girl fantasises about what sex would be
like with an older man, circumventing censorship
restrictions by assuring us it's all happening inside
her head. (See p109.)

HUMMINGBIRDS
(Eng title for IDOL BÖEITAI HUMMINGBIRD,
lit Idol Defence Band Hummingbird)

OAV series, 4 parts
JAPANESE CREDITS: 1993-95. Dir: Yasushi
Murayama. Original Story: Taira Yoshioka.
Anime dir: Kenichi Katsuro. Art dir: Torao
Arai. Prod co: Ashi Pro. © *Toho Video. Each*
c50 mins.
WESTERN CREDITS: UK video release 1995
on Western Connection, sub, trans
Jonathan Clements (first 2 episodes only,
on 1 tape).
POINTS OF INTEREST: As if the sibling
pilots weren't enough of a clue, the girls'

surname Toriishi is deliberately evocative
of Thunderbirds' Tracy family.
CATEGORIES: F
RATINGS: MAINSTREAM

Five sisters (from kiddie to late-teenager) are a
band of idol singers. They are also ace pilots sub-
contracted to the Self Defence Force. It's both a
satire on the eighties privatisation of Everything
and a tongue-in-cheek look at the music business, featuring some deliberately bad songs.
Later episodes lost the edge, as the series took
itself too seriously and became just another
example of the shows it was originally lampooning. One of the best examples of female anime
archetypes, with the five main girls forming a
carefully market-researched spread of teenage titillation, with more blatant sensuality bestowed
on their two Alien adversaries, the foxy, foreign
Fever Girls. (See pp94-96, 100, 108.)

I GIVE MY ALL
(Eng trans for MINNA AGECHAU)

OAV
JAPANESE CREDITS: 1987. Dir: Osamu
Uemura. Chara des: Masashi Tsukasa.
Storyboards: Osamu Uemura. Prod:
Minoru Takahashi. Prod co: Animate Film.
© *CBS Sony. 45 mins.*
ORIGINS: Based on the manga by Hikari
Yuzuki.
CATEGORIES: P, C
RATINGS: NN, XX, PORN

Yuno is a bored girl from a good family who
spends an afternoon snooping from her bedroom window with a pair of binoculars and
catches a young neighbour engaged in manual
activity with a pornographic magazine. Taking
pity on his solitary state, she drops round to see
him, and finds that he has problems only she
can solve. (See p48.)

JOKER MARGINAL CITY

OAV
JAPANESE CREDITS: 1992. Dir: Osamu
Yamazaki & Hidekage Hisashi. Screenplay:
Junichi Watanabe. Chara des: Chuichi
Iguchi. Storyboards: Takaaki Ishiyama.
Prod co: Studio Zyn. © *Michihara, Cyclone.*
45 mins.
ORIGINS: Manga by Katsumi Michihara,
serialised in Wings magazine.

CATEGORIES: SF
RATINGS: N, V, MAINSTREAM

The Jokers are genetically engineered beings whose remarkable attributes include the ability to switch genders at will. A victim of genetic experimentation goes on the run from a research facility, and the reporter who befriends him seeks the help of a Joker to keep the boy safe from his pursuers.

JUNK BOY
(Eng title for THE INCREDIBLE GYÖKAI VIDEO JUNK BOY, lit The Incredible Trade Video Junk Boy)

OAV
JAPANESE CREDITS: 1987. Dir: Katsuhisa Yamada. Screenplay: Tatsuhiko Urahata & Hiroyuki Fukushima. Chara des: Hiroshi Hamasaki. Chief animator: Hiroshi Hamasaki. Special Animation by: Yoshiaki Kawajiri. Music: Takashi Kudo.
© Y. Kunimoto, Futabasha, Victor Entertainment. 45 mins.
WESTERN CREDITS: UK & US video release 1996 on Manga Entertainment, dub, Eng rewrite George Roubicek.
ORIGINS: Manga by Yasuyuki Kunimoto, pub Futabasha.
CATEGORIES: P, C
RATINGS: NN, XX, EROTIC

Ryohei is a nerd and a creep with an overwhelmingly obvious interest in sex and correspondingly fashionable baggy pants. He talks his way into his dream job as dogsbody on *Potato Boy* magazine, where he has to evaluate photos (of naked girls), do investigative journalism (concerning naked girls who work in the sex trade) and attend celebrity photoshoots (with famous naked girls). Oh, and he gets to have a close encounter with his boss's underwear drawer. Reviewers with enough sense to know better have described this as amusing, sweet, or even inventive and sexy; the authors think it's a colossal yawn and would be offensive if it weren't so dumb. (See pp20, 87.)

KAMA SUTRA
(Eng title for TOKKYŌ NO SEX ADVENTURE KAMA SUTRA, lit Ultimate Sex Adventure Kama Sutra)

OAV
JAPANESE CREDITS: 1992. Dir: Masayuki Ozeki. Screenplay: Seiji Matsuoka. Chara
des: Shinsuke Taresawa. Art dir: Chihata Miyazaki. Music: Ken Yajima. Prod co: Animate. © Go Nagai, Dynamic Planning, Toho Video. 43 mins.
WESTERN CREDITS: UK video release 1994 on Western Connection, sub; US video release 1998 on Kitty Media, sub.
ORIGINS: Ancient Hindu erotic text; manga by Go Nagai.
CATEGORIES: F, C
RATINGS: X, N, EROTIC

Another of Nagai's saucy postcards, this time from India. A nineteen year-old virgin (whose girlfriend can't wait to remedy the situation) is on an archaeological dig when he discovers a beautiful Hindu princess who has been frozen for centuries, along with a magic cup which can give both endless pleasure and eternal life to those who drink from it. Of course, first the cup has to be filled with the right mix of bodily fluids. A harmless bit of smut with Nagai's characteristic good humour. (See pp57, 87.)

Hummingbirds

KEKKO KAMEN

(US title for KEKKÖ KAMEN; UK title KEKKOU KAMEN)

OAV series, 4 episodes
JAPANESE CREDITS: 1991-92. Dir: Nobuhiro Kondo. Screenplay: Masashi Sogo. Chara des: Tomo Hirayama. Opening animation dir: Koji Morimoto. Music: Keiji Ishikawa. Exec prod: Go Nagai & Genji Hiruta. Prod: Kenji Nagai, Yoshinaga Minami & Masaharu Takayama. Prod co: Studio Signal. © Go Nagai, Dynamic Planning. Each c27 mins.
WESTERN CREDITS: UK video release 1995 on East2West on 2 tapes, dub, trans Jonathan Clements; US video release 1995 on AD Vision, sub, trans Masako Arakawa & Chris Hutts.
ORIGINS: Manga by Go Nagai.
POINTS OF INTEREST: Note Memories' Koji Morimoto as director of opening animation.
SPINOFFS: A feature-length live action version directed by Go Nagai in 1991. It has been released on video in the US and stars Chris Aoki, Japan's Playmate of 1990.
CATEGORIES: C, F
RATINGS: NN, XX, V, SM, EROTIC

Go Nagai didn't single-handedly make sex funny, but he knows how to bring out the humour in any sexual situation. He points out the silliness of sex with a heart-warming absence of malice. Kekko Kamen, the 'Warrior of Love and Justice', fights to defend the innocent — no, make that hapless — Mayumi from the various perverts and sadists who make up the staff of her high school. The episode one torture scene, in which a girl is tied to a giant rotating swastika, was not popular with the British censor. (See pp46, 54-55, 87.)

KIRARA

OAV series
JAPANESE CREDITS: 1998. Dir: Yasushi Murayama. Screenplay: Noriko Hayasaka. Chara des: Shinya Takahashi. Prod co: Ashi. © Toho, Shueisha.
POINTS OF INTEREST: The part of the young Kirara was cast by open audition.
CATEGORIES: P, C
RATINGS: N, MAINSTREAM

A clever idea that approaches growing pains from both sides. Konpei is fantasising about his future wife, when he finds her ghost in his bed. Kirara Imai tells him that they're going to get married in eight years time, which will also be the day she dies in a traffic accident. Konpei and his future-dead-wife's-ghost have to join forces to save her younger self, who has just trans-ferred, oblivious, to Konpei's school. A time trav-el romance in which an Older Woman teaches a Maiden how to become a Girl Next Door, all for the benefit of the male viewer, who gets to enjoy the mature, sensual ghost as sexual initiatress, as well as her unsuspecting virgin incarnation as love interest.

KISS ME ON THE APPLE OF MY EYE

(Eng trans for KISS WA ME NI SHITE)

OAV
JAPANESE CREDITS: 1993. Dir: Takuji Endo. Script: Akinori Endo. Chara des: Kazuhiro Soeda. Prod co: Madhouse. © Ueda, Shueisha. c40 mins.
ORIGINS: Manga by Noriko Ueda, pub Shueisha in Margaret magazine. The previous release in the 6-part Margaret series was Sleepless Oedo.
SPINOFFS: The final release, A-Girl, came next.
CATEGORIES: P
RATINGS: MAINSTREAM

Ibuki is a high school girl with the usual dreams of love and romance. Then the boy of her dreams arrives to board with her family and join her class at school! Is this the answer to her prayers? Or will the whole romance be too fraught with problems and misunderstandings to really get off the ground?

KIZUNA

(Eng/Jpn title, lit Bonds)

OAV series, 2 episodes
JAPANESE CREDITS: 1994. Dir: Rin Hiro. Screenplay: Miyo Morita. Concept: Rin Hiro. Chara des: Ayako Mihashi. Anime dir: Ayako Mihashi. Art dir: Fumie Ayabe. Music: Fujio Takano. Prod co: SIDO. © K. Kodaka, Seiji Biblios, Daiei. Each 30 mins.
WESTERN CREDITS: US video release 1996 on CQC Pictures, sub.

ORIGINS: *Manga by Kazuma Kodaka,*
pub Be-Boy magazine.
POINTS OF INTEREST: *The first (and to*
date the only) shonen ai video released in
the English-speaking world.
CATEGORIES: *P*
RATINGS: *XX, NN, G, EROTIC*

A gay romance, with all its problems and tensions depicted frankly in the style Westerners are
more used to seeing in women's publications.
Ran has been involved in a hit-and-run 'accident' that may have been part of a shadowy
plot, and it takes him a long while to recover. He
and his friend Enjoji move in together. When a
college professor, a very nasty sort, tries to force
his attentions on Ran and break up the duo, he
bites off more than he can chew. Ran's friend
has a yakuza family — and a jealous half-broth-
er who also fancies Ran like mad. The course of
true love definitely doesn't run smooth. (See
pp32, 41.)

LA BLUE GIRL
(Eng title for INJÜ GAKUEN LA BLUE GIRL,
lit Lust-Beast Academy La Blue Girl)

OAV series, 6 parts
JAPANESE CREDITS: *1992-94. Dir: Raizo*
Kitakawa (1), Kan Fukumoto (2 & 3, 5 &
6), Rin'o Yanagikaze (4 & 6). Screenplay:
Megumi Ichiyanagi. Chara des: Kinji
Yoshimoto (1), Rin Shin (2-6). Art dir:
Bibimba Miyake (1), Taro Taki (2-6).
Music dir: Teruo Takahama. © T. Maeda,
Daiei. Each 45 mins except part 6,
60 mins.
WESTERN CREDITS: *US video release*
1995-96 on Anime 18, sub, dub; UK video
certificate refused by the BBFC, 1996.
ORIGINS: *Manga by Toshio Maeda.*
POINTS OF INTEREST: *The censoring*
digitisation imposed for the Japanese
market was removed in the US release.
SPINOFFS: *A sequel series entitled Lady*
Blue. A live-action version was also
released in Japan.
CATEGORIES: *F, H*
RATINGS: *XX, NN, VV, SM, PORN*

High school girls Miko Mido and her sister are
heirs to an ancient ninja clan. Clan rivalry
exposes them to attack by lust-crazed demons. It
turns out in the end that the girls are half-
demon themselves, which technically speaking
throws incest into the mix as well. The ongoing

adventures of Miko mix family problems, high
school friendships and girl rivalries with
sequences of multi-tentacled demonic rape
which, if they do nothing else, will put you off
eating squid for the rest of your life. (See pp79-
81, 99.)

LADY BLUE

OAV series, 4 parts
JAPANESE CREDITS: *1996-97. Dir: Kan*
Fukumoto. Script: Megumi Ichiryu. Chara
des: Rin Shin. Art dir: Shoji Hitachi.
Storyboards: Kan Fukumoto. Exec prod:
Rusher Ikeda. Prod: Smally Izumi &
Kento Maki. Prod co: Daiei. © Toshio
Maeda, Daiei. Each 60 mins.
WESTERN CREDITS: *US video release 1998*
on Anime 18, sub, trans Kevin McKeown.
ORIGINS: *Manga by Toshio Maeda; sequel*
to La Blue Girl.
POINTS OF INTEREST: *The digitisation*
imposed for the Japanese market was
removed in the US release.
CATEGORIES: *F, H*
RATINGS: *XX, NN, VV, SM, EROTIC*

Miko Mido is in college and falling in love for
the very first time, much to the jealousy and
frustration of her ninja sidekick Nin-Nin. But an
ancient curse, the result of a love affair gone
tragically wrong, puts her would-be boyfriend in
danger. Thanks to the BBFC, the people of
Britain will be forever protected from lines like:
'The flute strangely resounds through the
Shikima and forebodes the revived hatred of the
Anti-Shikima stemming from an incident that
happened 400 years ago'. And who can forget:
'In this world the flute makes a strange, intoxi-
cating sound that brings forth an amorous rap-
ture in young women'. (See pp20, 80-81.)

LEDA: FANTASTIC ADVENTURES OF YOKO
(Eng title for GENMUSENKI LEDA, lit Leda
Dream War)

OAV
JAPANESE CREDITS: *1985. Dir: Mamoru*
Oshii. Chara des: Mutsumi Inomata.
© Toho, Kaname Productions. 72 mins.
WESTERN CREDITS: *US video release 1997*
on US Manga Corps, dub.
CATEGORIES: *P, F*
RATINGS: *MAINSTREAM*

Yoko is a shy girl secretly in love with a high school classmate. In an effort to express her feelings she writes a passionate romantic melody for him, and unknowingly hits on the melodic key which will bring two different dimensions into harmony and make it possible for a sinister dictator on another world to cross into ours and take over. But as Yoko caused the problem, Yoko can prevent it, by becoming the chosen warrior of the Goddess Leda, (complete with battle-bikini and sword) and piloting the Wings of Leda into battle. So far, so conventional; yet this OAV has an erotic atmosphere which pervades even the gung-ho battle scenes and subverts what might have been just a teenage boy's dream into a meditation on the power and purity of first love and first sexual longing. (See pp28-29.)

LEGEND OF LEMNEAR
(Eng title for KYOKUGURO NO TSUBASA VALKISAS, lit Black Wings of Valkisas)

OAV
JAPANESE CREDITS: 1993. Dir: Kinji Yoshimoto. Screenplay: Kinji Yoshimoto. Chara des: Satoshi Urushibara. Music: Norimasa Yamanaka. Prod co: AIC.
© Soshin Pictures, AIC. 45 mins.
WESTERN CREDITS: US video release 1996, re-release 1998 on US Manga Corps, sub.
ORIGINS: Manga by Satoshi Urushibara.
CATEGORIES: F
RATINGS: N, V, MAINSTREAM

Lances and lechery rule. Warrior girl Silver is out to find her sister, who's become the tool of a power-crazed warlord. There's a slave trader's harem, a bar room brawl, a huge flying dino-bird and lots of other set-pieces nicked from all over the place and done very prettily by the designer of *Plastic Little*. Plenty of breast shots, not much else.

LEGEND OF LYON: FLARE
(Eng title/trans for LYON DENSETSU FLARE)

OAV series, 2 episodes
JAPANESE CREDITS: 1986 & 1990. Dir: Yorihisa Uchida. Chara des: Yorihisa Uchida & Yakihiro Makino. Prod co: Media Station. © Media Station.
Each 30 mins.
WESTERN CREDITS: US video release 1994 on AD Vision, sub, trans Doc Isaac (sic).

POINTS OF INTEREST: Described by one US reviewer as 'Urotsukidoji's drooling idiot cousin'.
CATEGORIES: F, H
RATINGS: X, V, NN, SM, PORN

Once again, the tentacled alien hordes are invading and they want our women. Luckily for the monstrous rapists, psychic lovely Flare doesn't use her considerable powers until after most of her friends have got closer to the calamares than they would have liked. Aided by her sword-slinging sidekick Neris, Flare finally makes sushi of the monsters. In part two, however, she learns that something is lurking in the woods and has to start the whole process again. Some people never learn, whether they're tentacled monsters or anime buyers.

LEGEND OF THE FOUR KINGS
(Eng title for SÖRYÜDEN, lit The Endragonning; aka SOHRYUDEN LEGEND OF THE DRAGON KINGS)

OAV series, 12 episodes
JAPANESE CREDITS: 1991-93. Dir: Shigeru Ueda & Yoshihiro Yamaguchi. Script: Akinori Endo. Chara des: Shunji Murata. Art dir: Shichiro Kobayashi & Jiro Kono. Prod co: Kitty Film Mitaka Studio.
© Tanaka, Kitty, Fuji, Kodansha.
Each c45 mins.
WESTERN CREDITS: US video release 1995 on US Manga Corps, sub, Eng rewrite Jay Parks; UK video release 1995 on Manga Video, dub.
ORIGINS: Novel by Yoshiki Tanaka.
CATEGORIES: P, F
RATINGS: V, MAINSTREAM

Four orphan brothers are avatars of ancient dragon kings of Chinese legend. When their powers awaken they can control the world, and unscrupulous men are out to use them for evil ends. The brothers are determined to stay free and remain together. There's a sequence in a restaurant where the second brother resists an all-out seduction attempt by a dazzling Older Woman who is very definitely not on the side of righteousness, just to prove that loyalty to family is the most important thing in life. (See pp87, 100.)

LEMON COCKTAIL — LOVE 30 S
(Eng trans for CHUHAI LEMON LOVE 30 S)

OAV
JAPANESE CREDITS: 1985. Prod co: Wonder
Kids. © Tsuchida. 45 mins.
ORIGINS: Manga of the same name by
Tsutomu Shinohara & Sho Shimura.
CATEGORIES: T
RATINGS: N, V, PORN

More cop show than strip show, this adventure has a musclebound policeman who uses his strength and apparent pig-headed stupidity to rescue his high school girlfriend from the scrapes she gets herself into. (See p47.)

LITTLE WITCH SALLY
(Eng trans for MAHŌTSUKAI SALLY)

TV series, 92 episodes
JAPANESE CREDITS: 1966-68. Series dir:
Osamu Kasai. Screenplay: Akiyoshi Sakai.
Chara des: Yoshiyuki Hane. Prod co: Toei.
© Hikari Pro, Toei Doga. Each c25 mins.
ORIGINS: Manga by Mitsuteru Yokoyama.
SPINOFFS: Does an entire genre count?
CATEGORIES: F, P
RATINGS: MAINSTREAM

The mother of all magical girls was created by the father of the giant robot. This charming irony isn't apparent anywhere in the series itself, which is pure little-girl magic. Sally is a trainee witch, sent to Earth to study humans and learn how to blend in among them, a task she accomplishes with more or less success and much humour and charm. (See pp23-24.)

LOLIKON ANGEL: PRETTY GIRL COMIC: SECRET EXPERIENCE
(Eng trans for LOLIKON ANGEL BISHŌJO COMIC HIMITSU NO AJI)

OAV
JAPANESE CREDITS: 1985. Prod co:
Pumpkin Pie. © Japan Home Video.
25 mins.
CATEGORIES: P
RATINGS: N, G, PORN

One of the *Cream Lemon* clones rushed out to cash in on the lolikon fad, this one is a thinly plotted excuse to get three underage girls under a shower together. Even the normally timid *Newtype* comments that: 'while there may be hard lesbian action, the animation and storyline are considerably below standard'.

LOVE'S WEDGE
(Eng trans for AI NO KUSABI, can also trans as Ties of Love, Loving Bond)

OAV series, 2 parts
JAPANESE CREDITS: 1992 & 1994. Dir:
Akira Nishimori (1), Kazuhito Akiyama
(2). Script: Naoko Hasegawa (1), Reiko
Yoshihara (2). Art dir: Yoichi Nango. Prod
co: AIC. © Yoshihara, AIC, Magazine. Each
60 mins.
ORIGINS: Novel by Reiko Yoshihara
illustrated by Katsumi Michihara, pub
June magazine.
CATEGORIES: SF
RATINGS: XX, N, V, G, EROTIC

Set in a future in which teenage 'Pets' are sex slaves to wealthy and powerful adults, this powerful shonen ai tale of doomed love, corruption and nobility is elegantly animated, though with major differences in style between the two episodes. (See pp36-38, 41.)

LUNATIC NIGHT

OAV, 2 episodes
JAPANESE CREDITS: 1996-97. Dir: Fuyumi
Shirakawa (1), Teruo Kigure (2).
Screenplay: Shinji Nishiyama & Haruka
Kaio. Chara des: Kiginmaru Oi. Gen prod:
Seiichi Nishino. Prod: Shigeyuki Hasegawa
& Noriko Nishino. Prod co: Knack. © Mii,
Mediax, Knack. Each 35 mins.
WESTERN CREDITS: US video release 1998
on Anime 18, sub, trans Kevin McKeown.
ORIGINS: Manga by Akira Mii.
POINTS OF INTEREST: US version removes
the censoring digitisation, giving the
characters infantile genitalia to match
their infantile behaviour.
CATEGORIES: P, SF, F, C
RATINGS: NN, XX, SM, PORN

Seemingly written by four drunken hacks taking turns on each page, this script begins on a moon-lit night when college boy Kanzaki gets a sex-crazed girl for a pet. She's there to remind him he's the lord of Atlantis and final incarnation of Krishna, forced to fight his satanic schoolmate Mutsuki for control of the world amidst innumerable jokey references to classic manga and anime like *Babel II*, *Giant Robo* and *Striker*. Watch in particular for V-girl, a robotic minion who is an evil, whip-wielding dominatrix when her batteries are inserted the wrong way round, but becomes a shy virginal schoolgirl when you follow the instructions in the manual. In part two, overindulgence has turned all Atlantean men into penises, and incredible power awaits the man who can pass the trials and give Queen Estelle the orgasm of a lifetime. Kanzaki also has to pleasure a giant Amazon who drowns him with her breasts and prompts the meaningful quote: 'She's huge! I could stick my whole head in there.' We would like to apologise for making this sound a lot more interesting than it is. (See p51.)

LUPIN III
(Eng title/trans for LUPIN SANSEI)

TV series, 23 episodes
JAPANESE CREDITS: 1971-72. Dir: Masaaki Okuma, Isao Takahata & Hayao Miyazaki. Screenplay: Tadaaki Yamazaki et al. Prod co: Tokyo Movie Shinsha. © Monkey Punch, NTV, YTV, TMS. Each c25 mins. WESTERN CREDITS: Several of the Lupin movies and videos that followed have had UK & US releases. ORIGINS: Novels by Maurice Leblanc; manga by Monkey Punch. SPINOFFS: 1977 and 1984 TV series totalling a further 205 episodes, movies, OAVs and annual TV specials. CATEGORIES: P, T RATINGS: V, N, MAINSTREAM

The capers of Monkey Punch's charming crook take him all over the world and lead to amorous encounters with a whole range of beautiful women. His ongoing love interest is the gorgeous and thoroughly unreliable Fujiko Mine, who almost sells him down the river for the promise of eternal youth in the movie *The Secret of Mamo*, but there are lots of others, from the elderly lush Rosetta of *The Gold of Babylon*, who turns out to be an alien sex goddess in disguise, to the innocent and courageous Clarisse of *Castle of Cagliostro*. Witty, fast-moving grown-up entertainment. (See pp13, 27, 42.)

LUST ALIEN
(Eng title for INJÜ ALIEN, lit Lust-Beast Alien)

OAV
JAPANESE CREDITS: 1997. Dir: Norio Takanami. Chara des: Ryu Tsukiyo. Storyboards: Shin Taira. Prod co: Pink Pineapple. © Pink Pineapple. 45 mins.

CATEGORIES: SF
RATINGS: N, V, PORN

A thousand light years from home, and without a man in sight, an all-female space crew resorts to lesbian sex to slake their sensual thirst. But when the ship is attacked by a multi-tentacled alien monster with a craving for female flesh, the scene is set for many tits and many tentacles, in what is supposedly an original contribution to the genre because it doesn't take place in a high school.

MACROSS PLUS

OAV series, 4 parts
JAPANESE CREDITS: 1994. Dir: Shoji Kawamori & Shinichiro Watanabe. Screenplay: Keiko Nobumo. Original story: Studio Nue & Shoji Kawamori. Chara des: Masayuki. Mecha des: Shoji Kawamori. Anime dir: Yuji Moriyama. Music: Yoko Kanno. Prod co: Triangle Staff. © Big West. 1 & 2 each 40 mins, 3 & 4 each 45 mins. WESTERN CREDITS: US video release 1994 on Manga Video, sub, dub, trans Neil Nadelman, Eng rewrite Raymond Garcia; UK video release 1995 on Manga Video, dub. ORIGINS: 1982 & 1993 TV series; 1984 Movie; 1987 & 1992 OAVs. SPINOFFS: Edited into the 'Movie Edition' in 1995, with new footage. CATEGORIES: SF RATINGS: N, V, MAINSTREAM

In this story of three seemingly unsympathetic characters — a hard man, a loudmouth and a self-pitying loser — we see how their past problems both create a crisis for their world and then help them solve it. A rape scene and a scary computer entity are combined with some stunning aerial footage to create a high-tech package which has more depth than is at first apparent.

MAD BULL 34

OAV series, 4 episodes
JAPANESE CREDITS: 1990-92. Dir: Tetsu Dezaki. Screenplay: Toshiaki Imaizumi. Art dir: Nobutaka Ike. Music dir: Katsunori Shimizu. Prod co: Magic Bus. © Koike, Inoue, Shueisha, Pony Canyon. Each 60 mins except part 4, 50 mins. WESTERN CREDITS: US & UK video release

Macross Plus

*1996 on Manga Video, dub, Eng rewrite
John Wolskel.
ORIGINS: Manga by Kazuo Koike &
Noriyoshi Inoue, pub Shueisha.
CATEGORIES: P, T
RATINGS: X, V, SM, MAINSTREAM*

One man's exotic location is another man's
home beat, but he wouldn't necessarily recognise
it as such. The New York of *Mad Bull 34* is a white
trash homeland of run-down brownstones
inhabited by pimps, junkies and hookers with
hearts of gold, where corrupt cops run the city
and wet-behind-the-ears rookies find out that
they're really the good guys, whatever police
academy may have told them. The mentor character Sleepy 'educates' his young partner on the
mean streets through such romps as transvestism
in the course of duty and running a hospital fund
for hookers. The sub-standard animation was bad
enough. The dub makes it worse. (See p40, 104.)

MAGICAL EMI
**(Eng title for MAHÖ NO STAR MAGICAL EMI,
lit Magic Star Magical Emi)**

*TV series, 38 episodes
JAPANESE CREDITS: 1985-86. Dir: Takashi
Ano. Screenplay: Mami Watanabe. Chara
des: Hiroshi Yamamoto & Yoshiyuki Kishi.
Prod co: Studio Pierrot. © Studio Pierrot,
NTV. Each c25 mins.
CATEGORIES: P, F
RATINGS: MAINSTREAM*

Another popular magical girl series following
much the same lines as *Creamy Mami*. (See p25.)

MAGICAL TWILIGHT

*OAV series, 3 episodes
JAPANESE CREDITS: 1994-95. Dir: Toshiaki
Kobayashi (1 & 2), Toshiaki Komura (3).
Chara des: Junichi Mihara. Prod co: AIC.
© Yuki, Pink Pineapple. Each 35 mins.
WESTERN CREDITS: US video release 1995-
96 on Softcel, sub, trans Doc Issaac. 1998
Softcel release The Hex Files is all 3
episodes on 1 tape.
ORIGINS: Based on characters created by
Yuki (Akane Shinshaken).*

POINTS OF INTEREST: *Non X-rated US version available, for people who want porn with the porn removed.*
CATEGORIES: *P, F*
RATINGS: *XX, NN, PORN*

Tsukasa Tachibana is a student with problems. His double exam failure is giving him nightmares; he's dreaming he's about to die. But he's not the only one with exams on his mind. Three young witches have to go to Earth to pass their final exam, and they all have the same project — Tsukasa. They'll affect his life in a weird variety of ways, though black witch Liv fails in her project: to kill him after horrendous tortures. This leaves Tsukasa with two young witches on his hands. Guess who's up for hands-on tuition?

MAGIC LIPSTICK
(Eng trans for MAHÖ NO ROUGE LIPSTICK)

OAV
JAPANESE CREDITS: *1985. Prod co: Fairy Dust. © Akushinsha. 25 mins.*
CATEGORIES: *P, F*
RATINGS: *NN, XX, PORN*

Yuma is given a magic lipstick with which she can transform herself into a grown woman. In this stunningly beautiful form, she decides to seduce her brother. (See p50.)

MEGAMI PARADISE
(Eng title for MEGAMI TENGOKU, lit Goddess Paradise)

OAV series, 2 episodes
JAPANESE CREDITS: *1995. Dir: Katsuhiko Nishijima. Screenplay: Mayori Sekijima. Original story: Akihiro Yoshimi. Scenario: Koji Shimana & Masaki Kawato. Chara*

Megami Paradise

des: *Noriyasu Yamauchi. Anime dir: Noriyasu Yamauchi. Art dir: Yoji Nakaza. Storyboards: Ko Matsuzono (1), Katsuhiko Nishijima (2). Prod co: Animate. © Megami Takada, Kensetsu Iinkai, Media Works, King Record, MOVIC. Each c30 mins.*
WESTERN CREDITS: *US video release 1996 on AD Vision, sub, trans Ichiro Arakaki.*
ORIGINS: *Video game and subsequent manga, pub Dengeki PC Engine magazine.*
CATEGORIES: *F*
RATINGS: *N, PORN*

Like the original game, this is an excuse to see girls in skimpy, see-through or collapsing outfits. There's an apology for a plot about the lovely shrine maidens having to defend the realm of peace and light from the followers of the Dark Goddess, but if you expect it to make much sense you've come to the wrong place. (See p25.)

MELANCHOLY SLAVE
(Eng trans for AI DÖRU, lit Melancholy Slave, but also pun on 'Idol' and 'Love Slave')

OAV
JAPANESE CREDITS: *1997. Dir: Raizo Kitagawa. Screenplay: Yuri Kanai & Naomi Hayakawa. Original story: Naomi Hayakawa. Chara des: Aidoru Project. Storyboards: Kazumasa Muraki. Prod co: Raishin Film. © Hayakawa, Raishin, JVC. 38 mins.*
CATEGORIES: *P*
RATINGS: *SM, N, PORN*

Bereft at her mother's death, Rachel goes into a convent, only to discover that the contemplative life is not quite as she imagined when she is bound, gagged and sexually assaulted by lust-crazy lesbian nuns.

MIDNIGHT ANIME LEMON ANGEL

TV series, 47 episodes
JAPANESE CREDITS: *1987-88. Art director: Yuji Moriyama. Prod co: Fairy Dust. © Aichi. Each 25 mins.*
CATEGORIES: *P*
RATINGS: *N, G, EROTIC*

Three lovely teenagers — and the three actresses

Miyuki-chan in Wonderland

who provide their voices — share their midnight confidences and fantasies with the television audience. (See p48.)

MIYUKI-CHAN IN WONDERLAND
(Eng title/trans for FUSHIGI NO KUNI NO MIYUKI-CHAN)

OAV series, 2 episodes
JAPANESE CREDITS: 1995. Dir: Masuo Maruyama. Prod: Masahiro Otake. Prod co: Mad House, Animate Film. © CLAMP, Sony Music Entertainment, Kadokawa, MOVIC. Each 35 mins.
WESTERN CREDITS: US video release 1997 on AD Vision, sub, trans Ichiro Arakaki.
ORIGINS: Lewis Carroll's novels Alice's Adventures in Wonderland & Through the Looking Glass; the manga Miyuki-chan in Wonderland by CLAMP.
CATEGORIES: F
RATINGS: NN, G, SM, EROTIC

Miyuki is an ordinary teenager who finds herself pulled into all kinds of strange situations when she follows a white rabbit and then again when she passes through a mirror — or has it all been a dream? All the scenes have some link with *Alice*, all seem to involve clothes falling off, and all are played entirely by and between saucy young women. Light-hearted fantasy with gorgeous art. (See p35.)

MOLDIVER

OAV series, 6 parts
JAPANESE CREDITS: 1993. Dir: Hirohide Fujiwara & Hiroyuki Kitazume. Screenplay: Manabu Nakamura (1, 4 & 6), Ryoei Tsukimura (2, 3 & 5). Original

story: Hiroyuki Kitazume. Chara des: Hiroyuki Kitazume. Art dir: Masumi Nishikawa. Music: Kei Wakakusa. Exec prod: Taro Maki. Prod co: AIC. © Pioneer LDC. Each 30 mins.
WESTERN CREDITS: US & UK video release 1994 on Pioneer, dub.
CATEGORIES: P, F
RATINGS: N, MAINSTREAM

The story of a girl genius who steals big brother's invention — a superhero chip — and uses it to right wrongs, fight for justice and find true love. Peppered with cute girls, knicker shots and nude transformation scenes. (See pp25, 39.)

MY MARIE
(Eng trans for BOKU NO MARIE)

OAV series, 3 episodes
JAPANESE CREDITS: 1996. Dir: Satoshi Mochizuki. Prod co: Studio Pierrot.
© Pierrot, Victor Entertainment.
CATEGORIES: P, F
RATINGS: MAINSTREAM

A boy has a robot girl as companion and toy, the perfect fantasy of a woman at his beck and call. Allegedly, she's a surrogate little sister, there to help him woo another Marie (the girl next door). Read into that what you will. (See p104.)

MY MY MAI
(Eng title for SONO KI NI SASETE YO, lit Get Me in the Mood)

OAV series, 4 episodes
JAPANESE CREDITS: 1993. Dir: Osamu Sekita. Chara des: Yumi Nakamura. Music: Koichi Ota & Koji Tajima. Prod co: Apple.
© M. Yamaguchi, Akita Shoten, Apple. Each 22 mins.
WESTERN CREDITS: US video release 1996 on US Manga Corps, on 2 tapes, dub.
ORIGINS: Manga by Masakazu Yamaguchi, pub Akita Shoten.
CATEGORIES: P
RATINGS: N, EROTIC

Mai runs a strange psychic detective-cum-consultancy agency — if you need it, she'll find it, from a surgeon to a cure for phobias. She solves most problems with a mix of pop psychobabble and flashes of her own bounteous charms in or out of lingerie. More innocently naughty than pornographic, and very, very weird with its parodies of horror classics like *Frankenstein* in unlikely situations.

MY SEXUAL HARASSMENT
(Eng trans for BOKU NO SEXUAL HARASSMENT)

OAV series, 4 episodes to date
JAPANESE CREDITS: 1994-. Dir: Yosei Morino. Script: Yosei Morino. Chara des: Aki Tsunaki. Art dir: Shigeru Ikehata. Prod co: Be-Boys Novels Video Project. © Momo, Be-Boys, Biblios. Each 45 mins.
ORIGINS: Novel by Sakura Momo, illustrated by Kazuma Kodaka, pub Be-Boys magazine.
CATEGORIES: P
RATINGS: X, EROTIC

A young businessman out to win the corporate war for his company travels extensively and meets male colleagues and competitors from many different countries and companies. This series lends a whole new emphasis to the cut and thrust of international business, since our hero seems to end up having sex with most of them. (See pp32, 35.)

NEON GENESIS EVANGELION
(Eng title for SHINSEIKI EVANGELION, lit New Century Evangelion)

TV series, 26 episodes
JAPANESE CREDITS: 1996-97. Dir: Hideaki Anno. Asst dir: Masayuki & Kazuya Tsurumaki. Original story: Gainax. Script: Hideaki Anno, Akio Satsugawa et al. Chara des: Yoshiyuki Sadamoto. Mecha des: Ikuto Yamashita & Hideaki Anno. Art dir: Hiroshi Kato. Music: Shiro Sagisu. Prod: Noriko Kobayashi & Yutaka Sugiyama. Prod co: Tatsunoko Productions, Gainax. © Gainax, Project EVA, TV Tokyo, NAS. Each c27 mins.
WESTERN CREDITS: US & UK video release 1997-98 on AD Vision, sub, dub, trans Kuni Kimura, Eng rewrite Matt Greenfield.
POINTS OF INTEREST: The original TV ending was replaced by a 'nicer' one. If you want to see how the makers really wanted to conclude the story, you'll have to see the movie edit, End of Evangelion.
SPINOFFS: Manga by Yoshiyuki Sadamoto, pub Kadokawa, Eng trans pub Viz (US), films Death, Rebirth and End of Evangelion.
CATEGORIES: SF
RATINGS: V, MAINSTREAM

Gainax reprise their seminal *Gunbuster* and ask exactly what it would feel like to be a kamikaze pilot in a giant robot. There are deep characterisations and some truly nasty reflections on family ties and Freudian psychology (even the music tracks have titles like 'Infantile Dependence, Adult Dependency' and 'Anxiety Avoidance Through Regression'). A beautiful, terrifying study of dysfunctional families, from the personal to the global, its underlying sexual themes include incest, child abuse, the Oedipus/Electra complexes and well observed studies of spinsterhood, co-dependency and romance gone stale. (See pp24, 84, 101-102, 111, 119.)

NEW ANGEL
(Eng title/trans for SHIN ANGEL)

OAV series, 4 parts
JAPANESE CREDITS: 1994-95. Dir: Kaoru Toyo'oka. Screenplay: Koji Sakakibara. Chara des: Rin Shin. Chief animator:

Masato Ijuin. Prod co: Pink Pineapple.
© Studio Angel, U-Jin, Pink Pineapple.
Parts 1 & 2 each 50 mins, parts 3 & 4
each 35 mins.
WESTERN CREDITS: US video release
1995-96 on AD Vision, sub, trans Masako
Arakawa, Chris Hutts & Doc Issaac, Eng
rewrite Matt Greenfield.
ORIGINS: Manga Angel by U-Jin.
CATEGORIES: P
RATINGS: XX, NN, PORN

Erotic adventure of Keisuke, a young man who
always manages to pull something good out of
an encounter with a girl — even if she's dead,
like the young lady in the first episode, or nude
and suicidal, like the one in the second. Not
tasteful, not tactful, but well animated with lots
of sex scenes.

NEW CREAM LEMON AMI — FROM THEN ON
(Eng trans for SHIN CREAM LEMON AMI SOREKARA...)

OAV series, 4 parts
JAPANESE CREDITS: 1988-90. Prod co:
Fairy Dust. © Soeishinsha. Each 40 mins.
ORIGINS: Follows on from a Cream
Lemon Special Ami Image White Shadow.
CATEGORIES: P
RATINGS: NN, XX, PORN

This four-part series is considered by Smet to
mark the end of the lolikon era. All the characters are in their twenties and Ami, the innocent
who was seduced by her older brother in the first
ever *Cream Lemon* story four years earlier, is now
nobody's baby, but a young woman in control of
her own destiny. The quality of art and animation is generally good, and certain stylistic similarities with *City Hunter* raise questions about the
identity of some members of staff. (See p50.)

NEW CREAM LEMON DREAM-COLOURED BUNNY
(Eng trans for SHIN CREAM LEMON YUME IRO BUNNY)
OAV
JAPANESE CREDITS: 1987. Prod co: Fairy
Dust. © Soeishinsha. 25 mins.
CATEGORIES: F, C
RATINGS: NN, XX, PORN

The hapless Takumi is forever hanging round

his local pet shop to ogle the girls who gather
there to coo at the cute little animals. One day
the pet shop owner tells him that if he's going
to keep chasing customers away, he'll have to
buy something himself. But the pet Takumi
buys isn't your run of the mill bunny. She's got
white ears, so he calls her Milk. She also has a
few hidden talents. Super-deformed parody
with no respect for anthropomorphics whatsoever. (See pp49-50.)

NEW CREAM LEMON ETUDE: SNOW HEARTBEAT
(Eng trans for SHIN CREAM LEMON E-TUDE YUKI NO KÖDÖ)

OAV
JAPANESE CREDITS: 1987. Prod co: Fairy
Dust. © Soeishinsha. 25 mins.
SPINOFFS: A second episode featuring the
same characters followed.
CATEGORIES: P
RATINGS: NN, XX, PORN

When fragile, beautiful Yurika, the child of a
wealthy family and a brilliant classical pianist,
falls in love with Ryo, her father isn't pleased.
Ryo is a biker and plays with a jazz band, not at
all the lover he had in mind for his little girl.
When Yurika's health begins to suffer, Dad tries
to break them up by telling Ryo it's because of
the strain of their affair. He could well have a
point. (See p49.)

NEW CREAM LEMON ETUDE 2: EARLY SPRING CONCERTO
(Eng trans for SHIN CREAM LEMON ETUDE II SÖSHUN CONCERTO)

OAV
JAPANESE CREDITS: 1988. Prod co:
Fairy Dust. © Soeishinsha.
25 mins.
ORIGINS: This is a sequel to New Cream
Lemon Etude: Snow Heartbeat.
CATEGORIES: P
RATINGS: NN, XX, PORN

Yurika has been very sad since her break-up with
Ryo. With her father away on business, her
mother invites a childhood friend along on the
school music club's summer trip, in an attempt
to matchmake. Meanwhile Ryo has embarked on
another passionate affair, with the singer in his
jazz band. (See p49.)

NEW CREAM LEMON PART ZERO

(Eng title for SHIN CREAM LEMON ESCALATION SÖSHÜHEN, lit New Cream Lemon Escalation Compilation)

OAV
JAPANESE CREDITS: 1988. Prod co: Fairy Dust. © Soeishinsha. 25 mins.
CATEGORIES: P
RATINGS: NN, XX, G, PORN

A compilation of scenes from two original *Cream Lemon* episodes, with less censorship. (See p50.)

NEW CREAM LEMON SUMMER WIND

(Eng trans for SHIN CREAM LEMON SUMMER WIND)

OAV
JAPANESE CREDITS: 1987. Prod co: Fairy Dust. © Soeishinsha. 25 mins.
CATEGORIES: P, F
RATINGS: NN, XX, PORN

Yo's girlfriend died a year ago. On holiday, he meets a girl called Mina and they decide to spend the rest of their vacation time together. But there's something strange and melancholy about her, and the affair begins to take on an aura of mystery. (See p49.)

NEW CREAM LEMON THE EVIL DOLL

(Eng trans for SHIN CREAM LEMON MANINGYÖ)
OAV
JAPANESE CREDITS: 1987. Dir: Ayako Mibashi. Chara des: Ayako Mibashi. Prod co: Fairy Dust. © Soeishinsha. 25 mins.
WESTERN CREDITS: Edited for US release by Excalibur Films as part of Pandora: An Erotic Trilogy.
CATEGORIES: P, D
RATINGS: NN, G, PORN

A classy, classic horror tale of the possession of a young man whose only mistake is to perform an act of kindness, then allow himself to be sucked into a web of dark fascination. This haunting modern fairy tale really belongs more in the horror genre than the erotic. (See pp46, 49.)

NEW CREAM LEMON TO MORIYAMA SPECIAL 1: FIVE HOUR VENUS

(Eng trans for SHIN CREAM LEMON GOJIKANME NO VENUS)

OAV
JAPANESE CREDITS: 1987. Dir: To Moriyama. Chara des: To Moriyama. Prod co: Fairy Dust. © Soeishinsha. 25 mins.
ORIGINS: Manga serialised in Penguin Club and Loli-pop magazines.
POINTS OF INTEREST: To Moriyama is the pseudonym of manga artist Naoki Yamamoto.
SPINOFFS: A second episode featuring the same characters followed.
CATEGORIES: P
RATINGS: NN, XX, G, PORN

When she was younger, Shimeji starred in a porno video because she needed the money. Now she's blackmailed to model nude for an art class, but is there more to it than that? With the help of her friend Yachio, Shimeji finds out what the true intentions of the art teacher are. (See p48.)

NEW CREAM LEMON TO MORIYAMA SPECIAL 2: AFTERSCHOOL XXX

(Eng trans for SHIN CREAM LEMON HÖKAGO NO XXX)

OAV
JAPANESE CREDITS: 1988. Dir: To Moriyama. Chara des: To Moriyama. Prod co: Fairy Dust. © Soeishinsha. 25 mins.
ORIGINS: A sequel to Five Hour Venus.
CATEGORIES: P
RATINGS: NN, XX, G, PORN

Shimeji has been blackmailed herself, so she knows just how Asuka feels, and naturally she wants to help. But those naughty pictures of Asuka are just too cute to resist, and besides, Shimeji and her friend Yachio have their own plans for one of the pictures. (See p48.)

NEW CREAM LEMON TWO PEOPLE'S LIFE OF HEARTBREAK

(Eng trans for SHIN CREAM LEMON FUTARI NO HEARTBREAK LIFE)

OAV

JAPANESE CREDITS: 1987. Prod co: Fairy Dust. © Soeishinsha. 25 mins.
ORIGINS: Magical girl genre TV shows, especially Creamy Mami.
POINTS OF INTEREST: Look for the version of the MGM lion. So far, they haven't sued.
CATEGORIES: F, C
RATINGS: NN, XX, PORN

Ruri has no interest in boys her own age. She's crazy about Koji, but he's madly in love with pop idol Saito Konami. If only Ruri could be in Saito's shoes... Then she meets a little blue fox and suddenly she can step right into the singer's body, getting exactly what she wants while giving Koji a chance with the girl of his dreams. (See p50.)

NEW CREAM LEMON WHITE SHADOW
(Eng trans for SHIN CREAM LEMON WHITE SHADOW)

OAV
JAPANESE CREDITS: 1987. Prod co: Fairy Dust. © Soeishinsha. 25 mins.
POINTS OF INTEREST: Not to be confused with Cream Lemon Special Ami Image White Shadow.
CATEGORIES: P, D
RATINGS: NN, XX, VV, PORN

Demons from another dimension are trying to enter into our world. When Shota gives a present to a girl he wants to impress, one of the demons uses it as a way to take over the girl's body, and thanks Shota in a way he never envisaged. Now she's going after his rival — and anyone else who crosses her path. (See pp48-49.)

NIGHTMARE CAMPUS
(Eng title for SOTOMICHI GAKUEN, lit Outer-Way College)

OAV series, 5 parts.
JAPANESE CREDITS: 1996. Dir: Koji Yoshikawa. Screenplay: Koji Yoshikawa. Chara des: Keiichi Sato & Kenji Hayama. Art dir: Takeshi Jinbo. Music: Masamichi Amano. Exec prod: Yasuhito Yamaki. Prod co: Phoenix Entertainment. © Maeda, Phoenix Entertainment. Each c50 mins.
WESTERN CREDITS: US video release 1998 on Anime 18, dub, trans Neil Nadelman.
ORIGINS: Manga by Toshio Maeda.

POINTS OF INTEREST: Note the variation of style in the chara designs, from the Giant Robo-style 'good guys', gag-manga high school grunts and Nagai demons, to girls ranging from American comic bimbo to conventionally cute Japanese schoolgirl.
CATEGORIES: H, P
RATINGS: XX, NN, V, PORN

Hero Tadao sees his mother murdered by marauding demons. When he shoots the creature that attacked her, he discovers it is his own father. Back at Tadao's school, wolves in sheep's clothing (adults disguised as children) prey on the nascent sexuality of the school kids, while in another echo of *Overfiend*, the geeky Tadao tries to forget his new-found demonic powers and woo his childhood sweetheart. A bloody series with some nasty punch-ups, assaults and other crude human activity, as well as the expected quota of demonic sex and violence. There's considerable variation in the depiction of genitals, from the suggested (shadows on a curtain or blank groins) to the realistic and the downright optimistic. The chara design and art also vary wildly. The translated script is pretty bad, with gratuitous obscenities thrown in, and the constant reference to American college terms seems aimed more at reinforcing Anime 18's insistence that everyone here is over school age than to render the original dialogue. The main weakness of the whole package, though, is that Toshio Maeda has done this kind of story so often he could do it in his sleep, and this plays as if he's started to do just that.

NINJA SCROLL
(Eng title for JUBEI NINPÖCHÖ, lit Jubei the Wind Ninja)

MOVIE
JAPANESE CREDITS: 1993. Dir: Yoshiaki Kawajiri. Screenplay: Yoshiaki Kawajiri. Chara des: Yutaka Minowa. Anime dir: Yutaka Minowa. Art dir: Hiromasa Ogura. Backgrounds: Hiromasa Ogura. Sound dir: Yasunori Honda. Music: Kaoru Wada. Prod co: Madhouse. © Y. Kawajiri, Madhouse, JVC, Toho Co Ltd, MOVIC. 90 mins.
WESTERN CREDITS: UK & US video release 1995-96 on Manga Video, dub, Eng rewrite Raymond Garcia.
CATEGORIES: H, D
RATINGS: N, X, VV, SM, MAINSTREAM

An exotic and electrifying mix of Madhouse's array of technical and artistic skills and Kawajiri's superbly paced direction, *Ninja Scroll* is set in the seventeenth century. It tells the story of a young ninja master battling political chicanery, supernatural evil and an array of villains ranging from your standard beefy goon to elegant, ice-hearted beings as powerful as himself. The love interest is a girl whose kiss is literally poison. There's some nudity and mild bondage, but the main point of the story is the atmospheric action. Magnificent. (See p86.)

OGENKI CLINIC
(Eng/Jpn title, lit Good Health Clinic)

OAV series, 3 parts
JAPANESE CREDITS: 1991-92. Dir: Takashi Watanabe. Chara des: Takashi Watanabe. Art dir: Hitoshi Nagao. Prod co: AC Create. © Inui, Somei Entertainment. Each 45 mins.
WESTERN CREDITS: US video release 1998 on Kitty Media, sub.
ORIGINS: Manga by Haruka Inui, serialised in Play Comic.
POINTS OF INTEREST: A well known British company allegedly asked for the BBFC's 'opinion' on this title several years ago. They were advised that submitting it would be a major waste of time. Each Japanese laserdisc is a minute longer than the video.
CATEGORIES: P
RATINGS: XX, N, PORN

Everyday life in a sex clinic is never dull. Patients come to have their problems solved, but the doctor and nurse have a big problem of their own — how are they ever going to get married while her mother thinks he's not good enough for her?

OGRE SLAYER
(Eng title/trans for ONIKIRIMARU)

OAV series, 4 parts
JAPANESE CREDITS: 1994-95. Dir: Yoshio Kato. Screenplay: Norifumi Terada. Chara des: Masayuki Goto. Anime dir: Masayuki Goto. Art dir: Katsuyoshi Kanemura. Music: Kazuhiko Sotoyama. Prod co: Pastel, OB Planning. © K. Kusunoki, Shogakukan, KSS, TBS. Each 30 mins.
WESTERN CREDITS: US video release 1995-96 on Viz Video, dub, trans William
Flanagan & Yuki Sato, Eng rewrite Danni Lyons.
ORIGINS: Manga by Kei Kusunoki, pub Shogakukan, Eng trans pub Viz.
CATEGORIES: P, H
RATINGS: VV, X, N, SM, MAINSTREAM

A boy who seems human, but is actually an ogre, roams the world, seeking to slay every one of his own kind so that he can become fully human. Among those he meets on his travels is a career woman who returns to her home town to help an old friend who has been raped, and finds herself in terrible danger.

OH MY GODDESS!
(Eng title/trans for AA MEGAMISAMA)

OAV series, 5 episodes
JAPANESE CREDITS: 1993-94. Dir: Hiroaki Goda. Chara des: Hidenori Matsubara. Anime dir: Hidenori Matsubara. Art dir: Hiroshi Kato. Music dir: Tomoaki Yamada. Prod co: AIC. © Fujishima, Kodansha, TBS, KSS. Each c30 mins except part 5, 40 mins.
WESTERN CREDITS: US video release 1994-96 on AnimEigo, sub, trans Shin Kurokawa & Michael House; UK video release 1995-96 on Anime Projects, same version.
ORIGINS: Manga by Kosuke Fujishima, pub Kodansha.
POINTS OF INTEREST: The 3 goddesses' names are borrowed from Norse myth.
CATEGORIES: F
RATINGS: MAINSTREAM

The telescoping and compressing of the much longer manga story loses most of the character development. What remains is the tale of a wimp and a doormat, whose only excuse is that they were predestined to be that way. The art, however, is stunning and gets more and more so through the five episodes. Fujishima's artistic skills are astonishing, and although the anime loses much of his technical facility, his design sense is largely preserved. Keiichi wishes for a dream girlfriend, and the goddess he has accidentally called into this dimension obliges by taking on the job herself. But the fulfilment of the dream brings problems — Keiichi gets kicked out of his dorm, he doesn't know how to explain to his family that he is now living with a foreign girl and he constantly worries about having enough money to live on. Other guys (some richer and better looking) try to steal her, and by episode two he still hasn't managed to get as far as holding her hand! Of course there is a reason why the two are destined to be together, dropped into the story by the actions of the ultimate *deus ex machina* right at the end. (See pp14, 23, 25 ,39, 106.)

PASTEL YUMI
(Eng title for MAHŌ NO IDOL PASTEL YUMI, lit Magic Idol Pastel Yumi)

TV series, 26 episodes
JAPANESE CREDITS: 1986. Prod co: Studio Pierrot. © Studio Pierrot, NTV. Each c25 mins.
CATEGORIES: P, F
RATINGS: MAINSTREAM

By now Studio Pierrot was widely regarded as the home of the magical girl, and even though the original audience for *Little Witch Sally* now had children of their own, the genre's popularity continued unabated. Yumi Hanazono, who loves nature and all living things, meets twin imps, gets a magic baton and can use it to bring the pictures she draws in the air to life.

PATALIRO!/I'M PATALIRO!
(Eng trans for PATALIRO!/BOKU PATALIRO!)

TV series, 52 episodes
JAPANESE CREDITS: 1982-83. Writer: Mineo Maya. Prod: Toei. © Toei Doga. Each c25 mins.
ORIGINS: Manga by Mineo Maya, pub Shueisha in Flowers & Dreams magazine.
POINTS OF INTEREST: Originally called just Pataliro!, the slightly longer version of the title was used from episode 27 on. The first series to introduce explicit homosexual themes to TV.
SPINOFFS: A movie, Pataliro! Stardust Project, was released in 1983.
CATEGORIES: F
RATINGS: G, MAINSTREAM

It's all down to the power of suggestion, and what a power it can be. This comic adventure series centres on the ten year-old despot magician Pataliro, prince of the tiny island of Marinella, and his reluctant bodyguard Jack Bankolan, an English secret agent with a double-0 rating, licence to kill, black hair right down to his backside and bedroom eyes. Most of the evil-doers sent against his royal charge are absolutely

drop-dead gorgeous, and the delicious irony of having a James Bond clone with a weakness for boys is only one among many neat jokes. (See pp34, 40.)

PATLABOR
(Eng title for KIDŌ KEISATSU PATLABOR, lit Mobile Police Patlabor)

OAV series, 7 episodes
JAPANESE CREDITS: 1988-89.
Dir: Mamoru Oshii. Script: Kazunori Ito. Chara des: Akemi Takada. Mecha des: Yutaka Izubuchi. Mus: Kenji Kawai. Prod co: Studio Dean.
© Headgear, TFC, Emotion.
Each 30 mins.
WESTERN CREDITS: US video release 1996 on US Manga Corps, sub, trans Pamela Parks, Eng rewrite Jay Parks.
ORIGINS: Manga by Masami Yuki, pub Shogakukan.
POINTS OF INTEREST: The OAV Tokyo Private Police takes similar story ele-ments and gives them a pornographic spin.
SPINOFFS: A further OAV series, TV series and 2 movies. A third movie is scheduled for release in 2000.
CATEGORIES: SF
RATINGS: MAINSTREAM

When police have robots, they won't be the main point of the story; they'll use them just like they use cars now. The joy of *Patlabor* is that it takes this as given from the start. In the very first video, the main focus of the action is in the characters, and the robot, impressive as it is, is just another bit of kit. When the show was released events started in 1998; now time has caught up with it, it still holds up as enjoy-able, intelligent entertainment, and features some marvellous observations on friendship and love, especially the non-relationship of the section chiefs Nagumo and Goto. They quarrel and bicker like a married couple, but never admit their feelings for each other in a back-ground saga of unconsummated romance that surpasses the very best Mulder/Scully ex-changes. (See pp24, 40, 88, 111.)

PHANTOM QUEST CORP
(Eng title/trans for YŪGEN KAISHA, pun on 'Limited Company' and 'Spirit-Phantasm Monster-Shrine')

OAV series, 4 episodes
JAPANESE CREDITS: 1994. Dir: Koichi
Chigira (1), Morio Asaka (2 & 4), Takuji
Endo (3). Screenplay: Mami Watanabe,
Tatsuhiko Urahata & Tetsu Kimura.
Original story: Juzo Mutsuki. Chara des:
Hitoshi Ueda. Music: Junichi Kanezaki.
Prod co: Madhouse. © Pioneer, AIC. Each
30 mins.
WESTERN CREDITS: US video release 1995
on Pioneer LDCA, sub, dub; UK video
release 1997 on Pioneer LDCE, dub.
POINTS OF INTEREST: Yoshiaki Kawajiri
directed the opening animation.
CATEGORIES: C, D
RATINGS: N, MAINSTREAM

Ayaka is a modern girl out to succeed in the cut-
throat world of big business with her very own
company — a freelance ghostbusting agency. But
somehow, despite a phenomenally successful
clear-up rate, she just can't seem to get ahead of
the game. Maybe her passion for designer clothes,
booze and karaoke has something to do with her

cashflow problems. The Older Woman as funny
failure, with plenty of asides about the nature of
freelance life. (See pp40, 102.)

PICTURES FROM HIGH SCHOOL
(Eng trans for KŌNAI SHASEI)

OAV series, 3 parts
JAPANESE CREDITS: 1990-92. Dir: Toshi
Sakurai (1 & 2), Takamasa Ikegami (3).
Screenplay: Toshi Sakurai. Original story:
U-Jin. Chara des: Yuji Moriyama (1 & 2),
Kinji Yoshimoto (2), Satoshi Urushihara
(3). Music: Takeshi Yasuda. Prod: Hisashi
Yoshida. Prod co: Studio Fantasia.
© U-Jin, Soeishinsha. Each 40 mins.
ORIGINS: Manga by U-Jin, serialised in
Leed/Read Comic.
POINTS OF INTEREST: Several famous
voice actresses on the cast list, without
pseudonyms.
CATEGORIES: P, C
RATINGS: NN, X, PORN

Phantom Quest Corp

Compilation of short erotic stories with a comic edge. The first tape includes 'Luck on the Long-Distance Commute', 'The Little Match Girl' and 'High school Nurse'. The second tape includes 'Take Me Back to My Childhood', 'How to Get a Free Pizza', 'Sailor-suited Akko-chan vs the Giant Dirty Old Man' and 'Qi Gong Girl'. The final tape contains 'Silver Lining', 'Back on Form', 'Aim for the A', 'The Scariest Story' and 'Come for World Peace'. (See pp108, 118-121.)

PLASTIC LITTLE

OAV
JAPANESE CREDITS: 1994. Dir: Kinji Yoshimoto. Writer: Satoshi Urushibara. Chara des: Satoshi Urushibara. Music: Tamiya Terashima. Prod co: Sony Music Entertainment. © Urushibara, Yoshimoto, MOVIC, Sony Music Entertainment Ltd. 55 mins.
WESTERN CREDITS: UK video release 1995 on Kiseki Films, sub, trans Jonathan Clements; US video release 1995 on AD Vision, sub, trans Ichiro Arakaki & Dwayne Jones.
POINTS OF INTEREST: Supposedly only a spinoff itself, designed to introduce fans to a larger story universe from an anime as yet unmade. An infamous advertisement in UK magazine Manga Mania removed the characters' nipples to avoid offending retailers.
CATEGORIES: SF
RATINGS: NN, V, X, MAINSTREAM

Massively maligned by some female fans, for obvious if inconsistent reasons, this gloriously pretty cream-puff is still the outstanding example of the perfect rendition of an artist's graphic style into animation. The story isn't much (but you could say that about lots of much less well executed OAVs) and there's lots of T&A and really big explosions. (See pp23, 40, 108.)

POLTERGEIST REPORT: YU YU HAKUSHO
(Eng trans for YÜ YÜ HAKUSHO)

MOVIE
JAPANESE CREDITS: 1994. Dir: Masakatsu Iijima. Script: Yoshihiro Togashi. Prod co: Studio Pierrot. © Togashi, Pierrot, Shueisha, Fuji TV. 93 mins.
WESTERN CREDITS: US video release 1998

on US Manga Corps, dub, trans nDa Language Services.
ORIGINS: Manga by Yoshihiro Togashi, pub Shueisha in Shonen Jump; 1992 & later TV series; 1993 movie.
POINTS OF INTEREST: Note that this Western release is actually the sequel to the film of the TV series of the comic. It shows.
CATEGORIES: D, F
RATINGS: V, MAINSTREAM

High production values on the art side are not matched by the script, in this story about a boy who comes back from the dead as an agent of the otherworld. Every key cast member is crowded into a film too small to give them all room. As a result, the tale of the fight by the King of the Netherworld to claim the earth as his new land is slowed down to an absurd degree. However, each of the regular team has to have his or her own particular problem to face, the most interesting being the fey fox spirit Kurama's. Long ago, when one of his thefts went wrong, Kurama's partner was caught by their pursuers and killed. Now his soul seems to have returned, bent on revenge. The pair of bishonen-types were certainly very close, and while a homosexual relationship is not explicitly stated, there are strong emotional ties between the two, even after they have been parted by death for many years.

POPS

OAV
JAPANESE CREDITS: 1993. Dir: Takuji Endo. Script: Akinori Endo. Chara des: Kazuhiro Soeda. Prod co: Madhouse. © Ikuemi, Shueisha. c40 mins.
ORIGINS: Manga by Aya Ikuemi, pub Shueisha in Margaret magazine. The previous release in the 6-part Margaret series was Singles.
SPINOFFS: Sleepless Oedo came next.
CATEGORIES: P
RATINGS: MAINSTREAM

Two high school students fall in love, but can they keep their romance alive with all the pressures of trying to study and get good grades, parental misunderstanding and classmates' teasing?

PRINCESS KNIGHT
(Eng title for RIBON NO KISHI, lit Ribbon Knight)

TV series, 52 episodes
JAPANESE CREDITS: 1967-68. Dir: Osamu
Tezuka & Masaki Tsuji. Screenplay: Osamu
Tezuka & Masaki Tsuji. Chara des: Kazuko
Anami & Sadao Miyamoto. Prod: Osamu
Tezuka. Prod co: Mushi Productions.
© Tezuka Productions. Each c25 mins.
ORIGINS: Manga by Osamu Tezuka.
POINTS OF INTEREST: The first ever shojo
anime series.
CATEGORIES: F
RATINGS: MAINSTREAM

Tezuka's beautiful story, of a princess brought up
as a prince so that she can inherit her parents'
throne, laid the foundations for shojo anime.
Inspired by Tezuka's love of the Takarazuka female
theatre troupe, where the stars take male roles.
(See pp11, 26, 27.)

PRIVATE PSYCHO LESSON
(Eng title for KOJIN JUGYŌ, lit Personal
Tuition)

OAV, 2 parts
JAPANESE CREDITS: 1996. Dir: Tetsuro
Amino. Script: Nagareboshi. Chara des:
Makoto Takahoko. Prod: JC Staff, Blue
Mantis. © U-Jin, Shogakukan, Gaga
Communications. Each c35 mins.
WESTERN CREDITS: US video release 1997
on Anime 18, sub, trans Kevin McKeown.
ORIGINS: Manga by U-Jin, pub Shogakukan
in Young Sunday Dynamo.
POINTS OF INTEREST: Amino also directed
the anime version of Starship Troopers.
CATEGORIES: P
RATINGS: XX, NN, G, EROTIC

Sara Iijima of Stunford University (sic) is a psy-
chotherapist who gets into a state of sexual excitement, rotates her breasts in opposite directions to
hypnotise her patients and then regresses them to
the point of trauma. This scholarly sex-solves-
everything school of analysis is very popular, and
makes her extremely successful — she travels to
assignments in her own helicopter gunship and
disciplines inadequate teachers with a few hundred well aimed bullets. Interesting in terms of
anime erotica because it makes the disposable
Alien/Older Woman the central character, as she
becomes a journeywoman sexual initiatress for
Boys and Girls Next Door. The script's treatment of
rape, especially as a punishment for *bad* Japanese
girls, dealt out by foreign men, is particularly distasteful.

THE PROFESSIONAL: GOLGO 13
(Eng title for GOLGO 13)

MOVIE
JAPANESE CREDITS: 1983. Dir: Osamu
Dezaki. Asst dir: Akio Sugino. Screenplay:
Hideyoshi Nagasaka. Chara des: Shichiro
Kobayashi. Anime dir: Shichiro Kobayashi.
Art dir: Shichiro Kobayashi. Music:
Toshiyuki Omori. Prod co: Tokyo Movie
Shinsha. © T. Saito, Saito Pro, TMS.
94 mins.
WESTERN CREDITS: US video release 1992
on Streamline Pictures, dub, Eng rewrite
Gregory Snegoff; UK video release 1993 on
Manga Video, dub.
ORIGINS: Manga by Takao Saito, Eng trans
pub Viz, graphic novel trans pub Lead
Publishing Co.
POINTS OF INTEREST: Director Osamu
Dezaki needlessly shows off with some
dated computer graphics, an error he was
to repeat in the 1996 Black Jack movie.
CATEGORIES: P, T
RATINGS: VV, N, X, SM, MAINSTREAM

If you showed a series of James Bond films to a
child and asked them to write their own, they'd
probably come up with something like this: sex,
death, sex, death, fight, the end. That's what this
is, a rather sad attempt by the Japanese to capture what *they* think *we* see in our action movies.
A good object lesson for those who think cultural misunderstanding is a one-way street. (See
pp14-15, 39.)

RANMA 1/2
(Eng title/trans for RANMA NIBBUNOICHI, lit
Lun-ma Half, pun on Japanese for 'half', lit
'One of Two', and Japlish word for a person
of mixed ancestry, as in 'half-caste'. Lun-ma
is Chinese for 'Wild-Horse')

TV series, 18 episodes
JAPANESE CREDITS: 1989-90. Dir: Tsutomu
Shibayama, Tomomitsu Mochizuki. Chara
des: Atsuko Nakajima. Music: Eiji Mori.
Prod co: Kitty Film. © Takahashi,
Shogakukan, Fuji TV, Kitty Film. Each
26 mins.
WESTERN CREDITS: US video release 1993-
95 on Viz Video, dub, sub, Eng rewrite
Trish Ledoux & Toshifumi Yoshida.
ORIGINS: Manga by Rumiko Takahashi,
Eng trans pub Viz (US), Boxtree (UK).
SPINOFFS: 2 further TV series, 2 movies,

ongoing OAV series.
CATEGORIES: F
RATINGS: N, MAINSTREAM

The story of Ranma Saotome, who is cursed to turn into a girl when doused with water, has lots of the slapstick and visual gags that made *Urusei Yatsura* so much fun, but is a more formulaic and cynical play on romantic stereotypes. Rumiko Takahashi is the richest female manga artist in Japan, but is this despite or because of the conservative, sexist stereotypes she gives her audience in this, one of her best-known works? (See pp14, 23, 24, 25, 98.)

REDDENING SNOW/GIRLS TORTURED WITH ROSES
(Eng title for YUKI NO KŌGESHŌ/SHŌJO BARAKEI, lit Blushing Snow in Scarlet [pun on 'rouge' and 'shame' and visual image of blood]/Girls Tortured With Roses)

OAV
JAPANESE CREDITS: 1984. Original story: Fumio Nakajima. Prod co: Wonder Kids. © F. Nakajima, Wonder Kids. 30 mins.
POINTS OF INTEREST: The first erotic OAV released in Japan. Torture with Roses is the title of a 1960 compilation of erotic photographs by Eiko Hosoe, featuring the author Yukio Mishima as a model.
SPINOFFS: The second Wonder Kids Lolita Anime release was Dying For a Girl/Altar of Sacrifice.
CATEGORIES: P
RATINGS: X, V, SM, PORN

Two short and distasteful stories of rape and sexual abuse. In the first, a girl is subjected to sexual assault by a gang of boys, including the one who secretly adores her. However, that doesn't stop him taking his turn. The second features older men introducing young girls to the pleasures of bondage. (See pp43, 108, 109.)

REI REI
(Eng title for UTSUKUSHIKI SEI NO DENDŌSHI REI REI, lit Li Li the Beauteous Sensual Evangelist)

OAV
JAPANESE CREDITS: 1993. Dir: Yoshiki Yamamoto. Screenplay: Mitsuru Mochizuki. Prod co: KSS. © T. Shimizu, Shonen Gahosha, Pink Pineapple. 60 mins.

WESTERN CREDITS: US video release 1995 on AD Vision, sub, trans Ichiro Arakaki & Dwayne Jones; UK video release 1997 on Kiseki, sub, trans Jonathan Clements.
ORIGINS: Manga by Toshimitsu Shimizu.
POINTS OF INTEREST: Edited US version available, for people who want to pretend they live in the UK.
CATEGORIES: F, P
RATINGS: NN, XX, V, SM, EROTIC

Relationship counselling courtesy of an undefined otherworld and a sexy superbeing called Kaguya. A real treat for psychoanalysts; listen carefully for the sound of Freud spinning in his grave. (See pp85, 97, 102-103.)

RG VEDA
(Eng title for SEIDEN RIG VEDA, lit The Myth of Rig Veda)

OAV series, 2 parts
JAPANESE CREDITS: 1992. Dir: Hiroyuki Ebata (1), Takamasa Ikegami (2). Script: Nanase Okawa. Chara des: Mokono Apapa (1), Tetsuro Aoki, Kiichi Takaoka & Futoshi Fujikawa (2). Anime dir: Tetsuro Aoki. Art dir: Yoji Nakazaka (1), Masuo Nakayama (2). Music: Nick Wood. Prod co: Animate Film. © CLAMP, Shinshokan, Sony Music Entertainment. Each 45 mins.
WESTERN CREDITS: US video release 1993 on 2 tapes by US Manga Corps, sub, Eng rewrite Jay Parks; UK video release 1993 on 1 tape on Manga Video, dub.
ORIGINS: Hindu myth, manga by CLAMP.

Rei Rei

CATEGORIES: F
RATINGS: MAINSTREAM

The Lord of Heaven, Ashura, is betrayed and murdered by his wife and the treacherous general Taishaku (Indra in the original myth). Now his daughter, rescued by his loyal general Yasha (Yaksha), assembles the group of warriors whom it is foretold will end Taishaku's reign as Heavenly Emperor. The anime ends with the finding of the sixth and last warrior, so the story is still unfinished unless you can read the manga in Japanese. The extreme prettiness of both male and female characters and the hothouse atmosphere of the whole piece make this a perfect example of CLAMP's earlier work in the 'pure shojo' mould, before their recent 'crossover' carrying shojo elements into mainstream series like *Magic Knight Rayearth*. (See pp33, 39.)

RIDING BEAN

OAV
JAPANESE CREDITS: 1989. Dir: Yasuo Hasegawa. Writer: Kenichi Sonoda. Chara des: Kenichi Sonoda. Mecha des: Keinchi Sonoda, Kinji Yoshimoto, Satoshi Urushibara, L. Lime & Yoshihisa Fujita. Supervisor: Kenichi Sonoda. Tech dir: Yasunori Ide. Anime dir: Masahiro Tanaka, Osamu Kamijo, Ohira Hiroya & Jun Okuda. Art dir: Hiroaki Sato. Prod: Toshimichi Suzuki. Prod co: Artmic, AIC. © Sonoda, Toshiba EMI. 45 mins. WESTERN CREDITS: US video release 1993 on AnimEigo, sub, dub, Eng rewrite Michael House & Shin Kurokawa; UK video release 1994 on Anime Projects, same version. POINTS OF INTEREST: AnimEigo's first ever English dub. SPINOFFS: The Gunsmith Cats manga and OAVs could be said to be spinoffs, since they feature a feisty female character called Rally Vincent as well as Bean Bandit himself. CATEGORIES: P, T RATINGS: V, G, SM, MAINSTREAM

This thrilling homage to the American movie post-*Blues Brothers* and pre-Tarantino is still very watchable. Its main interest for our purposes is the sado-masochistic lesbian relationship between the psychotic villain Semmerling and her Child sidekick, which is chilling in its conviction and realism without showing any sexual activity. One of the most powerful reminders on film in any country that sexual relationships between children and adults are always about abuse and exploitation. Should be compulsory viewing for anyone into lolikon. (See p39.)

RONIN WARRIORS
(Eng title for YOROIDEN, lit [Armoured Legend] Samurai Troopers)

TV series, 39 episodes
JAPANESE CREDITS: 1988-89. Dir: Shigeru Ikeda, Mamoru Hamazu. Original idea: 'Hajime Yatate'. Screenplay: Hideki Sonoda, Yuji Watanabe et al. Chara des: Tadashi Shioyama. Prod: Ryosuke Takahashi. Prod co: Sunrise, Inc. © Sunrise, Graz Entertainment. Each c25 mins. WESTERN CREDITS: US TV syndication 1995, dub, Eng rewrite Barry G. Hawkins, Michael Adams & Karen Kolus. SPINOFFS: Several OAVs were made but are as yet unreleased in the West. CATEGORIES: F RATINGS: VV, MAINSTREAM

Another series much beloved of shonen ai fan writers and artists, this was a hit with Japanese teenage girls for its heartthrob group of young fighters. The king of the phantom world was vanquished long ago by a holy man, but now is trying to conquer the real world once more. Five teenagers are called on to stand in his way, each given the powers of an ancient, magical suit of samurai armour and its related virtues. They face cruel and ruthless adversaries as they fight to keep the world free of phantom dominion. (See p35.)

ROSE OF VERSAILLES
(Eng trans for VERSAILLES NO BARA)

TV series, 40 episodes
JAPANESE CREDITS: 1979-80. Dir: Tadao Nagahama, Tetsu Dezaki & Tetsuo Imazawa. Screenplay: Yoshimi Shinozaki et al. Chara des: Shingo Araki. Art dir: Ken Kawai. Music: Koji Magakino. Prod co: Tokyo Movie Shinsha. © Ikeda, TMS. Each c25 mins. ORIGINS: Manga by Riyoko Ikeda. POINTS OF INTEREST: As this book went to press, we discovered the existence of a porno-pastiche, called Inma Yosei [Lust Faries] IV: Maya.

CATEGORIES: H
RATINGS: MAINSTREAM

This seminal series in the shojo tradition picks up the theme of Osamu Tezuka's *Princess Knight* — a girl forced to deny her own sexuality — and sets it in the years leading up to the French Revolution. Ikeda brilliantly interweaves the story of Oscar François de Jarjayes, the beautiful, powerful and female head of the Queen's Guard, with that of Marie Antoinette, the headstrong, silly, yet courageous Princess of France. Both have duties which prevent them following their hearts; both eventually lose their lives as a result of the Revolution; and both strive to understand and admit what they really seek, rather than simply accept what life has dealt them. The sweeping scale of the story and the romance of the setting can't overshadow its powerful characterisation, and some of the subplots would make a series in themselves. Magnificent and essential viewing for any student of shojo. (See pp26-27, 30, 31, 36.)

ROUGE
(Eng title for LADIES COMIC VIDEO ROUGE)

OAV series, 2 parts
JAPANESE CREDITS: 1998. Original story:
Haruko Kanzaki, Mizuki Iwase, Kei Mizugi,
Chiga Taniguchi et al. Prod co: Komine.
© Authors, Takeshobo, Komine
Communications, TDK Core. Each 40 mins.
ORIGINS: Stories in Comic Rouge
magazine.
CATEGORIES: M, F
RATINGS: NN, X, SM, PORN

Bereaved strangers lose themselves in a sordid double life of prostitution, but find love in each other. A loveless marriage blooms through bondage. A trainee gets more than she bargains for when the head nurse takes a biology lesson to the limit. And a male beautician uses unorthodox methods to put colour in a make-up artist's cheeks. Four erotically charged tales animated for a female audience.

SAILOR MOON
(Eng title for BISHŌJO SENSHI SAILOR MOON, lit Pretty Soldier Sailor Moon)

TV series, 46 episodes
JAPANESE CREDITS: 1992. Dir: Junichi
Sato. Music: Takanori Arisawa, Tetsuya
Komuro & Kazuo Sato. Prod co: Toei.

© Takeuchi, Kodansha, Toei, Bandai.
Each c25 mins.
WESTERN CREDITS: US TV syndication
1995, dub, Eng rewrite Mycheline Tremblay.
ORIGINS: Manga by Naoko Takeuchi.
POINTS OF INTEREST: The OAV Venus Five
is a porno-parody version of Sailor Moon.
SPINOFFS: 4 more TV series and 5 movies
followed.
CATEGORIES: F, P
RATINGS: MAINSTREAM

No sex, but passion and romance in bucketloads, from the apotheosis of the magical girl genre. Loved by millions of girls all over the world, Sailor Moon speaks Portuguese, Polish, Spanish and a whole linguistic institute of tongues as well as Japanese. The story of klutzy Usagi (known in the English-language version as Serena), her school chums and their destiny: fighting to save the world through the power of love and make-up. Luckily, the mysterious Tuxedo Mask is on hand to help the girls when the going gets tough, and with friendship on their side they'll always manage to win through somehow or (in a shock ending to the first series which was severely bowdlerised for the American audience) die trying. If the Famous Five had been played by Barbie dolls, this is how it might have looked; yet the heart of the series is pure, honest gold, a love story which is so genuinely touching that when our heroine finally finds words to tell the hero that she loves him, it reduces grown translators to teary-eyed mush. (See pp24, 25, 51, 95, 102.)

SAINT SEIYA

TV series, 114 episodes
JAPANESE CREDITS: 1986-89. Dir: Kozo
Morishita, Masayuki Akitaka, Tomoharu
Katsumata et al. Screenplay: Takashi
Koyama et al. Chara des: Shingo Araki &
Michi Himeno. Prod co: Toei. © Kurumada,
Shueisha, Toei. Each c25 mins.
ORIGINS: Manga by Masami Kurumada,
serialised in Weekly Shonen Jump.
SPINOFFS: Movies and OAVs.
CATEGORIES: F
RATINGS: VV, MAINSTREAM

One of the serials most often used as a base by writers of shonen ai fanzines, *Saint Seiya* has the same atmosphere of repressed sexuality and lurking cruelty as Lindsay Anderson's *If...*, without the black humour or the political dimension. It's a hothouse world of fighter elites dedicated to the service of

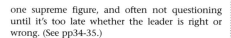

one supreme figure, and often not questioning until it's too late whether the leader is right or wrong. (See pp34-35.)

SAMURAI GOLD
(Eng title for TOYAMAZAKURA UCHÜCHÖ YATSU NO NA WA GOLD, lit Cosmic Commander of the Toyama Cherry Trees — The Guy's Name is Gold)

OAV
JAPANESE CREDITS: 1988. Dir: Atsutoshi Umezawa. Screenplay: Akiyoshi Sakai. Music: Kentaro Haneda. Prod co: Toei. © Toei, Tokuma Shoten. 60 mins
WESTERN CREDITS: UK video release 1994 on Western Connection, sub, trans Jonathan Clements.
ORIGINS: Japanese legendary/historical tales of Toyama No Kinsan; novel by Tatsuro Jinde & Kyosuke Yuki, pub Tokuma.
POINTS OF INTEREST: Compare Toyama no Benbo from U-Jin Brand.
CATEGORIES: SF
RATINGS: V, G, MAINSTREAM

Mentioned mostly for its blithe stereotyping of homosexuals, this also stereotypes women, rich kids, computers and almost every other element of its story. Pretty design, nice art, but the writing just doesn't hold up. The tale of a young man determined to find his father's attackers and unravel the mystery behind their motivation is set in the future, with an Earth controlled largely by an unfeeling computer called Edo. The idiot-savant

The Sensualist

Edo, despite being a machine, is given a female voice and character in the finalé. (See pp41, 99.)

THE SCARRED MAN
(Eng title for KIZUOIBITO, lit Marked Man/Running Scarred (sic))

OAV series, 5 parts
JAPANESE CREDITS: 1986-88. Dir: Toshio Takeuchi (1 & 2), Tetsu Dezaki (3-5). Chara des: Satoshi Kiyomizu. Prod: Madhouse for Bandai. Prod co: Madhouse (1), Magic Bus (2-5). © Koike, Ikegami, Shogakukan, Bandai. Part 1 40 mins, part 2 45 mins, parts 3-5 each 30 mins.
ORIGINS: Big Comic manga by Kazuo Koike & Ryoichi Ikegami.
CATEGORIES: T
RATINGS: X, N, VV, MAINSTREAM

Gold prospector Keisuke Ibaraki travels the dangerous corners of the world in search of wealth and adventure. Along the way women fall for him and get killed. The female of the species is treated throughout exactly like the females in Bond films, as a gratuitous story cipher cum decorative element, there to give our hero a chance to strut his stuff and then be disposed of so he can get down to the real business of action. Plot devices, like having one of the succession of love interests kidnapped by a gang of evil porn film-makers and forced to star in their latest production, keep on reminding us why this is intended for Men Only. (See p47.)

SEASIDE ANGEL MIYU
(Eng trans for MIU SEA SIDE ANGEL)

OAV
JAPANESE CREDITS: 1985. Original story: Fumio Nakajima. Prod co: Wonder Kids. © Nakajima, Wonder Kids. 60 mins.
ORIGINS: The previous Wonder Kids Lolita release was Surf Dreaming.
POINTS OF INTEREST: Miyu also 'stars' in Surf Dreaming & House of Kittens.
CATEGORIES: P
RATINGS: X, PORN

The sixth and last of the Wonder Kids Lolita Anime releases. A clever multiple-bind in this show helps the makers salve their consciences about producing child pornography. The animated heroine Miyu broadcasts a radio programme from Earth orbit, where she listens to the 'confessions' of various respondents who claim to have had their first sexual experience before reaching the age of consent. This makes the paedophilia animated, fictional, otherworldy and confessional, with the ultimate get-out clause that the callers might be lying. There is also an interesting montage, interesting because it is the most boring anime footage ever. For four minutes, nothing happens except still images of Miyu on the screen, presumably to bore underage viewers into turning off before they get to the action. The action itself is a show-reel of sequences from the other Wonder Kids releases, ending with the 'bonus' scene of Miyu having carnal relations with the captain of her spaceship.

THE SENSUALIST
(Eng title for IHARA SAIKAKU KÖSHOKU ICHIDAI OTOKO, lit Saikaku Ihara's The Life of an Amorous Man)

OAV
JAPANESE CREDITS: 1991. Dir: Yukio Abe. Screenplay: Eiichi Yamamoto. Art dir: Yukio Abe. Music: Keiji Ishikawa. Prod co: Groupier Productions. © Groupier. 53 mins.
WESTERN CREDITS: UK video release 1993 on Western Connection, sub using the spotting list (a very rough, invariably incomplete translation) provided by Japanese release company.
ORIGINS: Novel by Saikaku Ihara.
POINTS OF INTEREST: A sister-novel to the original, The Life of an Amorous Woman, was made into a live-action film by Kenji Mizoguchi, released in the West in 1952 as The Life of Oharu (aka Diary of Oharu).
CATEGORIES: H
RATINGS: N, EROTIC

Merchant Yonosuke takes pity on a simple yokel who has been conned into making a very unwise bet — that he will sleep with a top courtesan on first meeting. Any sophisticate could have told him he was onto a loser because the best geisha simply don't sleep with clients straight away, even if the client is important, wealthy or well connected. Luckily Yonosuke is an intimate friend of the lady in question and he appeals to her good nature to help the poor fool. Saturated in rich colour and languid atmosphere, each frame of film glows like a perfectly cut jewel. The pace is very slow and the sexuality subtle and erotically charged — this isn't a story for those

looking for 'action' in the usual twentieth-century sense of the word, but it's absolutely beautiful. (See pp15, 40.)

SHUTENDOJI
(Eng title for SHUTENDŌJI, lit The Foundling Child, US aka SHUTENDOJI: THE STAR HAND KID)

OAV series, 4 parts
JAPANESE CREDITS: 1989-91. Dir: Junji Nishimura (1), Hideyuki Motobashi (2), Jun Kawagoe (3 & 4). Screenplay: Masashi Sogo. Chara des: Satoshi Hirayama. Art dir: Hideyuki Motobashi. Prod co: Studio Signal. © Dynamic Production, Nippon Columbia. Each c50 mins.
WESTERN CREDITS: US video release 1996, on AD Vision, trans Ichiro Arakaki, Eng rewrite Matt Greenfield; UK video release 1998, same version.
ORIGINS: Manga by Go Nagai, pub Kodansha in Weekly Shonen Magazine.
CATEGORIES: D
RATINGS: N, VV, MAINSTREAM

Jiro Shutendo is different from the other kids. Adopted by a childless couple who have tried to forget that he was only on loan from time-travelling ogres, Jiro casts a giant's shadow. As he enters his fifteenth year, he finds himself changing, but into what? All hell breaks loose when the ogres return to reclaim him. An artful study of puberty, first love and family ties, as Jiro's adoptive clan proves to be more loving than the one that left him behind... (See pp55, 56.)

SINGLES

OAV
JAPANESE CREDITS: 1993. Dir: Takuji Endo. Script: Akinori Endo. Chara des: Kazuhiro Soeda. Prod co: Madhouse. © Fujimura, Shueisha. c40 mins.
ORIGINS: Manga by Mari Fujimura, pub Shueisha in Margaret magazine. The first OAV in the 6-part Margaret series was A-Plus for the Fashion Boy.
SPINOFFS: Pops was the next in the series.
CATEGORIES: P
RATINGS: MAINSTREAM

Saki leaves college with a secret — she loves her sister's boyfriend Yo. Even now she can't avoid him because they belong to the same social club, but really she knows it's just an excuse to be near him. Then she and another member, Daichi, take on a project for the club together and start to get to know each other better. Will Saki's feelings change? Can you love two men, or is it possible to love one man but make a happy life with another? (See p31.)

SLAM DUNK

TV series, c130 episodes
JAPANESE CREDITS: 1993-96. Dir: Hiroshi Kado & Nobuaki Nishizawa. Anime dir: Masaki Sato. Prod co: Toei. © Inoue, Shueisha, TV Asahi, Dentsu, ANB. Each c25 mins.
ORIGINS: Manga by Takehiko Inoue, pub Shueisha in Shonen Jump magazine.
SPINOFFS: Movies and OAVs followed.
CATEGORIES: P
RATINGS: MAINSTREAM

This series, featuring the ups and downs of a high school basketball team, was aimed at boys but attracted a large female audience swooning at all those anime hunks in baggy shorts.

SLEEPLESS OEDO
(Eng trans for O-EDO WA NEMURANAI)

OAV
JAPANESE CREDITS: 1993. Dir: Takuji Endo. Script: Akinori Endo. Chara des: Kazukuro Saeta. Prod co: Madhouse. © Honda, Shueisha. c40 mins.
ORIGINS: Manga by Keiko Honda, pub Shueisha in Margaret magazine. The previous release in the 6-part Margaret series was Pops.
SPINOFFS: Kiss Me on the Apple of My Eye came next.
CATEGORIES: H
RATINGS: N, MAINSTREAM

Set in Tokyo in days gone by (when the city was known as Edo), this period drama features an unlikely trio of friends — a famous courtesan, a thief and a gifted young doctor — and their adventures in and around the pleasure quarter. (See pp31.)

SLOW STEP

OAV series, 5 parts

JAPANESE CREDITS: 1991. Dir: Kunihiko Yuyama. Script: Toshimichi Saeki. Chara des: Tokuhiro Matsubara. Art dir: Mitsuki Nakamura. Music: Hiroya Watanabe. Prod co: OB Planning, Pastel. © Adachi, Toho Video. Each c45 mins.
WESTERN CREDITS: UK video release 1995 on Western Connection, sub, trans Jonathan Clements (on 3 tapes).
ORIGINS: Manga by Mitsuru Adachi, serialised in Monthly Ciao magazine.
CATEGORIES: P
RATINGS: MAINSTREAM

Minatsu is a terrific girl: a popular school sports star. So popular, in fact, that she has to fend off the boy next door, a suitor from a rival school, and the young softball coach. Wonderful characterisations include the svengali toddler Chika, who will do anything to find her uncle a wife, and the bad-girl with a heart of gold, Sawamura. Like Adachi's original, each part is set in a different season, finishing with a final resolution amid the spring cherry blossoms. A wonderful study of soap-style human relationships and everyday life in Japan, although production mix-ups involving several different drafts resulted in an English script that is at times simply awful. (See pp27, 41, 86.)

SOL BIANCA

OAV series, 2 parts
JAPANESE CREDITS: 1990-91. Dir: Katsuhito Akiyama (1), Hiroki Hayashi (2). Script: Mayori Sekijima. Chara des: Naoyuki Onda. Mecha des: Atsushi Takeuchi. Anime dir: Naoyuki Onda. Art dir: Shigemi Ikeda. Music: Kosei Kenjo. Prod co: AIC. © NEC Avenue. Each 60 mins.
WESTERN CREDITS: US video release 1993 on AD Vision, sub, trans Ichiro Arakaki & Dwayne Jones, dub forthcoming. UK video release 1995 on Kiseki Films, sub, trans Jonathan Clements.
ORIGINS: Concept by Toru Miura.
CATEGORIES: SF
RATINGS: V, MAINSTREAM

A clever space pirate tale with excellent characterisation and design. The original was a landmark lesson in non-sexist casting, but the second episode features a pathetically gratuitous excuse to get everyone's clothes off, purely (we assume) for some bra-and-panties shots to use in publicity photographs. A sad betrayal of an otherwise bold experiment in writing for female characters, by many of the crew who would later sell out completely on *Tenchi Muyo!* (See pp89-90, 111.)

SPACE ADVENTURE COBRA

TV series, 31 episodes
JAPANESE CREDITS: 1982-83. Dir: Osamu Dezaki & Yoshio Takeuchi. Screenplay: Kenji Terada, Haru Yamazaki, Kazuo Terada & Kosuke Miki. Prod co: Tokyo Movie Shinsha.
© Terasawa, TMS. Each c25 mins.
ORIGINS: Manga by Buichi Terasawa.
SPINOFFS: A movie was made in 1982 and had a 1995 UK release from Manga Video.
CATEGORIES: SF
RATINGS: V, N, MAINSTREAM

The adventures of Cobra, a space pirate and adventurer, and his android sidekick Lady, were heavily inspired by the 007 canon, though Cobra is more of a rough diamond than the university-educated Bond. A forerunner of the dream-within-a-dream of *Total Recall*, Cobra owes a lot of people, and now that he's back in action with a new face and a strange new weapon, the Psychogun, he's likely to get into more trouble than ever. (See p14.)

SPACE FIREBIRD
(Eng title for HI NO TORI 2772 AI NO COSMOZONE, lit Phoenix 2772 Love's Cosmozone)

MOVIE
JAPANESE CREDITS: 1980. Dir: Taki Sugiyama. Planning brains (sic!): Sakyo Komatsu, Jared Cook & Frederik Schodt. Screenplay: Osamu Tezuka. Art dir: Shinji Ito & Tsuyoshi Matsumoto. Prod: Osamu Tezuka. Prod co: Toho, Tezuka Productions.
© Tezuka Productions. 121 mins.
WESTERN CREDITS: UK video release 1993 on Western Connection, dub; US video release 1995 on Best Film & Video, dub.
ORIGINS: Manga by Osamu Tezuka.
POINTS OF INTEREST: A rare anime assignment for the peerless Fred Schodt, Tezuka's interpreter of choice, with his former Dadakai translation partner Cook, and science fiction author Komatsu.
CATEGORIES: SF
RATINGS: N, V, MAINSTREAM

In a repressive future society which has depleted

the Earth's resources, Godo sets out to find the legendary power source known as the Firebird and return it to Earth to regenerate the dying planet. On the way he encounters love, betrayal and adventure, and learns to recognise true friendship and loyalty and not to be deceived by appearances. (See pp11-13, 15.)

SPIRIT OF WONDER: MISS CHINA'S RING
(Eng title for THE SPIRIT OF WONDER: CHINA-SAN NO YÜTSU, lit The Spirit of Wonder: Miss China's Melancholy)

OAV
JAPANESE CREDITS: 1992. Dir: Mitsuru Hongo. Screenplay: Michiru Shimada. Chara des: Yoshiaki Yanagida. Art dir: Yoshiaki Yanagida. Music: Kohei Tanaka. Prod co: EMI.
© Tsuruta, Kodansha, Toshiba EMI.
45 mins.
WESTERN CREDITS: US video release 1996 on AminEigo, sub, dub.
ORIGINS: Manga by Kenji Tsuruta.
CATEGORIES: F
RATINGS: MAINSTREAM

A delicate love story of an Asian girl in a small town and her secret passion for the assistant to a local inventor. She thinks Jim is in love with another girl, the pretty florist Lily, but there's a happy ending for Miss China when the world finally learns that it's possible to go to the moon.

STREET FIGHTER II: THE ANIMATED MOVIE
(Eng title for STREET FIGHTER II)

MOVIE
JAPANESE CREDITS: 1994. Dir: Gisaburo Sugii. Screenplay: Kenichi Imai & Gisaburo Sugii. Prod co: Group TAC, AIC, O Productions. © Capcom.
c90 mins.
WESTERN CREDITS: US & UK video release 1995 on Manga Video, dub.
ORIGINS: Computer game.
SPINOFFS: Manga, Eng trans pub Viz (US), Titan Books (UK). A TV series, Streetfighter II V (for Victory) was made in 1996-97.
CATEGORIES: F
RATINGS: N, V, MAINSTREAM

A formulaic game-play story is enlivened by Sugii's directorial expertise. Hero Ken sets out to save his friend Ryu from the sinister Shadowlaw organisation, while Chun Li and American major Guile set out to crack their drugs and crime cartel. Lots of one-on-one combat, as you'd expect, the best of which is a chilling fight between Chun Li and Vega (Balrog in the Japanese). The whole sequence carries a huge erotic charge thanks to Sugii's skilful direction, which shows very little of the fight itself. It starts out in the shower (Chun Li without any clothes on, the dream of millions of game-freaks world-wide) and moves through a bloody and genuinely frightening ballet with the blond Hispanic psycho whose main concern is to keep the beautiful face behind his mask unscarred. (See pp86, 98, 112.)

SUIKODEN — DEMON CENTURY
(Eng title for YŌSEIKI SUIKŌDEN, lit Demon Century Water Margin)

OAV
JAPANESE CREDITS: 1993. Dir: Hiroshi Negishi. Original story: Ryohei Fukuoka. Original idea: Taira Yoshioka. Chara des: Nobuyuki Tsuru. Prod co: JC Staff.
© Yoshioka, Kadokawa, JVC, JC Staff. 45 mins.
WESTERN CREDITS: US video release 1996 on AD Vision, sub, dub; UK video release 1997, same version.
ORIGINS: The Chinese legends of the Water Margin.
POINTS OF INTEREST: Taira Yoshioka also created Irresponsible Captain Tylor.
CATEGORIES: SF
RATINGS: N, V, G, MAINSTREAM

'You kidnapped my sister and you must pay!' is the starting point for this tale of heroes reborn. Like the live-action *Water Margin* series, the first part of the OAV concerns itself with the getting-together of the band of heroes who are the reborn spirits of ancient warriors for justice. The second half has lots of highly satisfying rumbles, some transvestite martial arts hijinks, and some nudity. Never, ever rip off a nun's habit — you don't know what she's got underneath it. A scene in which the characters are unmasked as reincarnations of Lin Chung, Shih Chin, Hu San-Niang et al loses all of its resonance when the American translation merely transliterates the names into Japanese.

SUKEBAN DEKA
(Eng/Jpn title, lit Bad-Girl Cop)

OAV series, 3 episodes
JAPANESE CREDITS: 1991. Dir: Takeshi Hirota. Original story: Shinji Wada. Chara des: Noburteru Yuki. Music dir: Takashi Takao. Prod: Takeshi Hirota. Prod co: SIDO. © JVD, JH Project. Part 1 50 mins, parts 2 & 3 each 40 mins.
WESTERN CREDITS: US & UK video release 1996 on AD Vision, sub, dub, trans Ichiro Arakaki, Eng rewrite Matt Greenfield.
CATEGORIES: P, T
RATINGS: V, MAINSTREAM

A bad girl is taken out of borstal and put back into high school, to help crack a family crime syndicate using an exclusive educational establishment as a base for its operations. Her one weapon is a yo-yo, with which she manages to inflict enough severe injuries to make it no laughing matter. The villains are very nasty indeed and there is an unpleasant implied rape and murder sequence. (See p100.)

SUPERDIMENSIONAL CENTURY ORGUSS
(Eng title/trans for CHŌJIKU SEIKI ORGUSS)

TV series, 35 episodes
JAPANESE CREDITS: 1983-84. Dir: Noboru Ishiguro. Asst dir: Yasuyoshi Mikamoto. Original story: Studio Nue. Chara des: Haruhiko Mikimoto. Art dir: Yoshiyuki Yamamoto. Music: Kentaro Haneda. Prod: Toshitsuku Mukaitsubu. Prod co: Tokyo Movie Shinsha. © TMS, Big West. Each 27 mins.
WESTERN CREDITS: US video release 1992-94 on US Renditions, dub.
POINTS OF INTEREST: Future translation demi-gods Trish Ledoux and Raymond Garcia both worked on the US dub.
SPINOFFS: The almost completely unrelated Orguss 02.
CATEGORIES: SF
RATINGS: V, N, SM, MAINSTREAM

An involving and remarkably mature science fiction series whose hero does a runner after a one night stand, only to eventually meet his unknown daughter in an alternate universe on the opposite side in a war. He also has problems with his alien girlfriend — her species have to breed before they're seventeen or not at all, and time is running out for her. But her ex is still very much on the scene, and the whole emotional minefield teaches our hero that there's no such thing as a simple one night stand.

SUPERPOWERED GIRL BARABAMBA
(Eng trans for CHÖ NO RYOKU BARABAMBA)

OAV
JAPANESE CREDITS: 1985. Prod co: Fairy Dust. © Dynamic Planning. 30 mins.
ORIGINS: Manga by Go Nagai.
POINTS OF INTEREST: The first Nagai manga to be made into an OAV.
CATEGORIES: SF
RATINGS: N, X, V, G, EROTIC

Space pirate Baraba and her robot comrade Mia cross into our dimension fleeing a crime syndicate boss, and change forms. Baraba becomes a beautiful girl and Mia a cute fluffy animal. Magical girl series, anyone? No, this is Go Nagai's turf and things are a little more complicated than that. A young man, Hiro, steps in to save Baraba from the unwanted attention of some human thugs, and they start to fall in love. What's more, she likes her new shape and she's not sure Hiro will find her old one quite as attractive. The space fugitives and their human friend find shelter with a trio of lesbian sisters, but will they be able to stay on Earth with Baraba's past enemies still in pursuit? (See p52.)

SURF DREAMING

OAV
JAPANESE CREDITS: 1984. Original Story: Fumio Nakajima. Prod co: Wonder Kids. © F. Nakajima, Wonder Kids. 25 mins.
ORIGINS: The previous Wonder Kids release was Variation.
SPINOFFS: The next, and final Wonder Kids release was Seaside Angel Miyu.
CATEGORIES: P
RATINGS: N, PORN

Young love blooms between two teenagers who meet on a beach in this, the fifth Wonder Kids release. Essentially an erotic encounter, with the adult parts 'played' by two childish actors, allegedly to thwart the censorship restriction

Sword for Truth

(still powerful at the time) against depicting pubic hair. Nevertheless, sex between consenting children for the entertainment of adults is still paedophilia, however you try to dress it up.

SWORD FOR TRUTH
(Eng title for SHURANOSUKE ZANMAKEN, lit Demon-Slaying Sword of Shuranosuke)

OAV
JAPANESE CREDITS: 1991. Dir: Osamu Dezaki. Screenplay: Jo Toriumi. Chara des: Akio Sugino. Anime dir: Akio Sugino. Art dir: Yukio Abe. Prod: Naoko Takahashi, Takeshi Tamiya, Osamu Dezaki. Prod co: Toei. © Toriumi, Promise, Toei. c50 mins.
WESTERN CREDITS: US & UK video release 1998 on Manga Video, dub, trans Neil Nadelman.
ORIGINS: Novel by Jo Toriumi, pub Kadokawa.
CATEGORIES: H
RATINGS: NN, X, VV, EROTIC

Shuranosuke is a master swordsman who wanders seventeenth century Japan selling his skills. When a princess is abducted by a clan of ruthless ninja he is called on to get her back, but dark forces are at work and he must face not only ninja fighting skills but black magic. The violence exceeds the sex in quantity, but there are two longish sex scenes — one straight, one lesbian — and some nudity, mostly when female characters have their clothes slashed off. (See p9.)

THE TALE OF GENJI
(Eng title for MURASAKI SHIKIBU: GENJI MONOGATARI, lit Murasaki Shikibu: Tale of Genji)

MOVIE
JAPANESE CREDITS: 1987. Dir: Gisaburo Sugii. Screenplay: Tomomi Tsutsui. Chara des: Yasuhiro Nakura. Anime dir: Yasuo Maeda. Art dir: Mihoko Magori. Music: Harumi Hosono. Prod co: Group TAC. © Asahi, Nippon Herald, Group TAC. 105 mins.
WESTERN CREDITS: US video release 1995 on Central Park Media, sub, Eng rewrite Studio Phoenix.
ORIGINS: Novel by Murasaki Shikibu.
POINTS OF INTEREST: Composer Haruomi Hosono was one third of the Yellow Magic Orchestra with Ryuichi Sakamoto and Yukihiro Takahashi. Gainax's Yoshiyuki Sadamoto was among the animators.
CATEGORIES: H
RATINGS: N, X, MAINSTREAM

Based on what many regard as the world's earliest novel, an eleventh century text by a Heian court lady, this film tells only a small part of the original, and focuses on the principal loves of Prince Genji, a nobleman haunted by the death of his mother. Genji has lots of sex with many different women, but he's really still a little boy searching for a truly selfless love. This remarkably modern focus for the tale does not prevent director Sugii from slowing the pace of the film almost to a standstill in places, and packing in detail of Heian court life to make a visually beautiful package. (See p96.)

TENCHI MUYO! RYO OH KI
(Eng/Jpn title, lit This Way Up/No Need For Tenchi/Heaven And Earth Cannot Prevail, Ryo Oh Ki)

OAV series, 13 parts
JAPANESE CREDITS: 1992-95. Dir: Hiroki Hayashi. Screenplay: Naoko Hasegawa, Masaki Kajishima & Hiroki Hayashi. Chara des: Masaki Kajishima. Anime dir: Masaki Kajishima. Art dir: Takeshi Waki. Music dir: Yasunori Honda. Music: Seiko Nagaoka. Prod co: AIC. © Pioneer LDC. Each c30 mins.
WESTERN CREDITS: US video release 1994-95 on Pioneer LDCA, sub, dub, Eng rewrite
Jack Fletcher; UK video release 1994-96 on Pioneer LDCE, dub, same version.
SPINOFFS: Manga, a radio drama series, further OAVs, TV series and movies, plus a 'spinoff' TV show, Magical Girl Pretty Sammy and plenty of merchandise.
CATEGORIES: SF
RATINGS: N, MAINSTREAM

Another alien girlfriend story as average teen Tenchi Masaki gets not one, not two, but five gorgeous babes between about nine and eighteen years of age descending on his home and taking over his life. Lots of traditional Japanese hot spring scenes, much bitchy joshing about breasts, cookery and age between the girls. (See pp14, 23, 32, 33, 39, 108.)

TOKYO BABYLON

OAV series, two parts
JAPANESE CREDITS: 1992-93. Dir: Koichi Chiaki (1), Kumiko Takahashi (2). Screenplay: Tatsuhiko Urahata (1), Hiroaki Jinno (2). Chara des: Kumiko Takahashi. Anime dir: Kumiko Takahashi. Art dir: Yuji Ikeda. Music: Toshiyuki Honda. Prod co: Animate Film. © CLAMP, Shinshokan, MOVIC, SME. Part 1 50 mins, part 2 55 mins.
WESTERN CREDITS: UK video release 1994 on Manga Video, dub, trans Jay Parks, Eng rewrite George Roubicek; US video release 1995 on US Manga Corps.
ORIGINS: Manga by CLAMP
POINTS OF INTEREST: The central relationship of the manga is underplayed in the OAVs, but recurs in the CLAMP movie and manga X.
CATEGORIES: P, F
RATINGS: VV, MAINSTREAM

Psychic Subaru Sumeragi is heir to an ancient line of mystics and uses his powers to solve cases with a magical or otherworldly dimension in modern-day Tokyo. Each episode contrasts Subaru's unworldly gentleness with the cynical and self-seeking city dwellers he meets. The religious symbols are left-over eighties fashion statements rather than deep philosophical subtexts; the real importance of *Tokyo Babylon*, which emerges more clearly in the manga, is its part in the movement of shojo elements into the commercial mainstream, in which CLAMP have long been standard-bearers. (See pp35, 39.)

TOKYO PRIVATE POLICE
(Eng title for TOKIO KIDÖ POLICE, lit Tokio Mobile Police)

OAV, 2 episodes
JAPANESE CREDITS: 1997. Dir: Moriichi Higashi. Screenplay: Yu Yamato. Chara des: Harunaga Kazuki. Mecha des: Satoshi Teraoka. Prod co: Dandylion. © Hakage, Dandylion. Each 30 mins.
WESTERN CREDITS: US video release 1998 on Kitty Media.
ORIGINS: Pornographic novel allegedly inspired by Patlabor.
CATEGORIES: SF
RATINGS: N, X, PORN

The year is 2034, and Tokyo is beset with a crime-wave of giant robots. Section One of the robot division is on hand to deal with the problems, but they spend a lot of time screwing each other in the office. Much of the drama in *Patlabor* came from the suppressed emotion: Goto's doomed adoration for Nagumo, or Izumi's purely platonic friendship with Azuma. *Tokyo Private Police* just lets it all hang out, as new recruit Kazuko succumbs to the temptation to get off with the rest of her team on day one. There goes the suspense.

TOKYO REVELATION
(Eng title for SHIN MEGAMI TENSEI TÖKYÖ JIROKU, lit True Goddess Reborn Tokyo Revelation)

OAV, 2 parts
JAPANESE CREDITS: 1994. Dir: Osamu Yamazaki. Original story: Kazuya Suzuki & Chiaki Mikishima. Script: Mamiya Fujimura. Chara des: Kenichi Onuki. Monster des: Koichi Ohata & Hikaru Takanashi. Art dir: Chitose Asakura. Exec prod: Megumi Sugiyama. Prod: Yasuhisa Kazama & Kazumasa Fujiya. Prod co: Vap. © Sony Music Entertainment. Each 30 mins.
WESTERN CREDITS: US & UK video release 1997 on Manga Entertainment on 1 tape, dub, Eng rewrite Richard Epcar.
CATEGORIES: F
RATINGS: N, V, MAINSTREAM

When Kojiro was younger, he toyed with the idea of summoning a demon. For him it was just a game; but for his friend Akito, a lonely kid bullied or ignored by everyone else, anything his friend wants is to be taken very, very seriously. Once out of elementary school they are separated, but years later Akito comes back to Tokyo and Kojiro's high school. He's made some powerful new friends, but he still values his childhood playmate, and to prove it he's carried Kojiro's boyish experiments to extremes and endangered the whole human race. Akito's fey prettiness puts him right in the bishonen mould, and he tries to take the childhood friendship to a new level when he kisses Kojiro after school. Kojiro, of course, being a straight kind of guy, turns him down, but nicely. Akito decides to show him just how easy it is to call up a demon, and triggers a change in his old friend which is completely unexpected and not at all what he was hoping for. (See p35.)

TOUCH

TV series, 101 episodes
JAPANESE CREDITS: 1985-87. Dir: Gisaburo Sugii, Naoto Hashimoto & Akinori Nagaoka. Series dir: Hiroko Tokita. Screenplay: Yumiko Takahoshi, Shigeru Yanagawa & Satoko Kaneharu. Storyboards: Hiroko Tokita. Prod: Masamichi Fujiwara. Prod co: Toho. © Adachi, Shogakukan, Toho, Asatsu. Each c25 mins.
ORIGINS: Manga by Mitsuru Adachi.
SPINOFFS: 3 movies were edited from the series.
CATEGORIES: P
RATINGS: MAINSTREAM

As with Adachi's later *Slow Step*, school sports and everyday life form the background for an intensely emotional story. The love triangle between a girl and twin brothers is beautifully drawn and the resulting emotional chaos when one of the brothers dies has enormous impact. (See p42.)

TWIN DOLLS
(Eng title for INJÜ SEISEN TWIN ANGEL, lit Lust-Beast Crusade Twin Angel)

OAV series, 2 parts
JAPANESE CREDITS: 1994. Dir: Kan Fukumoto. Original story: Oji Miyako. Script: Oji Miyako. Chara des: Shin Rin. Art dir: Manami Matsumoto. Mus: Teruo Takahama. Exec Prod: Rusher Ikeda. Prod: Kento Maki & Smally Izumi. Prod co: Dandy Lion. © Daiei. Each 50 mins.
WESTERN CREDITS: US video release 1995-96 on SoftCel, sub, Eng rewrite Matt

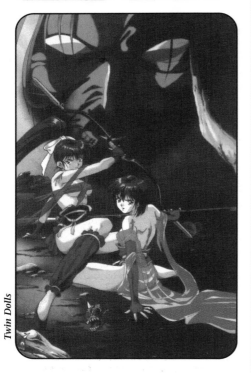

Twin Dolls

Greenfield.
CATEGORIES: P, D
RATINGS: XX, NN, VV, EROTIC

Demons want to invade Earth and rape our women. Luckily, two priestesses turn out to be the descendants of an immortal, and are appointed guardians of the child messiah, whether they like it or not. The Immortal Dialogue Sampler came up with: 'Feel the love nectar flow, gushing from your trembling vagina', and 'It's a treasure trove of tits and clits'. Real historical/mythical figures lie buried beneath the tits-and-tentacles plot, which is more concerned with the incestuous allure of twins, the rejected woman's quest for power through sex and the worship of His Majesty the Baby.

U-JIN BRAND

OAV
JAPANESE CREDITS: 1991. Dir: Osamu Okada. Writer: U-Jin. Original idea: Hideo Takano. Chief animator: Yumi Nakayama.

Music: Nobuo Ito. Prod co: Coconut Boy Project, Animate. © U-Jin, Seiyo, Animate Film. 45 mins.
WESTERN CREDITS: US video release 1994 on US Manga Corps, sub.
ORIGINS: Manga by U-Jin.
CATEGORIES: P
RATINGS: XX, NN, PORN

Short stories based on U-Jin's manga, similar in tone and style to *New Angel*, *Visionary* and *Pictures from High School*. There's the tale of a songwriter who produces hit after hit for teenage idol singers, but can only work if he really, really gets to know the girl. Seducing girl after girl, he still cherishes a secret love for the innocent Akiyo. So what will happen when he and Akiyo have to work together? Then we meet Sachiko, who made the common mistake of believing her boyfriend when he said he'd still love her just as much afterwards, only to find that he firmly intends to marry a virgin. Now he's dating the seemingly innocent Hitomi. The jilted Sachiko hires a renowned seducer, Toyama No Benbo, to get her revenge on her ex and find out if Hitomi is really as pure as she pretends to be. Lastly, a young man is trapped in a relationship with Tomoko, his boss's nymphomaniac daughter. Iwata really wants to marry sweet, gentle Kyoko, but he can't just dump the girl who holds his career prospects in the palm of her hand. More business for Toyama No Benbo as he's called in to sort out the insatiable Tomoko.

UROTSUKIDOJI I.1-II.2: LEGEND OF THE OVERFIEND/LEGEND OF THE DEMON WOMB
(Eng title for CHŌJIN DENSETSU UROTSUKIDŌJI, lit Legend of the Overfiend: The Wandering Child)

MOVIE/OAV series: 5 OAVs, 2 movies
JAPANESE CREDITS: 1987-91. Dir: Hideki Takayama. Screenplay: Noboru Aikawa & Goro Sanyo. Music: Jeffrey Jackson & Masamichi Amano. Prod co: JAVN, Angel. © Maeda, Westcape Corp. Part 1 c45 mins, parts 2-4 c55 mins, part 5 c50 mins. Movie versions: Legend of the Overfiend 108 mins, Legend of the Demon Womb 88 mins. WESTERN CREDITS: US video release 1993 on Anime 18, as edited movie versions of OAVs 1-3, (Legend of the Overfiend) & 4 & 5 (Legend of the Demon Womb), dub, Eng rewrite Michael Lawrence, & as Urotsukidoji Perfect Collection, all 5 OAVs

unedited in a box set, sub; UK video release 1993 on Manga Video, movie versions only, dub.
ORIGINS: Manga by Toshio Maeda.
SPINOFFS: 2 more OAV series, largely thanks to the overwhelming response from the Western market.
CATEGORIES: F, D
RATINGS: XX, NN, VV, SM, EROTIC

Violent and sexually explicit in the extreme, the video series was edited for movie release in Japan before the British censors got their hands on it. *Overfiend* has moments of real grandeur and terror heavily mired in enough schlock to sink a battleship, but it merits attention as much because of our own attitudes to it as because of its content or form. (See pp15, 20, 21, 38, 42, 48, 55, 58-81, 82, 86, 87-88, 91, 104, 108.)

UROTSUKIDOJI III: RETURN OF THE OVERFIEND
(Eng title for CHŌJIN DENSETSU UROTSUKIDŌJI MIRAI HEN, lit Legend of the Overfiend: The Wandering Child Future Chapter)

OAV series, 4 parts
JAPANESE CREDITS: 1993. Dir: Hideki Takayama. Screenplay: Noboru Aikawa (1), Hideki Takayama & Yasuhito Yamaki (2 & 3), Gonzo Satsuka (4). Chara des: Rikizo Sekime & Shiro Kasami. Monster des: Sumito Ioi. Art dir: Kenichi Harada. Music: Masamichi Amano. Prod co: Jupiter Films. © Maeda, Jupiter. Part 1 60 mins, parts 2-4 50 mins.
WESTERN CREDITS: UK video release 1994 on Kiseki Films, dub, trans Ryoichi Murata (1 & 2), Jonathan Clements (3 & 4); US video release 1994 on Anime 18, same version.
ORIGINS: Manga by Toshio Maeda, 1987-91 OAV series.
POINTS OF INTEREST: A 120-min, edited version with Eng subtitles is available as Urotsukidoji III: The Movie.
SPINOFFS: A further series was made 2 years later.
CATEGORIES: F, D
RATINGS: XX, NN, VV, SM, EROTIC

Amanojaku follows the Chojin's search for his nemesis, the Kyo-O, through a devastated wasteland, clinging desperately to the hope that all the violence and suffering he has wit-

nessed will lead to a better world. When humans like Caesar and Munchausen behave as badly as the bestial makemono, this seems unlikely, but there are still some rare (if futile) expressions of love in the midst of chaos. The poignant and foreboding passage in episode four, where little girl Himi unleashes the Kyo-O's Light of Judgement on the world, lingers in the mind more powerfully than the gross images of rape and torture which precede it. (See pp58-81, 92, 98.)

UROTSUKIDOJI IV: INFERNO ROAD
(Eng title for CHŌJIN DENSETSU UROTSUKIDŌJI INFERNO ROAD, lit Legend of the Overfiend: The Wandering Child Inferno Road)

OAV series, 3 parts
JAPANESE CREDITS: 1995. Dir: Hideki Takayama. Screenplay: Nobuaki Kishima. Storyboards: Hideki Takayama. Chara des: Keiichi Sato & Tetsuya Yanagisawa. Anime dir: Tetsuya Yanagisawa. Music: Masamichi Amano. Prod co: MW Films. © Maeda, Jupiter Films. Each 40 mins.
WESTERN CREDITS: UK version on Kiseki, trans Jonathan Clements, certificate refused by BBFC; US video release 1996 on Anime 18, sub.
ORIGINS: Manga by Toshio Maeda, 1987-91 and 1993 OAV series.
POINTS OF INTEREST: Kiseki are still attempting to get a UK release for the series.
CATEGORIES: F, D
RATINGS: XX, NN, VV, SM, EROTIC

The end of the *Overfiend* saga is literally its beginning, as the meeting of the Chojin and the Kyo-O turns time back on itself and restarts the cycle. Maeda drives home his message that the only escape from the self-centredness of childhood is the clumsy self-gratification of adulthood. In a world in which the only way to win is to die before your dreams, Amanojaku's ending is the saddest one possible. (See pp53, 58-81, 92, 101, 109.)

URUSEI YATSURA
(Eng/Jpn title, pun on Noisy People/ Obnoxious Aliens/Guys from Planet Uru)

TV series, 218 episodes

JAPANESE CREDITS: 1981-86. Dir: Kazuo Yamazaki & Mamoru Oshii. Story editor: Kazunori Ito. Screenplay: Kazunori Ito, Michiru Shimada, Shigeru Yanagawa, Mamoru Oshii et al. Chara des: Akemi Takada. Prod co: Kitty Film. © Takahashi, Shogakukan, Kitty Film. Each c25 mins. WESTERN CREDITS: US ongoing video release 1993-to date on AnimEigo, sub, trans Shin Kurokawa & Vincent Winiarski; UK partial video release 1994-96 on Anime Projects, same version. ORIGINS: Manga by Rumiko Takahashi. SPINOFFS: 5 movies and 11 OAVs followed. CATEGORIES: P, F RATINGS: N, V, MAINSTREAM

The ultimate cautionary tale of what happens to Japanese boys who hanker after alien babes, *Urusei Yatsura* remains one of the freshest, funniest stories of the unwelcome guest/alien girlfriend genre. (See pp14, 85, 96, 101, 105.)

USHI & TORA
(Eng title/trans for USHI TO TORA)

OAV series, 11 episodes JAPANESE CREDITS: 1992-93. Dir: Kunihiko Yuyama. Script: Kenji Terada. Art dir: Kachiyoshi Kanamura. Prod co: Pastel, Toho. © Fujita, Shogakukan, Toho, Toshiba EMI, OB Planning. Each c27 mins. WESTERN CREDITS: UK video release 1995 on Western Connection, sub, trans Jonathan Clements; US video release 1997 on AD Vision. ORIGINS: Manga by Kazuhiro Fujita. POINTS OF INTEREST: The lead characters' names are punning references to oriental astrology, the signs of the Ox (Ushi) and Tiger (Tora). CATEGORIES: P, F RATINGS: V, MAINSTREAM

An involving, edgy series about the ghostbusting relationship between a priest's son and the evil spirit he is supposed to guard, you could call this *Tenchi Muyo!* for sceptics (*Ushio & Tora's* manga origins give them a stronger background to draw on). Ushio and Tora are a great couple, and the unlikely beginnings of their friendship make their eventual alliance more powerful than your average buddy movie. Ghosts of the past leave space for comment on modern sexu-

al mores; Tora cannot eat modern people because they douse themselves in perfume. Ushio's love-hate relationship with Tora is mirrored in the real world by his constant sparring with the Tomboy Asako, a touching nod to the truth that Tora is Ushio's last childish escape from the world, before he wakes up and discovers there are more interesting things to do with Asako than fight.

VARIATION
(Eng trans for HENSÖKYOKU)

OAV JAPANESE CREDITS: 1984. Original Story: Fumio Nakajima. Prod co: Wonder Kids. © F. Nakajima, Wonder Kids. 25 mins. ORIGINS: The previous Wonder Kids release was House of Kittens. Variation is a direct sequel to Altar of Sacrifice, the story that followed Dying for a Girl in the second Lolita release. SPINOFFS: The next in the series was Surf Dreaming. CATEGORIES: P RATINGS: NN, XX, SM, PORN

The fourth Wonder Kids release, in which a young girl interested in art gets more than she bargains for when she accepts the art teacher's invitation to dinner. One of the most distasteful of the lolikon genre, because it seems less like fantasy than a beginner's guide to statutory rape. (See pp108-109.)

VENUS FIVE
(Eng title for SAILOR SENSHI VENUS FIVE, lit Sailor Soldiers Venus Five)

OAV series, 2 parts JAPANESE CREDITS: 1994. Dir: Kan Fukumoto. Screenplay: Wataru Amano. Chara des: Rin Shin. Art dir: Shoichiro Sugiura. Exec prod: Rusher Ikeda. Prod: Smally Izumi & Kento Maki. Prod co: Daiei Co Ltd. © Daiei Co Ltd. Each c45 mins. WESTERN CREDITS: US video release 1996 on Anime 18, sub, trans Moe I. Yada. ORIGINS: Parody manga by Jin Ara. CATEGORIES: F, P RATINGS: XX, NN, V, PORN

A *Sailor Moon* parody in which a team of heroic

schoolgirls are granted mystical powers to battle the evil invader Necros and her team of tasty young men. Of course, Necros and co are really nasty vicious slimy alien things in disguise, so there are lots of tentacles, and even a scene of bestiality (bringing new meaning to the phrase 'pussy-licking'). Set in the kind of cod-classical rooms you expect to find in places decorated by people with more money than taste, and larded with cod-classical references on the same level, the stories are patently absurd and serve mostly to remind us that nobody watches this kind of tape for the story.

VIOLENCE JACK

OAV series, 3 parts
JAPANESE CREDITS: 1986-90. Dir: Ichiro Itano. Script: Noboru Aikawa. Chara des: Takuya Wada. Anime dir: Takuya Wada. Art dir: Mitsuharu Miyamae. Music dir: Yasunori Honda. Prod: Kazufumi Nomura. Prod co: Ashi. © Dynamic Planning, Soeishinsha, Japan Home Video. Part 1 40 mins, parts 2 & 3 each 60 mins.
WESTERN CREDITS: US & UK video release 1996 on Manga Video, dub, trans Studio Nemo, Eng rewrite John Wolskel.
ORIGINS: Manga by Go Nagai.
CATEGORIES: SF, H
RATINGS: N, XX, VV, MAINSTREAM

Three episodes from the adventures of the elemental creature Violence Jack, set in a nightmare world following a huge earthquake which has destroyed most of the island of Honshu, and all the trappings of civilisation. Cannibalism, child murder, gang rape, sex slavery and casual violence are all featured. Even in the British versions, as approved by the BBFC, these stories are not at all nice. (See pp54, 55, 56.)

VIRUS
(Eng title for VIRUS BUSTER SERGE)

TV series, 13 episodes
JAPANESE CREDITS: 1997. Dir: Masami Obari. Screenplay: Masami Obari, Jiro Kaneko et al. Series supervision: Kazuhiko Soba & Jiro Kaneko. Chara des: Masami Obari. Mecha des: Natsuki Mamiya. Sound dir: Toshiki Kameyama. Music: Satoshi Komori. Exec prod: Masakazu

Kobayashi & Shigekazu Ochiai. Prod co: Plum. © Obari, Sega, Victor Entertainment. Each 25 mins.
ORIGINS: Computer game.
POINTS OF INTEREST: Archangel Thunderbird's Yasushi Nirasawa designed monsters for the Sega Saturn game.
CATEGORIES: SF
RATINGS: MAINSTREAM

Beautiful boys and curiously unattractive girls fight to save the world from deadly demonic viruses that leap from machine to brain. Yes, it's *Akira* meets *Doom*, with an international twist in the setting (Hong Kong) and the dialogue (English-soaked). This might not be the future of anime, but it's a well-lit path the industry may take: based on a computer game, with unisex appeal, ready-made foreign sales and fast cuts and flashy effects to hide the cheap animation. While still paying lip-service to the office-romance element of many police stories, *Virus* is noteworthy in the mainstream for carrying a barely concealed homoerotic charge. The gimlet-eyed women have courtesy breasts and a fair amount of screen time, but seem almost deliberately unappealing, whereas the men are all smouldering gods, pouting suggestively at each other. Even the opening music plays to a proto-gay disinterest in women, as a fey man, swamped beneath a hard-rock beat, sings sulkily about his girlfriend's heartless pleasure in dumping him, and his resolve to get on with his life. (See pp35, 40.)

VISIONARY

OAV series, 2 episodes
JAPANESE CREDITS: 1995. Dir: Teruo Kigure. Script: Toyohiro Ando. Gen prod: Seiichi Nishino. Prod: Shigeyuki Hasegawa & Noriko Nishino. Prod co: Knack. © U-Jin, Shiberu Publishing Co, Knack. Each c20 mins.
WESTERN CREDITS: US video release 1997 on Anime 18, sub, trans nDa Language Services.
ORIGINS: Manga by U-Jin, pub Shiberu.
POINTS OF INTEREST: The android catgirl from the future has a name which is very close to that of the robot cat Doraemon — most of whose original audience are now old enough to buy both nostalgia and porn.
CATEGORIES: F, C
RATINGS: NN, XX, SM, PORN

Nineteen year-old geek Ujita has no luck with women and gets grief from the local bully, until he hits the wrong key on his computer and the sexy Doreimon pops back from the future. (No, you can't do that with Windows 95.) Although Doreimon can give Ujita experiences beyond his wildest dreams, everything doesn't always go according to plan. (See pp39, 105.)

VOLTAGE FIGHTER GOWCAIZER

OAV series, 2 parts (to date)
JAPANESE CREDITS: 1996. Dir: Masami Obari. Screenplay: Kengo Asai. Chara des: Masami Obari. Art dir: Hiroshi Kato. Storyboards: Masami Obari. Exec prod: Hiroshi Yamaji & Yoshimasa Onishi. Gen prod: Yoshinori Chiba, Shinichi Hirai & Tomoko Kawasaki. Prod: Gaga Communications, Big West. Prod co: JC Staff. © Gaga Communications, Urban Plant. Each 45 mins.
WESTERN CREDITS: US video release 1997 on US Manga Corps, dub, trans Kevin McKeown.
POINTS OF INTEREST: One of the lead characters has the same name as Devilman's human form, Akira Fudo.
CATEGORIES: SF
RATINGS: N, V, MAINSTREAM

Isato Goka's athletic skills have won him a place at the Belnar Institute, a school for those with some outstanding gift. (All the female students seem to have at least two...) The Institute's founder, Shizuru Ozaki, has another agenda quite apart from education — he appears to be using the mysterious powers of his Caizer Stones to control his students and he reports in secret to a beautiful, seemingly female but certainly inhuman entity. Isato's friend Kash has given him a Caizer Stone, and with it the power to transform into armoured hero Gowcaizer. Isato's girlfriend and female chum are over-endowed to the point of absurdity, with more cels spent depicting each wiggle and jiggle than on any of the battle scenes, and tiny costumes which are shed at every opportunity. There's also some much more serious sex going on between a brother and sister. They serve Ozaki's nefarious ends because he saved the girl when she was on the point of death, after their family had abandoned the siblings in disgust at their forbidden love. This is evidently the kind of abnormality that deserves death. (See p25.)

WEATHER REPORT GIRL
(Eng title/trans for OTENKI OJÖSAMA)

OAV series, 2 parts
JAPANESE CREDITS: 1994-95. Dir: Kunihiko Yuyama (1), Takashi Watanabe (2). Prod co: OB Planning. © OB Planning, Toho Co. Each 45 mins.
WESTERN CREDITS: US video release 1996 on Critical Mass, sub.
ORIGINS: Manga by Tetsu Ando, pub Shogakukan in Weekly Young Magazine.
CATEGORIES: P
RATINGS: NN, MAINSTREAM

Keiko's big chance comes when regular weather-girl Michiko goes on vacation. She uses her body to illustrate the forecasts, baring strategic portions for warm fronts and peaks on the barometer. As ratings rise, Michiko comes back, but Keiko doesn't want to step down. Even the introduction of a classier rival in episode two doesn't faze her. Having come so far by showing so much determination, she'll show whatever it takes to keep her place in the spotlight.

THE WHITE SERPENT
(Eng trans for HAKUJADEN)

MOVIE
JAPANESE CREDITS: 1958. Dir: Taiji Yabushita. Screenplay: Taiji Yabushita. Prod co: Toei Doga. © Toei. 78 mins.
ORIGINS: Chinese legend.
POINTS OF INTEREST: Toei's first feature film, usually regarded as the first anime of the modern era.
CATEGORIES: F
RATINGS: MAINSTREAM

The story of a boy's love for a beautiful young girl who has lived before as a serpent goddess. In childhood he has a beautiful white snake as a pet, but his parents make him get rid of it. Later on when he meets his former pet again, this time in human form, he falls in love with her. Again, his parents are not happy, and nor is the local priest who suspects her of having demonic powers. In the end, the girl gives up her magic powers in order to be allowed to settle down to a life of ordinary human domesticity with the boy she loves.

WICKED CITY
(Eng title/trans for YŌJŪ TOSHI, aka MONSTER CITY, aka SUPERNATURAL BEAST CITY)

OAV
JAPANESE CREDITS: 1987. Dir: Yoshiaki Kawajiri. Screenplay: Kisei Cho. Chara des: Yoshiaki Kawajiri. Art dir: Yuji Kaeda. Music: Osamu Shoji. Prod co: Madhouse, Video Art. © Japan Home Video. 90 mins.
WESTERN CREDITS: US video release 1992 on Streamline, dub, Eng rewrite Greg Snegoff; UK video release 1993 on Manga Video, same version; also limited US & UK theatrical release 1993/94.
ORIGINS: Novel by Hideyuki Kikuchi.
SPINOFFS: A live-action version was made in Hong Kong and released on video in the UK by East2West.
CATEGORIES: P, H
RATINGS: N, X, V, SM, EROTIC

The human and demon worlds have enjoyed an uneasy truce for centuries, but now the deal is up for renegotiation and some don't want it renewed. In Kikuchi's tale of horror-political intrigue, representatives from the human and demon secret services are assigned to guard an interdimensional ambassador. But the human male and the demon female don't realise that they are being set up for a dynastic marriage to secure the union of opposites. The romantic angle is unintentionally ruined by the 'Oh, Maki', 'Oh, Taki' dialogue. (See pp30-31, 39, 86.)

WINGS OF HONNEAMISE
(Eng title for HONNEAMISE NO TSUBASA ŌRITSU UCHŪ GUN, lit Wings Of Honneamise — Royal Space Force)

MOVIE
JAPANESE CREDITS: 1987. Dir: Hiroyuki Yamaga. Writer: Hiroyuki Yamaga. Chara des: Yoshiyuki Sadamoto. Anime dir: Hideaki Anno, Yuji Moriyama, Fumio Iida & Yoshiyuki Sadamoto. Art dir: Hiromasa Ogura. Music: Ryuichi Sakamoto et al. Prod co: Gainax. © Gainax, Bandai Visual. 120 mins.
WESTERN CREDITS: US video release 1994 on Manga Video, sub, dub, trans Neil Nadelman, Taro Yoshida & Nobuhiro Hayashi, Eng rewrite Quint Lancaster & Mary Mason; UK video release 1995 on Manga Video, same version.
POINTS OF INTEREST: Gainax's preferred title is allegedly Royal Space Force; the name change was forced by executives who wanted 'The Something of Something' to subliminally suggest a non-existent relationship with Nausicaä of the Valley of Wind. TV announcers take note, the title is pronounced OH-NEE-AH-MISS.
CATEGORIES: SF
RATINGS: V, MAINSTREAM

This remarkable science fiction film, one of the best examples of world-building in the genre, is included here because of a scene in which the hero attempts to rape a girl who has befriended him and is dissuaded by the application of an ornament to the back of his head. It is a great movie and should be in every film-lover's collection, but the thrills it offers are of a very different nature from those offered by other titles in this list. (See p111.)

Wicked City

AFTERWORD

By Helen McCarthy

Golden Boy

This book is in part a response to the demonisation of anime in the British media, and to the restrictions placed on freedom of imagination in British society. Sex is the easiest and most obvious arena for this particular fight, but the fight itself is about other, more important issues.

It took the unexpected success of the film *Akira* on video, and a brilliant marketing campaign by Island World Entertainment, to turn anime into a journalistic scapegoat, as a contributory cause of violence, sexual misbehaviour and social decay in British society. In the last decade of the twentieth century, a Britain bankrupt of excuses for its own moral decline found an easy target: a nation which speaks a completely different language, has a different skin colour, a different social and cultural base, and (best of all) lost the War. The response of the British media and politicians to anime has all the hallmarks of one-nation chauvinism at its worst.

That all the sound and fury directed at anime had almost no factual basis was, of course, ignored by those making the noise. I took this complete failure to check the available facts about anime personally, since most of them were contained in my first book. It was obvious that the journalistic

community simply ignored it in the time-honoured tradition of refusing to allow the facts to get in the way of a good story.

But why should this worry fans of Japanese animation? Anime, after all, is a commercial entertainment, not a political or social movement. You buy a video, take it home and watch it. How does this simple action affect the security of your fellow citizens and the state? How can entertainment be a political arena and choice of entertainment a political choice?

In fairness, I should state my own position: I am entirely opposed to all forms of censorship of the private entertainment or thoughts of responsible adults. Jonathan has different views, but I believe that in a free society, anyone who is legally of age and mentally competent is able to decide what constitutes acceptable entertainment. Surely censoring some expressions of opinion because of the way in which they present sex, fantasy, violence, politics or anything else, is not the proper action of a free society. Yet we're told that we live in one. Do we or don't we? I could deal with an honest answer more easily than an inconsistent fudging of the truth.

I accept that anyone unable to give full and free consent — children, animals, the mentally incompetent or anyone similarly unable to accept full responsibility for their own actions — should be protected from sexual acts. However, I question whether the protection of individuals or society as a whole is served by implying that private fantasy is in some way an excuse or justification for behaviour towards real people in the real world.

Television is more accessible and more influential than video in terms of forming attitudes, particularly among children. Yet television soaps revolve around familiar characters living in a world like ours, whose moral code and social structure make anime look ludicrously old-fashioned. Serial adultery, partner-swapping, incest, murder, theft, deception and violence abound. These soaps are popular with children, yet the press, scourge of Japanese animation, broadly approves of them, to the extent that soap 'events' and stars are given more prominence than real news in many so-called newspapers.

Anime is demonised in the press as nothing but sex and violence. In just the same fashion, Japan is mythologised as a strange and exotic realm on the borders of reality. This results in a good deal of tosh being talked about both, mostly by people with a very limited knowledge of the subject. In this book we hope we have addressed some of the principal areas of misinformation and opened the way for a more balanced, reasoned discussion of anime and its various genres, of which the erotic is only one.

Writing this book has clarified many of my opinions on censorship and erotica. I have come to realise that the idea of censorship *per se* bothers me less than the clumsy reality of its present operation in the United Kingdom. I dislike the pretence that control of private individual expression is compatible with a free society, and I dislike the condescending dismissal of the ordinary person's ability to separate fact from fantasy, real life from wish-fulfilment, real people from the dream-figures of porn. If we are going to have censorship, let's be honest and admit why.

This is not about pornography, or taste, or decency or the protection of minors. It's not about preserving our decent Anglo-Saxon culture from these nasty, unprincipled oriental invaders. It's about control. Who controls what you can see on your screen and what you can see in your head? Here in Britain, it isn't us. ●

AFTERWORD

By Jonathan Clements

In Japan, the encyclopaedias and reference works often treat erotic anime quite cursorily, or even leave them out altogether. And yet these are the very anime that we in the West are most likely to see. It took a decade for Buena Vista to buy *Kiki's Delivery Service*, but Kiseki bought *Plastic Little* before it was even completed.

I am interested in neglected areas of anime criticism, but when it comes to the porn sector, many are already the subject of rights negotiations. As I look down the list of new anime in Japan, I see: *Lust Alien*, *Sex Jihad*, *Don't Call Me Amy*, *Secret Anima*, *Nonomura Hospital*, *Beast City* and *Pendant*, which will not only be available in Japan by the time you read this, but also stand a good chance of being available here in the West. There are so many, even in English, that we could easily write this book again without repeating ourselves. What is 'neglected' in this genre is not the availability of the titles themselves, but critical appraisal. I hope that we have somehow redressed the balance.

Helen sees this book as a meditation on freedom. What interests me is the craft of making anime, the many factors that combine to form a finished story. This is not my first book, but it is the first I have written under my own name. Like my colleagues in Japan, I have a pseudonymous shadow-career, writing, ghosting, and translating in the adult and children's market, producing works that I do not necessarily want attached to my biography.

Commercial work is never made for love. As

the name implies, it is made for money. No publisher has ever come up to me with £10,000 and said: 'Here you go, write something nice'. Instead, I am given a set of constraints, which can include time, resources, aims, audience, vocabulary, distribution, collaborators, legality, or just about anything. All these factors, plus talent (or lack of it), make a finished work. I can't teach talent, but I can discuss the many unseen influences that make anime art and writing what it is today, the chance to explain why without resorting to racist stereotype.

My attitude towards censorship is neither political nor moral, it is based in my own, emotional response to Japan. There are people alive today whose only encounter with Japanese culture has been with an *Overfiend* video. I think they deserve more. I think they are entitled to an *informed* opinion, if they can sift the information from the lies. Frankly, I think that Toshio Maeda deserves more, too. As a writer, I would hate to see my work only available in bastardised editions.

I do not believe for a moment that I am protecting the weak-minded from harm if I support the BBFC's actions. I do believe that I am helping to protect Japan from the weak-minded, since the media have provided an unrepresentative picture of the culture and people I love so dearly. What should bother you more: that Toshio Maeda has sick fantasies, or that 60,000 British men pay money for them?

If I may make a modest proposal, since many intellectual property laws in Europe are rationalising with the German model, we should perhaps consider adopting a German-style censorship system as well. Under such a system, if you wanted to buy *Overfiend* uncut, you could go into any sex shop and do so. Problem solved: if you want to buy *Overfiend* it's right there, in its place, among the porn of other cultures. But you wouldn't be able to see the sanitised, incomprehensible, cut version, because it wouldn't be sold in mainstream stores.

I know it affects people, because I know it affects me. But *Overfiend* doesn't turn me into a rapist, it just depresses me. When I translated *Overfiend* III.3 I was a nervous wreck for days. I had to watch it seventeen times, uncut. It took nearly a fortnight. Two years later when I translated *Overfiend* IV.3, it took me four hours, just long enough to watch it twice. Have I become a better, stronger person through prolonged exposure to this material? Or have I lost something precious and irreplaceable?

I think that eroticism is part, but only part, of human nature. If I want to lose sleep over

Plastic Little

anything, there are plenty of other options. I am not one of the hordes of inarticulate fanboys who see nothing unpleasant in *Overfiend*. Nor am I one of the misguided *chauvinistes* who believe that turning men into sex objects is some kind of feminist statement. I have translated pornography on several occasions, and have come to hold it in a kind of indulgent, catholic regard. I find rabble-rousing and demagoguery, deliberate misinformation as practised by the unscrupulous media, far more disturbing than watching two-dimensional cels feign sexual intercourse.

There is more to censorship than cuts imposed by a Government organisation. Japan, real Japan, is censored every time a Western newspaper editor drops a piece because the readers 'won't understand'. It is censored every time a video company fifteens a good script into an amateurish swearing match between bored actors with their eyes on the clock. It is censored every time a retailer refuses to stock subtitled anime because he believes that only teenage illiterates buy 'manga videos'.

You deserve more. You deserve to see *Overfiend* uncut if you can handle it, if you want to handle it. But don't put it on the shelf in Tower Records, not unless it is just one of ten thousand Japanese videos, across every genre, for every conceivable age-group.

Because the Japanese deserve more too, don't you think? ●

GLOSSARY

We have tried to keep our use of Japanese terms to a minimum, but you will encounter some of them throughout this book, so here is a very short list:

ANIME: The Japanese word for animation. In Japan this means animation of any kind; foreign fans use it to distinguish Japanese animation from that of any other nation.

BI: 'Pretty'. Often found as a prefix to SHONEN or SHOJO.

DOJINSHI: Amateur fanzine. The material can be original or based on popular ANIME, comics or novels. (Some dojinshi circles also put real-life characters in their work. One SHONEN AI fanzine in the mid-nineties chronicled the fantasy of life as a roadie for boy-band Take That.)

DOSEIAN: A term sometimes used in place of SHONEN AI for material in which the main romantic protagonists are male. From dosei ai, 'homosexual love'.

ECCHI: Abbreviated form of 'HENTAI' ('H'), signifying a mild level of perversion.

HENTAI: Perverse, pervert, person interested in explicit erotic story.

JUNE: (Two syllables.) The name of a magazine devoted to SHONEN AI material, another term for this kind of story.

LOLIKON: Also transliterated as rorikon — abbreviation for 'Lolita complex', used for material featuring girls who appear to be under the age of consent.

MANGA: Comics. 'Comics' is also often used.

OAV: Original Anime Video, ie first appearance on video, not television or film.

OTAKU: In Japan, a derogatory term for someone obsessed by any hobby, corresponding to fanboy/anorak. Some fans view the label as a compliment, especially in the West.

SENTAI: Battle team. As seen in team shows like *Battle of the Planets*, *Sailor Moon* and *Mighty Morphin' Power Rangers*. A great excuse for extra merchandise, and a handy shorthand for screenwriters pressed for time.

SHOJO MANGA: Girls' MANGA, directed at elementary and junior high school age groups where the main character is female. Stories usually have romantic themes. Shojo is not actually erotica, but there are grey areas.

SHONEN AI: A category of entertainment written for women where the main romantically involved characters are male, especially BISHONEN 'pretty boys'. These need not always be explicitly homosexual characters.

SHONEN MANGA: Boys' MANGA. Compare to SHOJO MANGA.

BIBLIOGRAPHY AND RECOMMENDED READING

ALLISON, A. (1996) *Permitted and Prohibited Desires: Mothers, Comics and Censorship in Japan*. Oxford: Westview Press.

[ANON] (1997) 'For Men Only Forbidden [Ikenai] Anime Catalogue' in *Anime V*, No.141 (December), pp40-43.

[ANON] (1998) 'Mania no Takarabako: Shin Seiki Tokyo Chushin: #12: Adult Anime' [Strongbox of Mania: New Century Tokyo Centre: #12: Adult Anime] in *SPA!*, No.2586 (25 March), p95.

[BBFC] (1995) *Annual Report for 1994/95*. London: British Board of Film Classification.

BEER, L. (1984) *Freedom of Expression in Japan: A Study in Comparative Law, Politics and Society*. Tokyo: Kodansha.

BENDAZZI, G. (1996) *Cartoons*. Bloomington, IN: University of Indiana Press.

BENEDICT, R. (1946) *The Chrysanthemum and the Sword*. New York: Houghton Mifflin.

BIODROWSKI, S. (1990) 'Japanese Animation: Wonder Overcoming Western Prejudice' in *Cinefantastique*, Vol.20, No.4 (March), p47.

BORNOFF, N. (1991) *Pink Samurai: The Pursuit and Politics of Sex in Japan*. London: Grafton.

[BSC] (1994), *A Code of Practice*. London: Broadcasting Standards Council.

BURUMA, I. (1984) *A Japanese Mirror: Heroes and Villains of Japanese Culture*. London: Penguin.

CLEMENTS, J. (1995) 'The Mechanics of the US Anime and Manga Industry' in *Foundation: The Review of Science Fiction*, No.64, pp32-44.

_____. (1995) 'Flesh and Metal: Marriage and Female Emancipation in the Science Fiction of Wei Yahua' in *Foundation: The Review of Science Fiction*, No.65, pp61-80.

CONSTANTINE, P. (1993) *Japan's Sex Trade: A Journey Through Japan's Erotic Subcultures*. Tokyo: Tuttle.

COTTA VAZ, M. ed. (1992) *Illusions of the Floating World*, exhibition catalogue, San Francisco: Cartoon Art Museum.

COURTNEY-GRIMWOOD, J. (1997) 'Virtual Girlfriends Versus Real Life', in *Focus*, September, pp78-82.

DUFFY, M. (1989) *The Erotic World of Faery*. London: Cardinal.

EVANS, P. (1992) 'An Interview with Go Nagai', in *Anime UK*, Vol.1, No.5 (December) pp28-32.

GROENSTEEN, T. (1991) *L'Univers des Mangas: Une introduction à la bande dessinée japonaise*. [Second edition.] Tournai: Casterman.

GROVE, V. (1998) 'What the Censors Saw', in *The Sunday Times*, 30 May, p21.

HARAGUCHI, T., ed. (1998) *Animage Pocket Data Notes*, in *Animage* (book supplement), March.

HASKELL, M. (1987) *From Reverence to Rape: The Treatment of Women in the Movies*. [Second edition.] Chicago: University of Chicago Press.

'HEART HAKASE.' (1996) 'Heart Mark OAV no Kosa' [Lectures on Heart Mark Video Anime] in *Anime V*, No.120 (December), pp40-41.

HELLEN, N. (1997) 'Censor Licenses Obscene Videos', in *The Sunday Times*, 23 November, p1.

HORN, M, (ed)(1980) *The World Encyclopaedia of Cartoons*. New York: Chelsea House.

HOWELL, T. (1996) 'Banned!' in *Manga Mania*, No.38, p15.

HUGHES, D. and CLEMENTS, J. (1997) 'Manga Goes to Hollywood' in the *Guardian* (G2), 14 April, pp10-11.

JENKINS, H. (1992) *Textual Poachers: Television Fans and Participatory Culture*. New York: Routledge.

KATO, S. (ed.) (1992) *B-Club Kyukyoku no Majokko Tokushu* [B-Club: The Ultimate Magical Girl Special Edition]. No.75 (Feb).

KAWAI, H. (1988). *The Japanese Psyche: Major Motifs in the Fairy Tales of Japan* [Mukashibanashi to Nihonjin no Kokoro, trans. Kawai and Reece.] Dallas: Spring Publications.

KISHIKAWA, O. (1996) *Gainax Himitsu Dai Hyakka* [Great Gainax Encyclopaedia], in *Animage* (book supplement), March.

KONDO, R (ed.) (1997) *Kusou Bishojo Tokuhon* [The Guide of Fantastic Beauties], Bessatsu Takarajima No.349. Tokyo: Takarajimasha.

LEDOUX, T. and RANNEY, D. (1996) *The Complete Anime Guide: Japanese Animation Video Directory and Resource Guide*. Issaquah, WA: Tiger Mountain Press.

_____. et al. (eds) (1997) *Anime Interviews: The First Five Years of Animerica, Anime and Manga Monthly (1992-1997)*. San Francisco: Cadence Books.

LEONARD, A. (1995). 'Anime Nations' in *Wired*, April, pp48-52.

LEVI, A. (1996) *Samurai from Outer Space: Understanding Japanese Animation*. Chicago: Open Court.

LISTER, D. (1993) 'Cartoon Cult with an Increasing Appetite for Sex and Violence', in the *Independent*, 15 October, p10.

LUBICH, D. (1995) 'Japanimation', in *The Guardian*, 20 January, p8.

MacKENZIE, D. (1994) *Myths and Legends: China and Japan*. London: Senate.

MALLORY, M. (1998) 'Princess Goes West' in *Daily Variety*, 13 February, p1.

MARCHETTI, G. (1993) *Romancing the "Yellow Peril": Race, Sex and Discursive Strategies in Hollywood Fiction*. Berkeley: University of California Press.

McALPINE, H & W. (1958) *Japanese Tales and Legends*. Oxford: Oxford University Press.

McCARTHY, H. (1993) 'The Voice of Anime: Interview with Hayashibara Megumi' in *Anime UK*, No.10 (October), pp8-9.

_____. (1996) *The Anime Movie Guide: Japanese Animation Since 1983*. London: Titan Books.

MILLAR, P. (1995) 'Titillation in Virgin Territory' in *The Sunday Times: The Culture*, December, pp8-9.

[MUSEUM OF CONTEMPORARY ART]. (1994) *Kaboom!: Explosive Animation from America and Japan*. Sydney: MCA.

NEWMARK, P. (1995) *A Textbook of Translation*. New York: Prentice Hall.

[NEWTYPE EDITORIAL STAFF] (1997) *Newtype's Almanac '97*, in *Newtype* (book supplement), February.

_____. (1998) *Newtype's Almanac '98*, in *Newtype* (book supplement), February.

NICHIREN (1979). *The Major Writings of Nichiren*

Daishonin, Volume One. (Trans, The Gosho Translation Committee.) Tokyo: Nichiren Shoshu International Centre.

NICHOLS, P. (1998) 'At Mickey's House, A Quiet Welcome for Distant Cousins' in the *New York Times* (Arts & Pleasure section), 1 February.

[NIKKEI BP PUBLISHING CENTRE] (1996) *Entertainment Keyword '95-'96*. Tokyo: Nikkei BP Publishing Centre.

OKADA, T. (1996) *Otakugaku Nyumon [Introduction to Otakuology.]* Tokyo: Ota.

OSHIMA, N. (1992) *Cinema, Censorship and the State: The Writings of Nagisa Oshima 1956-1978 [Écrits 1956-1978: Dissolution et jaillissement,* trans. Lawson.] Cambidge, MA: MIT Press.

PARKER, D. (1995) *Writing Erotic Fiction*. London: A & C Black.

RAYNS, T. (1995) 'Japan: Sex and Beyond' in *Sight & Sound*, Vol.5, No.6 (June), pp26-29.

RIDOUT, C. (1996) 'Anime in the UK' in *Manga Mania*, No. 30 (January), p120.

_____. & CLEMENTS, J. (1996) 'Sense and Censorship' in *Manga Mania*, No.30, pp118-121.

RICHIE, D. (1966) *The Japanese Movie: An Illustrated History*. London: Warde Lock & Co and Kodansha International.

RUBIN, J. (1984) *Injurious to Public Morals: Writers and the Meiji State*. Seattle: University of Washington Press.

SCHILLING, M. (1997) *The Encyclopedia of Japanese Pop Culture*. New York: Weatherhill.

SCHODT, F. (1980) 'Berusaiyu no Bara' in Horn (ed.) *The World Encyclopaedia of Cartoons*. New York: Chelsea House. pp14-15.

_____. (1987) *Manga! Manga!: The World of Japanese Comics*. Tokyo: Kodansha International.

_____. (1993) 'The Manga Kingdom' in *Japan: An Illustrated Encyclopaedia*. Tokyo: Kodansha International. pp216-217.

_____. (1996) *Dreamland Japan: Writings on Modern Manga*. Berkeley, CA: Stone Bridge Press.

SENGUPTA, K. (1993) 'Snuff Out These Sick Cartoons'

in the *Daily Star*, 25 January.

SERTORI, J. (1998) 'The Devil Inside' in *Manga Mania*, No.44, pp12-15.

SHARKEY, A. (1997) 'The Land of the Free', in *The Guardian Weekend*, 22 November, pp14-24.

SMET, S. (1994) 'Urotsuki Doji' in *JAMM: The Japanese Animation and Manga Magazine*, No.1, pp25-50 & No.2, pp35-47.

_____. (1995) 'Cream Lemon; An Almost Complete Overview' in *JAMM* no.4, pp38-46.

SMITH, A. (1995) 'Inside a Society Dominated by Rigid Codes of Public Conduct Exists a Parallel Universe Where Anything Goes,' in *Observer Life*, 19 November, pp20-23.

SMITH, T. (1996) 'The Red Light Zone: Manga's Erotic Past and Present' in *Manga Mania*, No.38, pp12-16.

TAKADA, A. (1995) *Anime no Samenai Maho: Doraemon kara Sailor Moon made Animetrauma kozo bunseki [Anime's Power to Deceive: Animetrauma Paradigms from Doraemon to Sailor Moon]*. Tokyo: PHP.

TAKAHASHI, M. and KATO, C. (eds) (1993) *Majokko Daizenshu Toei Doga Hen [The Magical Girl Companion: Toei Animation Edition]*. Tokyo: Bandai.

TAKAHASHI, R. (1990) *Lum: Urusei Yatsura Volume 2* [Trans. Jones and Fujii.] San Francisco: Viz.

TAKEFUJI, T. (ed) (1992) *Newtype Animesoft Kanzen [Complete] Catalogue*. Tokyo: Kadokawa.

TOMONO, T. and MOCHIZUKI, N. (1986) *Sekai Animation Eiga Shi [The Animation Films of the World]*. Tokyo: Pulp.

TWITCHELL, J. (1985) *Dreadful Pleasures: An Anatomy of Modern Horror*. New York: Oxford University Press.

UENO, C. (1992) *Skirt no Shita no Gekijo [The Theatre Beneath the Skirt]*. Tokyo: Kawade Bunko.

WESTFAHL, G. (1993) 'Wrangling Conversation: Linguistic Patterns in the Dialogue of Heroes and Villains' in Slusser and Rabkin (eds) *Fights of Fantasy: Armed Conflict in Science Fiction and Fantasy*. Athens, GA: University of Georgia Press. pp35-48.

INDEX OF JAPANESE AND ALTERNATE TITLES

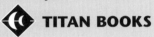